THE ENGLISH POETS

GENERAL EDITOR: CHRISTOPHER RICKS

Also available in this series

Ben Jonson
The Complete Poems

EDITED BY GEORGE PARFITT

NEW HAVEN AND LONDON
YALE UNIVERSITY PRESS

First published in 1975 in the United Kingdom in a paperback
edition by Penguin Books Limited in the series Penguin
English Poets. First published in 1982 in the United States of
America by Yale University Press.

Printed in the United States of America.

Library of Congress Cataloging in Publication Data

Jonson, Ben, 1573?–1637.
  The complete poems.

  (The English poets; 12)
  Bibliography: p.
  Includes indexes.
  I. Parfitt, George A. E.   II. Title   III. Series.
  PR2625.A2   1982   821'.3   81–15948
  ISBN 0–300–02825–3   AACR2
  ISBN 0–300–02828–8 (pbk.)

10   9   8   7   6   5   4   3   2   1

Contents

Collecting and editing Ben Jonson's poetry is, in some respects, a fairly straightforward task. For the *Epigrams* and *The Forest* there are few textual problems: both were printed in the 1616 folio of the poet's *Works* and it is clear that Jonson supervised that volume pretty carefully, so that we can be confident that the folio texts of both these collections represent the versions that the poet wished to stand as definitive. In both cases there are good reasons to believe that the poems are deliberately arranged in the order they are and there is no good reason for disturbing that order. The poems in *Epigrams*, as printed in the folio, have variety of length and tone which was clearly meant to reflect Jonson's knowledge of, and respect for, the example of Martial, and this variety could easily be lost if the poems were arranged by tone, for example, or alphabetically by title, or – a hopeless task – chronologically. *The Forest* is also a varied selection of poems: in fact it is almost an epitome of Jonson's achievement as a poet and, short though the collection is, serves as the best introduction to the range and quality of his non-dramatic work.

The third group of poems printed here, *Underwoods*, provides a more difficult problem. The collection was first printed in the two-volume folio put out by Kenelm Digby in 1640, about three years after Jonson's death, and we do not know how far the order in which the poems appear there reflects the poet's wishes. There is no clear evidence that Jonson had arranged them to his satisfaction, but there are obvious signs of purposive grouping, although in this case the purpose seems to be to bring poems of a similar type together rather than to provide the variety of *Epigrams* and *The Forest*. But although *Underwoods* is clearly more loosely organized than the earlier collections, I have, because of the grouping that does exist and for the sake of consistency, followed the

order of the 1640 folio. In this case, again, any attempt at chrono-
logical arrangement would soon founder.

With what I have labelled *Miscellaneous Poems* we meet a third
situation. This collection is exactly what its title suggests, a body
of pieces from a variety of sources: from the songs and masques,
from contemporary anthologies, from the prefatory material to
the publications of other writers, etc. These poems are largely at
an editor's mercy so far as arrangement goes and I have disposed
them primarily in terms of genre. I do not claim to have printed
here every piece of verse by Jonson which does not appear in one
or other of the three preceding collections. I was anxious to have
the songs from plays and masques more fully represented than in
other collections of Jonson's poetry, and I think that both the
lyric and the robust, popular sides of his verse emerge more
strongly as a result, but a number of songs have been left out,
usually because they are too fully integrated in their context to
make much sense in isolation from the relevant masque or play.

Horace, of the Art of Poetry survives in two versions and these –
with the Latin text that Jonson used – can be examined together in
volume VIII of Herford and Simpson's edition of Jonson's work.
For this present volume the obvious text was the second, that
which Jonson revised and improved.

I add, as appendixes, both *Timber: or Discoveries* and *Conver-
sations with William Drummond*. Both, in their different ways,
throw light on Jonson and his poetry; both are important docu-
ments of the period; neither is easily available in a modern and
reasonably inexpensive form. *Timber: or Discoveries* was first
printed in the 1640 folio but the text was not very carefully
arranged and so I have followed other modern editors in trying to
make my text as coherent as possible, bearing in mind that this
prose work lies somewhere between a group of essays on various
topics and a set of jottings from the poet's reading. The *Conversa-
tions with William Drummond* also poses editorial problems.
Drummond's manuscript is not extant but a transcript was made
of it by Sir Robert Sibbald which offers a markedly superior text
to the first printed one, the abridged version in Sage and Ruddi-
man's edition of Drummond's *Works* (1711). Here again I have
followed other modern editors in using Sibbald as the master text

and, bearing in mind that this version is an appendix and not a full-scale edition, have kept discussion of textual problems to a minimum.

Throughout this volume, following the editorial policy for the series, I have modernized spelling while leaving punctuation largely undisturbed. Jonson was a careful and heavy user of punctuation and I have occasionally lightened his text, but only where this seemed necessary to make the meaning clearer for a modern reader. Wherever the modernization of spelling has removed fruitful ambiguity I have used a note to alert the reader.

Jonson is not the easiest of poets to approach, partly because his best verse is spread across a broad range of genres and tones and partly because his plain-style manner means that his real strength only emerges gradually as the texts become familiar. Because of Jonson's ideals as a poet there are not many occasions where the sense needs elucidation in notes (except, of course, where a word has changed in meaning or dropped out of current usage). So the notes here concentrate mainly on two things. The first of these is the identification of persons and events addressed or alluded to, and here I have aimed to provide the minimum information necessary to clarify the reference. The second main category of note relates to Jonson's use of other authors, chiefly of classical ones. Everyone knows that Jonson was a 'classicist' (although little real effort has been made to find out just what the term indicates in his case) and he makes very frequent use of classical texts in his poems. Notes cannot really be used to show how Jonson uses this material, but it is important that a reader should know what is being used and where. Simple identification of borrowings is not very helpful, however, so I have printed in the notes the relevant passages of texts Jonson draws upon, and – bearing in mind that few of us have anything like Jonson's grasp of Latin and Greek – translations of such passages have been added, thus providing, I hope, the raw material for anyone who wishes to look at the ways in which Jonson makes English poetry from foreign material.

Any editor of any part of Jonson's writing stands, willingly or reluctantly, in debt to the remarkable edition of Herford and the Simpsons, editors who drew together the work of many earlier

scholars and added the results of their own researches to provide
the definitive picture of Jonson's achievement. I am as fully in
their debt as anyone could be, and finding occasional errors, in-
consistencies and failures of sympathy in their edition has only
made me more conscious of the very high standard they have set.
Beyond this it would be impossible for me to list all the scholars
whose work I have drawn upon, but I should like to thank Dr
John Wilders and Professor L. C. Knights for·initiating my in-
terest in Jonson; my wife, children and friends (colleagues and
students alike) for tolerating my obsession; and the University
of Nottingham for giving me a sabbatical term in which to finish
this edition. In addition I should like to thank my friend Mr
Richard Fishleigh for his help with a number of the translations
from classical material and the staff of the Cripps Health Centre,
University of Nottingham, for looking after me so well during an
illness which coincided with proof-reading.

Table of Dates

1572   Born, probably 11 June, probably in London. Father
            died about one month previously.
            Virtually nothing is known about Jonson's ancestry.
            Claims in *Conversations* that his paternal grandfather
            came from Annandale, served Henry VIII and 'was a
            gentleman'. Same source states father 'turned minister'
            after suffering loss of his estate under Queen Mary. The
            striking anecdote about his mother in *Conversations* is
            all we know of her character.

1574–5   ? Mother remarries. Second husband a Westminster
            bricklayer, of whom nothing useful is known.

1586–8   ? At Westminster School through the good offices of a
            friend, who may, or may not, have been his teacher
            William Camden.

1588   ? Brief, distasteful period at 'another craft',
            presumably bricklaying.

1591–2   ? Short period serving with the army in the
            Netherlands, possibly followed by more bricklaying.

1594   Marries Anne Lewis, 'a shrew yet honest': little else
            known.

1595   ? Death of Jonson's first daughter, Mary.

1597   In Henslowe's employ as actor–writer (probably
            preceded by a period of acting with a 'strolling
            company'). Imprisoned for acting in and part-writing
            the lost play *The Isle of Dogs*.

1598   ? Performance of *The Case is Altered* by the Children
            of the Chapel Royal.
            Every Man in His Humour performed by the Lord
            Chamberlain's Men.

Kills the actor Gabriel Spencer in a duel; imprisoned but released by pleading benefit of clergy; converted to Roman Catholicism while in gaol.

1599   *Every Man out of His Humour* performed by the Lord Chamberlain's Men.

1600–1601 *Cynthia's Revels* and *Poetaster* both performed by the Children of the Chapel Royal. Both part of the War of the Theatres (mainly Jonson versus Marston and Dekker).

1603   Failure of *Sejanus*, performed by the King's Men. Death of first son, Benjamin, then seven years old.

1605   *Masque of Blackness*, one of Jonson's first court commissions (Jonson wrote fairly regularly for the court for the next twenty-five years or so).

1605–6   *Eastward Ho* (written with Chapman and Marston) acted by the Children of the Queen's Revels. Jonson and Chapman imprisoned for alleged anti-Scots aspersions in the play.

1606   *Volpone* performed by the King's Men, and also probably at Oxford and Cambridge.

1609   *Epicoene* acted by the Children of the Queen's Revels.

1610   *Alchemist* acted by the King's Men.
           ? Returns to Anglicanism.

1611   *Catiline* (King's Men) fails.

1612–13   In France as tutor to Walter, son of Sir Walter Raleigh.

1614   *Bartholomew Fair* performed by Lady Elizabeth's Men.

1616   *The Devil is an Ass* performed by the King's Men. Publication of folio *Works*, which includes *Epigrams* and *The Forest*. This publication attracted derision as making pretentious claims for the importance of drama but was an important step in furthering recognition of plays as serious writing.
           Granted royal pension.

1618–19   Walks to Scotland and back; meets Drummond in Scotland.

1619	Honorary MA of Oxford.
1623	? Teaches at Gresham College, London. Fire at lodgings destroys books and papers.
1626	*Staple of News* acted by the King's Men.
1628	Made City Chronologer. Paralysed by a stroke.
1629	Failure of *The New Inn* (King's Men).
1631	Beginning of feud with Inigo Jones (though the two men seem to have quarrelled earlier).
1632	*Magnetic Lady* performed by the King's Men.
1633	Revised *Tale of a Tub* acted by Queen Henrietta's Men.
1635	Death of a second son.
1637	Dies in Westminster; buried in Westminster Abbey, 9 August.
1638	Publication of commemorative volume *Jonsonus Virbius*.
1640	Publication of two-volume folio *Works* put out by Sir Kenelm Digby (includes *Underwoods* and *Discoveries*).

Further Reading

EDITIONS

C. H. Herford, Percy and Evelyn Simpson (eds.), *Ben Jonson*, 11 vols., Clarendon Press, 1925–51.

Poems

W. B. Hunter (ed.), *The Complete Poetry of Ben Jonson*, Anchor, 1963.
G. B. Johnston (ed.), *Poems of Ben Jonson*, Routledge & Kegan Paul, 1954.

Timber: or Discoveries
F. C. Schelling (ed.), Ginn, 1892.

Conversations with William Drummond
R. F. Patterson (ed.), Blackie, 1924.

Plays and Masques
A. P. Kernan and R. B. Young (general editors), *The Yale Ben Jonson*, Yale University Press. This edition is in progress: volumes so far published include Stephen Orgel (ed.), *Ben Jonson: The Complete Masques*, 1969, which is now the standard edition.

BIOGRAPHY

There is no full and satisfactory biography of Jonson. Volume I of the Herford and Simpson edition contains an account of his life, together with full annotation and reproduction of contemporary notes and anecdotes (of varying reliability), of letters by Jonson and of relevant 'legal and official documents'.

CRITICISM

Books on Jonson's Poems

G. B. Johnston, *Ben Jonson: Poet*, Columbia University Press, 1945.

J. G. Nichols, *The Poetry of Ben Jonson*, Routledge & Kegan Paul, 1969.

W. Trimpi, *Ben Jonson's Poems*, Stanford University Press, 1962.

Other Relevant Books

J. B. Bamborough, *Ben Jonson*, Hutchinson, 1970.

J. A. Barish (ed.), *Ben Jonson: A Collection of Critical Essays*, Prentice-Hall, 1963.

J. F. Bradley and J. Q. Adams (eds.), *The Jonson Allusion Book*, Yale University Press, 1922.

L. C. Knights, *Drama and Society in the Age of Jonson*, Chatto & Windus, 1937.

E. Miner, *The Cavalier Mode from Jonson to Cotton*, Princeton University Press, 1971.

S. Orgel, *The Jonsonian Masque*, Harvard University Press, 1965.

E. B. Partridge, *The Broken Compass*, Columbia University Press, 1958.

A. C. Swinburne, *A Study of Ben Jonson*, Chatto & Windus, 1889.

J. A. Symonds, *Ben Jonson*, Longman, 1886.

C. F. Wheeler, *Classical Mythology in the Plays, Masques and Poems of Ben Jonson*, Princeton University Press, 1938.

Essays Relevant to the Poems

F. W. Bradbrook, 'Ben Jonson's Poetry', in *A Guide to English Literature*, ed. B. Ford, vol. 3, Penguin, 1956.

P. M. Cubeta, 'Ben Jonson's Religious Lyrics', *Journal of English and Germanic Philology* (LXII), 1947.

T. S. Eliot, 'Ben Jonson', in *The Sacred Wood*, Methuen, 1920.

D. J. Enright, 'Poetic Satire and Satire in Verse', *Scrutiny* (XVIII), 1952.

H. Maclean, 'Ben Jonson's Poems: Notes on the Ordered Society', in *Seventeenth-Century English Poetry*, ed. W. R. Keast, Oxford University Press, 1962.

J. H. Neumann, 'Notes on Ben Jonson's English', *Publications of the Modern Language Association* (LIV), 1939.

G. A. E. Parfitt, 'The Poetry of Ben Jonson', *Essays in Criticism* (XVIII), 1968.

G. A. E. Parfitt, 'Ethical Thought and Ben Jonson's Poetry', *Studies in English Literature* (IX), 1969.

G. A. E. Parfitt, 'Compromise Classicism . . .', *Studies in English Literature* (XI), 1971.

G. A. E. Parfitt, 'The nature of translation in Ben Jonson's poetry', *Studies in English Literature* (XIII), 1973.

Edward Partridge, 'Jonson's *Epigrammes*: the named and the nameless', *Studies in the Literary Imagination* (VI), 1973.

R. S. Walker, 'Jonson's Lyric Poetry', *Criterion* (XIII), 1933–4 (reprinted in Keast).

E. Wilson, 'Morose Ben Jonson', in *The Triple Thinkers*, Scribner, 1948.

Epigrams

Dedication

TO THE GREAT EXAMPLE OF HONOUR AND VIRTUE,
THE MOST NOBLE WILLIAM, EARL OF PEMBROKE, LORD
CHAMBERLAIN, ETC.

My lord. While you cannot change your merit, I dare not change your title: it was that made it, and not I. Under which name, I here offer to your lordship the ripest of my studies, my *Epigrams*; which, though they carry danger in the sound, do not therefore seek your shelter: for, when I made them, I had nothing in my conscience, to expressing of which I did need a cipher. But, if I be fallen into those times, wherein, for the likeness of vice, and facts, everyone thinks another's ill deeds objected to him; and that in their
10 ignorant and guilty mouths, the common voice is (for their security) 'Beware the poet', confessing, therein, so much love to their diseases, as they would rather make a party for them, than be either rid, or told of them: I must expect, at your [lordship's] hand, the protection of truth, and liberty, while you are constant to your own goodness. In thanks whereof, I return you the honour of leading forth so many good, and great names (as my verses mention on the better part) to their remembrance with posterity. Amongst whom, if I have praised, unfortunately, anyone, that doth not de-
20 serve; or, if all answer not, in all numbers, the pictures I have made of them: I hope it will be forgiven me, that they are no ill pieces, though they be not like the persons. But I foresee a nearer fate to my book, than this: that the vices therein will be owned before the virtues (though, there, I have avoided all particulars, as I have done names) and that some will be so ready to discredit me, as they will have the impudence to

belie themselves. For, if I meant them not, it is so. Nor, can I hope otherwise. For, why should they remit anything of their riot, their pride, their self-love, and other inherent
30 graces, to consider truth or virtue; but, with the trade of the world, lend their long ears against men they love not: and hold their dear mountebank, or jester, in far better condition, than all the study, or studiers of humanity? For such, I would rather know them by their vizards, still, than they should publish their faces, at their peril, in my theatre, where Cato, if he lived, might enter without scandal.

Your lo[rdship's] most faithful honourer,
Ben. Jonson.

I To the Reader

Pray thee, take care, that tak'st my book in hand,
To read it well: that is, to understand.

II To My Book

It will be looked for, book, when some but see
Thy title, *Epigrams*, and named of me,
Thou should'st be bold, licentious, full of gall,
Wormwood, and sulphur, sharp, and toothed withal;
Become a petulant thing, hurl ink, and wit,
As madmen stones: not caring whom they hit.
Deceive their malice, who could wish it so.
And by thy wiser temper, let men know
Thou are not covetous of least self-fame.
10 Made from the hazard of another's shame:
Much less with lewd, profane, and beastly phrase,
To catch the world's loose laughter, or vain gaze.
He that departs with his own honesty
For vulgar praise, doth it too dearly buy.

III To My Bookseller

Thou, that mak'st gain thy end, and wisely well,
Call'st a book good, or bad, as it doth sell,
Use mine so, too: I give thee leave. But crave
For the luck's sake, it thus much favour have,
To lie upon thy stall, till it be sought;
Not offered, as it made suit to be bought;
Nor have my title-leaf on posts, or walls,
Or in cleft sticks, advancèd to make calls
For termers, or some clerk-like serving-man,
10 Who scarce can spell the hard names: whose knight less can.
If, without these vile arts, it will not sell,
Send it to Bucklersbury, there 'twill, well.

36

IV To King James

How, best of kings, dost thou a sceptre bear!
How, best of poets, dost thou laurel wear!
But two things, rare, the Fates had in their store,
And gave thee both, to show they could no more.
For such a poet, while thy days were green,
Thou wert, as chief of them are said t'have been.
And such a prince thou art, we daily see,
As chief of those still promise they will be.
Whom should my muse then fly to, but the best
10 Of kings for grace; of poets for my test?

V On the Union

When was there contract better driven by Fate?
Or celebrated with more truth of state?
The world the temple was, the priest a king,
The spousèd pair two realms, the sea the ring.

VI To Alchemists

If all you boast of your great art be true;
Sure, willing poverty lives most in you.

VII On the New Hot-House

Where lately harboured many a famous whore,
A purging bill, now fixed upon the door,
Tells you it is a hot-house: so it may,
And still be a whore house. They are *synonima*.

VIII On a Robbery

Ridway robbed Duncote of three hundred pound,
Ridway was ta'en, arraigned, condemned to die;
But, for this money was a courtier found,
Begged Ridway's pardon: Duncote, now, doth cry,
Robbed both of money, and the law's relief,
The courtier is become the greater thief.

IX To All, to Whom I Write

May none, whose scattered names honour my book,
For strict degrees of rank, or title look:
'Tis 'gainst the manners of an epigram:
And, I a poet here, no herald am.

X To My Lord Ignorant

Thou call'st me poet, as a term of shame:
But I have my revenge made, in thy name.

XI On Something, that Walks Somewhere

At court I met it, in clothes brave enough,
To be a courtier; and looks grave enough,
To seem a statesman: as I near it came,
It made me a great face, I asked the name.
A lord, it cried, buried in flesh, and blood,
And such from whom let no man hope least good,
For I will do none: and as little ill,
For I will dare none. Good lord, walk dead still.

XII On Lieutenant Shift

Shift here, in town, not meanest among squires,
That haunt Pikthatch, Marshlambeth, and Whitefriars,
Keeps himself, with half a man, and defrays
The charge of that state, with this charm, god pays.
By that one spell he lives, eats, drinks, arrays
Himself: his whole revénue is, god pays.
The quarter-day is come; the hostess says,
She must have money: he returns, god pays.
The tailor brings a suit home; he it 'ssays,
10   Looks o'er the bill, likes it: and says, god pays.
He steals to ordinaries; there he plays
At dice his borrowed money: which, god pays.
Then takes up fresh commodity, for days;
Signs to new bond, forfeits: and cries, god pays.
That lost, he keeps his chamber, reads essays,
Takes physic, tears the papers: still god pays.
Or else by water goes, and so to plays;
Calls for his stool, adorns the stage: god pays.
To every cause he meets, this voice he brays:
20   His only answer is to all, god pays.
Not his poor cockatrice but he betrays
Thus: and for his lechery, scores, god pays.
But see! The old bawd hath served him in his trim,
Lent him a pocky whore. She hath paid him.

XIII To Doctor Empiric

When men a dangerous disease did 'scape,
Of old, they gave a cock to Aesculape;
Let me give two; that doubly am got free,
From my disease's danger, and from thee.

XIV To William Camden

Camden, most reverend head, to whom I owe
All that I am in arts, all that I know,
(How nothing's that?) to whom my country owes
The great renown, and name wherewith she goes.
Than thee the age sees not that thing more grave,
More high, more holy, that she more would crave.
What name, what skill, what faith hast thou in things!
What sight in searching the most antique springs!
What weight, and what authority in thy speech!
10 Man scarce can make that doubt, but thou canst teach.
Pardon free truth, and let thy modesty,
Which conquers all, be once overcome by thee.
Many of thine this better could, than I,
But for their powers, accept my piety.

XV On Court-Worm

All men are worms: but this no man. In silk
'Twas brought to court first wrapped, and white as milk;
Where, afterwards, it grew a butterfly:
Which was a caterpillar. So 'twill die.

XVI To Brain-Hardy

Hardy, thy brain is valiant, 'tis confessed,
Thou more; that with it every day, dar'st jest
Thyself into fresh brawls: when, called upon,
Scarce thy week's swearing brings thee off, of one.
So, in short time, th'art in arrearage grown
Some hundred quarrels, yet dost thou fight none;
Nor need'st thou: for those few, by oath released,
Make good what thou dar'st do in all the rest.
Keep thyself there, and think thy valour right,
10 He that dares damn himself, dares more than fight.

XVII To the Learnèd Critic

May others fear, fly, and traduce thy name,
As guilty men do magistrates: glad I,
That wish my poems a legitimate fame,
Charge them, for crown, to thy sole censure high.
And, but a sprig of bays, given by thee,
Shall outlive garlands, stol'n from the chaste tree.

XVIII To My Mere English Censurer

To thee, my way in epigrams seems new,
When both it is the old way, and the true.
Thou say'st, that cannot be: for thou hast seen
Davies, and Weever, and the best have been,
And mine come nothing like. I hope so. Yet,
As theirs did with thee, mine might credit get:
If thou'ld'st but use thy faith, as thou didst then,
When thou wert wont t'admire, not censure men.
Prithee believe still, and not judge so fast,
10   Thy faith is all the knowledge that thou hast.

XIX On Sir Cod the Perfumed

That Cod can get no widow, yet a knight,
I scent the cause: he woos with an ill sprite.

XX To the Same Sir Cod

Th'expense in odours is a most vain sin,
Except thou could'st, Sir Cod, wear them within.

XXI On Reformed Gamester

Lord, how is gamester changed! His hair close cut!
His neck fenced round with ruff! His eyes half shut!
His clothes two fashions off, and poor! His sword
Forbid' his side! And nothing, but the Word
Quick in his lips! Who hath this wonder wrought?
The late ta'en bastinado. So I thought.
What several ways men to their calling have!
The body's stripes, I see, the soul may save.

XXII On My First Daughter

Here lies to each her parents' ruth,
Mary, the daughter of their youth:
Yet, all heaven's gifts, being heaven's due,
It makes the father, less, to rue.
At six months' end, she parted hence
With safety of her innocence;
Whose soul heaven's queen, (whose name she bears)
In comfort of her mother's tears,
Hath placed amongst her virgin train:
10 Where, while that severed doth remain,
This grave partakes the fleshly birth.
Which cover lightly, gentle earth.

XXIII To John Donne

Donne, the delight of Phoebus, and each muse,
Who, to thy one, all other brains refuse;
Whose every work, of thy most early wit,
Came forth example, and remains so, yet:
Longer a-knowing, than most wits do live,
And which no affection praise enough can give!
To it, thy language, letters, arts, best life,
Which might with half mankind maintain a strife.

All which I meant to praise, and, yet, I would;
10   But leave, because I cannot as I should!

XXIV *To the Parliament*

There's reason good, that you good laws should make:
Men's manners ne'er were viler, for your sake.

XXV *On Sir Voluptuous Beast*

While Beast instructs his fair, and innocent wife,
In the past pleasures of his sensual life,
Telling the motions of each petticoat,
And how his Ganymede moved, and how his goat,
And now, her (hourly) her own cucqueen makes,
In varied shapes, which for his lust she takes:
What doth he else, but say, leave to be chaste,
Just wife, and, to change me, make woman's haste.

XXVI *On the Same Beast*

Than his chaste wife, though Beast now know no more,
He adulters still: his thoughts lie with a whore.

XXVII *On Sir John Roe*

In place of scutcheons, that should deck thy hearse,
Take better ornaments, my tears, and verse.
If any sword could save from Fates, Roe's could;
If any muse outlive their spite, his can;
If any friend's tears could restore, his would;
If any pious life e'er lifted man
To heaven, his hath: O happy state! wherein
We, sad for him, may glory, and not sin.

XXVIII On Don Surly

Don Surly, to aspire the glorious name
Of a great man, and to be thought the same,
Makes serious use of all great trade he knows.
He speaks to men with a rhinocerote's nose,
Which he thinks great; and so reads verses, too;
And, that is done, as he saw great men do.
H'has tympanies of business, in his face,
And, can forget men's names, with a great grace.
He will both argue, and discourse in oaths,
10 Both which are great. And laugh at ill-made clothes;
That's greater, yet: to cry his own up neat.
He doth, at meals, alone, his pheasant eat,
Which is main greatness. And, at his still board,
He drinks to no man: that's too, like a lord.
He keeps another's wife, which is a spice
Of solemn greatness. And he dares, at dice,
Blaspheme God, greatly. Or some poor hind beat,
That breathes in his dog's way: and this is great.
Nay more, for greatness' sake, he will be one
20 May hear my epigrams, but like of none.
Surly, use other arts, these only can
Style thee a most great fool, but no great man.

XXIX To Sir Annual Tilter

Tilter, the most may admire thee, though not I:
And thou, right guiltless, mayst plead to it, why?
For thy late sharp device. I say 'tis fit
All brains, at times of triumph, should run wit.
For then, our water-conduits do run wine;
But that's put in, thou'lt say. Why, so is thine.

XXX To Person Guilty

Guilty, be wise; and though thou know'st the crimes
Be thine, I tax, yet do not own my rhymes:
'Twere madness in thee, to betray thy fame,
And person to the world; ere I thy name.

XXXI On Bank the Usurer

Bank feels no lameness of his knotty gout,
His monies travel for him, in and out:
And though the soundest legs go every day,
He toils to be at hell, as soon as they.

XXXII On Sir John Roe

What two brave perils of the private sword
Could not effect, not all the furies do,
That self-divided Belgia did afford;
What not the envy of the seas reached to,
The cold of Moscow, and fat Irish air,
His often change of clime (though not of mind)
What could not work; at home in his repair
Was his blessed fate, but our hard lot to find.
Which shows, wherever death doth please t'appear,
10 Seas, serenes, swords, shot, sickness, all are there.

XXXIII To the Same

I'll not offend thee with a vain tear more,
Glad-mentioned Roe: thou art but gone before,
Whither the world must follow. And I, now,
Breathe to expect my when, and make my how.
Which if most gracious heaven grant like thine,
Who wets my grave, can be no friend of mine.

XXXIV Of Death

He that fears death, or mourns it, in the just,
Shows of the resurrection little trust.

XXXV To King James

Who would not be thy subject, James, t'obey
A prince, that rules by example, more than sway?
Whose manners draw, more than thy powers constrain.
And in this short time of thy happiest reign,
Hast purged thy realms, as we have now no cause
Left us of fear, but first our crimes, then laws.
Like aids 'gainst treasons who hath found before?
And than in them, how could we know God more?
First thou preservèd wert, our king to be,
10 And since, the whole land was preserved for thee.

XXXVI To the Ghost of Martial

Martial, thou gav'st far nobler epigrams
To thy Domitian, than I can my James:
But in my royal subject I pass thee,
Thou flattered'st thine, mine cannot flattered be.

XXXVII On Cheveril the Lawyer

No cause, nor client fat, will Cheveril leese,
But as they come, on both sides he takes fees,
And pleaseth both. For while he melts his grease
For this: that wins, for whom he holds his peace.

XXXVIII To Person Guilty

Guilty, because I bad you late be wise,
And to conceal your ulcers, did advise,
You laugh when you are touched, and long before
Any man else, you clap your hands, and roar,
And cry good! good! This quite perverts my sense,
And lies so far from wit, 'tis impudence.
Believe it, Guilty, if you lose your shame,
I'll lose my modesty, and tell your name.

XXXIX On Old Colt

For all night sins, with others' wives, unknown,
Colt, now, doth daily penance in his own.

XL On Margaret Ratcliffe

M arble, weep, for thou dost cover
A dead beauty underneath thee,
R ich, as nature could bequeath thee:
G rant then, no rude hand remove her.
A ll the gazers on the skies
R ead not in fair heaven's story,
E xpresser truth, or truer glory,
T han they might in her bright eyes.
R are, as wonder, was her wit;
10 A nd like Nectar ever flowing:
T ill time, strong by her bestowing,
C onquered hath both life and it.
L ife, whose grief was out of fashion,
I n these times. Few so have rued
F ate, in a brother. To conclude,
F or wit, feature, and true passion,
E arth, thou hast not such another.

XLI On Gypsy

Gypsy, new bawd, is turned physician,
And gets more gold, than all the college can:
Such her quaint practice is, so it allures,
For what she gave, a whore; a bawd, she cures.

XLII On Giles and Joan

Who says that Giles and Joan at discord be?
The observing neighbours no such mood can see.
Indeed, poor Giles repents he married ever.
But that his Joan doth too. And Giles would never,
By his free will, be in Joan's company.
No more would Joan he should. Giles riseth early,
And having got him out of doors is glad.
The like is Joan. But turning home, is sad.
And so is Joan. Oft-times, when Giles doth find
10 Harsh sights at home, Giles wisheth he were blind.
All this doth Joan. Or that his long-yarned life
Were quite out-spun. The like wish hath his wife.
The children, that he keeps, Giles swears are none
Of his begetting. And so swears his Joan.
In all affections she concurreth still.
If, now, with man and wife, to will, and nill
The selfsame things, a note of concord be:
I know no couple better can agree!

XLIII To Robert, Earl of Salisbury

What need hast thou of me, or of my muse,
Whose actions so themselves do celebrate?
Which should thy country's love to speak refuse,
Her foes enough would fame thee in their hate.
'Tofore, great men were glad of poets: now,
I, not the worst, am covetous of thee.

Yet dare not, to my thought, least hope allow
Of adding to thy fame; thine may to me,
When in my book, men read but Cecil's name,
10   And what I write thereof find far, and free
From servile flattery (common poets' shame)
As thou stand'st clear of the necessity.

XLIV On Chuff, Banks the Usurer's Kinsman

Chuff, lately rich in name, in chattels, goods,
And rich in issue to inherit all,
Ere blacks were bought for his own funeral,
Saw all his race approach the blacker floods:
He meant they thither should make swift repair,
When he made him executor, might be heir.

XLV On My First Son

Farewell, thou child of my right hand, and joy;
My sin was too much hope of thee, loved boy,
Seven years thou wert lent to me, and I thee pay,
Exacted by thy fate, on the just day.
O, could I lose all father, now. For why
Will man lament the state he should envy?
To have so soon 'scaped world's, and flesh's rage,
And, if no other misery, yet age!
Rest in soft peace, and, asked, say here doth lie
10   Ben Jonson his best piece of poetry.
For whose sake, henceforth, all his vows be such,
As what he loves may never like too much.

XLVI To Sir Luckless Woo-All

Is this the sir, who, some waste wife to win,
A knighthood bought, to go a-wooing in?

'Tis Luckless, he that took up one on band
To pay at's day of marriage. By my hand
The knight-wright's cheated then: he'll never pay.
Yes, now he wears his knighthood every day.

XLVII To the Same

Sir Luckless, troth, for luck's sake pass by one:
He that woos every widow, will get none.

XLVIII On Mongrel Esquire

His bought arms Mong' not liked; for his first day
Of bearing them in field, he threw 'hem away:
And hath no honour lost, our duellists say.

XLIX To Playwright

Playwright me reads, and still my verses damns,
He says, I want the tongue of epigrams;
I have no salt: no bawdry he doth mean.
For witty, in his language, is obscene.
Playwright, I loathe to have thy manners known
In my chaste book: profess them in thine own.

L To Sir Cod

Leave Cod, tobacco-like, burnt gums to take,
Or fumy clysters, thy moist lungs to bake:
Arsenic would thee fit for society make.

LI *To King James*

*(UPON THE HAPPY FALSE RUMOUR OF HIS DEATH,
THE TWO AND TWENTIETH DAY OF MARCH, 1607)*

That we the loss might know, and thou our love,
Great heaven did well, to give ill fame free wing;
Which though it did but panic terror prove,
And far beneath least pause of such a king,
Yet give thy jealous subjects leave to doubt:
Who this thy 'scape from rumour gratulate,
No less than if from peril; and devout,
Do beg thy care unto thy after-state.
For we, that have our eyes still in our ears,
10 Look not upon thy dangers, but our fears.

LII *To Censorious Courtling*

Courtling, I rather thou shouldst utterly
Dispraise my work, than praise it frostily:
When I am read, thou feign'st a weak applause,
As if thou wert my friend, but lackd'st a cause.
This but thy judgement fools: the other way
Would both thy folly, and thy spite betray.

LIII *To Old-End Gatherer*

Long-gathering Old-end, I did fear thee wise,
When having pilled a book, which no man buys,
Thou wert content the author's name to lose:
But when (in place) thou didst the patron's choose,
It was as if thou printed hadst an oath,
To give the world assurance thou wert both;
And that, as puritans at baptism do,
Thou wert the father, and the witness too,
For but thyself, where, out of motley, 's he
10 Could save that line to dedicate to thee?

LIV On Cheveril

Cheveril cries out, my verses libels are;
And threatens the Star Chamber, and the bar:
What are thy petulant pleadings, Cheveril, then,
That quitt'st the cause so oft, and rail'st at men?

LV To Francis Beaumont

How I do love thee Beaumont, and thy muse,
That unto me dost such religion use!
How I do fear myself, that am not worth
The least indulgent thought thy pen drops forth!
At once thou mak'st me happy, and unmak'st;
And giving largely to me, more thou tak'st.
What fate is mine, that so itself bereaves?
What art is thine, that so thy friend deceives?
When even there, where most thou praisest me,
10 For writing better, I must envy thee.

LVI On Poet-Ape

Poor Poet-Ape, that would be thought our chief,
Whose works are e'en the frippery of wit,
From brocage is become so bold a thief,
As we, the robbed, leave rage, and pity it.
At first he made low shifts, would pick and glean,
Buy the reversion of old plays; now grown
To a little wealth, and credit in the scene,
He takes up all, makes each man's wit his own.
And, told of this, he slights it. Tut, such crimes
10 The sluggish gaping auditor devours;
He marks not whose 'twas first: and after-times
May judge it to be his, as well as ours.
Fool, as if half-eyes will not know a fleece
From locks of wool, or shreds from the whole piece!

LVII On Bawds and Usurers

If, as their ends, their fruits were so, the same,
Bawdry, and usury were one kind of game.

LVIII To Groom Idiot

Idiot, last night, I prayed thee but forbear
To read my verses; now I must to hear:
For offering, with thy smiles, my wit to grace,
Thy ignorance still laughs in the wrong place.
And so my sharpness thou no less disjoints,
Than thou didst late my sense, losing my points.
So have I seen at Christmas sports one lost,
And, hood-winked, for a man, embrace a post.

LIX On Spies

Spies, you are lights in state, but of base stuff,
Who, when you have burnt yourselves down to the snuff,
Stink, and are thrown away. End fair enough.

LX To William, Lord Mounteagle

Lo, what my country should have done (have raised
An obelisk, or column to thy name,
Or, if she would but modestly have praised
Thy fact, in brass or marble writ the same)
I, that am glad of thy great chance, here do!
And proud, my work shall outlast common deeds,
Durst think it great, and worthy wonder too,
But thine, for which I do it, so much exceeds!
My country's parents I have many known;
10 But saver of my country thee alone.

LXI To Fool, or Knave

Thy praise, or dispraise is to me alike,
One doth not stroke me, nor the other strike.

LXII To Fine Lady Would-Be

Fine Madam Would-be, wherefore should you fear,
That love to make so well, a child to bear?
The world reputes you barren: but I know
Your 'pothecary, and his drug says no.
Is it the pain affrights? That's soon forgot.
Or your complexion's loss? You have a pot,
That can restore that. Will it hurt your feature?
To make amends, you're thought a wholesome creature.
What should the cause be? Oh, you live at court:
10 And there's both loss of time, and loss of sport
In a great belly. Write, then on thy womb,
Of the not born, yet buried, here's the tomb.

LXIII To Robert, Earl of Salisbury

Who can consider thy right courses run,
With what thy virtue on the times hath won,
And not thy fortune; who can clearly see
The judgement of the king so shine in thee;
And that thou seek'st reward of thy each act,
Not from the public voice, but private fact;
Who can behold all envy so declined
By constant suffering of thy equal mind;
And can to these be silent, Salisbury,
10 Without his, thine, and all times' injury?
Cursed be his muse, that could lie dumb, or hid
To so true worth, though thou thyself forbid.

LXIV *To The Same*

(UPON THE ACCESSION OF THE TREASURERSHIP TO
HIM)

Not glad, like those that have new hopes, or suits,
With thy new place, bring I these early fruits
Of love, and what the golden age did hold
A treasure, art: contemned in th'age of gold.
Nor glad as those, that old dependants be,
To see thy father's rights new laid on thee.
Nor glad for fashion. Nor to show a fit
Of flattery to thy titles. Nor of wit.
But I am glad to see that time survive,
10   Where merit is not sepulchered alive.
Where good men's virtues them to honours bring,
And not to dangers. When so wise a king
Contends to have worth enjoy, from his regard,
As her own conscience, still, the same reward.
These (noblest Cecil) laboured in my thought,
Wherein what wonder see thy name hath wrought!
That whilst I meant but thine to gratulate,
I have sung the greater fortunes of our state.

LXV *To My Muse*

Away, and leave me, thou thing most abhorred
That hast betrayed me to a worthless lord;
Made me commit most fierce idolatry
To a great image through thy luxury.
Be thy next master's more unlucky muse,
And, as thou hast mine, his hours, and youth abuse.
Get him the time's long grudge, the court's ill will;
And, reconciled, keep him suspected still.
Make him lose all his friends; and, which is worse,
10   Almost all ways, to any better course.
With me thou leav'st an happier muse than thee,
And which thou brought'st me, welcome poverty.

She shall instruct my after-thoughts to write
Things manly, and not smelling parasite.
But I repent me: stay. Whoe'er is raised,
For worth he has not, he is taxed, not praised.

LXVI To Sir Henry Cary

That neither fame, nor love might wanting be
To greatness, Cary, I sing that, and thee.
Whose house, if it no other honour had,
In only thee, might be both great, and glad.
Who, to upbraid the sloth of this our time,
Durst valour make, almost, but not a crime.
Which deed I know not, whether were more high,
Or thou more happy, it to justify
Against thy fortune: when no foe, that day,
10　Could conquer thee, but chance, who did betray.
Love thy great loss, which a renown hath won,
To live when Broeck not stands, nor Ruhr doth run.
Love honours, which of best example be,
When they cost dearest, and are done most free,
Though every fortitude deserves applause.
It may be much, or little, in the cause.
He's valiant'st, that dares fight, and not for pay:
That virtuous is, when the reward's away.

LXVII To Thomas, Earl of Suffolk

Since men have left to do praiseworthy things,
Most think all praises flatteries. But truth brings
That sound, and that authority with her name,
As, to be raised by her, is only fame.
Stand high, then, Howard, high in eyes of men,
High in thy blood, thy place, but highest then,
When, in men's wishes, so thy virtues wrought,
As all thy honours were by them first sought:

And thou designed to be the same thou art,
10 Before thou wert it, in each good man's heart.
Which, by no less confirmed, than thy king's choice,
Proves, that is God's, which was the people's voice.

LXVIII On Playwright

Playwright convict of public wrongs to men,
Takes private beatings, and begins again.
Two kinds of valour he doth show, at once;
Active in 's brain, and passive in his bones.

LXIX To Pertinax Cob

Cob, thou nor soldier, thief, nor fencer art,
Yet by thy weapon liv'st! Th'hast one good part.

LXX To William Roe

When Nature bids us leave to live, 'tis late
Then to begin, my Roe: he makes a state
In life, that can employ it; and takes hold
On the true causes, ere they grow too old.
Delay is bad, doubt worse, depending worst;
Each best day of our life escapes us, first.
Then, since we (more than many) these truths know;
Though life be short, let us not make it so.

LXXI On Court-Parrot

To pluck down mine, Poll sets up new wits still,
Still, 'tis his luck to praise me 'gainst his will.

LXXII To Courtling

I grieve not, Courtling, thou art started up
A chamber-critic, and dost dine, and sup
At madam's table, where thou mak'st all wit
Go high, or low, as thou wilt value it.
'Tis not thy judgement breeds the prejudice,
Thy person only, Courtling, is the vice.

LXXIII To Fine Grand

What is't, fine Grand, makes thee my friendship fly,
Or take an epigram so fearfully:
As 'twere a challenge, or a borrower's letter?
The world must know your greatness is my debtor.
In primis, Grand, you owe me for a jest,
I lent you, on mere acquaintance, at a feast.
Item, a tale or two, some fortnight after;
That yet maintains you, and your house in laughter.
Item, the Babylonian song you sing;
10 *Item*, a fair Greek posy for a ring:
With which a learnèd madam you belie.
Item, a charm surrounding fearfully,
Your *partie per pale* picture, one half drawn
In solemn cypress, the other cobweb lawn.
Item, a gulling imprese for you, at tilt.
Item, your mistress' anagram, in your hilt.
Item, your own, sewed in your mistress' smock.
Item, an epitaph on my lord's cock,
In most vile verses, and cost me more pain,
20 Than had I made them good, to fit your vein.
Forty things more, dear Grand, which you know true,
For which, or pay me quickly, or I'll pay you.

LXXIV To Thomas, Lord Chancellor

Whilst thy weighed judgments, Egerton, I hear,
And know thee, then, a judge, not of one year;
Whilst I behold thee live with purest hands;
That no affection in thy voice commands;
That still th'art present to the better cause;
And no less wise, than skilful in the laws;
Whilst thou art certain to thy words, once gone,
As is thy conscience, which is always one:
The virgin, long since fled from earth, I see,
10 T'our times returned, hath made her heaven in thee.

LXXV On Lip the Teacher

I cannot think there's that antipathy
'Twixt puritans, and players, as some cry;
Though Lip, at Paul's, ran from his text away,
T'inveigh 'gainst players: what did he then but play?

LXXVI On Lucy, Countess of Bedford

This morning, timely rapt with holy fire,
I thought to form unto my zealous muse,
What kind of creature I could most desire,
To honour, serve, and love; as poets use.
I meant to make her fair, and free, and wise,
Of greatest blood, and yet more good than great;
I meant the day-star should not brighter rise,
Nor lend like influence from his lucent seat.
I meant she should be courteous, facile, sweet,
10 Hating that solemn vice of greatness, pride;
I meant each softest virtue, there should meet,
Fit in that softer bosom to reside.
Only a learnèd, and a manly soul
I purposed her; that should, with even powers,

The rock, the spindle, and the shears control
Of destiny, and spin her own free hours.
Such when I meant to feign, and wished to see,
My muse bad, *Bedford* write, and that was she.

LXXVII *To One that Desired Me Not to Name Him*

Be safe, nor fear thyself so good a fame,
That, any way, my book should speak thy name:
For, if thou shame, ranked with my friends, to go,
I'm more ashamed to have thee thought my foe.

LXXVIII *To Hornet*

Hornet, thou hast thy wife dressed, for the stall,
To draw thee custom: but herself gets all.

LXXIX *To Elizabeth, Countess of Rutland*

That poets are far rarer births than kings,
Your noblest father proved: like whom, before,
Or then, or since, about our muses' springs,
Came not that soul exhausted so their store.
Hence was it, that the destinies decreed
(Save that most masculine issue of his brain)
No male unto him: who could so exceed
Nature, they thought, in all, that he would feign.
At which, she happily displeased, made you:
10 On whom, if he were living now, to look,
He should those rare, and absolute numbers view,
As he would burn, or better far his book.

LXXX Of Life and Death

The ports of death are sins; of life, good deeds:
Through which, our merit leads us to our meeds.
How wilful blind is he then, that would stray,
And hath it, in his powers, to make his way!
This world death's region is, the other life's:
And here, it should be one of our first strifes,
So to front death, as men might judge us past it.
For good men but see death, the wicked taste it.

LXXXI To Prowl the Plagiary

Forbear to tempt me, Prowl, I will not show
A line unto thee, till the world it know;
Or that I have by, two good sufficient men,
To be the wealthy witness of my pen:
For all thou hear'st, thou swear'st thyself didst do.
Thy wit lives by it, Prowl, and belly too.
Which, if thou leave not soon (though I am loath)
I must a libel make, and cozen both.

LXXXII On Cashiered Capt[ain] Surly

Surly's old whore in her new silks doth swim:
He cast, yet keeps her well! No, she keeps him.

LXXXIII To a Friend

To put out the word, whore, thou dost me woo,
Throughout my book. 'Troth put out woman too.

LXXXIV To Lucy, Countess of Bedford

Madam, I told you late how I repented,
I asked a lord a buck, and he denied me;
And, ere I could ask you, I was prevented:
For your most noble offer had supplied me.
Straight went I home; and there most like a poet,
I fancied to myself, what wine, what wit
I would have spent: how every muse should know it,
And Phoebus' self should be at eating it.
O madam, if your grant did thus transfer me,
10 Make it your gift. See whither that will bear me.

LXXXV To Sir Henry Goodyere

Goodyere, I am glad, and grateful to report,
Myself a witness of thy few days' sport:
Where I both learned, why wise men hawking follow,
And why that bird was sacred to Apollo.
She doth instruct men by her gallant flight,
That they to knowledge so should tower upright,
And never stoop, but to strike ignorance:
Which if they miss, they yet should readvance
To former height, and there in circle tarry,
10 Till they be sure to make the fool their quarry.
Now, in whose pleasures I have this discerned,
What would his serious actions me have learned?

LXXXVI To the Same

When I would know thee Goodyere, my thought looks
Upon thy well-made choice of friends, and books;
Then do I love thee, and behold thy ends
In making thy friends books, and thy books friends:
Now, I must give thy life, and deed, the voice
Attending such a study, such a choice.

Where, though't be love, that to thy praise doth move,
It was a knowledge, that begat that love.

LXXXVII On Captain Hazard the Cheater

Touched with the sin of false play, in his punk,
Hazard a month forswore his; and grew drunk,
Each night, to drown his cares: but when the gain
Of what she had wrought came in, and waked his brain,
Upon the account, hers grew the quicker trade.
Since when he's sober again, and all play's made.

LXXXVIII On English Monsieur

Would you believe, when you this monsieur see,
That his whole body should speak French, not he?
That so much scarf of France, and hat, and feather,
And shoe, and tie, and garter should come hither,
And land on one, whose face durst never be
Toward the sea, farther than halfway tree?
That he, untravelled, should be French so much,
As Frenchmen in his company, should seem Dutch?
Or had his father, when he did him get,
10 The French disease, with which he labours yet?
Or hung some monsieur's picture on the wall,
By which his dam conceived him, clothes and all?
Or is it some French statue? No: 't doth move,
And stoop, and cringe. O then, it needs must prove
The new French tailor's motion, monthly made,
Daily to turn in Paul's, and help the trade.

LXXXIX To Edward Alleyn

If Rome so great, and in her wisest age,
Feared not to boast the glories of her stage,

As skilful Roscius, and grave Aesop, men,
Yet crowned with honours, as with riches, then;
Who had no less a trumpet of their name,
Than Cicero, whose every breath was fame:
How can so great example die in me,
That, Alleyn, I should pause to publish thee?
Who both their graces in thyself hast more
10 Outstripped, than they did all that went before:
And present worth in all dost so contract,
As others speak, but only thou dost act.
Wear this renown. 'Tis just, that who did give
So many poets life, by one should live.

XC On Mill, My Lady's Woman

When Mill first came to court, the unprofiting fool,
Unworthy such a mistress, such a school,
Was dull, and long, ere she would go to man:
At last, ease, appetite, and example wan
The nicer thing to taste her lady's page;
And, finding good security in his age,
Went on: and proving him still, day by day,
Discerned no difference of his years, or play.
Not though that hair grew brown, which once was amber,
10 And he grown youth, was called to his lady's chamber,
Still Mill continued: nay, his face growing worse,
And he removed to gent'man of the horse,
Mill was the same. Since, both his body and face
Blown up; and he (too unwieldy for that place)
Hath got the steward's chair; he will not tarry
Longer a day, but with his Mill will marry.
And it is hoped, that she, like Milo, wull
First bearing him a calf, bear him a bull.

XCI To Sir Horace Vere

Which of thy names I take, not only bears
A Roman sound, but Roman virtue wears,
Illustrious Vere, or Horace; fit to be
Sung by a Horace, or a muse as free;
Which thou art to thyself: whose fame was won
In the eye of Europe, where thy deeds were done,
When on thy trumpet she did sound a blast,
Whose relish to eternity shall last.
I leave thy acts, which should I prosecute
10 Throughout, might flattery seem; and to be mute
To any one, were envy: which would live
Against my grave, and time could not forgive.
I speak thy other graces, not less shown,
Nor less in practice; but less marked, less known:
Humanity, and piety, which are
As noble in great chiefs, as they are rare.
And best become the valiant man to wear,
Who more should seek men's reverence, than fear.

XCII The New Cry

Ere cherries ripe, and strawberries be gone,
Unto the cries of London I'll add one;
Ripe statesmen ripe: they grow in every street.
At six and twenty, ripe. You shall them meet,
And have them yield no savour, but of state.
Ripe are their ruffs, their cuffs, their beards, their gait,
And grave as ripe, like mellow as their faces,
They know the states of Christendom, not the places:
Yet have they seen the maps, and bought them too,
10 And understand them, as most chapmen do.
The councils, projects, practices they know,
And what each prince doth for intelligence owe,
And unto whom: they are the almanacs
For twelve years yet to come, what each state lacks.

They carry in their pockets Tacitus,
And the gazetti, or *Gallo-Belgicus*:
And talk reserved, locked up, and full of fear,
Nay, ask you, how the day goes, in your ear.
Keep a Star Chamber sentence close, twelve days:
20   And whisper what a proclamation says.
They meet in sixes, and at every mart,
Are sure to con the catalogue by heart;
Or, every day, some one at Rimee's looks,
Or Bills', and there he buys the names of books.
They all get Porta, for the sundry ways
To write in cipher, and the several keys,
To ope' the character. They have found the sleight
With juice of lemons, onions, piss, to write.
To break up seals, and close them. And they know,
30   If the States make peace, how it will go
With England. All forbidden books they get.
And of the powder plot, they will talk yet.
At naming the French king, their heads they shake,
And at the pope, and Spain slight faces make.
Or 'gainst the bishops, for the Brethren, rail,
Much like those Brethren; thinking to prevail
With ignorance on us, as they have done
On them: and therefore do not only shun
Others more modest, but contemn us too,
40   That know not so much state, wrong, as they do.

XCIII *To Sir John Radcliffe*

How like a column, Radcliffe, left alone
For the great mark of virtue, those being gone
Who did, alike with thee, thy house upbear,
Stand'st thou, to show the times what you all were!
Two bravely in the battle fell, and died,
Upbraiding rebels' arms, and barbarous pride;
And two, that would have fallen as great, as they,
The Belgic fever ravishèd away.

Thou, that art all their valour, all their spirit,
10   And thine own goodness to increase thy merit,
Than whose I do not know a whiter soul,
Nor could I, had I seen all Nature's roll,
Thou yet remain'st, unhurt in peace or war,
Though not unproved: which shows, thy fortunes are
Willing to expiate the fault in thee,
Wherewith, against thy blood, they offenders be.

XCIV To Lucy, Countess of Bedford, with Mr Donne's Satires

Lucy, you brightness of our sphere, who are
Life of the muses' day, their morning star!
If works (not th'authors) their own grace should look,
Whose poems would not wish to be your book?
But these, desired by you, the maker's ends
Crown with their own. Rare poems ask rare friends.
Yet, satires, since the most of mankind be
Their unavoided subject, fewest see:
For none e'er took that pleasure in sin's sense,
10   But, when they heard it taxed, took more offence.
They, then, that living where the matter is bred,
Dare for these poems, yet, both ask, and read,
And like them too; must needfully, though few,
Be of the best: and 'mongst those, best are you.
Lucy, you brightness of our sphere, who are
The muses' evening, as their morning star.

XCV To Sir Henry Savile

If, my religion safe, I durst embrace
That stranger doctrine of Pythagoras,
I should believe the soul of Tacitus
In thee, most weighty Savile, lived to us:
So hast thou rendered him in all his bounds,

And all his numbers, both of sense, and sounds.
But when I read that special piece, restored,
Where Nero falls, and Galba is adored,
To thine own proper I ascribe then more;
10 And gratulate the breach, I grieved before:
Which Fate (it seems) caused in the history,
Only to boast thy merit in supply.
O, wouldst thou add like hand, to all the rest!
Or, better work, were thy glad country blessed,
To have her story woven in thy thread;
Minerva's loom was never richer spread.
For who can master those great parts like thee,
That liv'st from hope, from fear, from faction free;
That hast thy breast so clear of present crimes,
20 Thou need'st not shrink at voice of aftertimes;
Whose knowledge claimeth at the helm to stand;
But, wisely, thrusts not forth a forward hand,
No more than Sallust in the Roman state!
As, then, his cause, his glory emulate.
Although to write be lesser than to do,
It is the next deed, and a great one too.
We need a man that knows the several graces
Of history, and how to apt their places;
Where brevity, where splendour, and where height,
30 Where sweetness is required, and where weight;
We need a man, can speak of the intents,
The councils, actions, orders, and events
Of state, and censure them: we need his pen
Can write the things, the causes, and the men.
But most we need his faith (and all have you)
That dares nor write things false, nor hide things true.

XCVI To John Donne

Who shall doubt, Donne, where I a poet be,
When I dare send my epigrams to thee?
That so alone canst judge, so alone dost make:

And, in thy censures, evenly, dost take
As free simplicity, to disavow,
As thou hast best authority, to allow.
Read all I send: and, if I find but one
Marked by thy hand, and with the better stone,
My title's sealed. Those that for claps do write,
10   Let puisnees', porters', players' praise delight,
And, till they burst, their backs, like asses' load:
A man should seek great glory, and not broad.

XCVII *On the New Motion*

See you yond' motion? Not the old fading,
Nor Captain Pod, nor yet the Eltham thing;
But one more rare, and in the case so new:
His cloak with orient velvet quite lined through,
His rosy ties and garters so o'er-blown,
By his each glorious parcel to be known!
He wont was to encounter me, aloud,
Where e'er he met me; now he's dumb, or proud.
Know you the cause? He has neither land, nor lease,
10   Nor bawdy stock, that travels for increase,
Nor office in the town, nor place in court,
Nor 'bout the bears, nor noise to make lords sport.
He is no favourite's favourite, no dear trust
Of any madams, hath neadd squires, and must.
Nor did the king of Denmark him salute,
When he was here. Nor hath he got a suit,
Since he was gone, more than the one he wears.
Nor are the queen's most honoured maids by th'ears
About his form. What then so swells each limb?
20   Only his clothes have over-leavened him.

XCVIII To Sir Thomas Roe

Thou hast begun well, Roe, which stand well too,
And I know nothing more thou hast to do.
He that is round within himself, and straight,
Need seek no other strength, no other height;
Fortune upon him breaks herself, if ill,
And what would hurt his virtue makes it still.
That thou at once, then, nobly may'st defend
With thine own course the judgement of thy friend,
Be always to thy gathered self the same:
10 And study conscience, more than thou wouldst fame.
Though both be good, the latter yet is worst,
And ever is ill got without the first.

XCIX To the Same

That thou hast kept thy love, increased thy will,
Bettered thy trust to letters; that thy skill;
Hast taught thyself worthy thy pen to tread,
And that to write things worthy to be read:
How much of great example wert thou, Roe,
If time to facts, as unto men would owe?
But much it now avails, what's done, of whom:
The selfsame deeds, as diversely they come,
From place, or fortune, are made high, or low,
10 And even the praiser's judgement suffers so.
Well, though thy name less than our great ones' be,
Thy fact is more: let truth encourage thee.

C On Playwright

Playwright, by chance, hearing some toys I had writ,
Cried to my face, they were the elixir of wit:
And I must now believe him: for, today,
Five of my jests, then stolen, passed him a play.

CI *Inviting a Friend to Supper*

Tonight, grave sir, both my poor house, and I
Do equally desire your company:
Not that we think us worthy such a guest,
But that your worth will dignify our feast,
With those that come; whose grace may make that seem
Something, which, else, could hope for no esteem.
It is the fair acceptance, sir, creates
The entertainment perfect: not the cates.
Yet shall you have, to rectify your palate,
10 An olive, capers, or some better salad
Ush'ring the mutton; with a short-legged hen,
If we can get her, full of eggs, and then,
Lemons, and wine for sauce: to these, a cony
Is not to be despaired of, for our money;
And, though fowl, now, be scarce, yet there are clerks,
The sky not falling, think we may have larks.
I'll tell you of more, and lie, so you will come:
Of partridge, pheasant, woodcock, of which some
May yet be there; and godwit, if we can:
20 Knat, rail, and ruff too. Howsoe'er, my man
Shall read a piece of Virgil, Tacitus,
Livy, or of some better book to us,
Of which we'll speak our minds, amidst our meat;
And I'll profess no verses to repeat:
To this, if aught appear, which I not know of,
That will the pastry, not my paper, show of.
Digestive cheese, and fruit there sure will be;
But that, which most doth take my muse, and me,
Is a pure cup of rich canary wine,
30 Which is the Mermaid's, now, but shall be mine:
Of which had Horace, or Anacreon tasted,
Their lives, as do their lines, till now had lasted.
Tobacco, nectar, or the Thespian spring,
Are all but Luther's beer, to this I sing.
Of this we will sup free, but moderately,
And we will have no Pooly, or Parrot by;

Nor shall our cups make any guilty men:
But, at our parting, we will be, as when
We innocently met. No simple word,
40   That shall be uttered at our mirthful board,
Shall make us sad next morning: or affright
The liberty, that we'll enjoy tonight.

CII   To William, Earl of Pembroke

I do but name thee Pembroke, and I find
It is an epigram, on all mankind;
Against the bad, but of, and to the good:
Both which are asked, to have thee understood.
Nor could the age have missed thee, in this strife
Of vice, and virtue; wherein all great life
Almost, is exercised: and scarce one knows,
To which, yet, of the sides himself he owes.
They follow virtue, for reward, today;
10   Tomorrow vice, if she give better pay:
And are so good, and bad, just at a price,
As nothing else discerns the virtue or vice.
But thou, whose noblesse keeps one stature still,
And one true posture, though besieged with ill
Of what ambition, faction, pride can raise;
Whose life, even they, that envy it, must praise;
That art so reverenced, as thy coming in,
But in the view, doth interrupt their sin;
Thou must draw more: and they, that hope to see
20   The commonwealth still safe, must study thee.

CIII   To Mary, Lady Wroth

How well, fair crown of your fair sex, might he,
That but the twilight of your sprite did see,
And noted for what flesh such souls were framed,
Know you to be a Sidney, though unnamed?

And, being named, how little doth that name
Need any muse's praise to give it fame?
Which is, itself, the imprese of the great,
And glory of them all, but to repeat!
Forgive me then, if mine but say you are
10   A Sidney: but in that extend as far
As loudest praisers, who perhaps would find
For every part a character assigned.
My praise is plain, and wheresoe'er professed,
Becomes none more than you, who need it least.

CIV To Susan, Countess of Montgomery

Were they that named you, prophets? Did they see,
Even in the dew of grace, what you would be?
Or did our times require it, to behold
A new Susanna, equal to that old?
Or, because some scarce think that story true,
To make those faithful, did the Fates send you?
And to your scene lent no less dignity
Of birth, of match, of form, of chastity?
Or, more than born for the comparison
10   Of former age, or glory of our own,
Were you advanced, past those times, to be
The light, and mark unto posterity?
Judge they, that can: here I have raised to show
A picture, which the world for yours must know,
And like it too; if they look equally:
If not, 'tis fit for you, some should envy.

CV To Mary, Lady Wroth

Madam, had all antiquity been lost,
All history sealed up, and fables crossed;
That we had left us, nor by time, nor place,

Least mention of a nymph, a muse, a grace,
But even their names were to be made anew,
Who could not but create them all, from you?
He, that but saw you wear the wheaten hat,
Would call you more than Ceres, if not that:
And, dressed in shepherd's 'tire, who would not say:
10 You were the bright Oenone, Flora, or May?
If dancing, all would cry the Idalian queen,
Were leading forth the graces on the green:
And armèd to the chase, so bare her bow
Diana alone, so hit, and hunted so.
There's none so dull, that for your stile would ask,
That saw you put on Pallas' pluméd casque:
Or, keeping your due state, that would not cry,
There Juno sat, and yet no peacock by.
So are you Nature's index, and restore,
20 In yourself, all treasure lost of th'age before.

CVI *To Sir Edward Herbert*

If men get name, for some one virtue: then,
What man art thou, that art so many men,
All-virtuous Herbert? On whose every part
Truth might spend all her voice, fame all her art.
Whether thy learning they would take, or wit,
Or valour, or thy judgement seasoning it,
Thy standing upright to thyself, thy ends
Like straight, thy piety to God, and friends:
Their latter praise would still the greatest be,
10 And yet, they, altogether, less than thee.

CVII *To Captain Hungry*

Do what you come for, captain, with your news;
That's, sit, and eat: do not my ears abuse.
I oft look on false coin, to know it from true:

Not that I love it, more, than I will you.
Tell the gross Dutch those grosser tales of yours,
How great you were with their two emperors;
And yet are with their princes: fill them full
Of your Moravian horse, Venetian bull.
Tell them, what parts you've ta'en, whence run away,
10   What states you've gulled, and which yet keeps you in pay.
Give them your services, and embassies
In Ireland, Holland, Sweden, pompous lies,
In Hungary, and Poland, Turkey too;
What at Ligorne, Rome, Florence you did do:
And, in some year, all these together heaped,
For which there must more sea, and land be leaped,
If but to be believed you have the hap,
Than can a flea at twice skip in the map.
Give your young statesmen (that first make you drunk,
20   And then lie with you, closer, than a punk,
For news) your Villeroys, and Silleries,
Janins, your nuncios, and your Tuilleries,
Your Arch Duke's agents, and your Beringhams,
That are your words of credit. Keep your names
Of Hanou, Shieter-Huissen, Popenheim,
Hans-spiegle, Rotenberg, and Boutersheim,
For your next meal: this you are sure of. Why
Will you part with them, here, unthriftily?
Nay, now you puff, tusk, and draw up your chin,
30   Twirl the poor chain you run a-feasting in.
Come, be not angry, you are hungry; eat;
Do what you come for, captain, there's your meat.

CVIII *To True Soldiers*

Strength of my country, whilst I bring to view
Such as are miscalled captains, and wrong you;
And your high names: I do desire, that thence
Be nor put on you, nor you take offence.
I swear by your true friend, my muse, I love

Your great profession; which I once did prove:
And did not shame it with my actions, then,
No more, than I dare now do, with my pen.
He that not trusts me, having vowed thus much,
10 But's angry for the captain, still: is such.

CIX To Sir Henry Nevil

Who now calls on thee, Nevil, is a muse,
That serves nor fame, nor titles; but doth choose
Where virtue makes them both, and that's in thee:
Where all is fair, beside thy pedigree.
Thou art not one, seek'st miseries with hope,
Wrestlest with dignities, or feign'st a scope
Of service to the public, when the end
Is private gain, which hath long guilt to friend.
Thou rather striv'st the matter to possess,
10 And elements of honour, than the dress;
To make thy lent life, good against the Fates:
And first to know thine own state, then the State's.
To be the same in root, thou art in height;
And that thy soul should give thy flesh her weight.
Go on, and doubt not, what posterity,
Now I have sung thee thus, shall judge of thee.
Thy deeds, unto thy name, will prove new wombs,
Whilst others toil for titles to their tombs.

CX To Clement Edmonds, on His Caesar's Commentaries Observed, and Translated

Not Caesar's deeds, nor all his honours won,
In these west parts, nor when that war was done,
The name of Pompey for an enemy,
Cato's to boot, Rome, and her liberty,
All yielding to his fortune, nor, the while,
To have engraved these acts, with his own stile,

And that so strong and deep, as't might be thought,
He wrote, with the same spirit that he fought,
Nor that his work lived in the hands of foes,
10 Unargued then, and yet hath fame from those;
Not all these, Edmonds, or what else put to,
Can so speak Caesar, as thy labours do.
For, where his person lived scarce one just age,
And that, midst envy and parts; then fell by rage:
His deeds too dying, but in books (whose good
How few have read! how fewer understood!)
Thy learnéd hand, and true Promethean art
(As by a new creation) part by part,
In every council, stratagem, design,
20 Action, or engine, worth a note of thine,
To all future time, not only doth restore
His life, but makes, that he can die no more.

CXI *To the Same; on the Same*

Who Edmonds, reads thy book, and doth not see
What the antique soldiers were, the moderns be?
Wherein thou show'st, how much the latter are
Beholding, to this master of the war;
And that, in action, there is nothing new,
More, than to vary what our elders knew:
Which all, but ignorant captains, will confess:
Nor to give Caesar this, makes ours the less.
Yet thou, perhaps, shall meet some tongues will grutch,
10 That to the world thou should'st reveal so much,
And thence, deprave thee, and thy work. To those
Caesar stands up, as from his urn late rose,
By thy great help: and doth proclaim by me,
They murder him again, that envy thee.

CXII To a Weak Gamester in Poetry

With thy small stock, why are thou vent'ring still,
At this so subtle sport: and play'st so ill?
Think'st thou it is mere fortune, that can win?
Or thy rank setting? That thou dar'st put in
Thy all, at all: and whatsoe'er I do,
Art still at that, and think'st to blow me up too?
I cannot for the stage a drama lay,
Tragic, or comic; but thou writ'st the play.
I leave thee there, and giving way, intend
10 An epic poem; thou hast the same end.
I modestly quit that, and think to write,
Next morn, an ode: thou mak'st a song ere night.
I pass to elegies; thou meet'st me there:
To satires; and thou dost pursue me. Where,
Where shall I 'scape thee? In an epigram?
O (thou cry'st out) that is thy proper game.
Troth, if it be, I pity thy ill luck;
That both for wit, and sense, so oft dost pluck,
And never art encountered, I confess:
20 Nor scarce dost colour for it, which is less.
Prithee, yet save thy rest; give o'er in time:
There's no vexation, that can make thee prime.

CXIII To Sir Thomas Overbury

So Phoebus makes me worthy of his bays,
As but to speak thee, Overbury, is praise:
So, where thou liv'st, thou mak'st life understood!
Where, what makes others great, doth keep thee good!
I think, the Fate of court thy coming craved,
That the wit there, and manners might be saved:
For since, what ignorance, what pride is fled!
And letters, and humanity in the stead!
Repent thee not of thy fair precedent,
10 Could make such men, and such a place repent:

Nor may any fear, to lose of their degree,
Who in such ambition can but follow thee.

CXIV *To Mrs Philip Sidney*

I must believe some miracles still be,
When Sidney's name I hear, or face I see:
For Cupid, who (at first) took vain delight,
In mere out-forms, until he lost his sight,
Hath changed his soul, and made his object you:
Where finding so much beauty met with virtue,
He hath not only gained himself his eyes,
But, in your love, made all his servants wise.

CXV *On the Town's Honest Man*

You wonder, who this is! And, why I name
Him not, aloud, that boasts so good a fame:
Naming so many, too! But, this is one,
Suffers no name, but a description:
Being no vicious person, but the Vice
About the town; and known too, at that price.
A subtle thing, that doth affections win
By speaking well of the company it's in.
Talks loud, and bawdy, has a gathered deal
10 Of news, and noise, to sow out a long meal.
Can come from Tripoli, leap stools, and wink,
Do all, that 'longs to the anarchy of drink,
Except the duel. Can sing songs, and catches;
Give every one his dose of mirth: and watches
Whose name's unwelcome to the present ear,
And him it lays on; if he be not there,
Tells of him, all the tales, itself then makes;
But, if it shall be questioned, undertakes,
It will deny all; and forswear it too:
20 Not that it fears, but will not have to do

With such a one. And therein keeps its word.
'Twill see its sister naked, ere a sword.
At every meal, where it doth dine, or sup,
The cloth's no sooner gone, but it gets up
And shifting of its faces, doth play more
Parts, than the Italian could do, with his dore.
Acts old Iniquity, and in the fit
Of miming gets the opinion of a wit.
Executes men in picture. By defect,
30 From friendship, is its own fame's architect.
An engineer, in slanders, of all fashions,
That seeming praises, are, yet accusations.
Described, it's thus: defined would you it have?
Then, the town's honest man's her errant'st knave.

CXVI To Sir William Jephson

Jephson, thou man of men, to whose loved name
All gentry, yet, owe part of their best flame!
So did thy virtue inform, thy wit sustain
That age, when thou stood'st up the master brain:
Thou wert the first, mad'st merit know her strength,
And those that lacked it, to suspect at length,
'Twas not entailed on title. That some word
Might be found out as good, and not 'my lord'.
That Nature no such difference had impressed
10 In men, but every bravest was the best:
That blood not minds, but minds did blood adorn:
And to live great, was better, than great born.
These were thy knowing arts: which who doth now
Virtuously practise must at least allow
Them in, if not from thee; or must commit
A desperate solecism in truth and wit.

CXVII On Groin

Groin, come of age, his state sold out of hand
For his whore: Groin doth still occupy his land.

CXVIII On Gut

Gut eats all day, and lechers all the night,
So all his meat he tasteth over, twice:
And, striving so to double his delight,
He makes himself a thoroughfare of vice.
Thus, in his belly, can he change a sin,
Lust it comes out, that gluttony went in.

CXIX To Sir Ra[l]ph Shelton

Not he that flies the court for want of clothes,
At hunting rails, having no gift in oaths,
Cries out 'gainst cocking, since he cannot bet,
Shuns prease, for two main causes, pox, and debt,
With me can merit more, than that good man,
Whose dice not doing well, to a pulpit ran.
No, Shelton, give me thee, canst want all these,
But dost it out of judgement, not disease;
Dar'st breathe in any air; and with safe skill,
10   Till thou canst find the best, choose the least ill.
That to the vulgar canst thyself apply,
Treading a better path, not contrary;
And, in their errors' maze, thine own way know:
Which is to live to conscience, not to show.
He, that, but living half his age, dies such;
Makes the whole longer, than 'twas given him, much.

CXX Epitaph on S.P., a Child of Q[ueen] El[izabeth's] Chapel

Weep with me all you that read
    This little story:
And know, for whom a tear you shed,
    Death's self is sorry.
'Twas a child, that so did thrive
    In grace, and feature,
As Heaven and Nature seemed to strive
    Which owned the creature.
Years he numbered scarce thirteen
10   When Fates turned cruel,
Yet three filled zodiacs had he been
    The stage's jewel;
And did act (what now we moan)
    Old men so duly,
As, sooth, the Parcae thought him one,
    He played so truly.
So, by error, to his fate
    They all consented;
But viewing him since (alas, too late)
20   They have repented.
And have sought (to give new birth)
    In baths to steep him;
But, being so much too good for earth,
    Heaven vows to keep him.

CXXI To Benjamin Rudyerd

Rudyerd, as lesser dames, to great ones use,
My lighter comes, to kiss thy learnèd muse;
Whose better studies while she emulates,
She learns to know long difference of their states.
Yet is the office not to be despised,
If only love should make the action prized:

Nor he, for friendship, to be thought unfit,
That strives, his manners should precede his wit.

CXXII *To the Same*

If I would wish, for truth, and not for show,
The agèd Saturn's age, and rites to know;
If I would strive to bring back times, and try
The world's pure gold, and wise simplicity;
If I would virtue set, as she was young,
And hear her speak with one, and her first tongue;
If holiest friendship, naked to the touch,
I would restore, and keep it ever such;
I need no other arts, but study thee:
10   Who prov'st, all these were, and again may be.

CXXIII *To the Same*

Writing thyself, or judging others' writ,
I know not which thou hast most, candour, or wit:
But both thou hast so, as who affects the state
Of the best writer, and judge, should emulate.

CXXIV *Epitaph on Elizabeth, L.H.*

Wouldst thou hear, what man can say
In a little? Reader, stay.
Underneath this stone doth lie
As much beauty, as could die:
Which in life did harbour give
To more virtue, than doth live.
If, at all, she had a fault,
Leave it buried in this vault.
One name was Elizabeth,
10   The other let it sleep with death:

Fitter, where it died, to tell,
Than that it lived at all. Farewell.

CXXV To Sir William Uvedale

Uvedale, thou piece of the first times, a man
Made for what Nature could, or virtue can;
Both whose dimensions, lost, the world might find
Restoréd in thy body, and thy mind!
Who sees a soul, in such a body set,
Might love the treasure for the cabinet.
But I, no child, no fool, respect the kind,
The full, the flowing graces there enshrined;
Which (would the world not miscall 't flattery)
10 I could adore, almost t'idolatry.

CXXVI To His Lady, Then Mrs Cary

Retired, with purpose your fair worth to praise,
'Mongst Hampton shades, and Phoebus' grove of bays,
I plucked a branch; the jealous god did frown,
And bad me lay the usurpèd laurel down:
Said I wronged him, and (which was more) his love.
I answered, 'Daphne now no pain can prove.'
Phoebus replied: 'Bold head, it is not she:
Cary my love is, Daphne but my tree.'

CXXVII To Esmé, Lord Aubigny

Is there a hope, that man would thankful be,
If I should fail, in gratitude, to thee
To whom I am so bound, loved Aubigny?
No, I do, therefore, call posterity
Into the debt; and reckon on her head,
How full of want, how swallowed up, how dead

I, and this muse had been, if thou hadst not
Lent timely succours, and new life begot:
So, all reward, or name, that grows to me
10 By her attempt, shall still be owing thee.
And, than this same, I know no abler way
To thank thy benefits: which is, to pay.

CXXVIII To William Roe

Roe (and my joy to name) th'art now, to go
Countries, and climes, manners, and men to know,
To extract, and choose the best of all these known,
And those to turn to blood, and make thine own:
May winds as soft as breath of kissing friends,
Attend thee hence; and there, may all thy ends,
As the beginnings here, prove purely sweet,
And perfect in a circle always meet.
So, when we, blest with thy return, shall see
10 Thyself, with thy first thoughts, brought home by thee,
We each to other may this voice inspire;
This is that good Aeneas, passed through fire,
Through seas, storms, tempests: and embarked for hell,
Came back untouched. This man hath travelled well.

CXXIX To Mime

That, not a pair of friends each other see,
But the first question is, when one saw thee?
That there's no journey set, or thought upon,
To Brainford, Hackney, Bow, but thou mak'st one;
That scarce the town designeth any feast
To which th'art not a week, bespoke a guest;
That still th'art made the supper's flag, the drum,
The very call, to make all others come:
Think'st thou, Mime, this is great? Or, that they strive
10 Whose noise shall keep thy miming most alive,

Whilst thou dost raise some player, from the grave,
Outdance the babion, or outboast the brave,
Or (mounted on a stool) thy face doth hit
On some new gesture, that's imputed wit?
O, run not proud of this. Yet, take thy due.
Thou dost outzany Cokely, Pod; nay Gue:
And thine own Coriat too. But (wouldst thou see)
Men love thee not for this: they laugh at thee.

CXXX To Alphonso Ferrabosco, on His Book

To urge, my loved Alphonso, that bold fame
Of building towns, and making wild beasts tame,
Which music had; or speak her known effects,
That she removeth cares, sadness ejects,
Declineth anger, persuades clemency,
Doth sweeten mirth, and heighten piety,
And is t' a body, often, ill inclined,
No less a sovereign cure, than to the mind;
To allege, that greatest men were not ashamed,
10   Of old, even by her practice, to be famed;
To say, indeed, she were the soul of heaven,
That the eight spheres, no less, than planets seven,
Moved by her order, and the ninth more high,
Including all, were thence called harmony:
I, yet, had uttered nothing on thy part,
When these were but the praises of the art.
But when I have said, the proofs of all these be
Shed in thy songs; 'tis true: but short of thee.

CXXXI To the Same

When we do give, Alphonso, to the light,
A work of ours, we part with our own right;
For, then, all mouths will judge, and their own way:
The learned have no more privilege, than the lay.

And though we could all men, all censures hear,
We ought not give them taste, we had an ear.
For, if the humorous world will talk at large,
They should be fools, for me, at their own charge.
Say, this, or that man they to thee prefer;
10   Even those for whom they do this, know they err:
And would (being asked the truth) ashamèd say,
They were not to be named on the same day.
Then stand unto thyself, not seek without
For fame, with breath soon kindled, soon blown out.

CXXXII *To Mr Joshua Sylvester*

If to admire were to commend, my praise
Might then both thee, thy work and merit raise:
But, as it is (the child of ignorance,
And utter stranger to all air of France)
How can I speak of thy great pains, but err?
Since they can only judge, that can confer.
Behold! The reverend shade of Bartas stands
Before my thought, and (in thy right) commands
That to the world I publish, for him, this:
10   Bartas doth wish thy English now were his.
So well in that are his inventions wrought,
As his will now be the translation thought,
Thine the original; and France shall boast,
No more, those maiden glories she hath lost.

CXXXIII *On the Famous Voyage*

No more let Greece her bolder fables tell
Of Hercules, or Theseus going to hell,
Orpheus, Ulysses: or the Latin muse,
With tales of Troy's just knight, our faiths abuse:
We have a Shelton, and a Heyden got,
Had power to act, what they to feign had not.

All, that they boast of Styx, of Acheron,
Cocytus, Phlegeton, our have proved in one;
The filth, stench, noise: save only what was there
10 Subtly distinguished, was confusèd here.
Their wherry had no sail, too; ours had none:
And in it, two more horrid knaves than Charon.
Arses were heard to croak, instead of frogs;
And for one Cerberus, the whole coast was dogs.
Furies there wanted not: each scold was ten.
And, for the cries of ghosts, women, and men,
Laden with plague-sores, and their sins, were heard,
Lashed by their consciences, to die, afeared.
Then let the former age, with this content her,
20 She brought the poets forth, but ours the adventer.

THE VOYAGE ITSELF

I sing the brave adventure of two wights,
And pity 'tis, I cannot call them knights:
One was; and he, for brawn, and brain, right able
To have been stylèd of King Arthur's table.
The other was a squire, of fair degree;
But, in the action, greater man than he:
Who gave, to take at his return from Hell,
His three for one. Now, lordings, listen well.
   It was the day, what time the powerful moon
30 Makes the poor Bankside creature wet its shoon,
In its own hall; when these (in worthy scorn
Of those, that put out monies, on return
From Venice, Paris, or some inland passage
Of six times to, and fro, without embassage,
Or him that backward went to Berwick, or which
Did dance the famous Morris, unto Norwich)
At Bread Street's Mermaid, having dined, and merry,
Proposed to go to Holborn in a wherry:
A harder task, than either his to Bristo',
40 Or his to Antwerp. Therefore, once more list ho.
   A dock there is, that called is Avernus,

Of some Bridewell, and may, in time, concern us
All, that are readers: but, methinks 'tis odd,
That all this while I have forgot some god,
Or goddess to invoke, to stuff my verse;
And with both bombard style, and phrase, rehearse
The many perils of this port, and how
Sans help of Sybil, or a golden bough,
Or magic sacrifice, they passed along!
50 Alcides, be thou succouring to my song.
Thou hast seen hell (some say) and know'st all nooks there,
Canst tell me best, how every Fury looks there,
And art a god, if Fame thee not abuses,
Always at hand, to aid the merry muses.
Great club-fist, though thy back, and bones be sore,
Still, with thy former labours; yet, once more,
Act a brave work, call it thy last adventry:
But hold my torch, while I describe the entry
To this dire passage. Say, thou stop thy nose:
60 'Tis but light pains: indeed this dock's no rose.
   In the first jaws appeared that ugly monster,
Ycleped Mud, which, when their oars did once stir,
Belched forth an air, as hot, as at the muster
Of all your night-tubs, when the carts do cluster,
Who shall discharge first his merd-urinous load:
Thorough her womb they make their famous road,
Between two walls; where, on one side, to scar men,
Were seen your ugly centaurs, ye call car-men,
Gorgonian scolds, and harpies: on the other
70 Hung stench, diseases, and old filth, their mother,
With famine, wants, and sorrows many a dozen,
The least of which was to the plague a cousin.
But they unfrighted pass, though many a privy
Spake to them louder, than the ox in Livy;
And many a sink poured out her rage anenst 'hem;
But still their valour, and their virtue fenced 'hem,
And, on they went, like Castor brave, and Pollux:
Ploughing the main. When see (the worst of all lucks)
They met the second prodigy, would fear a

80   Man, that had never heard of a Chimera.
One said, it was bold Briareüs, or the beadle,
(Who hath the hundred hands when he doth meddle)
The other thought it Hydra, or the rock
Made of the trull, that cut her father's lock:
But, coming near, they found it but a lighter,
So huge, it seemed, they could by no means quit her.
'Back', cried their brace of Charons: they cried, 'No,
No going back; on still you rogues, and row.
How hight the place?' A voice was heard, 'Cocytus.'
90   'Row close then, slaves.' 'Alas, they will beshite us.'
'No matter, stinkards, row. What croaking sound
Is this we hear? Of frogs?' 'No, guts wind-bound,
Over your heads': 'Well, row.' At this a loud
Crack did report itself, as if a cloud
Had burst with storm, and down fell, *ab excelsis*,
Poor Mercury, crying out on Paracelsus,
And all his followers, that had so abused him:
And, in so shitten sort, so long had used him:
For (where he was the god of eloquence,
100 And subtlety of metals) they dispense
His spirits, now, in pills, and eke in potions,
Suppositories, cataplasms, and lotions.
But many moons there shall not wane (quoth he)
(In the meantime, let them imprison me)
But I will speak (and know I shall be heard)
Touching this cause, where they will be afeared
To answer me. And sure, it was the intent
Of the grave fart, late let in parliament,
Had it been seconded, and not in fume
110 Vanished away: as you must all presume
Their Mercury did now. By this the stem
Of the hulk touched, and, as by Polypheme
The sly Ulysses stole in a sheepskin,
The well-greased wherry now had got between,
And bad her farewell sough, unto the lurden:
Never did bottom more betray her burden;
The meat-boat of Bears' college, Paris garden,

Stunk not so ill; nor, when she kissed, Kate Arden.
Yet, one day in the year, for sweet 'tis voiced,
120   And that is when it is the Lord Mayor's foist.
        By this time had they reached the Stygian pool,
By which the masters swear, when, on the stool
Of worship, they their nodding chins do hit
Against their breasts. Here, several ghosts did flit
About the shore, of farts, but late departed,
White, black, blue, green, and in more forms outstarted,
Than all those *atomi* ridiculous,
Whereof old Democrite, and Hill Nicholas,
One said, the other swore, the world consists.
130   These be the cause of those thick frequent mists
Arising in that place, through which, who goes,
Must try the unused valour of a nose:
And that ours did. For, yet, no nare was tainted,
Nor thumb, nor finger to the stop acquainted,
But open, and unarmed encountered all:
Whether it languishing stuck upon the wall,
Or were precipitated down the jakes,
And, after, swom abroad in ample flakes,
Or, that it lay, heaped like an usurer's mass,
140   All was to them the same, they were to pass,
And so they did, from Styx, to Acheron:
The ever-boiling flood. Whose banks upon
Your Fleet Lane Furies; and hot cooks do dwell,
That, with still-scalding steams, make the place hell.
The sinks ran grease, and hair of measled hogs,
The heads, houghs, entrails, and the hides of dogs:
For, to say truth, what scullion is so nasty,
To put the skins, and offal in a pasty?
Cats there lay divers had been flayed and roasted,
150   And, after mouldy grown, again were toasted,
Then, selling not, a dish was ta'en to mince them,
But still, it seemed, the rankness did convince them.
For, here they were thrown in with the melted pewter,
Yet drowned they not. They had five lives in future.
        But 'mongst these Tiberts, who do you think there was?

Old Banks the juggler, our Pythagoras,
Grave tutor to the learnéd horse. Both which,
Being, beyond sea, burnéd for one witch:
Their spirits transmigrated to a cat:
160 And, now, above the pool, a face right fat
With great grey eyes, are lifted up, and mewed;
Thrice did it spit; thrice dived. At last, it viewed
Our brave heroes with a milder glare,
And, in a piteous tune, began. 'How dare
Your dainty nostrils (in so hot a season,
When every clerk eats artichokes, and peason,
Laxative lettuce, and such windy meat)
'Tempt such a passage? When each privy's seat
Is filled with buttock? And the walls do sweat
170 Urine, and plasters? When the noise doth beat
Upon your ears, of discords so unsweet?
And outcries of the damnéd in the Fleet?
Cannot the plague-bill keep you back? Nor bells
Of loud sepúlchres with their hourly knells,
But you will visit grisly Pluto's hall?
Behold where Cerberus, reared on the wall
Of Holborn (three sergeants' heads) looks o'er,
And stays but till you come unto the door!
Tempt not his fury, Pluto is away:
180 And madam Caesar, great Proserpina,
Is now from home. You lose your labours quite,
Were you Jove's sons, or had Alcides' might'.
They cried out puss. He told them he was Banks,
That had, so often, showed them merry pranks.
They laughed, at his laugh-worthy fate. And passed
The triple head without a sop. At last,
Calling for Radamanthus, that dwelt by,
A soap-boiler; and Aeacus him nigh,
Who kept an ale-house; with my little Minos,
190 An ancient purblind fletcher, with a high nose;
They took them all to witness of their action:
And so went bravely back, without protraction.
    In memory of which most liquid deed,

The city since hath raised a pyramid.
And I could wish for their eternized sakes,
My muse had ploughed with his, that sung A-JAX.

The Forest

I Why I Write Not of Love

Some act of Love's bound to rehearse,
I thought to bind him, in my verse:
Which when he felt, Away (quoth he)
Can poets hope to fetter me?
It is enough, they once did get
Mars, and my mother, in their net:
I wear not these my wings in vain.
With which he fled me: and again,
Into my rhymes could ne'er be got
10   By any art. Then wonder not,
That since, my numbers are so cold,
When Love is fled, and I grow old.

II To Penshurst

Thou art not, Penshurst, built to envious show,
Of touch, or marble; nor canst boast a row
Of polished pillars, or a roof of gold:
Thou hast no lanthern, whereof tales are told;
Or stair, or courts; but stand'st an ancient pile,
And these grudged at, art reverenced the while.
Thou joy'st in better marks, of soil, of air,
Of wood, of water: therein thou art fair.
Thou hast thy walks for health, as well as sport:
10   Thy Mount, to which the dryads do resort,
Where Pan, and Bacchus their high feasts have made,
Beneath the broad beech, and the chestnut shade;
That taller tree, which of a nut was set,
At his great birth, where all the muses met.
There, in the writhèd bark, are cut the names
Of many a Sylvan, taken with his flames.
And thence, the ruddy satyrs oft provoke
The lighter fauns, to reach thy lady's oak.
Thy copse, too, named of Gamage, thou hast there,
20   That never fails to serve thee seasoned deer,

When thou would'st feast, or exercise thy friends.
The lower land, that to the river bends,
Thy sheep, thy bullocks, kine, and calves do feed:
The middle grounds thy mares, and horses breed.
Each bank doth yield thee conies; and the tops
Fertile of wood, Ashore, and Sidney's copse,
To crown thy open table, doth provide
The purpled pheasant, with the speckled side:
The painted partridge lies in every field,
30   And, for thy mess, is willing to be killed.
And if the high-swoll'n Medway fail thy dish,
Thou hast thy ponds, that pay thee tribute fish,
Fat, agéd carps, that run into thy net.
And pikes, now weary their own kind to eat,
As loth, the second draught, or cast to stay,
Officiously, at first, themselves betray.
Bright eels, that emulate them, and leap on land,
Before the fisher, or into his hand.
Then hath thy orchard fruit, thy garden flowers,
40   Fresh as the air, and new as are the hours.
The early cherry, with the later plum,
Fig, grape, and quince, each in his time doth come:
The blushing apricot, and woolly peach
Hang on thy walls, that every child may reach.
And though thy walls be of the country stone,
They are reared with no man's ruin, no man's groan,
There's none, that dwell about them, wish them down;
But all come in, the farmer, and the clown:
And no one empty-handed, to salute
50   Thy lord, and lady, though they have no suit.
Some bring a capon, some a rural cake,
Some nuts, some apples; some that think they make
The better cheeses, bring them; or else send
By their ripe daughters, whom they would commend
This way to husbands; and whose baskets bear
An emblem of themselves, in plum, or pear.
But what can this (more than express their love)
Add to thy free provisions, far above

The need of such ? Whose liberal board doth flow,
60 With all, that hospitality doth know!
Where comes no guest, but is allowed to eat,
Without his fear, and of thy lord's own meat:
Where the same beer, and bread, and self-same wine,
That is his lordship's, shall be also mine.
And I not fain to sit (as some, this day,
At great men's tables) and yet dine away.
Here no man tells my cups; nor, standing by,
A waiter, doth my gluttony envy;
But gives me what I call, and lets me eat,
70 He knows, below, he shall find plenty of meat,
Thy tables hoard not up for the next day,
Nor, when I take my lodging, need I pray
For fire, or lights, or livery: all is there;
As if thou, then, wert mine, or I reigned here:
There's nothing I can wish, for which I stay.
That found King James, when hunting late, this way,
With his brave son, the prince, they saw thy fires
Shine bright on every hearth as the desires
Of thy Penates had been set on flame,
80 To entertain them; or the country came,
With all their zeal, to warm their welcome here.
What (great, I will not say, but) sudden cheer
Didst thou, then, make them! And what praise was heaped
On thy good lady, then! Who, therein, reaped
The just reward of her high huswifery;
To have her linen, plate, and all things nigh,
When she was far: and not a room, but dressed,
As if it had expected such a guest!
These, Penshurst, are thy praise, and yet not all.
90 Thy lady's noble, fruitful, chaste withal.
His children thy great lord may call his own:
A fortune, in this age, but rarely known.
They are, and have been taught religion: thence
Their gentler spirits have sucked innocence.
Each morn, and even, they are taught to pray,
With the whole household, and may, every day,

Read, in their virtuous parents' noble parts,
The mysteries of manners, arms, and arts.
Now, Penshurst, they that will proportion thee
100 With other edifices, when they see
Those proud, ambitious heaps, and nothing else,
May say, their lords have built, but thy lord dwells.

III *To Sir Robert Wroth*

How blessed art thou, canst love the country, Wroth,
  Whether by choice, or fate, or both;
And, though so near the city, and the court,
  Art ta'en with neither's vice, nor sport:
That at great times, art no ambitious guest
  Of sheriff's dinner, or mayor's feast.
Nor com'st to view the better cloth of state;
  The richer hangings, or crown plate;
Nor throng'st (when masquing is) to have a sight
10   Of the short bravery of the night;
To view the jewels, stuffs, the pains, the wit
  There wasted, some not paid for yet!
But canst, at home, in thy securer rest,
  Live, with unbought provision blessed;
Free from proud porches, or their gilded roofs,
  'Mongst lowing herds, and solid hoofs:
Alongst the curléd woods, and painted meads,
  Through which a serpent river leads
To some cool, courteous shade, which he calls his,
20   And makes sleep softer than it is!
Or, if thou list the night in watch to break,
  Abed canst hear the loud stag speak,
In spring, oft rouséd for thy master's sport,
  Who, for it, makes thy house his court;
Or with thy friends, the heart of all the year,
  Divid'st, upon the lesser deer;
In autumn, at the partridge makes a flight,
  And giv'st thy gladder guests the sight;

And, in the winter, hunt'st the flying hare,
30   More for thy exercise, than fare;
While all, that follow, their glad ears apply
    To the full greatness of the cry:
Or hawking at the river, or the bush,
    Or shooting at the greedy thrush,
Thou dost with some delight the day outwear,
    Although the coldest of the year!
The whilst, the several seasons thou hast seen
    Of flowery fields, of copses green,
The mowèd meadows with the fleecèd sheep,
40   And feasts that either shearers keep;
The ripened ears, yet humble in their height,
    And furrows laden with their weight;
The apple harvest, that doth longer last;
    The hogs returned home fat from mast;
The trees cut out in log; and those boughs made
    A fire now, that lent a shade!
Thus Pan, and Sylvan, having had their rites,
    Comus puts in, for new delights;
And fills thy open hall with mirth, and cheer,
50   As if in Saturn's reign it were;
Apollo's harp, and Hermes' lyre resound,
    Nor are the muses strangers found:
The rout of rural folk come thronging in,
    (Their rudeness then is thought no sin)
Thy noblest spouse affords them welcome grace;
    And the great heroes, of her race,
Sit mixed with loss of state, or reverence.
    Freedom doth with degree dispense.
The jolly wassail walks the often round,
60   And in their cups, their cares are drowned:
They think not, then, which side the cause shall leese,
    Nor how to get the lawyer fees.
Such, and no other, was that age, of old,
    Which boasts to have had the head of gold.
And such since thou canst make thine own content,
    Strive, Wroth, to live long innocent.

Let others watch in guilty arms, and stand
　　The fury of a rash command,
Go enter breaches, meet the cannons' rage,
70　　That they may sleep with scars in age.
And show their feathers shot, and colours torn,
　　And brag, that they were therefore born.
Let this man sweat, and wrangle at the bar,
　　For every price, in every jar,
And change possessions, oft'ner with his breath,
　　Than either money, war, or death:
Let him, than hardest sires, more disinherit,
　　And eachwhere boast it as his merit,
To blow up orphans, widows, and their states;
80　　And think his power doth equal Fate's.
Let that go heap a mass of wretched wealth,
　　Purchased by rapine, worse than stealth,
And brooding o'er it sit, with broadest eyes,
　　Not doing good, scarce when he dies.
Let thousands more go flatter vice, and win,
　　By being organs to great sin,
Get place, and honour, and be glad to keep
　　The secrets, that shall break their sleep:
And, so they ride in purple, eat in plate,
90　　Though poison, think it a great fate.
But thou, my Wroth, if I can truth apply,
　　Shalt neither that, nor this envy:
Thy peace is made; and, when man's state is well,
　　'Tis better, if he there can dwell.
God wisheth, none should wrack on a strange shelf:
　　To him, man's dearer, than t'himself.
And, howsoever we may think things sweet,
　　He always gives what he knows meet;
Which who can use is happy: such be thou.
100　　Thy morning's, and thy evening's vow
Be thanks to him, and earnest prayer, to find
　　A body sound, with sounder mind;
To do thy country service, thyself right;
　　That neither want do thee affright,

Nor death; but when thy latest sand is spent,
    Thou mayst think life, a thing but lent.

IV To the World

(A FAREWELL FOR A GENTLEWOMAN, VIRTUOUS
AND NOBLE)

False world, goodnight: since thou hast brought
    That hour upon my morn of age,
Henceforth I quit thee from my thought,
    My part is ended on thy stage.
Do not once hope, that thou canst tempt
    A spirit so resolved to tread
Upon thy throat, and live exempt
    From all the nets that thou canst spread.
I know thy forms are studied arts,
10   Thy subtle ways, be narrow straits;
Thy courtesy but sudden starts,
    And what thou call'st thy gifts are baits.
I know too, though thou strut, and paint,
    Yet art thou both shrunk up, and old,
That only fools make thee a saint,
    And all thy good is to be sold.
I know thou whole art but a shop
    Of toys, and trifles, traps, and snares,
To take the weak, or make them stop:
20   Yet art thou falser than thy wares.
And, knowing this, should I yet stay,
    Like such as blow away their lives,
And never will redeem a day,
    Enamoured of their golden gyves?
Or, having 'scaped, shall I return,
    And thrust my neck into the noose,
From whence, so lately, I did burn,
    With all my powers, myself to loose?
What bird, or beast, is known so dull,

30 That fled his cage, or broke his chain,
And tasting air, and freedom, wull
 Render his head in there again?
If these, who have but sense, can shun
 The engines, that have them annoyed;
Little, for me, had reason done,
 If I could not thy gins avoid.
Yes, threaten, do. Alas I fear
 As little, as I hope from thee:
I know thou canst nor show, nor bear
40 More hatred, than thou hast to me.
My tender, first, and simple years
 Thou didst abuse, and then betray;
Since stirred'st up jealousies and fears,
 When all the causes were away.
Then, in a soil hast planted me,
 Where breathe the basest of thy fools;
Where envious arts professéd be,
 And pride, and ignorance the schools,
Where nothing is examined, weighed,
50 But, as 'tis rumoured, so believed:
Where every freedom is betrayed,
 And every goodness taxed, or grieved.
But, what we are born for, we must bear:
 Our frail condition it is such,
That, what to all may happen here,
 If't chance to me, I must not grutch.
Else, I my state should much mistake,
 To harbour a divided thought
From all my kind: that, for my sake,
60 There should a miracle be wrought.
No, I do know, that I was born
 To age, misfortune, sickness, grief:
But I will bear these, with that scorn,
 As shall not need thy false relief.
Nor for my peace will I go far,
 As wanderers do, that still do roam,

> But make my strengths, such as they are,
> Here in my bosom, and at home.

V Song. To Celia

> Come my Celia, let us prove,
> While we may, the sports of love;
> Time will not be ours, for ever:
> He, at length, our good will sever.
> Spend not then his gifts in vain.
> Suns, that set, may rise again:
> But if once we lose this light,
> 'Tis, with us, perpetual night.
> Why should we defer our joys?
> 10 Fame, and rumour are but toys.
> Cannot we delude the eyes
> Of a few poor household spies?
> Or his easier ears beguile,
> So removèd by our wile?
> 'Tis no sin, love's fruit to steal,
> But the sweet theft to reveal:
> To be taken, to be seen,
> These have crimes accounted been.

VI To the Same

> Kiss me, sweet: the wary lover
> Can your favours keep, and cover,
> When the common courting jay
> All your bounties will betray.
> Kiss again: no creature comes.
> Kiss, and score up wealthy sums
> On my lips, thus hardly sundered,
> While you breathe. First give a hundred,
> Then a thousand, then another
> 10 Hundred, then unto the tother

Add a thousand, and so more:
Till you equal with the store,
All the grass that Romney yields,
Or the sands in Chelsea fields,
Or the drops in silver Thames,
Or the stars, that gild his streams,
In the silent summer nights,
When youths ply their stol'n delights.
That the curious may not know
20 How to tell them as they flow,
And the envious ,when they find,
What their number is, be pined.

VII Song. That Women Are But Men's Shadows

Follow a shadow, it still flies you;
Seem to fly it, it will pursue:
So court a mistress, she denies you;
Let her alone, she will court you.
Say, are not women truly, then,
Styled but the shadows of us men?
At morn, and even, shades are longest;
At noon, they are or short, or none:
So men at weakest, they are strongest,
10 But grant us perfect, they're not known.
Say, are not women truly, then,
Styled but the shadows of us men?

VIII To Sickness

Why, disease, dost thou molest
Ladies, and of them the best?
Do not men, ynow of rites
To thy altars, by their nights
Spent in surfeits: and their days,

And nights too, in worser ways?
Take heed, sickness, what you do,
I shall fear, you'll surfeit too.
Live not we, as, all thy stalls,
10   Spittles, pest-house, hospitals,
Scarce will take our present store?
And this age will build no more:
Pray thee, feed contented, then,
Sickness, only on us men.
Or if needs thy lust will taste
Womankind; devour the waste
Livers, round about the town.
But, forgive me, with thy crown
They maintain the truest trade,
20   And have more diseases made.
What should, yet, thy palate please?
Daintiness, and softer ease,
Sleekéd limbs, and finest blood?
If thy leanness love such food,
There are those, that, for thy sake,
Do enough; and who would take
Any pains; yea, think it price,
To become thy sacrifice.
That distil their husbands' land
30   In decoctions; and are manned
With ten emp'rics, in their chamber,
Lying for the spirit of amber.
That for the oil of Talc, dare spend
More than citizens dare lend
Them, and all their officers.
That, to make all pleasure theirs,
Will by coach, and water go,
Every stew in town to know;
Dare entail their loves on any,
40   Bald, or blind, or ne'er so many:
And, for thee, at common game,
Play away, health, wealth, and fame.
These, disease, will thee deserve:

And will, long ere thou shouldst starve,
On their beds, most prostitute,
Move it, as their humblest suit,
In thy justice to molest
None but them, and leave the rest.

IX Song. To Celia

Drink to me, only, with thine eyes,
   And I will pledge with mine;
Or leave a kiss but in the cup,
   And I'll not look for wine.
The thirst, that from the soul doth rise,
   Doth ask a drink divine:
But might I of Jove's nectar sup,
   I would not change for thine.
I sent thee, late, a rosy wreath,
10   Not so much honouring thee,
As giving it a hope, that there
   It could not withered be.
But thou thereon didst only breathe,
   And send'st it back to me:
Since when it grows, and smells, I swear,
   Not of itself, but thee.

X 'And must I sing? What subject shall I choose?'

And must I sing? What subject shall I choose?
Or whose great name in poets' heaven use,
For the more countenance to my active muse?

Hercules? Alas his bones are yet sore,
With his old earthly labours. T'exact more,
Of his dull godhead, were sin. I'll implore

Phoebus. No? Tend thy cart still. Envious day
Shall not give out, that I have made thee stay,
And foundered thy hot team, to tune my lay.

10 Nor will I beg of thee, lord of the vine,
To raise my spirits with thy conjuring wine,
In the green circle of thy ivy twine.

Pallas, nor thee I call on, mankind maid,
That, at thy birth, mad'st the poor smith afraid,
Who, with his axe, thy father's midwife played.

Go, cramp dull Mars, light Venus, when he snorts,
Or, with thy tribade trine, invent new sports,
Thou, nor thy looseness, with my making sorts.

Let the old boy, your son, ply his old task,
20 Turn the stale prologue to some painted masque,
His absence in my verse, is all I ask.

Hermes, the cheater, shall not mix with us,
Though he would steal his sisters' Pegasus,
And riffle him: or pawn his Petasus.

Nor all the ladies of the Thespian lake,
(Though they were crushed into one form) could make
A beauty of that merit, that should take

My muse up by commission: no, I bring
My own true fire. Now my thought takes wing,
30 And now an epode to deep ears I sing.

XI Epode

Not to know vice at all, and keep true state,
  Is virtue, and not Fate:
Next, to that virtue, is to know vice well,
  And her black spite expel.
Which to effect (since no breast is so sure,
  Or safe, but she'll procure

Some way of entrance) we must plant a guard
    Of thoughts to watch, and ward
At the eye and ear (the ports unto the mind)
10   That no strange, or unkind
Object arrive there, but the heart (our spy)
    Give knowledge instantly,
To wakeful reason, our affections' king:
    Who (in the examining)
Will quickly taste the treason, and commit
    Close, the close cause of it.
'Tis the securest policy we have,
    To make our sense our slave.
But this true course is not embraced by many:
20   By many? Scarce by any.
For either our affections do rebel,
    Or else the sentinel
(That should ring 'larum to the heart) doth sleep,
    Or some great thought doth keep
Back the intelligence, and falsely swears,
    They are base, and idle fears
Whereof the loyal conscience so complains.
    Thus, by these subtle trains,
Do several passions still invade the mind,
30   And strike our reason blind.
Of which usurping rank, some have thought love
    The first; as prone to move
Most frequent tumults, horrors, and unrests,
    In our inflamèd breasts:
But this doth from the cloud of error grow,
    Which thus we overblow,
The thing, they here call love, is blind desire,
    Armed with bow, shafts, and fire;
Inconstant, like the sea, of whence 'tis born,
40   Rough, swelling, like a storm:
With whom who sails, rides on the surge of fear,
    And boils, as if he were
In a continual tempest. Now, true love
    No such effects doth prove;

That is an essence far more gentle, fine,
    Pure, perfect, nay divine;
It is a golden chain let down from heaven,
    Whose links are bright, and even,
That falls like sleep on lovers, and combines
50   The soft, and sweetest minds
In equal knots: this bears no brands, nor darts,
    To murther different hearts,
But, in a calm, and god-like unity,
    Preserves community.
O, who is he, that (in this peace) enjoys
    The elixir of all joys?
A form more fresh, than are the Eden bowers,
    And lasting, as her flowers:
Richer than time, and as time's virtue, rare:
60   Sober, as saddest care:
A fixéd thought, an eye untaught to glance;
    Who (blessed with such high chance)
Would, at suggestion of a steep desire,
    Cast himself from the spire
Of all his happiness? But soft: I hear
    Some vicious fool draw near,
That cries, we dream, and swears, there's no such thing,
    As this chaste love we sing.
Peace, luxury, thou art like one of those
70   Who, being at sea, suppose,
Because they move, the continent doth so:
    No, vice, we let thee know
Though thy wild thoughts with sparrows' wings do fly
    Turtles can chastely die;
And yet (in this to express ourselves more clear)
    We do not number, here,
Such spirits as are only continent,
    Because lust's means are spent:
Or those, who doubt the common mouth of fame,
80   And for their place, and name,
Cannot so safely sin. Their chastity
    Is mere necessity.

Nor mean we those, whom vows and conscience
    Have filled with abstinence:
Though we acknowledge, who can so abstain,
    Makes a most blessèd gain.
He that for love of goodness hateth ill,
    Is more crown-worthy still,
Than he, which for sin's penalty forbears.
90   His heart sins, though he fears.
But we propose a person like our dove,
    Graced with a phoenix love;
A beauty of that clear, and sparkling light,
    Would make a day of night,
And turn the blackest sorrows to bright joys:
    Whose odorous breath destroys
All taste of bitterness, and makes the air
    As sweet, as she is fair.
A body so harmoniously composed,
100   As if nature disclosed
All her best symmetry in that one feature!
    O, so divine a creature
Who could be false to? Chiefly, when he knows
    How only she bestows
The wealthy treasure of her love on him;
    Making his fortunes swim
In the full flood of her admired perfection?
    What savage, brute affection,
Would not be fearful to offend a dame
110   Of this excelling frame?
Much more a noble, and right generous mind
    (To virtuous moods inclined)
That knows the weight of guilt: he will refrain
    From thoughts of such a strain.
And to his sense object this sentence ever,
    Man may securely sin, but safely never.

XII Epistle to Elizabeth, Countess of Rutland

Madam,
Whilst that, for which, all virtue now is sold,
And almost every vice, almighty gold,
That which, to boot with hell, is thought worth heaven,
And, for it, life, conscience, yea, souls are given,
Toils, by grave custom, up and down the court,
To every squire, or groom, that will report
Well, or ill, only, all the following year,
Just to the weight their this day's presents bear;
While it makes huishers serviceable men,
10   And some one apteth to be trusted, then,
Though never after; whiles it gains the voice
Of some grand peer, whose air doth make rejoice
The fool that gave it; who will want, and weep,
When his proud patron's favours are asleep;
While thus it buys great grace, and hunts poor fame;
Runs between man, and man; 'tween dame, and dame;
Solders cracked friendship; makes love last a day;
Or perhaps less: whilst gold bears all this sway,
I, that have none (to send you) send you verse.
20   A present, which (if elder writs rehearse
The truth of times) was once of more esteem,
Than this, our gilt, nor golden age can deem,
When gold was made no weapon to cut throats,
Or put to flight Astrea, when her ingots
Were yet unfound, and better placed in earth,
Than, here, to give pride fame, and peasants birth.
But let this dross carry what price it will
With noble ignorants, and let them still,
Turn, upon scorned verse, their quarter-face:
30   With you, I know, my offering will find grace.
For what a sin 'gainst your great father's spirit,
Were it to think, that you should not inherit
His love unto the muses, when his skill
Almost you have, or may have, when you will?
Wherein wise Nature you a dowry gave,

Worth an estate, treble to that you have.
Beauty, I know, is good, and blood is more;
Riches thought most: but, madam, think what store
The world hath seen, which all these had in trust,
40 And now lie lost in their forgotten dust.
It is the muse, alone, can raise to heaven,
And, at her strong arms' end, hold up, and even,
The souls, she loves. Those other glorious notes,
Inscribed in touch or marble, or the coats
Painted, or carved upon our great men's tombs,
Or in their windows; do but prove the wombs,
That bred them, graves: when they were born, they died,
That had no muse to make their fame abide.
How many equal with the Argive queen,
50 Have beauty known, yet none so famous seen?
Achilles was not first, that valiant was,
Or, in an army's head, that, locked in brass,
Gave killing strokes. There were brave men, before
Ajax, or Idomen, or all the store,
That Homer brought to Troy; yet none so live:
Because they lacked the sacred pen, could give
Like life unto them. Who heaved Hercules
Unto the stars? Or the Tyndarides?
Who placèd Jason's Argo in the sky?
60 Or set bright Ariadne's crown so high?
Who made a lamp of Berenice's hair?
Or lifted Cassiopea in her chair?
But only poets, rapt with rage divine?
And such, or my hopes fail, shall make you shine.
You, and that other star, that purest light,
Of all Lucina's train; Lucy the bright.
Than which a nobler heaven itself knows not.
Who, though she have a better verser got,
(Or poet, in the court account) than I,
70 And, who doth me (though I not him) envy,
Yet, for the timely favours she hath done,
To my less sanguine muse, wherein she hath won
My grateful soul, the subject of her powers,

I have already used some happy hours,
To her remembrance; which when time shall bring
To curious light, the notes I then shall sing,
Will prove old Orpheus' act no tale to be:
For I shall move stocks, stones, no less than he.
Then all, that have but done my muse least grace,
80 Shall thronging come, and boast the happy place
They hold in my strange poems, which, as yet,
Had not their form touched by an English wit.
There like a rich, and golden pyramid,
Borne up by statues, shall I rear your head,
Above your under-carvéd ornaments,
And show, how, to the life, my soul presents
Your form impressed there: not with tickling rhymes,
Or commonplaces, filched, that take these times,
But high, and noble matter, such as flies
90 From brains entranced, and filled with ecstasies;
Moods, which the godlike Sidney oft did prove,
And your brave friend, and mine so well did love.
Who wheresoe'er he be, on what dear coast,
Now thinking on you, though to England lost,
For that firm grace he holds in your regard,
I, that am grateful for him, have prepared
This hasty sacrifice, wherein I rear
A vow as new, and ominous as the year,
Before his swift and circled race be run,
100 My best of wishes, may you bear a son.

XIII Epistle. To Katherine, Lady Aubigny

'Tis grown almost a danger to speak true
Of any good mind, now: there are so few.
The bad, by number, are so fortified,
As what they have lost to expect, they dare deride.
So both the praised, and praisers suffer: yet,
For others' ill, ought none their good forget.
I, therefore, who profess myself in love

With every virtue, wheresoe'er it move,
And howsoever; as I am at feud
10 With sin and vice, though with a throne endued;
And, in this name, am given out dangerous
By arts, and practice of the vicious,
Such as suspect themselves, and think it fit
For their own cap'tal crimes, t'indict my wit;
I, that have suffered this; and, though forsook
Of Fortune, have not altered yet my look,
Or so myself abandoned, as because
Men are not just, or keep no holy laws
Of nature, and society, I should faint;
20 Or fear to draw true lines, 'cause others paint:
I, madam, am become your praiser. Where,
If it may stand with your soft blush to hear
Yourself but told unto yourself, and see
In my chárácter, what your features be,
You will not from the paper slightly pass:
No lady, but, at some time, loves her glass.
And this shall be no false one, but as much
Removed, as you from need to have it such.
Look then, and see yourself. I will not say
30 Your beauty; for you see that every day:
And so do many more. All which can call
It perfect, proper, pure, and natural,
Not taken up o' the doctors, but as well
As I, can say, and see it doth excel.
That asks but to be censured by the eyes;
And, in those outward forms, all fools are wise.
Nor that your beauty wanted not a dower,
Do I reflect. Some alderman has power,
Or cozening farmer of the customs so,
40 To advance his doubtful issue, and o'erflow
A prince's fortune: these are gifts of chance,
And raise not virtue; they may vice enhance.
My mirror is more subtle, clear, refined,
And takes, and gives the beauties of the mind.
Though it reject not those of Fortune: such

As blood, and match. Wherein, how more than much
Are you engagèd to your happy fate,
For such a lot! That mixed you with a state
Of so great title, birth, but virtue most,
50 Without which, all the rest were sounds, or lost.
'Tis only that can time, and chance defeat:
For he, that once is good, is ever great.
Wherewith, then, madam, can you better pay
This blessing of your stars, than by that way
Of virtue, which you tread? What if alone?
Without companions? 'Tis safe to have none.
In single paths, dangers with ease are watched:
Contagion in the press is soonest catched.
This makes, that wisely you decline your life,
60 Far from the maze of custom, error, strife,
And keep an even, and unaltered gait;
Not looking by, or back (like those, that wait
Times, and occasions, to start forth, and seem)
Which though the turning world may disesteem,
Because that studies spectacles, and shows,
And after varied, as fresh objects goes,
Giddy with change, and therefore cannot see
Right, the right way: yet must your comfort be
Your conscience, and not wonder, if none asks
70 For truth's complexion, where they all wear masks.
Let who will follow fashions, and attires,
Maintain their liegers forth, for foreign wires,
Melt down their husbands' land, to pour away
On the close groom, and page, on New Year's Day,
And almost all days after, while they live;
(They find it both so witty, and safe to give).
Let them on powders, oils, and paintings, spend,
Till that no usurer, nor his bawds dare lend
Them, or their officers: and no man know,
80 Whether it be a face they wear, or no.
Let them waste body, and state; and after all,
When their own parasites laugh at their fall,
May they have nothing left, whereof they can

Boast, but how oft they have gone wrong to man:
And call it their brave sin. For such there be
That do sin only for the infamy:
And never think, how vice doth every hour,
Eat on her clients, and some one devour.
You, madam, young have learned to shun these shelves,
90   Whereon the most of mankind wrack themselves,
And, keeping a just course, have early put
Into your harbour, and all passage shut
'Gainst storms, or pirates, that might charge your peace;
For which you worthy are the glad increase
Of your blessed womb, made fruitful from above,
To pay your lord the pledges of chaste love:
And raise a noble stem, to give the fame
To Clifton's blood, that is denied their name.
Grow, grow, fair tree, and as thy branches shoot,
100   Hear, what the muses sing about thy root,
By me, their priest (if they can aught divine)
Before the moons have filled their triple trine,
To crown the burthen which you go withall,
It shall a ripe and timely issue fall,
To expect the honours of great Aubigny:
And greater rites, yet writ in mystery,
But which the Fates forbid me to reveal.
Only, thus much, out of a ravished zeal,
Unto your name, and goodness of your life,
110   They speak; since you are truly that rare wife,
Other great wives may blush at: when they see
What your tried manners are, what theirs should be.
How you love one, and him you should; how still
You are depending on his word, and will;
Not fashioned for the court, or strangers' eyes;
But to please him, who is the dearer prize
Unto himself, by being so dear to you.
This makes, that your affections still be new,
And that your souls conspire, as they were gone
120   Each into other, and had now made one.
Live that one, still; and as long years do pass,

Madam, be bold to use this truest glass:
Wherein, your form, you still the same shall find;
Because nor it can change, nor such a mind.

XIV Ode. To Sir William Sidney,
on His Birthday

Now that the hearth is crowned with smiling fire,
  And some do drink, and some do dance,
      Some ring,
      Some sing,
  And all do strive to advance
The gladness higher:
      Wherefore should I
      Stand silent by,
        Who not the least,
10   Both love the cause, and authors of the feast?

Give me my cup, but from the Thespian well,
  That I may tell to Sidney, what
      This day
      Doth say,
  And he may think on that
Which I do tell:
      When all the noise
      Of these forced joys,
        Are fled and gone,
20   And he, with his best genius left alone.

This day says, then, the number of glad years
  Are justly summed, that make you man;
      Your vow
      Must now
  Strive all right ways it can,
To outstrip your peers:
      Since he doth lack
      Of going back

   Little, whose will
30   Doth urge him to run wrong, or to stand still.

Nor can a little of the common store,
  Of nobles' virtue, show in you;
   Your blood
   So good
  And great, must seek for new,
  And study more:
   Not weary, rest
   On what's deceased.
   For they, that swell
40   With dust of ancestors, in graves but dwell.

'Twill be exacted of your name, whose son,
  Whose nephew, whose grand-child you are;
   And men
   Will, then,
  Say you have followed far,
  When well begun:
   Which must be now,
   They teach you, how.
   And he that stays
50   To live until tomorrow hath lost two days.

So may you live in honour, as in name,
  If with this truth you be inspired,
   So may
   This day
  Be more, and long desired:
  And with the flame,
   Of love be bright,
   As with the light
   Of bone-fires. Then
60   The birthday shines, when logs not burn, but men.

XV To Heaven

Good, and great God, can I not think of thee,
But it must, straight, my melancholy be?
Is it interpreted in me disease,
That, laden with my sins, I seek for ease?
O, be thou witness, that the reins dost know,
And hearts of all, if I be sad for show,
And judge me after: if I dare pretend
To aught but grace, or aim at other end.
As thou art all, so be thou all to me,
10   First, midst, and last, converted one, and three;
My faith, my hope, my love: and in this state,
My judge, my witness, and my advocate.
Where have I been this while exiled from thee?
And whither rapt, now thou but stoop'st to me?
Dwell, dwell here still: O, being everywhere,
How can I doubt to find thee ever, here?
I know my state, both full of shame, and scorn,
Conceived in sin, and unto labour born,
Standing with fear, and must with horror fall,
20   And destined unto judgment, after all.
I feel my griefs too, and there scarce is ground,
Upon my flesh to inflict another wound.
Yet dare I not complain, or wish for death
With holy Paul, lest it be thought the breath
Of discontent; or that these prayers be
For weariness of life, not love of thee.

Underwoods

CONSISTING OF DIVERSE POEMS

To the Reader

With the same leave the ancients called that kind of body
Sylva, or *Hule*, in which there were works of diverse
nature, and matter congested; as the multitude call timber-
trees, promiscuously growing, a wood, or forest: so am I
bold to entitle these lesser poems, of later growth, by this
of *Underwood*, out of the analogy they hold to the *Forest*,
in my former book, and no otherwise.

Ben Jonson.

I Poems of Devotion

1 The Sinner's Sacrifice

(TO THE HOLY TRINITY)

1. O holy, blessèd, glorious Trinity
   Of persons, still one God, in unity,
   The faithful man's believèd mystery,
       Help, help to lift

2. Myself up to thee, harrowed, torn, and bruised
   By sin, and Satan; and my flesh misused,
   As my heart lies in pieces, all confused,
       O take my gift.

3. All-gracious God, the sinner's sacrifice,
   A broken heart thou wert not wont despise,
   But 'bove the fat of rams, or bulls, to prize
       An offering meet,

4. For thy acceptance. O, behold me right,
   And take compassion on my grievous plight.
   What odour can be, than a heart contrite,
       To thee more sweet?

5. Eternal Father, God, who didst create
   This all of nothing, gav'st it form, and fate,
   And breath'st into it, life, and light, with state
       To worship thee.

6. Eternal God the Son, who not denied'st
   To take our nature; becam'st man, and died'st,
   To pay our debts, upon thy cross, and cried'st
       All's done in me.

10

20

7. Eternal Spirit, God from both proceeding,
   Father and Son; the comforter, in breeding
   Pure thoughts in man: with fiery zeal them feeding
     For acts of grace.

8. Increase those acts, O glorious Trinity
30   Of persons, still one God in unity;
   Till I attain the longed-for mystery
     Of seeing your face.

9. Beholding one in three, and three in one,
   A Trinity, to shine in union;
   The gladdest light, dark man can think upon;
     O grant it me!

10. Father, and Son, and Holy Ghost, you three
   All coëternal in your majesty,
   Distinct in persons, yet in unity
40   One God to see.

11. My maker, saviour, and my sanctifier,
   To hear, to mediate, sweeten my desire,
   With grace, with love, with cherishing entire,
     O, then how blessed;

12. Among thy saints elected to abide,
   And with thy angels, placèd side by side,
   But in thy presence truly glorified
     Shall I there rest!

2 *A Hymn to God the Father*

Hear me, O God!
   A broken heart,
   Is my best part:
Use still thy rod,
   That I may prove
   Therein, thy love.

If thou hadst not
    Been stern to me,
    But left me free,
10 I had forgot
    Myself and thee.

For, sin's so sweet,
    As minds ill bent
    Rarely repent,
Until they meet
    Their punishment.

Who more can crave
    Than thou hast done:
    That gav'st a Son,
20 To free a slave?
    First made of nought;
    With all since bought.

Sin, death, and hell,
    His glorious name
    Quite overcame,
Yet I rebel,
    And slight the same.

But, I'll come in,
    Before my loss
30   Me farther toss,
As sure to win
    Under his cross.

3 *A Hymn on the Nativity of My Saviour*

I sing the birth, was born tonight,
The author both of life, and light;
    The angels so did sound it,
And like the ravished shepherds said,
Who saw the light, and were afraid,
    Yet searched, and true they found it.

The son of God, the eternal king,
That did us all salvation bring,
   And freed the soul from danger;
10 He whom the whole world could not take,
The Word, which heaven, and earth did make;
   Was now laid in a manger.

The Father's wisdom willed it so,
The Son's obedience knew no no,
   Both wills were in one stature;
And as that wisdom had decreed,
The word was now made flesh indeed,
   And took on him our nature.

What comfort by him do we win,
20 Who made himself the price of sin,
   To make us heirs of glory?
To see this babe, all innocence;
A martyr born in our defence;
   Can man forget this story?

II *A Celebration of Charis in Ten Lyric Pieces*

I HIS EXCUSE FOR LOVING

Let it not your wonder move,
Less your laughter; that I love.
Though I now write fifty years,
I have had, and have my peers;
Poets, though divine, are men:
Some have loved as old again.
And it is not always face,
Clothes, or fortune gives the grace;
Or the feature, or the youth:
10 But the language, and the truth,
With the ardour, and the passion,
Gives the lover weight and fashion.
If you then will read the story,

First prepare you to be sorry,
That you never knew till now,
Either whom to love, or how:
But be glad, as soon with me,
When you know, that this is she,
Of whose beauty it was sung,
20   She shall make the old man young,
Keep the middle age at stay,
And let nothing high decay,
Till she be the reason why,
All the world for love may die.

2 HOW HE SAW HER

I beheld her, on a day,
When her look outflourished May:
And her dressing did out-brave
All the pride the fields then have:
Far I was from being stupid,
For I ran and called on Cupid:
Love if thou wilt ever see
Mark of glory, come with me;
Where's thy quiver? Bend thy bow:
10   Here's a shaft, thou art too slow!
And (withal) I did untie
Every cloud about his eye;
But, he had not gained his sight
Sooner, than he lost his might,
Or his courage; for away
Straight he ran, and durst not stay,
Letting bow and arrow fall,
Nor for any threat, or call,
Could be brought once back to look.
20   I fool-hardy, there uptook
Both the arrow he had quit,
And the bow: with thought to hit
This my object. But she threw
Such a lightning (as I drew)

At my face, that took my sight,
And my motion from me quite;
So that there, I stood a stone,
Mocked of all: and called of one
(Which with grief and wrath I heard)
30   Cupid's statue with a beard,
Or else one that played his ape,
In a Hercules his shape.

3 WHAT HE SUFFERED

After many scorns like these,
Which the prouder beauties please,
She content was to restore
Eyes and limbs, to hurt me more,
And would on conditions, be
Reconciled to love, and me:
First, that I must kneeling yield
Both the bow, and shaft I held
Unto her; which Love might take
10   At her hand, with oath, to make
Me, the scope of his next draught
Aimèd, with that self-same shaft.
He no sooner heard the law,
But the arrow home did draw
And (to gain her by his art)
Left it sticking in my heart:
Which when she beheld to bleed,
She repented of the deed,
And would fain have changed the fate,
20   But the pity comes too late.
Loser-like, now, all my wreak
Is, that I have leave to speak,
And in either prose, or song,
To revenge me with my tongue,
Which how dexterously I do
Hear and make example too.

4 HER TRIUMPH

See the chariot at hand here of Love
   Wherein my lady rideth!
Each that draws, is a swan, or a dove,
   And well the car Love guideth.
As she goes, all hearts do duty
    Unto her beauty;
And enamoured, do wish, so they might
    But enjoy such a sight,
That they still were, to run by her side,
10 Through swords, through seas, whither she would ride.

Do but look on her eyes, they do light
   All that Love's world compriseth!
Do but look on her hair, it is bright
   As Love's star when it riseth!
Do but mark her forehead's smoother
    Than words that sooth her!
And from her archèd brows, such a grace
    Sheds itself through the face,
As alone there triumphs to the life
20 All the gain, all the good, of the elements' strife.

Have you seen but a bright lily grow,
   Before rude hands have touched it?
Ha' you marked but the fall o' the snow
   Before the soil hath smutched it?
Ha' you felt the wool o' the beaver,
    Or swansdown ever?
Or have smelt o' the bud o' the briar,
    Or the nard in the fire?
Or have tasted the bag of the bee?
30 O so white! O so soft! O so sweet is she!

5 HIS DISCOURSE WITH CUPID

Noblest Charis, you that are
Both my fortune, and my star!
And do govern more my blood,

Than the various moon the flood!
Hear, what late discourse of you,
Love, and I have had; and true.
'Mongst my muses finding me,
Where he chanced your name to see
Set, and to this softer strain;
10 Sure, said he, if I have brain,
This here sung, can be no other
By description, but my mother!
So hath Homer praised her hair;
So, Anacreon drawn the air
Of her face, and made to rise
Just about her sparkling eyes,
Both her brows, bent like my bow.
By her looks I do her know,
Which you call my shafts. And see!
20 Such my mother's blushes be,
As the bath your verse discloses
In her cheeks, of milk, and roses;
Such as oft I wanton in!
And, above her even chin,
Have you placed the bank of kisses,
Where, you say, men gather blisses,
Ripened with a breath more sweet,
Than when flowers, and west winds meet.
Nay, her white and polished neck,
30 With the lace that doth it deck,
Is my mother's! Hearts of slain
Lovers, made into a chain!
And between each rising breast,
Lies the valley, called my nest,
Where I sit and proin my wings
After flight; and put new stings
To my shafts! Her very name,
With my mother's is the same.
I confess all, I replied,
40 And the glass hangs by her side,
And the girdle 'bout her waist,

All is Venus: save unchaste.
But alas, thou see'st the least
Of her good, who is the best
Of her sex; but couldst thou, Love,
Call to mind the forms, that strove
For the apple, and those three
Make in one, the same were she.
For this beauty yet doth hide,
50   Something more than thou hast spied.
Outward grace weak love beguiles:
She is Venus, when she smiles,
But she's Juno, when she walks,
And Minerva, when she talks.

6 CLAIMING A SECOND KISS BY DESERT

Charis, guess, and do not miss,
Since I drew a morning kiss
From your lips, and sucked an air
Thence, as sweet, as you are fair,
What my muse and I have done:
Whether we have lost, or won,
If by us, the odds were laid,
That the bride (allowed a maid)
Looked not half so fresh, and fair,
10   With the advantage of her hair,
And her jewels, to the view
Of the assembly, as did you!
Or, that did you sit, or walk,
You were more the eye, and talk
Of the court, today, than all
Else that glistered in Whitehall;
So, as those that had your sight,
Wished the bride were changed tonight,
And did think, such rites were due
20   To no other grace but you!
Or, if you did move tonight
In the dances, with what spite

Of your peers, you were beheld,
That at every motion swelled
So to see a lady tread,
As might all the Graces lead,
And was worthy (being so seen)
To be envied of the queen.
Or if you would yet have stayed,
30   Whether any would upbraid
To himself his loss of time;
Or have charged his sight of crime,
To have left all sight for you:
Guess of these, which is the true;
And, if such a verse as this,
May not claim another kiss.

7 BEGGING ANOTHER, ON COLOUR OF MENDING THE FORMER

For Love's sake, kiss me once again,
     I long, and should not beg in vain,
     Here's none to spy, or see;
          Why do you doubt, or stay?
     I'll taste as lightly as the bee,
That doth but touch his flower, and flies away.
     Once more, and (faith) I will be gone.
     Can he that loves, ask less than one?
          Nay, you may err in this,
10   And all your bounty wrong:
     This could be called but half a kiss.
What w'are but once to do, we should do long.
     I will but mend the last, and tell
     Where, how it would have relished well;
          Join lip to lip, and try:
               Each sucks out other's breath.
          And whilst our tongues perplexèd lie,
Let who will think us dead, or wish our death.

8 URGING HER OF A PROMISE

Charis one day in discourse
Had of Love, and of his force,
Lightly promised, she would tell
What a man she could love well:
And that promise set on fire
All that heard her, with desire.
With the rest, I long expected,
When the work would be effected:
But we find that cold delay,
10 And excuse spun every day,
As, until she tell her one,
We all fear, she loveth none.
Therefore, Charis, you must do't,
For I will so urge you to't
You shall neither eat, nor sleep,
No, nor forth your window peep,
With your emissary eye,
To fetch in the forms go by:
And pronounce, which band or lace,
20 Better fits him, than his face;
Nay I will not let you sit
'Fore your idol glass a whit,
To say over every purl
There; or to reform a curl;
Or with secretary Sis
To consult, if fucus this
Be as good, as was the last:
All your sweet of life is past,
Make account unless you can,
30 (And that quickly) speak your man.

9 HER MAN DESCRIBED BY HER OWN DICTAMEN

Of your trouble, Ben, to ease me,
I will tell what man would please me.
I would have him if I could,

Noble; or of greater blood:
Titles, I confess, do take me;
And a woman God did make me.
French to boot, at least in fashion,
And his manners of that nation.
Young I'd have him too, and fair,
10 Yet a man; with crispèd hair
Cast in thousand snares, and rings
For Love's fingers, and his wings:
Chestnut colour, or more slack
Gold, upon a ground of black.
Venus', and Minerva's eyes
For he must look wanton-wise.
Eye-brows bent like Cupid's bow,
Front, an ample field of snow;
Even nose, and cheek (withal)
20 Smooth as is the billiard ball:
Chin, as woolly as the peach;
And his lip should kissing teach,
Till he cherished too much beard,
And make Love or me afeared.
He would have a hand as soft
As the down, and show it oft;
Skin as smooth as any rush,
And so thin to see a blush
Rising through it ere it came;
30 All his blood should be a flame
Quickly fired as in beginners
In love's school, and yet no sinners.
'Twere too long to speak of all:
What we harmony do call
In a body should be there.
Well he should his clothes to wear;
Yet no tailor help to make him;
Dressed, you still for man should take him;
And not think he'd eat a stake,
40 Or were set up in a brake.
Valiant he should be as fire,

Showing danger more than ire;
Bounteous as the clouds to earth;
And as honest as his birth.
All his actions to be such,
As to do no thing too much.
Nor o'er-praise, nor yet condemn;
Nor out-value, nor contemn:
Nor do wrongs, nor wrongs receive;
50 Nor tie knots, nor knots unweave;
And from baseness to be free,
As he durst love truth and me.
Such a man, with every part,
I could give my very heart;
But of one, if short he came,
I can rest me where I am.

10 ANOTHER LADY'S EXCEPTION,
PRESENT AT THE HEARING

For his mind, I do not care,
That's a toy, that I could spare:
Let his title be but great,
His clothes rich, and band sit neat,
Himself young, and face be good,
All I wish is understood.
What you please, you parts may call,
'Tis one good part I'd lie withal.

III The Musical Strife; in a Pastoral Dialogue

(SHE)
Come with our voices, let us war,
    And challenge all the spheres,
Till each of us be made a star,
    And all the world turn ears.

(HE)
At such a call, what beast or fowl,
   Of reason empty is?
What tree or stone doth want a soul?
   What man but must lose his?

(SHE)
Mix then your notes, that we may prove
10   To stay the running floods,
To make the mountain quarries move,
   And call the walking woods!

(HE)
What need of me? Do you but sing,
   Sleep, and the grave will wake.
No tunes are sweet, nor words have sting,
   But what those lips do make.

(SHE)
They say the angels mark each deed,
   And exercise below,
And out of inward pleasure feed
20   On what they viewing know.

(HE)
O sing not you then, lest the best
   Of angels should be driven
To fall again; at such a feast,
   Mistaking earth for heaven.

(SHE)
Nay, rather both our souls be strained
   To meet their high desire;
So they in state of grace retained,
   May wish us of their choir.

IV 'Oh do not wanton with those eyes'

Oh do not wanton with those eyes,
   Lest I be sick with seeing;
Nor cast them down, but let them rise,
   Lest shame destroy their being:
O, be not angry with those fires,
   For then their threats will kill me;
Nor look too kind on my desires,
   For then my hopes will spill me;
O, do not steep them in thy tears,
10   For so will sorrow slay me;
Nor spread them as distract with fears,
   Mine own enough betray me.

V In the Person of Womankind

(A SONG APOLOGETIC)

Men, if you love us, play no more
   The fools, or tyrants with your friends,
To make us still sing o'er, and o'er,
   Our own false praises for your ends:
     We have both wits, and fancies too,
     And if we must, let's sing of you.

Nor do we doubt, but that we can,
   If we would search with care, and pain,
Find some one good, in some one man;
10   So going thorough all your strain:
     We shall at last, of parcels make
     One good enough for a song's sake.

And as a cunning painter takes
   In any curious piece you see
More pleasure while the thing he makes
   Than when 'tis made, why so will we.
     And having pleased our art, we'll try
     To make a new, and hang that by.

VI Another. In Defence of Their Inconstancy. A Song

Hang up those dull, and envious fools
  That talk abroad of woman's change,
We were not bred to sit on stools,
  Our proper virtue is to range:
    Take that away, you take our lives,
    We are no women then, but wives.

Such as in valour would excel
  Do change, though man, and often fight,
Which we in love must do as well,
10 If ever we will love aright.
    The frequent varying of the deed,
    Is that which doth perfection breed.

Nor is't inconstancy to change
  For what is better, or to make
(By searching) what before was strange,
  Familiar, for the use's sake;
    The good, from bad, is not descried,
    But as 'tis often vexed, and tried.

And this profession of a store
20 In love, doth not alone help forth
Our pleasure; but preserves us more
  From being forsaken, than doth worth,
    For were the worthiest woman cursed
    To love one man, he'd leave her first.

VII A Nymph's Passion

I love, and he loves me again,
  Yet dare I not tell who;
For if the nymphs should know my swain,
  I fear they'd love him too;
    Yet if it be not known,

The pleasure is as good as none,
For that's a narrow joy is but our own.

I'll tell, that if they be not glad,
    They yet may envy me:
10 But then if I grow jealous mad,
      And of them pitied be,
        It were a plague 'bove scorn,
        And yet it cannot be forborn,
Unless my heart would as my thought be torn.

He is, if they can find him, fair,
    And fresh, and fragrant too,
As summer's sky, or purgèd air,
    And looks as lilies do,
      That are this morning blown,
20   Yet, yet I doubt he is not known,
And fear much more, that more of him be shown.

But he hath eyes so round, and bright,
    As make away my doubt,
Where Love may all his torches light,
    Though hate had put them out;
      But then t'increase my fears,
      What nymph so e'er his voice but hears
Will be my rival, though she have but ears.

I'll tell no more, and yet I love,
30   And he loves me; yet no
One unbecoming thought doth move
    From either heart, I know;
      But so exempt from blame,
      As it would be to each a fame:
If love, or fear, would let me tell his name.

VIII The Hour-Glass

Do but consider this small dust,
   Here running in the glass,
     By atoms moved;
   Could you believe, that this,
     The body was
       Of one that loved?
And in his mistress' flame, playing like a fly,
   Turned to cinders by her eye?
   Yes; and in death as life unblessed,
10   To have't expressed,
   Even ashes of lovers find no rest.

IX My Picture Left in Scotland

I now think, Love is rather deaf, than blind,
   For else it could not be,
     That she,
Whom I adore so much, should so slight me,
   And cast my love behind:
I'm sure my language to her, was as sweet,
     And every close did meet
     In sentence, of as subtle feet,
       As hath the youngest he,
10   That sits in shadow of Apollo's tree.
Oh, but my conscious fears,
     That fly my thoughts between,
     Tell me that she hath seen
    My hundreds of grey hairs,
    Told seven and forty years,
   Read so much waist, as she cannot embrace
   My mountain belly, and my rocky face,
And all these through her eyes, have stopped her ears.

141

X *Against Jealousy*

Wretched and foolish jealousy,
How cam'st thou thus to enter me?
   I ne'er was of thy kind;
  Nor have I yet the narrow mind
   To vent that poor desire,
That others should not warm them at my fire:
   I wish the sun should shine
On all men's fruit, and flowers, as well as mine.

But under the disguise of love
10 Thou say'st, thou only cam'st to prove
   What my affections were.
  Think'st thou that love is helped by fear?
   Go, get thee quickly forth;
Love's sickness, and his noted want of worth,
   Seek doubting men to please;
I ne'er will owe my health to a disease.

XI *The Dream*

Or scorn, or pity on me take,
I must the true relation make,
  I am undone tonight;
  Love in a subtle dream disguised,
  Hath both my heart and me surprised,
Whom never yet he durst attempt awake;
Nor will he tell me for whose sake
   He did me the delight,
    Or spite,
10   But leaves me to inquire,
  In all my wild desire
   Of sleep again; who was his aid;
   And sleep so guilty and afraid,
As since he dares not come within my sight.

XII *An Epitaph on Master Vincent Corbet*

I have my piety too, which could
It vent itself, but as it would,
Would say as much, as both have done
Before me here, the friend and son;
For I both lost a friend and father,
Of him whose bones this grave doth gather:
Dear Vincent Corbet, who so long
Had wrestled with diseases strong,
That though they did possess each limb,
10   Yet he broke them, ere they could him,
With the just canon of his life,
A life that knew nor noise, nor strife:
But was by sweetening so his will,
All order, and disposure, still.
His mind as pure, and neatly kept,
As were his nurseries; and swept
So of uncleanness, or offence,
That never came ill odour thence:
And add his actions unto these,
20   They were as specious as his trees.
'Tis true, he could not reprehend;
His very manners taught t'amend,
They were so even, grave, and holy;
No stubbornness so stiff, nor folly
To licence ever was so light,
As twice to trespass in his sight,
His looks would so correct it, when
It chid the vice, yet not the men.
Much from him I profess I won,
30   And more, and more, I should have done,
But that I understood him scant;
Now I conceive him by my want,
And pray who shall my sorrows read,
That they for me their tears will shed;
For truly, since he left to be,
I feel, I'm rather dead than he!

Reader, whose life, and name, did e'er become
   An epitaph, deserved a tomb:
Nor wants it here through penury, or sloth,
40   Who makes the one, so it be first makes both.

XIII *An Epistle to Sir Edward Sackville, now Earl of Dorset*

If Sackville, all that have the power to do
Great and good turns, as well could time them too,
And knew their how, and where: we should have, then
Less list of proud, hard, or ingrateful men.
For benefits are owed with the same mind
As they are done, and such returns they find:
You then whose will not only, but desire
To succour my necessities took fire,
Not at my prayers, but your sense; which laid
10 The way to meet, what others would upbraid;
And in the act did so my blush prevent,
As I did feel it done, as soon as meant:
You cannot doubt, but I who freely know
This good from you, as freely will it owe;
And though my fortune humble me, to take
The smallest courtesies with thanks, I make
Yet choice from whom I take them; and would shame
To have such do me good, I durst not name:
They are the noblest benefits, and sink
20 Deepest in man, of which when he doth think,
The memory delights him more, from whom
Than what he hath received. Gifts stink from some,
They are so long a coming, and so hard;
Where any deed is forced, the grace is marred.
   Can I owe thanks, for courtesies received
Against his will that does them? That hath weaved
Excuses, or delays? Or done them scant,
That they have more oppressed me, than my want?
Or if he did it not to succour me,

30 But by mere chance? For interest? Or to free
Himself of further trouble, or the weight
Of pressure, like one taken in a strait?
All this corrupts the thanks; less hath he won,
That puts it in his debt-book ere it be done;
Or that doth sound a trumpet, and doth call
His grooms to witness; or else lets it fall
In that proud manner: as a good so gained
Must make me sad for what I have obtained.
    No! Gifts and thanks should have one cheerful face,
40 So each, that's done, and ta'en, becomes a brace.
He neither gives, or does, that doth delay
A benefit: or that doth throw't away,
No more than he doth thank, that will receive
Naught but in corners; and is loth to leave
Least air, or print, but flies it: such men would
Run from the conscience of it if they could.
    As I have seen some infants of the sword
Well known, and practised borrowers on their word,
Give thanks by stealth, and whispering in the ear,
50 For what they straight would to the world forswear;
And speaking worst of those, from whom they went
But then, fist filled, to put me off the scent.
Now damn me, sir, if you shall not command
My sword ('tis but a poor sword understand)
As far as any poor sword in the land;
Then turning unto him is next at hand,
Damns whom he damned too, is the veriest gull,
Has feathers, and will serve a man to pull.
    Are they not worthy to be answered so,
60 That to such natures let their full hands flow,
And seek not wants to succour: but inquire
Like money-brokers, after names, and hire
Their bounties forth, to him that last was made,
Or stands to be in commission of the blade?
Still, still, the hunters of false fame apply
Their thoughts and means to making loud the cry;
But one is bitten by the dog he fed,

And hurt seeks cure; the surgeon bids take bread,
And sponge-like with it dry up the blood quite:
70 Then give it to the hound that did him bite;
Pardon, says he, that were a way to see
All the town curs take each their snatch at me.
O, is it so? Knows he so much? And will
Feed those, at whom the table points at still?
I not deny it, but to help the need
Of any, is a great and generous deed:
Yea, of the ingrateful; and he forth must tell
Many a pound, and piece will place one well;
But these men ever want: their very trade
80 Is borrowing; that but stopped they do invade
All as their prize, turn pirates here at land,
Have their Bermudas, and their straits in the Strand:
Man out their boats to the Temple, and not shift
Now, but command; make tribute, what was gift;
And it is paid them with a trembling zeal,
And superstition I dare scarce reveal
If it were clear, but being so in cloud
Carried and wrapped, I only am allowed
My wonder why the taking a clown's purse,
90 Or robbing the poor market folks should nurse
Such a religious horror in the breasts
Of our town gallantry! Or why there rests
Such worship due to kicking of a punk!
Or swaggering with the watch, or drawer drunk;
Or feats of darkness acted in mid-sun,
And told of with more licence than they were done!
Sure there is mystery in it, I not know,
That men such reverence to such actions show!
And almost deify the authors! Make
100 Loud sacrifice of drink, for their health' sake
Rear-suppers in their names! And spend whole nights
Unto their praise, in certain swearing rites;
Cannot a man be reckoned in the state
Of valour, but at this idolatrous rate?
I thought that fortitude had been a mean

'Twixt fear and rashness: not a lust obscene,
Or appetite of offending, but a skill,
Or science of discerning good and ill.
And you, sir, know it well to whom I write,
110　That with these mixtures we put out her light.
Her ends are honesty, and public good!
And where they want, she is not understood.
No more are these of us, let them then go,
I have the list of mine own faults to know,
Look to and cure; he's not a man hath none,
But like to be, that every day mends one,
And feels it; else he tarries by the beast.
Can I discern how shadows are decreased,
Or grown, by height or lowness of the sun?
120　And can I less of substance? When I run,
Ride, sail, am coached, know I how far I have gone,
And my mind's motion not? Or have I none?
No! he must feel and know, that will advance.
Men have been great, but never good by chance,
Or on the sudden. It were strange that he
Who was this morning such a one, should be
Sidney ere night! Or that did go to bed
Coriat, should rise the most sufficient head
Of Christendom! And neither of these know
130　Were the rack offered them how they came so;
'Tis by degrees that men arrive at glad
Profit in aught; each day some little add,
In time 'twill be a heap; this is not true
Alone in money, but in manners too.
Yet we must more than move still, or go on,
We must accomplish; 'tis the last key-stone
That makes the arch. The rest that there were put
Are nothing till that comes to bind and shut.
Then stands it a triumphal mark! Then men
140　Observe the strength, the height, the why, and when,
It was erected; and still walking under
Meet some new matter to look up and wonder!
Such notes are virtuous men! They live as fast

As they are high; are rooted and will last.
They need no stilts, nor rise upon their toes,
As if they would belie their stature; those
Are dwarfs of honour, and have neither weight
Nor fashion; if they chance aspire to height,
'Tis like light canes, that first rise big and brave,
150 Shoot forth in smooth and comely spaces; have
But few and fair divisions: but being got
Aloft, grow less and straitened; full of knot;
And last, go out in nothing: you that see
Their difference, cannot choose which you will be.
You know (without my flattering you) too much
For me to be your indice. Keep you such,
That I may love your person (as I do)
Without your gift, though I can rate that too,
By thanking thus the courtesy to life,
160 Which you will bury, but therein, the strife
May grow so great to be example, when
(As their true rule or lesson) either men
Donors or donees to their practice shall
Find you to reckon nothing, me owe all.

XIV An Epistle to Master John Selden

I know to whom I write. Here, I am sure,
Though I am short, I cannot be obscure:
Less shall I for the art or dressing care;
Truth, and the Graces, best when naked are.
Your book, my Selden, I have read, and much
Was trusted, that you thought my judgement such
To ask it: though in most of works it be
A penance, where a man may not be free,
Rather than office, when it doth or may
10 Chance that the friend's affection proves allay
Unto the censure. Yours all need doth fly
Of this so vicious humanity,
Than which there is not unto study, a more

Pernicious enemy; we see before
A many of books, even good judgements wound
Themselves through favouring what is there not found:
But I on yours far otherwise shall do,
Not fly the crime, but the suspicion too:
Though I confess (as every muse hath erred,
20 And mine not least) I have too oft preferred
Men past their terms, and praised some names too much,
But 'twas with purpose to have made them such.
Since being deceived, I turn a sharper eye
Upon myself, and ask to whom, and why,
And what I write? And vex it many days
Before men get a verse: much less a praise;
So that my reader is assured, I now
Mean what I speak: and still will keep that vow.
Stand forth my object, then, you that have been
30 Ever at home: yet, have all countries seen:
And like a compass keeping one foot still
Upon your centre, do your circle fill
Of general knowledge; watched men, manners too,
Heard what times past have said, seen what ours do:
Which grace shall I make love to first? Your skill,
Or faith in things? Or is't your wealth and will
To instruct and teach? Or your unwearied pain
Of gathering? Bounty in pouring out again?
What fables have you vexed! What truth redeemed!
40 Antiquities searched! Opinions disesteemed!
Impostures branded! And authorities urged!
What blots and errors have you watched and purged
Records, and authors of! How rectified
Times, manners, customs! Innovations spied!
Sought out the fountains, sources, creeks, paths, ways,
And noted the beginnings and decays!
Where is that nominal mark, or real rite,
Form, act or ensign, that hath 'scaped your sight?
How are traditions there examined: how
50 Conjectures retrieved! And a story now
And then of times (besides the bare conduct

Of what it tells us) weaved in to instruct.
I wondered at the richness, but am lost,
To see the workmanship so exceed the cost!
To mark the excellent seasoning of your style!
And manly elocution, not one while
With horror rough, then rioting with wit!
But to the subject, still the colours fit
In sharpness of all search, wisdom of choice,
60   Newness of sense, antiquity of voice!
      I yield, I yield, the matter of your praise
Flows in upon me, and I cannot raise
A bank against it. Nothing but the round
Large clasp of nature, such a wit can bound.
Monarch in letters! 'Mongst thy titles shown
Of others' honours, thus, enjoy thine own.
I first salute thee so; and gratulate
With that thy style, thy keeping of thy state,
In offering this thy work to no great name,
70   That would, perhaps, have praised, and thanked the same,
But naught beyond. He thou hast given it to,
Thy learnèd chamber-fellow, knows to do
It true respects. He will not only love,
Embrace, and cherish; but he can approve
And estimate thy pains; as having wrought
In the same mines of knowledge; and thence brought
Humanity enough to be a friend,
And strength to be a champion, and defend
Thy gift 'gainst envy. O how I do count
80   Among my comings in, and see it mount,
The grain of your two friendships! Hayward and
Selden! Two names that so much understand!
On whom I could take up, and ne'er abuse
The credit, what would furnish a tenth muse!
But here's no time, nor place, my wealth to tell,
You both are modest. So am I. Farewell.

XV An Epistle to a Friend, to Persuade
Him to the Wars

Wake, friend, from forth thy lethargy: the drum
Beats brave, and loud in Europe, and bids come
All that dare rouse: or are not loth to quit
Their vicious ease, and be o'erwhelmed with it.
It is a call to keep the spirits alive
That gasp for action, and would yet revive
Man's buried honour, in his sleepy life:
Quickening dead nature, to her noblest strife.
All other acts of worldlings, are but toil
10   In dreams, begun in hope, and end in spoil.
Look on the ambitious man, and see him nurse
His unjust hopes, with praises begged, or (worse)
Bought flatteries, the issue of his purse,
Till he become both their, and his own curse!
Look on the false, and cunning man, that loves
No person, nor is loved: what ways he proves
To gain upon his belly; and at last
Crushed in the snaky brakes, that he had passed!
See, the grave, sour, and supercilious sir
20 In outward face, but inward, light as fur,
Or feathers: lay his fortune out to show
Till envy wound, or maim it at a blow!
See him, that's called, and thought the happiest man,
Honoured at once, and envied (if it can
Be honour is so mixed) by such as would
For all their spite be like him if they could:
No part or corner man can look upon,
But there are objects, bid him to be gone
As far as he can fly, or follow day,
30   Rather than here so bogged in vices stay.
The whole world here leavened with madness swells;
And being a thing, blown out of naught, rebels
Against his Maker; high alone with weeds,
And impious rankness of all sects and seeds:
Not to be checked, or frighted now with fate,

But more licentious made, and desperate!
Our delicacies are grown capital,
And even our sports are dangers! What we call
Friendship is now masked hatred! Justice fled,
40 And shamefastness together! All laws dead
That kept man living! Pleasures only sought!
Honour and honesty, as poor things thought
As they are made! Pride and stiff clownage mixed
To make up greatness! And man's whole good fixed
In bravery, or gluttony, or coin,
All which he makes the servants of the groin,
Thither it flows; how much did Stallion spend
To have his court-bred filly there commend
His lace and starch? And fall upon her back
50 In admiration, stretched upon the rack
Of lust, to his rich suit and title, Lord?
Aye, that's a charm and half! She must afford
That all respect; she must lie down: nay more,
'Tis there civility to be a whore;
He's one of blood, and fashion! And with these
The bravery makes, she can no honour leese:
To do it with cloth, or stuffs, lust's name might merit;
With velvet, plush, and tissues, it is spirit.
    O, these so ignorant monsters! Light, as proud,
60 Who can behold their manners, and not cloud-
Like upon them lighten? If nature could
Not make a verse; anger; or laughter would
To see them aye discoursing with their glass,
How they may make someone that day an ass,
Planting their purls, and curls spread forth like net,
And every dressing for a pitfall set
To catch the flesh in, and to pound a prick;
Be at their visits, see them squeamish, sick,
Ready to cast, at one, whose band sits ill,
70 And then, leap mad on a neat pickardil,
As if a brise were gotten in their tail,
And firk, and jerk, and for the coachman rail,
And jealous each of other, yet think long

To be abroad chanting some bawdy song,
And laugh, and measure thighs, then squeak, spring, itch,
Do all the tricks of a saut lady bitch;
For t'other pound of sweetmeats, he shall feel
That pays, or what he will. The dame is steel,
For these with her young company she'll enter,
80 Where Pitts, or Wright, or Modet would not venter,
And comes by these degrees, the style t'inherit
Of woman of fashion, and a lady of spirit:
Nor is the title questioned with our proud,
Great, brave, and fashioned folk, these are allowed
Adulteries now, are not so hid, or strange,
They're grown commodity upon Exchange;
He that will follow but another's wife,
Is loved, though he let out his own for life:
The husband now's called churlish, or a poor
90 Nature, that will not let his wife be a whore;
Or use all arts, or haunt all companies
That may corrupt her, even in his eyes.
The brother trades a sister; and the friend
Lives to the lord, but to the lady's end.
Less must not be thought on than mistress: or
If it be thought, killed like her embrions; for,
Whom no great mistress hath as yet infamed
A fellow of coarse lechery, is named
The servant of the serving woman in scorn,
100 Ne'er came to taste the plenteous marriage horn.
    Thus they do talk. And are these objects fit
For man to spend his money on? His wit?
His time? Health? Soul? Will he for these go throw
Those thousands on his back, shall after blow
His body to the Counters, or the Fleet?
Is it for these that Fine-man meets the street
Coached, or on foot-cloth, thrice-changed every day?
To teach each suit, he has the ready way
From Hyde Park to the stage, where at the last
110 His dear and borrowed bravery he must cast;
When not his combs, his curling irons, his glass,

Sweet bags, sweet powders, nor sweet words will pass
For less security. O, friend, for these
Is it that man pulls on himself disease?
Surfeit? And quarrel? Drinks the tother health?
Or by damnation voids it? Or by stealth?
What fury of late is crept into our feasts?
What honour given to the drunkenest guests?
What reputation to bear one glass more?
120   When oft the bearer is borne out of door?
This hath our ill-used freedom, and soft peace
Brought on us, and will every hour increase.
Our vices do not tarry in a place,
But being in motion still (or rather in race)
Tilt one upon another, and now bear
This way, now that, as if their number were
More than themselves, or than our lives could take,
But both fell pressed under the load they make.
    I'll bid thee look no more, but flee, flee friend,
130   This precipice, and rocks, that have no end,
Or side, but threatens ruin. The whole day
Is not enough now, but the night's to play:
And whilst our states, strength, body, and mind we waste;
Go make ourselves the usurer's at a cast.
He that no more for age, cramps, palsies, can
Now use the bones, we see doth hire a man
To take the box up for him; and pursues
The dice with glassen eyes, to the glad views
Of what he throws: like lechers grown content
140   To be beholders, when their powers are spent.
    Can we not leave this worm? Or will we not?
Is that the truer excuse? Or have we got
In this, and like, an itch of vanity,
That scratching now's our best felicity?
Well, let it go. Yet this is better, than
To lose the forms, and dignities of men
To flatter my good lord, and cry his bowl
Runs sweetly, as it had his lordship's soul.
Although, perhaps it has, what's that to me,

150   That may stand by, and hold my peace? Will he
       When I am hoarse, with praising his each cast,
       Give me but that again, that I must waste
       In sugar candied, or in buttered beer,
       For the recovery of my voice? No, there
       Pardon his lordship. Flattery's grown so cheap
       With him, for he is followed with that heap
       That watch, and catch, at what they may applaud,
       As a poor single flatterer, without bawd,
       Is nothing, such scarce meat and drink he'll give,
160   But he that's both, and slave to boot, shall live,
       And be beloved, while the whores last. O times,
       Friend fly from hence; and let these kindled rhymes
       Light thee from hell on earth: where flatterers, spies,
       Informers, masters both of arts and lies;
       Lewd slanderers, soft whisperers that let blood
       The life, and fame-veins (yet not understood
       Of the poor sufferers); where the envious, proud,
       Ambitious, factious, superstitious, loud
       Boasters, and perjured, with the infinite more
170   Prevaricators swarm. Of which the store
       (Because they are everywhere amongst mankind
       Spread through the world) is easier far to find,
       Than once to number, or bring forth to hand,
       Though thou wert muster-master of the land.
           Go quit them all. And take along with thee,
       Thy true friend's wishes, Colby, which shall be,
       That thine be just, and honest, that thy deeds
       Not wound thy conscience, when thy body bleeds;
       That thou dost all things more for truth, than glory,
180   And never but for doing wrong be sorry;
       That by commanding first thyself, thou mak'st
       Thy person fit for any charge thou tak'st;
       That fortune never make thee to complain,
       But what she gives, thou dar'st give her again;
       That whatsoever face thy fate puts on,
       Thou shrink or start not; but be always one;
       That thou think nothing great, but what is good,

And from that thought strive to be understood.
So, 'live or dead, thou wilt preserve a fame
190 Still precious, with the odour of thy name.
And last, blaspheme not; we did never hear
Man thought the valianter, 'cause he durst swear,
No more, than we should think a lord had had
More honour in him, 'cause we have known him mad:
These take, and now go seek thy peace in war:
Who falls for love of God, shall rise a star.

XVI *An Epitaph on Master Philip Gray*

     Reader, stay,
And if I had no more to say,
But here doth lie till the last day,
All that is left of Philip Gray,
It might thy patience richly pay:
   For, if such men as he could die,
    What surety of life have thou, and I?

XVII *Epistle to a Friend*

They are not, sir, worst owers, that do pay
Debts when they can: good men may break their day,
And yet the noble nature never grudge;
'Tis then a crime, when the usurer is judge,
And he is not in friendship. Nothing there
Is done for gain: if't be 'tis not sincere.
Nor should I at this time protested be,
But that some greater names have broke with me,
And their words too; where I but break my band.
10 I add that 'but' because I understand
That as the lesser breach: for he that takes
Simply my band, his trust in me forsakes,
And looks unto the forfeit. If you be
Now so much friend, as you would trust in me,

Venter a longer time, and willingly:
All is not barren land, doth fallow lie.
Some grounds are made the richer, for the rest;
And I will bring a crop, if not the best.

XVIII An Elegy

Can beauty that did prompt me first to write,
Now threaten, with those means she did invite?
Did her perfections call me on to gaze,
Then like, then love; and now would they amaze?
Or was she gracious afar off, but near
A terror? Or is all this but my fear?
That as the water makes things, put in't, straight,
Crookèd appear; so that doth my conceit:
I can help that with boldness; and love sware,
10 And fortune once, to assist the spirits that dare.
But which shall lead me on? Both these are blind:
Such guides men use not, who their way would find,
Except the way be error to those ends:
And then the best are, still, the blindest friends!
O how a lover may mistake! To think,
Or love, or fortune blind, when they but wink
To see men fear: or else for truth, and state,
Because they would free justice imitate,
Veil their own eyes, and would impartially
20 Be brought by us to meet our destiny.
If it be thus; come love, and fortune go,
I'll lead you on; or if my fate will so,
That I must send one first, my choice assigns,
Love to my heart, and fortune to my lines.

XIX An Elegy

By those bright eyes, at whose immortal fires
Love lights his torches to inflame desires,

By that fair stand, your forehead, whence he bends
His double bow, and round his arrows sends;
By that tall grove, your hair; whose globy rings
He flying curls, and crispeth, with his wings;
By those pure baths your either cheek discloses,
Where he doth steep himself in milk and roses;
And lastly by your lips, the bank of kisses,
10   Where men at once may plant, and gather blisses:
.Tell me (my loved friend) do you love or no?
So well as I may tell in verse, 'tis so?
You blush, but do not: friends are either none,
(Though they may number bodies) or but one.
I'll therefore ask no more, but bid you love;
And so that either may example prove
Unto the other; and live patterns, how
Others in time may love, as we do now.
Slip no occasion; as time stands not still,
20   I know no beauty, nor no youth that will.
To use the present, then, is not abuse;
You have a husband is the just excuse
Of all that can be done him; such a one
As would make shift, to make himself alone,
That which we can, who both in you, his wife,
His issue, and all circumstance of life,
As in his place, because he would not vary,
Is constant to be extraordinary.

XX A Satirical Shrub

A woman's friendship! God whom I trust in,
Forgive me this one foolish deadly sin;
Amongst my many other, that I may
No more, I am sorry for so fond cause, say
At fifty years, almost, to value it,
That ne'er was known to last above a fit!
Or have the least of good, but what it must
Put on for fashion, and take up on trust:

Knew I all this afore? Had I perceived,
10 That their whole life was wickedness, though weaved
Of many colours; outward fresh from spots,
But their whole inside full of ends, and knots?
Knew I, that all their dialogues, and discourse,
Were such as I will now relate, or worse?

        . . . Here, something is wanting . . .

Knew I this woman? Yes; and you do see,
How penitent I am, or I should be!
Do not you ask to know her; she is worse
Than all ingredients made into one curse,
And that poured out upon mankind can be!
20 Think but the sin of all her sex, 'tis she!
I could forgive her being proud! A whore!
Perjured! And painted! If she were no more –
But she is such, as she might, yet, forestall
The devil; and be the damning of us all.

XXI   A Little Shrub Growing By

Ask not to know this man. If fame should speak
His name in any metal, it would break.
Two letters were enough the plague to tear
Out of his grave, and poison every ear.
A parcel of court-dirt, a heap, and mass
Of all vice hurled together, there he was,
Proud, false, and treacherous, vindictive, all
That thought can add, unthankful, the lay-stall
Of putrid flesh alive! Of blood, the sink!
10 And so I leave to stir him, lest he stink.

XXII   An Elegy

Though beauty be the mark of praise,
        And yours of whom I sing be such

As not the world can praise too much,
Yet is't your virtue now I raise.

A virtue, like alloy, so gone
    Throughout your form: as though that move,
    And draw, and conquer all men's love,
This subjects you to love of one.

Wherein you triumph yet: because
10   'Tis of yourself, and that you use
    The noblest freedom, not to choose
Against or faith or honour's laws.

But who should less expect from you,
    In whom alone love lives again?
    By whom he is restored to men:
And kept, and bred, and brought up true?

His falling temples you have reared,
    The withered garlands ta'en away;
    His altars kept from the decay,
20 That envy wished, and nature feared.

And on them burn so chaste a flame,
    With so much loyalty's expense
    As love, to acquit such excellence,
Is gone himself into your name.

And you are he: the deity
    To whom all lovers are designed;
    That would their better objects find:
Among which faithful troop am I.

Who as an offering at your shrine,
30   Have sung this hymn, and here entreat
    One spark of your diviner heat
To light upon a love of mine.

Which if it kindle not, but scant
    Appear, and that to shortest view,
    Yet give me leave to adore in you
What I, in her, am grieved to want.

XXIII An Ode. To Himself

Where dost thou careless lie
    Buried in ease and sloth?
Knowledge, that sleeps, doth die;
And this security,
    It is the common moth,
That eats on wits, and arts, and oft destroys them both.

Are all the Aonian springs
    Dried up? Lies Thespia waste?
Doth Clarius' harp want strings,
10 That not a nymph now sings?
    Or droop they as disgraced,
To see their seats and bowers by chattering pies defaced?

If hence thy silence be,
    As 'tis too just a cause;
Let this thought quicken thee,
Minds that are great and free,
    Should not on fortune pause,
'Tis crown enough to virtue still, her own applause.

What though the greedy fry
20   Be taken with false baits
Of worded balladry,
And think it poesy?
    They die with their conceits,
And only piteous scorn, upon their folly waits.

Then take in hand thy lyre,
    Strike in thy proper strain,
With Japhet's line, aspire
Sol's chariot for new fire,
    To give the world again:
30 Who aided him, will thee, the issue of Jove's brain.

And since our dainty age
    Cannot endure reproof,
Make not thyself a page,

To that strumpet the stage,
　　But sing high and aloof,
Safe from the wolf's black jaw, and the dull ass's hoof.

XXIV *The Mind of the Frontispiece to a Book*

From death and dark oblivion (near the same)
　　The mistress of man's life, grave history,
Raising the world to good or evil fame,
　　Doth vindicate it to eternity.
Wise providence would so; that nor the good
　　Might be defrauded, nor the great secured,
But both might know their ways were understood,
　　When vice alike in time with virtue dured.
Which makes that (lighted by the beamy hand
10　　Of truth, that searcheth the most hidden springs,
And guided by experience, whose straight wand
　　Doth mete, whose line doth sound the depth of things)
She cheerfully supporteth what she rears;
　　Assisted by no strengths, but are her own,
Some note of which each varied pillar bears,
　　By which as proper titles she is known
Time's witness, herald of antiquity,
　　The light of truth, and life of memory.

XXV *An Ode to James, Earl of Desmond*

(WRIT IN QUEEN ELIZABETH'S TIME, SINCE LOST
AND RECOVERED)

　　　Where art thou, genius? I should use
　　　　Thy present aid: arise invention,
　　Wake, and put on the wings of Pindar's muse,
　　　　To tower with my intention
　　　　High, as his mind, that doth advance

Her upright head, above the reach of chance,
   Or the times' envy:
   Cynthius, I apply
My bolder numbers to thy golden lyre:
10   O, then inspire
Thy priest in this strange rapture; heat my brain
   With Delphic fire:
That I may sing my thoughts, in some unvulgar strain.

   Rich beam of honour, shed your light
   On these dark rhymes; that my affection
May shine (through every chink) to every sight
   Graced by your reflection!
   Then shall my verses, like strong charms
Break the knit circle of her stony arms,
20   That holds your spirit:
   And keeps your merit
Locked in her cold embraces, from the view
   Of eyes more true,
Who would with judgement search, searching conclude,
   (As proved in you)
True noblesse. Palm grows straight, though handled ne'er so
 rude!

   Nor think yourself unfortunate,
   If subject to the jealous errors
Of politic pretext, that wries a state,
30   Sink not beneath these terrors:
   But whisper; O glad innocence
Where only a man's birth is his offence;
   Or the disfavour,
   Of such as savour
Nothing, but practise upon honour's thrall.
   O virtue's fall,
When her dead essence (like the anatomy
   In Surgeons' Hall)
Is but a statist's theme, to read phlebotomy.

40   Let Brontes, and black Steropes
          Sweat at the forge, their hammers beating;
      Pyracmon's hour will come to give them ease,
              Though but while metal's heating:
                  And, after all the Etnean ire,
      Gold, that is perfect, will outlive the fire.
                  For fury wasteth,
                  As patience lasteth.
      No armour to the mind! He is shot-free
                  From injury,
50   That is not hurt; not he, that is not hit;
                  So fools we see,
      Oft scape an imputation, more through luck, than wit.

          But to yourself, most loyal lord,
              (Whose heart in that bright sphere flames clearest,
      Though many gems be in your bosom stored,
                  Unknown which is the dearest)
                  If I auspiciously divine,
      (As my hope tells) that our fair Phoebe's shine,
                  Shall light those places,
60   With lustrous graces,
      Where darkness with her gloomy sceptered hand,
                  Doth now command;
      O then (my best-best loved) let me importune,
                  That you will stand,
      As far from all revolt, as you are now from fortune.

XXVI An Ode

          High-spirited friend,
      I send nor balms, nor corsives to your wound;
              Your fate hath found
      A gentler, and more agile hand, to tend
      The cure of that, which is but corporal,
      And doubtful days (which were named critical),

Have made their fairest flight,
And now are out of sight.
Yet doth some wholesome physic for the mind,
10   Wrapped in this paper lie,
Which in the taking if you misapply,
        You are unkind.

        Your covetous hand,
Happy in that fair honour it hath gained,
        Must now be reined.
True valour doth her own renown command
In one full action; nor have you now more
To do, than be a husband of that store.
        Think but how dear you bought
20   This same which you have caught,
Such thoughts will make you more in love with truth:
        'Tis wisdom and that high,
For men to use their fortune reverently,
        Even in youth.

XXVII *An Ode*

Helen, did Homer never see
Thy beauties, yet could write of thee?
Did Sappho on her seven-tongued lute,
So speak (as yet it is not mute)
Of Phao's form? Or doth the boy
In whom Anacreon once did joy,
Lie drawn to life, in his soft verse,
As he whom Maro did rehearse?
Was Lesbia sung by learned Catullus?
10 Or Delia's graces, by Tibullus?
Doth Cynthia, in Propertius' song
Shine more, than she the stars among?
Is Horace his each love so high
Rapt from the earth, as not to die?
With bright Lycoris, Gallus' choice,

Whose fame hath an eternal voice?
Or hath Corinna, by the name
Her Ovid gave her, dimmed the fame
Of Caesar's daughter, and the line
20 Which all the world then styled divine?
Hath Petrarch since his Laura raised
Equal with her? Or Ronsard praised
His new Cassandra, 'bove the old,
Which all the fate of Troy foretold?
Hath our great Sidney, Stella set,
Where never star shone brighter yet?
Or Constable's ambrosiac muse
Made Dian not his notes refuse?
Have all these done (and yet I miss
30 The swan so relished Pancharis)
And shall not I my Celia bring,
Where men may see whom I do sing?
Though I, in working of my song,
Come short of all this learnèd throng,
Yet sure my tunes will be the best,
So much my subject drowns the rest.

XXVIII A Sonnet, to the Noble Lady, the Lady Mary Wroth

I that have been a lover, and could show it,
  Though not in these, in rhymes not wholly dumb,
  Since I exscribe your sonnets, am become
A better lover, and much better poet.
Nor is my muse, or I ashamed to owe it
  To those true numerous graces; whereof some
  But charm the senses, others overcome
Both brains and hearts; and mine now best do know it:
For in your verse all Cupid's armory,
10 His flames, his shafts, his quiver, and his bow,
  His very eyes are yours to overthrow.

But then his mother's sweets you so apply,
   Her joys, her smiles, her loves, as readers take
   For Venus' ceston, every line you make.

XXIX   A Fit of Rhyme against Rhyme

Rhyme, the rack of finest wits,
That expresseth but by fits,
        True conceit,
Spoiling senses of their treasure,
Cozening judgement with a measure,
        But false weight.
Wresting words, from their true calling;
Propping verse, for fear of falling
        To the ground.
10 Jointing syllabes, drowning letters,
Fastening vowels, as with fetters
        They were bound!
Soon as lazy thou wert known,
All good poetry hence was flown,
        And art banished.
For a thousand years together,
All Parnassus' green did wither,
        And wit vanished.
Pegasus did fly away,
20 At the wells no muse did stay,
        But bewailed
So to see the fountain dry,
And Apollo's music die,
        All light failed!
Starveling rhymes did fill the stage,
Not a poet in an age,
        Worth crowning.
Not a work deserving bays,
Nor a line deserving praise,
30   Pallas frowning.
Greek was free from rhyme's infection,

Happy Greek, by this protection,
      Was not spoiled,
Whilst the Latin, queen of tongues,
Is not yet free from rhyme's wrongs,
      But rests foiled.
Scarce the hill again doth flourish,
Scarce the world a wit doth nourish,
      To restore
40 Phoebus to his crown again;
And the muses to their brain;
      As before.
Vulgar languages that want
Words, and sweetness, and be scant
      Of true measure,
Tyran rhyme hath so abused,
That they long since have refused
      Other caesure.
He that first invented thee,
50 May his joints tormented be,
      Cramped forever;
Still may syllabes jar with time,
Still may reason war with rhyme,
      Resting never.
May his sense, when it would meet
The cold tumour in his feet,
      Grow unsounder.
And his title be long fool,
That, in rearing such a school,
60   Was the founder.

XXX An Epigram on William, Lord Burl[eigh], Lo[rd] High Treasurer of England

(PRESENTED UPON A PLATE OF GOLD TO HIS SON
ROB[ERT], E[ARL] OF SALISBURY, WHEN HE WAS ALSO
TREASURER)

If thou wouldst know the virtues of mankind,
Read here in one, what thou in all canst find,
And go no farther: let this circle be
Thy universe, though his epitome.
Cecil the grave, the wise, the great, the good,
What is there more that can ennoble blood?
The orphan's pillar, the true subject's shield,
The poor's full storehouse, and just servant's field.
The only faithful watchman for the realm,
10   That in all tempests, never quit the helm,
But stood unshaken in his deeds, and name,
And laboured in the work; not with the fame:
That still was good for goodness' sake, nor thought
Upon reward, till the reward him sought.
Whose offices and honours did surprise,
Rather than meet him: and, before his eyes
Closed to their peace, he saw his branches shoot,
And in the noblest families took root
Of all the land; who now at such a rate,
20   Of divine blessing, would not serve a state?

XXXI An Epigram. To Thomas Lo[rd] Ellesmere, the Last Term He Sat Chancellor

(FOR A POOR MAN)

So justest lord, may all your judgements be
Laws; and no change e'er come to one decree:
So, may the king proclaim your conscience is
Law, to his law; and think your enemies his:
So, from all sickness, may you rise to health,

The care, and wish still of the public wealth:
So may the gentler muses, and good fame
Still fly about the odour of your name;
As with the safety, and honour of the laws,
10   You favour truth, and me, in this man's cause.

XXXII *Another to Him*

(FOR THE SAME)

The judge his favour timely then extends,
When a good cause is destitute of friends,
Without the pomp of council; or more aid,
Than to make falsehood blush, and fraud afraid:
When those good few, that her defenders be,
Are there for charity, and not for fee.
Such shall you hear today, and find great foes
Both armed with wealth, and slander to oppose,
Who thus long safe, would gain upon the times
10   A right by the prosperity of their crimes;
Who, though their guilt, and perjury they know,
Think, yea and boast, that they have done it so
As though the court pursues them on the scent,
They will come off, and 'scape the punishment.
When this appears, just lord, to your sharp sight,
He does you wrong, that craves you to do right.

XXXIII *An Epigram to the Councillor that Pleaded and Carried the Cause*

That I, hereafter, do not think the bar,
The seat made of a more than civil war;
Or the great hall at Westminster, the field
Where mutual frauds are fought, and no side yield;
That, henceforth, I believe nor books, nor men,
Who 'gainst the law, weave calumnies, my Benn;

But when I read or hear the names so rife
Of hirelings, wranglers, stitchers-to of strife,
Hook-handed harpies, gownèd vultures, put
10 Upon the reverend pleaders; do now shut
All mouths, that dare entitle them (from hence)
To the wolf's study, or dog's eloquence;
Thou art my cause: whose manners since I knew,
Have made me to conceive a lawyer new.
So dost thou study matter, men, and times,
Mak'st it religion to grow rich by crimes!
Dar'st not abuse thy wisdom, in the laws,
Or skill to carry out an evil cause!
But first dost vex, and search it! If not sound,
20 Thou prov'st the gentler ways, to cleanse the wound,
And make the scar fair; if that will not be,
Thou hast the brave scorn, to put back the fee!
But in a business, that will bide the touch,
What use, what strength of reason! And how much
Of books, of precedents, hast thou at hand?
As if the general store thou didst command
Of argument, still drawing forth the best,
And not being borrowed by thee, but possessed.
So com'st thou like a chief into the court
30 Armed at all pieces, as to keep a fort
Against a multitude; and (with thy stile
So brightly brandished) wound'st, defend'st! The while
Thy adversaries fall, as not a word
They had, but were a reed unto thy sword.
Then com'st thou off with victory and palm,
Thy hearer's nectar, and thy client's balm,
The court's just honour, and thy judge's love.
And (which doth all achievements get above)
Thy sincere practice, breeds not thee a fame
40 Alone, but all thy rank a reverend name.

XXXIV An Epigram. To the Small-Pox

Envious and foul disease, could there not be
One beauty in an age, and free from thee?
What did she worth thy spite? Were there not store
Of those that set by their false faces more
Than this did by her true? She never sought
Quarrel with Nature, or in balance brought
Art, her false servant; nor, for Sir Hugh Plat,
Was drawn to practise other hue, than that
Her own blood gave her: she ne'er had, nor hath
10 Any belief, in Madam Baud-bee's bath,
Or Turner's oil of Talc. Nor ever got
Spanish receipt, to make her teeth to rot.
What was the cause then? Thought'st thou in disgrace
Of beauty, so to nullify a face,
That heaven should make no more; or should amiss
Make all hereafter, had'st thou ruined this?
Ay, that thy aim was; but her fate prevailed:
And scorned, thou hast shown thy malice, but hast failed.

XXXV An Epitaph

What beauty would have lovely styled,
What manners pretty, nature mild,
What wonder perfect, all were filed
Upon record in this blessed child.
      And, till the coming of the soul
        To fetch the flesh, we keep the roll.

XXXVI A Song

(LOVER)
Come, let us here enjoy the shade,
For love in shadow best is made.
Though envy oft his shadow be,
None brooks the sunlight worse than he.

(MISTRESS)
Where love doth shine, there needs no sun,
All lights into his one doth run;
Without which all the world were dark;
Yet he himself is but a spark.

(ARBITER)
A spark to set whole worlds afire,
10   Who more they burn, they more desire,
And have their being, their waste to see;
And waste still, that they still might be.

(CHORUS)
Such are his powers, whom time hath styled,
Now swift, now slow, now tame, now wild;
Now hot, now cold, now fierce, now mild:
The eldest god, yet still a child.

XXXVII *An Epistle to a Friend*

Sir, I am thankful, first, to heaven, for you;
Next to yourself, for making your love true:
Then to your love, and gift. And all's but due.

You have unto my store added a book,
On which with profit, I shall never look,
But must confess from whom what gift I took.

Not like your country neighbours, that commit
Their vice of loving for a Christmas fit;
Which is indeed but friendship of the spit:

10   But, as a friend, which name yourself receive,
And which you (being the worthier) gave me leave
In letters, that mix spirits, thus to weave.

Which, how most sacred I will ever keep,
So may the fruitful vine my temples steep,
And Fame wake for me, when I yield to sleep.

Though you sometimes proclaim me too severe,
Rigid, and harsh, which is a drug austere
In friendship, I confess: but dear friend, hear.

Little know they, that prófess amity,
20   And seek to scant her comely liberty,
How much they lame her in her property.

And less they know, who being free to use
That friendship which no chance but love did choose,
Will unto licence that fair leave abuse.

It is an act of tyranny, not love,
In practiced friendship wholly to reprove,
As flattery with friends' humours still to move.

From each of which I labour to be free,
Yet if with either's vice I tainted be,
30   Forgive it, as my frailty, and not me.

For no man lives so out of passion's sway
But shall sometimes be tempted to obey
Her fury, yet no friendship to betray.

XXXVIII An Elegy

'Tis true, I'm broke! Vows, oaths, and all I had
Of credit lost. And I am now run mad:
Or do upon myself some desperate ill;
This sadness makes no approaches, but to kill.
It is a darkness hath blocked up my sense,
And drives it in to eat on my offence,
Or there to starve it. Help, O you that may
Alone lend succours, and this fury stay.
Offended mistress, you are yet so fair,
10   As light breaks from you, that affrights despair,
And fills my powers with persuading joy,
That you should be too noble to destroy.
There may some face or menace of a storm
Look forth, but cannot last in such a form.

If there be nothing worthy you can see
Of graces, or your mercy here in me,
Spare your own goodness yet; and be not great
In will and power, only to defeat.
God, and the good, know to forgive, and save.
20   The ignorant, and fools, no pity have.
I will not stand to justify my fault,
Or lay the excuse upon the vintner's vault;
Or in confessing of the crime be nice,
Or go about to countenance the vice,
By naming in what company 'twas in,
As I would urge authority for sin.
No, I will stand arraigned, and cast, to be
The subject of your grace in pardoning me,
And (styled your mercy's creature) will live more
30   Your honour now, than your disgrace before.
Think it was frailty, mistress, think me man,
Think that yourself like heaven forgive me can:
Where weakness doth offend, and virtue grieve,
There greatness takes a glory to relieve.
Think that I once was yours, or may be now;
Nothing is vile, that is a part of you:
Error and folly in me may have crossed
Your just commands; yet those, not I be lost.
I am regenerate now, become the child
40   Of your compassion; parents should be mild:
There is no father that for one demerit,
Or two, or three, a son will disinherit –
That is the last of punishments is meant:
No man inflicts that pain, till hope be spent.
An ill-affected limb (whate'er it ail)
We cut not off, till all cures else do fail:
And then with pause; for severed once, that's gone,
Would live his glory that could keep it on;
Do not despair my mending ; to distrust
50   Before you prove a medicine, is unjust.
You may so place me, and in such an air
As not alone the cure, but scar be fair.

That is, if still your favours you apply,
And not the bounties you have done, deny.
Could you demand the gifts you gave, again?
Why was it? Did e'er the clouds ask back their rain?
The sun his heat, and light, the air his dew?
Or winds the spirit, by which the flower so grew?
That were to wither all, and make a grave
60 Of that wise nature would a cradle have!
Her order is to cherish, and preserve,
Consumption's nature to destroy, and starve.
But to exact again what once is given,
Is nature's mere obliquity! As heaven
Should ask the blood, and spirits he hath infused
In man, because man hath the flesh abused.
O may your wisdom take example hence,
God lightens not at man's each frail offence,
He pardons slips, goes by a world of ills,
70 And then his thunder frights more, than it kills.
He cannot angry be, but all must quake,
It shakes even him, that all things else doth shake.
And how more fair, and lovely looks the world
In a calm sky; than when the heaven is hurled
About in clouds, and wrapped in raging weather,
As all with storm and tempest ran together.
O imitate that sweet serenity
That makes us live, not that which calls to die.
In dark, and sullen morns; do we not say
80 This looketh like an execution day?
And with the vulgar doth it not obtain
The name of cruel weather, storm, and rain?
Be not affected with these marks too much
Of cruelty, lest they do make you such.
But view the mildness of your Maker's state,
As I the penitent's here emulate:
He, when he sees a sorrow such as this,
Straight puts off all his anger, and doth kiss
The contrite soul, who hath no thought to win
90 Upon the hope to have another sin

Forgiven him; and in that line stand I,
Rather than once displease you more, to die,
To suffer tortures, scorn, and infamy,
What fools, and all their parasites can apply;
The wit of ale, and genius of the malt
Can pump for; or a libel without salt
Produce; though threatening with a coal, or chalk
On every wall, and sung where e'er I walk.
I number these as being of the chore
100 Of contumely, and urge a good man more
Than sword, or fire, or what is of the race
To carry noble danger in the face:
There is not any punishment, or pain,
A man should fly from, as he would disdain.
Then mistress, here, here let your rigour end,
And let your mercy make me ashamed t'offend.
I will no more abuse my vows to you,
Than I will study falsehood, to be true.
O, that you could but by dissection see
110 How much you are the better part of me!
How all my fibres by your spirit do move,
And that there is no life in me, but love.
You would be then most confident, that though
Public affairs command me now to go
Out of your eyes, and be awhile away;
Absence, or distance, shall not breed decay.
Your form shines here, here fixèd in my heart:
I may dilate myself, but not depart.

Others by common stars their courses run,
120 When I see you, then I do see my sun,
Till then 'tis all but darkness, that I have;
Rather than want your light, I wish a grave.

XXXIX

See note, p. 530

XL An Elegy

That love's a bitter sweet, I ne'er conceive
Till the sour minute comes of taking leave,
And then I taste it. But as men drink up
In haste the bottom of a medicined cup,
And take some syrup after; so do I,
To put all relish from my memory
Of parting, drown it in the hope to meet
Shortly again: and make our absence sweet.
This makes me, mistress, that sometime by stealth
10 Under another name, I take your health;
And turn the ceremonies of those nights
I give, or owe my friends, into your rites,
But ever without blazon, or least shade
Of vows so sacred, and in silence made;
For though love thrive, and may grow up with cheer,
And free society, he's born elsewhere,
And must be bred, so to conceal his birth,
As neither wine do rack it out, or mirth.
Yet should the lover still be airy and light,
20 In all his actions rarified to sprite;
Not like a Midas shut up in himself,
And turning all he toucheth into pelf,
Keep in reserved in his dark-lantern face,
As if that excellent dulness were love's grace;
No, mistress, no, the open merry man
Moves like a sprightly river, and yet can
Keep secret in his channels what he breeds
'Bove all your standing waters, choked with weeds.
They look at best like cream bowls, and you soon
30 Shall find their depth: they're sounded with a spoon.
They may say grace, and for love's chaplains pass;

But the grave lover ever was an ass;
Is fixed upon one leg, and dares not come
Out with the other, for he's still at home;
Like the dull, wearied crane that (come on land)
Doth, while he keeps his watch, betray his stand.
Where he that knows will like a lapwing fly
Far from the nest, and so himself belie
To others, as he will deserve the trust
40   Due to that one, that doth believe him just.
And such your servant is, who vows to keep
The jewel of your name, as close as sleep
Can lock the sense up, or the heart a thought,
And never be by time, or folly brought,
Weakness of brain, or any charm of wine,
The sin of boast, or other countermine
(Made to blow up love's secrets) to discover
That article, may not become your lover:
Which in assurance to your breast I tell,
50   If I had writ no word, but 'dear', farewell.

XLI An Elegy

Since you must go, and I must bid farewell,
Hear, mistress, your departing servant tell
What it is like: and do not think they can
Be idle words, though of a parting man;
It is as if a night should shade noon-day,
Or that the sun was here, but forced away;
And we were left under that hemisphere,
Where we must feel it dark for half a year.
What fate is this to change men's days and hours,
10   To shift their seasons, and destroy their powers!
Alas I have lost my heat, my blood, my prime,
Winter is come a quarter ere his time,
My health will leave me; and when you depart,
How shall I do, sweet mistress, for my heart?
You would restore it? No, that's worth a fear,

As if it were not worthy to be there:
O, keep it still; for it had rather be
Your sacrifice, than here remain with me.
And so I spare it. Come what can become
20 Of me, I'll softly tread unto my tomb;
Or like a ghost walk silent amongst men,
Till I may see both it and you again.

XLII An Elegy

Let me be what I am, as Virgil cold;
As Horace fat; or as Anacreon old;
No poet's verses yet did ever move,
Whose readers did not think he was in love.
Who shall forbid me then in rhythm to be
As light, and active as the youngest he
That from the muses' fountains doth endorse
His lines, and hourly sits the poet's horse?
Put on my ivy garland, let me see
10 Who frowns, who jealous is, who taxeth me.
Fathers and husbands, I do claim a right
In all that is called lovely: take my sight
Sooner than my affection from the fair.
No face, no hand, proportion, line, or air
Of beauty; but the muse hath interest in:
There is not worn that lace, purl, knot or pin,
But is the poet's matter: and he must
When he is furious, love, although not lust.
But then content, your daughters and your wives,
20 (If they be fair and worth it) have their lives
Made longer by our praises. Or, if not,
Wish, you had foul ones, and deformèd got;
Cursed in their cradles, or there changed by elves,
So to be sure you do enjoy yourselves.
Yet keep those up in sackcloth too, or leather,
For silk will draw some sneaking songster thither.
It is a rhyming age, and verses swarm

At every stall; the city cap's a charm.
But I who live, and have lived twenty year
30 Where I may handle silk, as free, and near,
As any mercer; or the whalebone man
That quilts those bodies, I have leave to span:
Have eaten with the beauties, and the wits,
And braveries of court, and felt their fits
Of love, and hate: and came so nigh to know
Whether their faces were their own, or no:
It is not likely I should now look down
Upon a velvet petticoat, or a gown,
Whose like I have known the tailor's wife put on
40 To do her husband's rites in, ere 'twere gone
Home to the customer: his lechery
Being, the best clothes still to preoccupy.
Put a coach-mare in tissue, must I horse
Her presently? Or leap thy wife of force,
When by thy sordid bounty she hath on,
A gown of that was the caparison?
So I might dote upon thy chairs, and stools
That are like clothed: must I be of those fools
Of race accounted, that no passion have
50 But when thy wife (as thou conceiv'st) is brave?
Then ope thy wardrobe, think me that poor groom
That from the footman, when he was become
An officer there, did make most solemn love,
To every petticoat he brushed, and glove
He did lay up, and would adore the shoe,
Or slipper was left off, and kiss it too,
Court every hanging gown, and after that,
Lift up some one, and do, I tell not what.
Thou didst tell me; and wert o'erjoyed to peep
60 In at a hole, and see these actions creep
From the poor wretch, which though he played in prose,
He would have done in verse , with any of those
Wrung on the withers, by lord Love's despite,
Had he had the faculty to read, and write!
Such songsters there are store of; witness he

That chanced the lace, laid on a smock, to see,
And straightway spent a sonnet; with that other
That (in pure madrigal) unto his mother
Commended the French hood, and scarlet gown
70 The Lady Mayoress passed in through the town,
Unto the Spittle sermon. O, what strange
Variety of silks were on the Exchange!
Or in Moorfields! This other night, sings one,
Another answers, 'Las those silks are none,
In smiling *l'envoy*, as he would deride
Any comparison had with his Cheapside.
And vouches both the pageant, and the day,
When not the shops, but windows do display
The stuffs, the velvets, plushes, fringes, lace,
80 And all the original riots of the place:
Let the poor fools enjoy their follies, love
A goat in velvet; or some block could move
Under that cover; an old midwife's hat!
Or a close-stool so cased; or any fat
Bawd, in a velvet scabbard! I envy
None of their pleasures! Nor will ask thee, why
Thou art jealous of thy wife's, or daughter's case:
More than of either's manners, wit, or face!

XLIII An Execration upon Vulcan

And why to me this, thou lame lord of fire,
What had I done that might call on thine ire?
Or urge thy greedy flame, thus to devour
So many my years' labours in an hour?
I ne'er attempted, Vulcan, 'gainst thy life;
Nor made least line of love to thy loose wife;
Or in remembrance of thy affront, and scorn,
With clowns, and tradesmen, kept thee closed in horn.
'Twas Jupiter that hurled thee headlong down,
10 And Mars, that gave thee a lantern for a crown:
Was it because thou wert of old denied

By Jove to have Minerva for thy bride,
That since thou tak'st all envious care and pain,
To ruin any issue of the brain?
Had I wrote treason there, or heresy,
Imposture, witchcraft, charms, or blasphemy,
I had deserved, then, thy consuming looks,
Perhaps, to have been burnèd with my books.
But, on thy malice, tell me, didst thou spy
20 Any, least loose, or scurrile paper, lie
Concealed or kept there, that was fit to be,
By thy own vote, a sacrifice to thee?
Did I there wound the honours of the crown?
Or tax the glories of the church, and gown?
Itch to defame the state? Or brand the times?
And myself most, in some self-boasting rhymes?
If none of these, then why this fire? Or find
A cause before; or leave me one behind.
Had I compiled from *Amadis de Gaul*,
30 The *Esplandians, Arthurs, Palmerins*, and all
The learnèd library of Don Quixote;
And so some goodlier monster had begot,
Or spun out riddles, and weaved fifty tomes
Of logogriphs, and curious palindromes,
Or pomped for those hard trifles anagrams,
Or eteostichs, or those finer flammes
Of eggs, and halberds, cradles, and a hearse,
A pair of scissors, and a comb in verse;
Acrostichs, and telestichs, on jump names,
40 Thou then hadst had some colour for thy flames,
On such my serious follies; but, thou'lt say,
There were some pieces of as base allay,
And as false stamp there; parcels of a play,
Fitter to see the firelight, than the day;
Adulterate monies, such as might not go:
Thou shouldst have stayed, till public fame said so.
She is the judge, thou executioner:
Or if thou needs wouldst trench upon her power,
Thou mightst have yet enjoyed thy cruelty

50 With some more thrift, and more variety:
  Thou mightst have had me perish, piece by piece,
  To light tobacco, or save roasted geese,
  Singe capons, or poor pigs, dropping their eyes:
  Condemned me to the ovens with the pies;
  And so, have kept me dying a whole age,
  Not ravished all hence in a minute's rage.
  But that's a mark, whereof thy rites do boast,
  To make consumption, ever, where thou go'st;
  Had I foreknown of this thy least desire
60 To have held a triumph, or a feast of fire,
  Especially in paper: that, that steam
  Had tickled your large nostril: many a ream,
  To redeem mine, I had sent in; enough,
  Thou shouldst have cried, and all been proper stuff.
  The *Talmud*, and the *Alcoran* had come,
  With pieces of the *Legend*; the whole sum
  Of errant knighthood, with the dames, and dwarfs;
  The charmèd boats, and the enchanted wharfs;
  The Tristrams, Lancelots, Turpins, and the Peers,
70 All the mad Rolands, and sweet Oliveers;
  To Merlin's marvels, and his cabal's loss,
  With the chimera of the Rosy-Cross,
  Their seals, their characters, hermetic rings,
  Their gem of riches, and bright stone, that brings
  Invisibility, and strength, and tongues:
  The art of kindling the true coal, by lungs;
  With Nicholas Pasquil's *Meddle with your match*,
  And the strong lines, that so the time do catch,
  Or Captain Pamphlet's horse, and foot, that sally
80 Upon the Exchange, still out of Pope's Head Alley.
  The weekly corrants, with Paul's seal; and all
  The admired discourses of the prophet Ball:
  These, hadst thou pleased either to dine, or sup,
  Had made a meal for Vulcan to lick up.
  But in my desk, what was there to excite
  So ravenous, and vast an appetite?
  I dare not say a body, but some parts

There were of search, and mastery in the arts.
All the old Venusine, in poetry,
90   And lighted by the Stagerite, could spy,
Was there made English: with the Grammar too,
To teach some that, their nurses could not do –
The purity of language; and among
The rest, my journey into Scotland sung,
With all the adventures; three books not afraid
To speak the fate of the Sicilian màid
To our own ladies; and in story there
Of our fifth Henry, eight of his nine year;
Wherein was oil, beside the succour spent,
100   Which noble Carew, Cotton, Selden lent:
And twice twelve years stored up humanity,
With humble gleanings in divinity;
After the Fathers, and those wiser guides
Whom faction had not drawn to study sides.
How in these ruins, Vulcan, thou dost lurk,
All soot, and embers! Odious, as thy work!
I now begin to doubt, if ever grace,
Or goddess, could be patient of thy face.
Thou woo Minerva! Or to wit aspire!
110   'Cause thou canst halt, with us, in arts, and fire!
Son of the wind! For so thy mother gone
With lust conceived thee; father thou hadst none:
When thou wert born, and that thou look'st at best,
She durst not kiss, but flung thee from her breast.
And so did Jove, who ne'er meant thee his cup:
No mar'l the clowns of Lemnos took thee up,
For none but smiths would have made thee a god.
Some alchemist there may be yet, or odd
Squire of the squibs, against the pageant day,
120   May to thy name a Vulcanale say;
And for it lose his eyes with gunpowder,
As the other may his brains with quicksilver.
Well fare the wise men yet, on the Bankside,
My friends, the watermen! They could provide
Against thy fury, when to serve their needs,

They made a Vulcan of a sheaf of reeds,
Whom they durst handle in their holiday coats,
And safely trust to dress, not burn their boats.
But, O those reeds! Thy mere disdain of them,
130   Made thee beget that cruel stratagem,
(Which, some are pleased to style but thy mad prank)
Against the Globe, the glory of the Bank,
Which, though it were the fort of the whole parish,
Flanked with a ditch, and forced out of a marish,
I saw with two poor chambers taken in
And razed; ere thought could urge, this might have been!
See the world's ruins! Nothing but the piles
Left! And wit since to cover it with tiles.
The Brethren, they straight noised it out for news,
140   'Twas verily some relic of the stews:
And this a sparkle of that fire let loose
That was locked up in the Winchestrian goose
Bred on the Bank, in time of popery,
When Venus there maintained the mystery.
But, others fell, with that conceit by the ears,
And cried, it was a threatening to the bears;
And that accursèd ground, the Parish Garden:
Nay (sighed a sister) 'twas the nun, Kate Arden,
Kindled the fire! But, then did one return,
150   No fool would his own harvest spoil, or burn!
If that were so, thou rather wouldst advance
The place, that was thy wife's inheritance.
O no, cried all. Fortune, for being a whore,
Scaped not his justice any jot the more:
He burnt that idol of the Revels too:
Nay, let Whitehall with Revels have to do,
Though but in dances, it shall know his power;
There was a judgement shown too in an hour.
He is true Vulcan still! He did not spare
160   Troy, though it were so much his Venus' care.
Fool, wilt thou let that in example come?
Did she not save from thence, to build a Rome?
And what hast thou done in these petty spites,

More than advanced the houses, and their rites?
I will not argue thee, from those of guilt,
For they were burnt, but to be better built.
'Tis true, that in thy wish they were destroyed,
Which thou hast only vented, not enjoyed.
So wouldst thou have run upon the Rolls by stealth,
170 And didst invade part of the Commonwealth,
In those records, which were all chronicles gone,
Will be remembered by six clerks, to one.
But, say all six, good men, what answer ye?
Lies there no writ, out of the Chancery,
Against this Vulcan? No injunction?
No order? No decree? Though we be gone
At Common Law: methinks in his despite
A court of Equity should do us right,
But to confine him to the brew-houses,
180 The glasshouse, dye-fats, and their furnaces;
To live in sea coal, and go forth in smoke;
Or lest that vapour might the city choke,
Condemn him to the brick kilns, or some hill-
Foot (out in Sussex) to an iron mill;
Or in small faggots have him blaze about
Vile taverns, and the drunkards piss him out;
Or in the bellman's lantern, like a spy,
Burn to a snuff, and then stink out, and die:
I could invent a sentence, yet were worse;
190 But I'll conclude all in a civil curse.
Pox on your flameship, Vulcan; if it be
To all as fatal as't hath been to me,
And to Paul's steeple; which was unto us
'Bove all your fireworks had at Ephesus,
Or Alexandria; and though a divine
Loss remains yet, as unrepaired as mine.
Would you had kept your forge, at Etna still,
And there made swords, bills, glaives, and arms your fill;
Maintained the trade at Bilbo; or elsewhere;
200 Struck in at Mílan with the cutlers there;
Or stayed but where the friar, and you first met,

Who from the devil's arse did guns beget;
Or fixed in the Low Countries, where you might
On both sides do your mischiefs with delight;
Blow up, and ruin, mine, and countermine,
Make your petards, and granats, all your fine
Engines of murder, and receive the praise
Of massacring mankind so many ways.
We ask your absence here, we all love peace,
210 And pray the fruits thereof, and the increase;
So doth the king, and most of the king's men
That have good places: therefore once again,
Pox on thee, Vulcan, thy Pandora's pox,
And all the evils that flew out of her box
Light on thee: or if those plagues will not do,
Thy wife's pox on thee, and Bess Braughton's too.

XLIV A Speech according to Horace

Why yet, my noble hearts, they cannot say,
But we have powder still for the king's day,
And ordinance too: so much as from the tower
To have waked, if sleeping, Spain's ambassador,
Old Aesop Gondomar: the French can tell,
For they did see it the last tilting well,
That we have trumpets, armour, and great horse,
Lances, and men, and some a breaking force.
They saw too store of feathers, and more may,
10 If they stay here, but till Saint George's Day.
All ensigns of a war are not yet dead,
Nor marks of wealth so from our nation fled,
But they may see gold chains, and pearl worn then,
Lent by the London dames, to the lords' men;
Withal, the dirty pains those citizens take,
To see the pride at court, their wives do make:
And the return those thankful courtiers yield
To have their husbands drawn forth to the field,
And coming home, to tell what acts were done

20 Under the auspice of young Swinnerton.
What a strong fort old Pimlico had been!
How it held out! How (last) 'twas taken in!
Well, I say thrive, thrive brave Artillery yard,
Thou seed-plot of the war, that hast not spared
Powder, or paper, to bring up the youth
Of London, in the military truth,
These ten years' day; as all may swear that look
But on thy practice, and the posture book:
He that but saw thy curious captain's drill,
30 Would think no more of Flushing, or the Brill:
But give them over to the common ear
For that unnecessary charge they were.
Well did thy crafty clerk, and knight, Sir Hugh
Supplant bold Panton; and brought there to view
Translated Aelian *Tactics* to be read,
And the Greek discipline (with the modern) shed
So, in that ground. as soon it grew to be
The city-question, whether Tilly, or he,
Were now the greater captain! For they saw
40 The Berghen siege, and taking in Breda,
So acted to the life, as Maurice might,
And Spinola have blushèd at 'he sight.
O happy art! And wise epitome
Of bearing arms! Most civil soldiery!
Thou canst draw forth thy forces, and fight dry
The battles of thy aldermanity;
Without the hazard of a drop of blood:
More than the surfeits, in thee, that day stood.
Go on, increase in virtue and in fame:
50 And keep the glory of the English name,
Up among nations. In the stead of bold
Beauchamps, and Nevills, Cliffords, Audleys old;
Insert thy Hodges, and those newer men,
As Stiles, Dike, Ditchfield, Millar, Crips, and Fen:
That keep the war, though now't be grown more tame,
Alive yet, in the noise; and still the same;
And could (if our great men would let their sons

Come to their schools) show them the use of guns.
And there instruct the noble English heirs
60 In politic and militar' affairs;
But he that should persuade, to have this done
For education of our lordings; soon
Should he not hear of billow, wind, and storm,
From the tempestuous grandlings? 'Who'll inform
Us, in our bearing, that are thus, and thus,
Born, bred, allied! What's he dare tutor us?
Are we by bookworms to be awed? Must we
Live by their scale, that dare do nothing free?
Why are we rich, or great, except to show
70 All licence in our lives? What need we know?
More than to praise a dog or horse? Or speak
The hawking language? Or our day to break
With citizens? Let clowns, and tradesmen breed
Their sons to study arts, the laws, the creed:
We will believe, like men of our own rank,
In so much land a year, or such a bank,
That turns us so much monies, at which rate
Our ancestors imposed on prince and state.
Let poor nobility be virtuous: we,
80 Descended in a rope of titles, be
From Guy, or Bevis, Arthur, or from whom
The herald will. Our blood is now become
Past any need of virtue. Let them care,
That in the cradle of their gentry are,
To serve the state by councils, and by arms:
We neither love the troubles, nor the harms.'
What love you then? Your whore? What study? Gait,
Carriage, and dressing? There is up of late
The academy, where the gallants meet –
90 What, to make legs? Yes, and to smell most sweet.
All that they do at plays. O, but first here
They learn and study; and then practise there.
But why are all these irons in the fire
Of several makings? Helps, helps, to attire
His lordship. That is for his band, his hair

This, and that box his beauty to repair;
This other for his eyebrows; hence, away,
I may no longer on these pictures stay,
These carcasses of honour; tailors' blocks,
100 Covered with tissue, whose prosperity mocks
The fate of things: whilst tottered virtue holds
Her broken arms up, to their empty moulds.

XLV An Epistle to Master Arth[ur] Squib

What I am not, and what I fain would be,
Whilst I inform myself, I would teach thee,
My gentle Arthur; that it might be said
One lesson we have both learned, and well read;
I neither am, nor art thou one of those
That hearkens to a jack's pulse, when it goes.
Nor ever trusted to that friendship yet
Was issue of the tavern, or the spit:
Much less a name would we bring up, or nurse,
10 That could but claim a kindred from the purse.
Those are poor ties, depend on those false ends,
'Tis virtue alone, or nothing that knits friends:
And as within your office, you do take
No piece of money, but you know, or make
Enquiry of the worth: so must we do,
First weigh a friend, then touch, and try him too:
For there are many slips, and counterfeits.
Deceit is fruitful. Men have masks and nets,
But these with wearing will themselves unfold:
20 They cannot last. No lie grew ever old.
Turn him, and see his threads: look, if he be
Friend to himself, that would be friend to thee.
For that is first required, a man be his own.
But he that's too much that, is friend of none.
Then rest, and a friend's value understand:
It is a richer purchase than of land.

XLVI An Epigram on Sir Edward Coke, when He was Lord Chief Justice of England

He that should search all glories of the gown,
And steps of all raised servants of the crown,
He could not find, than thee of all that store
Whom Fortune aided less, or virtue more.
Such, Coke, were thy beginnings, when thy good
In others' evil best was understood:
When, being the stranger's help, the poor man's aid,
Thy just defences made the oppressor afraid.
Such was thy process, when integrity,
10 And skill in thee, now, grew authority;
That clients strove, in question of the laws,
More for thy patronage, than for their cause,
And that thy strong and manly eloquence
Stood up thy nation's fame, her crown's defence,
And now such is thy stand; while thou dost deal
Desirèd justice to the public weal
Like Solon's self; explat'st the knotty laws
With endless labours, whilst thy learning draws
No less of praise, than readers in all kinds
20 Of worthiest knowledge, that can take men's minds.
Such is thy all; that (as I sung before)
None Fortune aided less, or virtue more.
Of if chance must, to each man that doth rise,
Needs lend an aid, to thine she had her eyes.

XLVII An Epistle answering to One that Asked to be Sealed of the Tribe of Ben

Men that are safe, and sure, in all they do,
Care not what trials they are put unto;
They meet the fire, the test, as martyrs would;
And though opinion stamp them not, are gold.
I could say more of such, but that I fly
To speak myself out too ambitiously,

And showing so weak an act to vulgar eyes,
Put conscience and my right to compromise.
Let those that merely talk, and never think,
10   That live in the wild anarchy of drink
Subject to quarrel only; or else such
As make it their proficiency, how much
They have glutted in, and lechered out that week,
That never yet did friend, or friendship seek
But for a sealing: let these men protest.
Or the other on their borders, that will jest
On all souls that are absent: even the dead;
Like flies, or worms, which man's corrupt parts fed:
That to speak well, think it above all sin,
20   Of any company but that they are in,
Call every night to supper in these fits,
And are received for the covy of wits;
That censure all the town, and all the affairs,
And know whose ignorance is more than theirs;
Let these men have their ways, and take their times
To vent their libels, and to issue rhymes:
I have no portion in them, nor their deal
Of news they get, to strew out the long meal.
I study other friendships, and more one,
30   Than these can ever be; or else wish none.
What is't to me whether the French design
Be, or be not, to get the Valtelline?
Or the States' ships sent forth belike to meet
Some hopes of Spain in their West Indian fleet?
Whether the dispensation yet be sent,
Or that the match from Spain was ever meant?
I wish all well, and pray high heaven conspire
My prince's safety, and my king's desire,
But if for honour, we must draw the sword,
40   And force back that, which will not be restored,
I have a body, yet, that spirit draws
To live, or fall, a carcass in the cause.
So far without inquiry what the States,
Brunsfield, and Mansfield do this year, my fates

Shall carry me at call; and I'll be well,
Though I do neither hear these news, nor tell
Of Spain or France; or were not pricked down one
Of the late mystery of reception,
Although my fame, to his, not underhears,
50 That guides the motions, and directs the bears.
But that's a blow, by which in time I may
Lose all my credit with my Christmas clay,
And animated porcelain of the court;
Ay, and for this neglect, the coarser sort
Of earthen jars, there may molest me too:
Well, with mine own frail pitcher, what to do
I have decreed; keep it from waves, and press;
Lest it be jostled, cracked, made naught, or less:
Live to that point I will, for which I am man,
60 And dwell as in my centre, as I can,
Still looking to, and ever loving heaven;
With reverence using all the gifts thence given.
'Mongst which, if I have any friendships sent
Such as are square, well-tagged, and permanent,
Not built with canvas, paper, and false lights
As are the glorious scenes, at the great sights;
And that there be no fevery heats, nor colds,
Oily expansions, or shrunk dirty folds,
But all so clear, and led by reason's flame,
70 As but to stumble in her sight were shame.
These I will honour, love, embrace, and serve:
And free it from all question to preserve.
So short you read my character, and theirs
I would call mine, to which not many stairs
Are asked to climb. First give me faith, who know
Myself a little. I will take you so,
As you have writ yourself. Now stand, and then,
Sir, you are sealèd of the tribe of Ben.

XLVIII The Dedication of the
King's New Cellar. To Bacchus

Since, Bacchus, thou art father
Of wines, to thee the rather
We dedicate this cellar,
Where new, thou art made dweller;
And seal thee thy commission:
But 'tis with a condition,
That thou remain here taster
Of all to the great master.
And look unto their faces,
10 Their qualities, and races,
That both, their odour take him,
And relish merry make him.
  For Bacchus, thou art freer
Of cares, and overseer
Of feast, and merry meeting,
And still begin'st the greeting:
See then thou dost attend him,
Lyaeus, and defend him,
By all the arts of gladness
20 From any thought like sadness.
  So mayst thou still be younger
Than Phoebus; and much stronger
To give mankind their eases,
And cure the world's diseases:
  So may the muses follow
Thee still, and leave Apollo,
And think thy stream more quicker
Than Hippocrenè's liquor;
And thou make many a poet,
30 Before his brain do know it;
So may there never quarrel
Have issue from the barrel;
But Venus and the graces
Pursue thee in all places,
And not a song be other

Than Cupid, and his mother.
That when King James, above here
Shall feast it, thou mayst love there
The causes and the guests too,
40 And have thy tales and jests too,
Thy circuits, and thy rounds free
As shall the feast's fair grounds be.
    Be it he hold communion
In great Saint George's union;
Or gratulates the passage
Of some well-wrought embassage:
Whereby he may knit sure up
The wishèd peace of Europe:
Or else a health advances,
50 To put his court in dances,
And set us all on skipping,
When with his royal shipping
The narrow seas are shady,
And Charles brings home the lady.

Accessit fervor Capiti, Numerusque Lucernis.

XLIX An Epigram on the Court Pucell

Does the court pucell then so censure me,
And thinks I dare not her? Let the world see.
What though her chamber be the very pit
Where fight the prime cocks of the game, for wit?
And that as any are struck, her breath creates
New in their stead, out of the candidates?
What though with tribade lust she force a muse,
And in an epicoene fury can write news
Equal with that, which for the best news goes,
10 As airy light, and as like wit as those?
What though she talk, and cannot once with them
Make state, religion, bawdry, all a theme?
And as lip-thirsty, in each word's expense,

Doth labour with the phrase more than the sense?
What though she ride two mile on holidays
To church, as others do to feasts and plays,
To show their tires? To view, and to be viewed?
What though she be with velvet gowns endued,
And spangled petticoats brought forth to eye,
20 As new rewards of her old secrecy?
What though she hath won on trust, as many do,
And that her truster fears her? Must I too?
I never stood for any place: my wit
Thinks itself naught, though she should value it.
I am no statesman, and much less divine;
For bawdry, 'tis her language, and not mine.
Farthest I am from the idolatry
To stuffs and laces, those my man can buy.
And trust her I would least, that hath forswore
30 In contract twice; what can she perjure more?
Indeed, her dressing some man might delight,
Her face there's none can like by candle-light.
Not he, that should the body have, for case
To his poor instrument, now out of grace.
Shall I advise thee, pucell? Steal away
From court, while yet thy fame hath some small day;
The wits will leave you, if they once perceive
You cling to lords; and lords, if them you leave
For sermoneers: of which now one, now other,
40 They say you weekly invite with fits o'th'mother,
And practise for a miracle; take heed,
This age would lend no faith to Dorrel's deed.
Or if it would, the court is the worst place,
Both for the mothers and the babes of grace,
For there the wicked in the chair of scorn,
Will call it a bastard, when a prophet's born.

L An Epigram. To the Honoured —,
Countess of —

The wisdom, Madam, of your private life,
Wherewith this while you live a widowed wife,
And the right ways you take unto the right,
To conquer rumour, and triumph on spite;
Not only shunning by your act, to do
Aught that is ill, but the suspicion too,
Is of so brave example, as he were
No friend to virtue, could be silent here.
The rather, when the vices of the time
10 Are grown so fruitful, and false pleasures climb
By all oblique degrees, that killing height
From whence they fall, cast down with their own weight.
And though all praise bring nothing to your name,
Who (herein studying conscience, and not fame)
Are in yourself rewarded; yet 'twill be
A cheerful work to all good eyes, to see
Among the daily ruins that fall foul,
Of state, of fame, of body, and of soul,
So great a virtue stand upright to view,
20 As makes Penelope's old fable true,
Whilst your Ulysses hath ta'en leave to go,
Countries, and climes, manners, and men to know.
Only your time you better entertain,
Than the great Homer's wit, for her, could feign;
For you admit no company, but good,
And when you want those friends, or near in blood,
Or your allies, you make your books your friends,
And study them unto the noblest ends,
Searching for knowledge, and to keep your mind
30 The same it was, inspired, rich, and refined.
These graces, when the rest of ladies view
Not boasted in your life, but practised true,
As they are hard, for them to make their own,
So are they profitable to be known:

For when they find so many meet in one,
It will be shame for them, if they have none.

LI Lord Bacon's Birthday

Hail, happy genius of this ancient pile!
How comes it all things so about thee smile?
The fire, the wine, the men! And in the midst,
Thou stand'st as if some mystery thou didst!
Pardon, I read it in thy face, the day
For whose returns, and many, all these pray:
And so do I. This is the sixtieth year
Since Bacon, and thy lord was born, and here;
Son to the grave wise Keeper of the Seal,
10 Fame, and foundation of the English weal.
What then his father was, that since is he,
Now with a title more to the degree;
England's high Chancellor: the destined heir
In his soft cradle to his father's chair,
Whose even thread the Fates spin round and full,
Out of their choicest, and their whitest wool.
      'Tis a brave cause of joy, let it be known,
For 'twere a narrow gladness, kept thine own.
Give me a deep-crowned bowl, that I may sing
20 In raising him the wisdom of my king.

LII (A Poem Sent Me by Sir William Burlase)

THE PAINTER TO THE POET

To paint thy worth, if rightly I did know it,
And were but painter half like thee, a poet;
      Ben, I would show it:
But in this skill, my unskilful pen will tire,
Thou, and thy worth, will still be found far higher;
      And I a liar.
Then, what a painter's here? Or what an eater

Of great attempts? When as his skill's no greater,
    And he a cheater?
10 Then what a poet's here? Whom, by confession
Of all with me, to paint without digression
    There's no expression.

My Answer
THE POET TO THE PAINTER
Why? Though I seem of a prodigious waist,
I am not so voluminous, and vast,
But there are lines, wherewith I might be embraced.

'Tis true, as my womb swells, so my back stoops,
And the whole lump grows round, deformed, and droops,
But yet the tun at Heidelberg had hoops.

You were not tied, by any painter's law
To square my circle, I confess; but draw
My superficies: that was all you saw.

10 Which if in compass of no art it came
To be describèd by a monogram,
With one great blot, you had formed me as I am.

But whilst you curious were to have it be
An archetype, for all the world to see,
You made it a brave piece, but not like me.

O, had I now your manner, mastery, might,
Your power of handling shadow, air, and sprite,
How I would draw, and take hold, and delight.

But, you are he can paint; I can but write:
20 A poet hath no more but black and white,
Ne knows he flattering colours, or false light.

Yet when of friendship I would draw the face,
A lettered mind, and a large heart would place
To all posterity; I will write *Burlase*.

LIII *An Epigram. To William, Earl of Newcastle*

When first, my lord, I saw you back your horse,
Provoke his mettle, and command his force
To all the uses of the field, and race,
Methought I read the ancient art of Thrace,
And saw a centaur, past those tales of Greece,
So seemed your horse and you, both of a piece!
You showed like Perseus upon Pegasus;
Or Castor mounted on his Cyllarus:
Or what we hear our home-born legend tell,
10 Of bold Sir Bevis, and his Arundel:
Nay, so your seat his beauties did endorse,
As I began to wish myself a horse:
And surely had I but your stable seen
Before, I think my wish absolved had been.
For never saw I yet the muses dwell,
Nor any of their household half so well.
So well, as when I saw the floor, and room,
I looked for Hercules to be the groom!
And cried, away with the Caesarian bread,
20 At these immortal mangers Virgil fed.

LIV *Epistle to Mr Arthur Squib*

I am to dine, friend, where I must be weighed
For a just wager, and that wager paid
If I do lose it: and, without a tale
A merchant's wife is regent of the scale,
Who, when she heard the match, concluded straight,
An ill commodity! 'T must make good weight.
So that upon the point, my corporal fear
Is, she will play Dame Justice, too severe;
And hold me to it close; to stand upright
10 Within the balance; and not want a mite;
But rather with advantage to be found
Full twenty stone; of which I lack two pound:

That's six in silver; now within the socket
Stinketh my credit, if into the pocket
It do not come: one piece I have in store,
Lend me, dear Arthur, for a week five more,
And you shall make me good, in weight and fashion,
And then to be returned; or protestation
To go out after – till when take this letter
20 For your security. I can no better.

LV To Mr John Burges

Would God, my Burges, I could think
Thoughts worthy of thy gift, this ink,
Then would I promise here to give
Verse, that should thee, and me outlive.
But since the wine hath steeped my brain,
I only can the paper stain;
Yet with a dye, that fears no moth,
But scarlet-like outlasts the cloth.

LVI Epistle. To My Lady Covell

You won not verses, Madam, you won me,
When you would play so nobly, and so free,
A book to a few lines: but, it was fit
You won them too, your odds did merit it.
So have you gained a servant, and a muse:
The first of which I fear, you will refuse;
And you may justly, being a tardy, cold,
Unprofitable chattel, fat and old,
Laden with belly, and doth hardly approach
10 His friends, but to break chairs, or crack a coach.
His weight is twenty stone within two pound;
And that's made up as doth the purse abound.
Marry, the muse is one, can tread the air,
And stroke the water, nimble, chaste, and fair,

Sleep in a virgin's bosom without fear,
Run all the rounds in a soft lady's ear,
Widow or wife, without the jealousy
Of either suitor, or a servant by.
Such (if her manners like you) I do send:
20 And can for other graces her commend,
To make you merry on the dressing stool,
A-mornings, and at afternoons, to fool
Away ill company, and help in rhyme
Your Joan to pass her melancholy time.
By this, although you fancy not the man,
Accept his muse; and tell, I know you can,
How many verses, Madam, are your due!
I can lose none in tendering these to you.
I gain, in having leave to keep my day.
30 And should grow rich, had I much more to pay.

LVII *To Master John Burges*

Father John Burges,
Necessity urges
My woeful cry,
To Sir Robert Pie:
And that he will venter
To send my debentur.
Tell him his Ben
Knew the time, when
He loved the muses;
10 Though now he refuses
To take apprehension
Of a year's pension,
And more is behind:
Put him in mind
Christmas is near;
And neither good cheer,
Mirth, fooling, nor wit,
Nor any least fit

Of gambol, or sport
20 Will come at the court.
If there be no money,
No plover, or cony
Will come to the table,
Or wine to enable
The muse, or the poet,
The parish will know it.
Nor any quick-warming pan help him to bed,
If the 'chequer be empty, so will be his head.

LVIII Epigram to My Bookseller

Thou, friend, wilt hear all censures; unto thee
All mouths are open, and all stomachs free:
Be thou my book's intelligencer, note
What each man says of it, and of what coat
His judgement is; if he be wise, and praise,
Thank him: if other, he can give no bays.
If his wit reach no higher, but to spring
Thy wife a fit of laughter; a cramp ring
Will be reward enough: to wear like those,
10 That hang their richest jewels in their nose;
Like a rung bear, or swine: grunting out wit
As if that part lay for a (   ) most fit!
If they go on, and that thou lov'st a-life
Their perfumed judgements, let them kiss thy wife.

LIX An Epigram. To William, Earl of Newcastle

They talk of fencing, and the use of arms,
The art of urging, and avoiding harms,
The noble science, and the mastering skill
Of making just approaches how to kill:
To hit in angles, and to clash with time;
As all defence, or óffence were a chime!

I hate such measured, give me mettled fire
That trembles in the blaze, but (then) mounts higher!
A quick, and dazzling motion! When a pair
10 Of bodies meet like rarified air!
Their weapons shot out, with that flame, and force,
As they outdid the lightning in the course;
This were a spectacle! A sight to draw
Wonder to valour! No, it is the law
Of daring, not to do a wrong is true
Valour! To slight it, being done to you!
To know the heads of danger! Where 'tis fit
To bend, to break, provoke, or suffer it!
All this (my lord) is valour! This is yours!
20 And was your father's! All your ancestors!
Who durst live great, 'mongst all the colds, and heats,
Of human life! As all the frosts, and sweats
Of fortune! When, or death appeared, or bands!
And valiant were, with, or without their hands.

LX An Epitaph, on Henry L[ord] La-ware. To the Passer-By

If, passenger, thou canst but read:
Stay, drop a tear for him that's dead,
Henry, the brave young Lord La-ware,
Minerva's and the muses' care!
What could their care do 'gainst the spite
Of a disease, that loved no light
Of honour, nor no air of good?
But crept like darkness through his blood?
Offended with the dazzling flame
10 Of virtue, got above his name?
No noble furniture of parts,
No love of action, and high arts,
No aim at glory, or in war,
Ambition to become a star,
Could stop the malice of this ill,

That spread his body o'er, to kill:
And only, his great soul envied,
Because it durst have noblier died.

LXI An Epigram

That you have seen the pride, beheld the sport,
And all the games of fortune, played at court;
Viewed there the mercat, read the wretched rate
At which there are, would sell the prince, and state:
That scarce you hear a public voice alive,
But whispered councils, and those only thrive;
Yet are got off thence, with clear mind, and hands
To lift to heaven: who is't not understands
Your happiness, and doth not speak you blessed,
10   To see you set apart, thus, from the rest,
To obtain of God, what all the land should ask?
A nation's sin got pardoned! 'Twere a task
Fit for a bishop's knees! O bow them oft,
My lord, till felt grief make our stone hearts soft,
And we do weep, to water, for our sin.
He, that in such a flood, as we are in
Of riot, and consumption, knows the way
To teach the people, how to fast, and pray,
And do their penance, to avert God's rod,
20   He is the man, and favourite of God.

LXII An Epigram. To K[ing] Charles for a Hundred Pounds He Sent Me in My Sickness. 1629

Great Charles, among the holy gifts of grace
Annexéd to thy person, and thy place,
'Tis not enough (thy piety is such)
To cure the called King's evil with thy touch;
But thou wilt yet a kinglier mastery try,

To cure the poet's evil, poverty:
And, in these cures, dost so thyself enlarge,
As thou dost cure our evil, at thy charge.
Nay, and in this, thou show'st to value more
10 One poet, than of other folk ten score.
O piety! So to weigh the poor's estates!
O bounty! So to difference the rates!
What can the poet wish his king may do,
But, that he cure the people's evil too?

*LXIII To K[ing] Charles and Q[ueen] Mary,
for the Loss of Their First-Born.
An Epigram Consolatory. 1629*

Who dares deny, that all first fruits are due
To God, denies the God-head to be true:
Who doubts, those fruits God can with gain restore,
Doth, by his doubt, distrust his promise more.
He can, he will, and with large interest pay,
What (at his liking) he will take away.
Then royal Charles, and Mary, do not grutch
That the Almighty's will to you is such:
But thank his greatness, and his goodness too;
10 And think all still the best, that he will do.
That thought shall make, he will this loss supply
With a long, large, and blessed posterity!
For God, whose essence is so infinite,
Cannot but heap that grace, he will requite.

*LXIV An Epigram. To our Great and Good
K[ing] Charles on His Anniversary Day. 1629*

How happy were the subject if he knew,
Most pious king, but his own good in you!
How many times, live long, Charles, would he say,
If he but weighed the blessings of this day?

And as it turns our joyful year about,
For safety of such majesty, cry out?
Indeed, when had great Britain greater cause
Than now, to love the sovereign, and the laws?
When you that reign, are her example grown,
10 And what are bounds to her, you make your own?
When your assiduous practice doth secure
That faith, which she professeth to be pure?
When all your life's a precedent of days,
And murmur cannot quarrel at your ways?
How is she barren grown of love! Or broke!
That nothing can her gratitude provoke!
O times! O manners! Surfeit bred of ease,
The truly epidemical disease!
'Tis not alone the merchant, but the clown,
20 Is bankrupt turned! The cassock, cloak, and gown
Are lost upon account! And none will know
How much to heaven for thee, great Charles, they owe!

LXV An Epigram on the Prince's Birth. 1630

And art thou born, brave babe? Blessed be thy birth!
That so hath crowned our hopes, our spring, and earth,
The bed of the chaste lily, and the rose!
What month than May, was fitter to disclose
This prince of flowers? Soon shoot thou up, and grow
The same that thou art promised, but be slow,
And long in changing. Let our nephews see
Thee, quickly come the garden's eye to be,
And there to stand so. Haste now, envious moon,
10 And interpose thyself, (care not how soon)
And threat' the great eclipse. Two hours but run,
Sol will reshine. If not, Charles hath a son.
    ... *Non displicuisse meretur*
    Festinat Caesar qui placuisse tibi.

LXVI *An Epigram to the Queen, then Lying in.*
1630

Hail Mary, full of grace, it once was said,
And by an angel, to the blessed'st maid,
The mother of our Lord: why may not I
(Without profaneness) yet, a poet, cry
Hail Mary, full of honours, to my queen,
The mother of our prince? When was there seen
(Except the joy that the first Mary brought,
Whereby the safety of mankind was wrought)
So general a gladness to an isle,
10 To make the hearts of a whole nation smile,
As in this prince? Let it be lawful, so
To compare small with great, as still we owe
Glory to God. Then, hail to Mary! Spring
Of so much safety to the realm, and king.

LXVII *An Ode, or Song, by All the Muses*

IN CELEBRATION OF HER MAJESTY'S BIRTHDAY.
1630

1 CLIO.
Up public joy, remember
This sixteenth of November,
    Some brave uncommon way:
And though the parish steeple
Be silent, to the people
    Ring thou it holiday.

2 MEL.
What, though the thrifty tower
And guns there, spare to pour
    Their noises forth in thunder:
10 As fearful to awake
This city, or to shake
    Their guarded gates asunder?

3 THAL.

Yet, let our trumpets sound;
And cleave both air and ground,
   With beating of our drums:
Let every lyre be strung,
Harp, lute, theorbo sprung,
   With touch of dainty thumbs!

4 EUT.

That when the choir is full,
20 The harmony may pull
   The angels from their spheres:
And each intelligence
May wish itself a sense,
   Whilst it the ditty hears.

5 TERP.

Behold the royal Mary,
The daughter of great Harry!
   And sister to just Lewis!
Comes in the pomp, and glory
Of all her brother's story,
30   And of her father's prowess!

6 ERAT.

She shows so far above
The feignèd queen of love,
   This sea-girt isle upon:
As here no Venus were;
But, that she reigning here,
   Had got the Ceston on!

7 CALLI.

See, see our active king
Hath taken twice the ring
   Upon his pointed lance:
40 Whilst all the ravished rout
Do mingle in a shout,
   Hey! for the flower of France!

8 URA.

This day the court doth measure
Her joy in state, and pleasure;
   And with a reverend fear,
The revels, and the play,
Sum up this crownèd day,
   Her two and twentieth year!

9 POLY.

Sweet happy Mary! All
50 The people her do call!
   And this the womb divine!
So fruitful and so fair,
Hath brought the land an heir!
   And Charles a Caroline!

LXVIII *An Epigram. To the Household. 1630*

What can the cause be, when the king hath given
His poet sack, the Household will not pay?
Are they so scanted in their store, or driven
For want of knowing the poet, to say him nay?
Well, they should know him, would the king but grant
His poet leave to sing his Household true;
He'ld frame such ditties of their store, and want,
Would make the very green-cloth to look blue:
And rather wish, in their expense of sack,
10 So, the allowance from the king to use,
As the old bard, should no canary lack,
'Twere better spare a butt, than spill his muse.
For in the genius of a poet's verse,
The king's fame lives. Go now, deny his tierce.

LXIX Epigram. To a Friend and Son

Son, and my friend, I had not called you so
To me; or been the same to you; if show,
Profit, or chance had made us: but I know
What, by that name, we each to other owe,
Freedom, and truth; with love from those begot:
Wise crafts, on which the flatterer ventures not.
His is more safe commodity, or none:
Nor dares he come in the comparison.
But as the wretched painter, who so ill
10   Painted a dog, that now his subtler skill
Was, t'have a boy stand with a club, and fright
All live dogs from the lane, and his shop's sight,
Till he had sold his piece, drawn so unlike:
So doth the flatterer, with far cunning strike
At a friend's freedom, proves all circling means
To keep him off; and howsoe'er he gleans
Some of his forms, he lets him not come near
Where he would fix, for the distinction's fear.
For as at distance, few have faculty
20   To judge; so all men coming near can spy,
Though now of flattery, as of picture are
More subtle works, and finer pieces far,
Than knew the former ages: yet to life,
All is but web, and painting; be the strife
Never so great to get them: and the ends,
Rather to boast rich hangings, than rare friends.

LXX To the Immortal Memory and Friendship of that Noble Pair, Sir Lucius Cary and Sir H. Morison

THE TURN
Brave infant of Saguntum, clear
Thy coming forth in that great year,
When the prodigious Hannibal did crown

His rage, with razing your immortal town.
Thou looking then about,
Ere thou wert half got out,
Wise child, didst hastily return,
And mad'st thy mother's womb thine urn.
How summed a circle didst thou leave mankind
10   Of deepest lore, could we the centre find!

THE COUNTER-TURN
Did wiser nature draw thee back,
From out the horror of that sack,
Where shame, faith, honour, and regard of right
Lay trampled on; the deeds of death, and night,
Urged, hurried forth, and hurled
Upon the affrighted world:
Sword, fire, and famine, with fell fury met;
And all on utmost ruin set;
As, could they but life's miseries foresee,
20   No doubt all infants would return like thee?

THE STAND
For, what is life, if measured by the space,
Not by the act?
Or maskèd man, if valued by his face,
Above his fact?
Here's one outlived his peers,
And told forth fourscore years;
He vexèd time, and busied the whole state;
Troubled both foes, and friends;
But ever to no ends:
30   What did this stirrer, but die late?
How well at twenty had he fallen, or stood!
For three of his four score, he did no good.

THE TURN
He entered well, by virtuous parts,
Got up and thrived with honest arts:
He purchased friends, and fame, and honours then,
And had his noble name advanced with men:

But weary of that flight,
He stooped in all men's sight
To sordid flatteries, acts of strife,
40 And sunk in that dead sea of life
So deep, as he did then death's waters sup;
But that the cork of title buoyed him up.

THE COUNTER-TURN
Alas, but Morison fell young:
He never fell, thou fall'st, my tongue.
He stood, a soldier to the last right end,
A perfect patriot, and a noble friend,
But most a virtuous son.
All offices were done
By him, so ample, full, and round,
50 In weight, in measure, number, sound,
As though his age imperfect might appear,
His life was of humanity the sphere.

THE STAND
Go now, and tell out days summed up with fears,
And make them years;
Produce thy mass of miseries on the stage,
To swell thine age:
Repeat of things a throng,
To show thou hast been long,
Not lived; for life doth her great actions spell,
60 By what was done and wrought
In season, and so brought
To light: her measures are, how well
Each syllabe answered, and was formed, how fair;
These make the lines of life, and that's her air.

THE TURN
It is not growing like a tree
In bulk, doth make man better be;
Or standing long an oak, three hundred year,
To fall a log, at last, dry, bald, and sere:
A lily of a day,

70 Is fairer far, in May,
   Although it fall, and die that night;
   It was the plant, and flower of light.
   In small proportions, we just beauties see:
   And in short measures, life may perfect be.

THE COUNTER-TURN
Call, noble Lucius, then for wine,
And let thy looks with gladness shine:
Accept this garland, plant it on thy head,
And think, nay know, thy Morison's not dead.
He leapt the present age,
80 Possessed with holy rage,
   To see that bright eternal day:
   Of which we priests, and poets say
   Such truths, as we expect for happy men,
   And there he lives with memory: and Ben

THE STAND
Jonson! Who sung this of him, ere he went
Himself to rest,
Or taste a part of that full joy he meant
To have expressed,
In this bright asterism:
90 Where it were friendship's schism,
   (Were not his Lucius long with us to tarry)
   To separate these twi-
   Lights, the Dioscuri;
   And keep the one half from his Harry.
   But fate doth so alternate the design,
   Whilst that in heaven, this light on earth must shine.

THE TURN
And shine as you exalted are;
Two names of friendship, but one star:
Of hearts the union. And those not by chance
100 Made, or indenture, or leased out to advance
    The profits for a time.
    No pleasures vain did chime,

Of rhymes, or riots, at your feasts,
Orgies of drink, or feigned protests:
But simple love of greatness, and of good;
That knits brave minds, and manners, more than blood.

THE COUNTER-TURN
This made you first to know the why
You liked, then after, to apply
That liking; and approach so one the tother,
110 Till either grew a portion of the other:
Each stylèd by his end,
The copy of his friend.
You lived to be the great surnames,
And titles, by which all made claims
Unto the virtue. Nothing perfect done,
But as a Cary, or a Morison.

THE STAND
And such a force the fair example had,
As they that saw
The good, and durst not practise it, were glad
120 That such a law
Was left yet to mankind;
Where they might read, and find
Friendship, in deed, was written, not in words:
And with the heart, not pen,
Of two so early men,
Whose lines her rolls were, and records,
Who, ere the first down bloomèd on the chin,
Had sowed these fruits, and got the harvest in.

*LXXI To the Right Honourable, the Lord High
Treasurer of England. An Epistle Mendicant. 1631*

My lord;
Poor wretched states, pressed by extremities,
Are fain to seek for succours, and supplies
Of princes' aids, or good men's charities.

Disease, the enemy, and his engineers,
Wants, with the rest of his concealed compeers,
Have cast a trench about me, now five years.

And made those strong approaches, by false braies,
Reduicts, half-moons, horn-works, and such close ways,
The muse not peeps out, one of hundred days;

10 But lies blocked up, and straitened, narrowed in,
Fixed to the bed, and boards, unlike to win
Health, or scarce breath, as she had never bin.

Unless some saving honour of the crown,
Dare think it, to relieve, no less renown,
A bedrid wit, than a besiegèd town.

LXXII To the King. On His Birthday. An Epigram Anniversary. Novem[ber] 19, 1632

This is King Charles his day. Speak it, thou tower,
Unto the ships, and they from tier, to tier,
Discharge it 'bout the island, in an hour,
As loud as thunder, and as swift as fire.
Let Ireland meet it out at sea, half way,
Repeating all Great Britain's joy, and more,
Adding her own glad accents, to this day,
Like Echo playing from the other shore.
What drums or trumpets, or great ordinance can,
10 The poetry of steeples, with the bells,
Three kingdoms' mirth, in light, and airy man,
Made lighter with the wine. All noises else,
At bonfires, rockets, fireworks, with the shouts
That cry that gladness, which their hearts would pray,
Had they but grace, of thinking, at these routes,
On the often coming of this holiday:
      And ever close the burden of the song,
      Still to have such a Charles, but this Charles long.
The wish is great; but where the prince is such,
20 What prayers (people) can you think too much?

LXXIII On the Right Honourable and Virtuous
Lord Weston, L[ord] High Treasurer of England,
upon the Day He was Made Earl of Portland,
17. Febr. 1632. To the Envious

Look up, thou seed of envy, and still bring
Thy faint, and narrow eyes, to read the king
In his great actions: view whom his large hand,
Hath raised to be the port unto his land!
Weston! That waking man! That eye of state!
Who seldom sleeps! Whom bad men only hate!
Why do I irritate, or stir up thee,
Thou sluggish spawn, that canst, but wilt not see!
Feed on thyself for spite, and show thy kind:
10 To virtue, and true worth, be ever blind.
Dream thou couldst hurt it, but before thou wake,
To effect it; feel, thou hast made thine own heart ache.

LXXIV To the Right Hon[oura]ble Hierome,
L[ord] Weston. An Ode Gratulatory for His
Return from His Embassy. 1632

Such pleasure as the teeming earth
Doth take in easy nature's birth,
    When she puts forth the life of everything:
And in a dew of sweetest rain,
She lies delivered without pain,
    Of the prime beauty of the year, the spring.
The rivers in their shores do run;
The clouds rack clear before the sun,
    The rudest winds obey the calmest air:
10 Rare plants from every bank do rise,
And every plant the sense surprise,
    Because the order of the whole is fair!
The very verdure of her nest,
Wherein she sits so richly dressed,

As all the wealth of season, there was spread;
Doth show, the Graces, and the Hours
Have multiplied their arts, and powers,
    In making soft her aromatic bed.
Such joys, such sweets doth your return
20 Bring all your friends (fair lord) that burn
        With love, to hear your modesty relate,
    The business of your blooming wit,
    With all the fruit shall follow it,
        Both to the honour of the king and state.
    O how will then our court be pleased,
    To see great Charles of travail eased,
        When he beholds a graft of his own hand,
    Shoot up an olive, fruitful, fair,
    To be a shadow to his heir,
30   And both a strength, and beauty to his land!

LXXV *Epithalamion: or, a Song*

CELEBRATING THE NUPTIALS OF THAT NOBLE
GENTLEMAN, MR HIEROME WESTON, SON, AND HEIR,
OF THE LORD WESTON, LORD HIGH TREASURER OF
ENGLAND, WITH THE LADY FRANCES STUART,
DAUGHTER OF ESMÉ D[UKE] OF LENNOX DECEASED,
AND SISTER OF THE SURVIVING DUKE OF THE SAME
NAME

Though thou hast passed thy summer standing, stay
    Awhile with us, bright sun, and help our light;
Thou canst not meet more glory, on the way,
    Between thy tropics, to arrest thy sight,
        Than thou shalt see today:
            We woo thee, stay
        And see, what can be seen,
The bounty of a king, and beauty of his queen!

See, the procession! What a holiday
10 (Bearing the promise of some better fate)

Hath filled, with caroches, all the way,
　　From Greenwich, hither, to Roehampton gate!
　　　　When looked the year, at best,
　　　　　　So like a feast?
　　　　Or were affairs in tune,
By all the spheres' consent, so in the heart of June?

What bevy of beauties, and bright youths at charge
　　Of summer's liveries, and gladding green:
Do boast their loves, and braveries so at large,
20　　As they came all to see, and to be seen!
　　　　When looked the earth so fine,
　　　　　　Or so did shine,
　　　　In all her bloom, and flower;
To welcome home a pair, and deck the nuptial bower?

It is the kindly season of the time,
　　The month of youth, which calls all creatures forth
To do their offices in nature's chime,
　　And celebrate (perfection at the worth)
　　　　Marriage, the end of life,
30　　　　　That holy strife,
　　　　And the allowèd war:
Through which not only we, but all our species are.

Hark how the bells upon the waters play
　　Their sister-tunes, from Thames his either side,
As they had learned new changes, for the day,
　　And all did ring the approaches of the bride;
　　　　The Lady Frances, dressed
　　　　　　Above the rest
　　　　Of all the maidens fair;
40 In graceful ornament of garland, gems, and hair.

See, how she paceth forth in virgin white,
　　Like what she is, the daughter of a duke,
And sister: darting forth a dazzling light
　　On all that come her simpless to rebuke!
　　　　Her tresses trim her back,
　　　　　　As she did lack

Naught of a maiden queen,
With modesty so crowned, and adoration seen.

Stay, thou wilt see what rites the virgins do!
50   The choicest virgin-troop of all the land!
Porting the ensigns of united two,
    Both crowns, and kingdoms in their either hand;
        Whose majesties appear,
           To make more clear
        This feast, than can the day
Although that thou, O sun, at our entreaty stay!

See, how with roses', and with lilies' shine,
    (Lilies and roses, flowers of either sex)
The bright bride's paths, embellished more than thine
60   With light of love, this pair doth intertex!
        Stay, see the virgins sow,
           (Where she shall go)
        The emblems of their way.
O, now thou smil'st, fair sun, and shin'st, as thou wouldst
    stay!

With what full hands, and in how plenteous showers
    Have they bedewed the earth, where she doth tread,
As if her airy steps did spring the flowers,
    And all the ground were garden, where she led!
        See, at another door,
70   On the same floor,
        The bridegroom meets the bride
With all the pomp of youth, and all our court beside.

Our court, and all the grandees; now, sun, look,
    And looking with thy best inquiry, tell,
In all thy age of journals thou hast took,
    Saw'st thou that pair, became these rites so well,
        Save the preceding two?
           Who, in all they do,
        Search, sun, and thou wilt find
80 They are the exampled pair, and mirror of their kind.

Force from the phoenix then, no rarity
   Of sex, to rob the creature; but from man,
The king of creatures, take his parity
    With angels, muse, to speak these: nothing can
      Illustrate these, but they
        Themselves today,
      Who the whole act express;
All else we see beside, are shadows, and go less.

It is their grace, and favour, that makes seen,
90   And wondered at, the bounties of this day:
All is a story of the king and queen!
    And what of dignity, and honour may
      Be duly done to those
        Whom they have chose,
      And set the mark upon
To give a greater name, and title to! Their own!

Weston, their treasure, as their treasurer,
    That mine of wisdom, and of councils deep,
Great 'say-master of state, who cannot err,
100   But doth his carract, and just standard keep
      In all the proved assays,
        And legal ways
      Of trials, to work down
Men's loves unto the laws, and laws to love the crown.

And this well moved the judgement of the king
    To pay with honours, to his noble son
Today, the father's service; who could bring
    Him up, to do the same himself had done.
      That far all-seeing eye
110   Could soon espy
      What kind of waking man
He had so highly set; and, in what barbican.

Stand there; for when a noble nature's raised,
    It brings friends joy, foes grief, posterity fame;
In him the times, no less than prince, are praised,
    And by his rise, in active men, his name

Doth emulation stir;
To the dull, a spur
It is: to the envious meant
120 A mere upbraiding grief, and tort'ring punishment.

See, now the chapel opens; where the king
And bishop stay, to consummate the rites;
The holy prelate prays, then takes the ring,
Asks first, who gives her (I, Charles) then he plights
One in the other's hand,
Whilst they both stand
Hearing their charge, and then
The solemn choir cries, joy; and they return, Amen.

O happy bands! And thou more happy place,
130 Which to this use, wert built and consecrate!
To have thy God to bless, thy king to grace,
And this their chosen bishop celebrate,
And knit the nuptial knot,
Which time shall not,
Or cankered jealousy,
With all corroding arts, be able to untie!

The chapel empties, and thou mayst be gone
Now, sun, and post away the rest of day:
These two, now holy church hath made them one,
140 Do long to make themselves, so, another way:
There is a feast behind,
To them of kind,
Which their glad parents taught
One to the other, long ere these to light were brought.

Haste, haste, officious sun, and send them night
Some hours before it should, that these may know
All that their fathers, and their mothers might
Of nuptial sweets, at such a season, owe,
To propagate their names,
150 And keep their fames
Alive, which else would die,
For fame keeps virtue up, and it posterity.

The ignoble never lived, they were awhile
    Like swine, or other cattle here on earth:
Their names are not recorded on the file
    Of life, that fall so; Christians know their birth,
        Alone, and such a race,
          We pray may grace
        Your fruitful spreading vine,
160 But dare not ask our wish in language *fescennine*:

Yet, as we may, we will, wish chaste desires,
    (The holy perfumes of the marriage bed)
Be kept alive, those sweet, and sacred fires
    Of love between you, and your lovelihead:
        That when you both are old,
          You find no cold
        There; but, renewèd, say,
(After the last child born); this is our wedding day.

Till you behold a race to fill your hall,
170   A Richard, and a Hierome, by their names
Upon a Thomas, or a Francis call;
    A Kate, a Frank, to honour their grand-dames,
        And 'tween their grandsire's thighs,
          Like pretty spies,
        Peep forth a gem; to see
How each one plays his part, of the large pedigree.

And never may there want one of the stem,
    To be a watchful servant for this state;
But like an arm of eminence, 'mongst them,
180   Extend a reaching virtue, early and late:
        Whilst the main tree still found
          Upright and sound,
        By this sun's noonstead's made
So great; his body now alone projects the shade.

They both are slipped to bed; shut fast the door,
    And let them freely gather love's first-fruits,
He's master of the office; yet no more
    Exacts than she is pleased to pay: no suits,

Strifes, murmurs, or delay,
190   Will last till day:
Night, and the sheets will show
The longing couple, all that elder lovers know.

LXXVI The Humble Petition of Poor Ben to the Best of Monarchs, Masters, Men, King Charles

... Doth most humbly show it,
To your majesty your poet:

That whereas your royal father,
James the blessèd, pleased the rather,
Of his special grace to letters,
To make all the muses debtors
To his bounty; by extension
Of a free poetic pension,
A large hundred marks annuity,
10 To be given me in gratuity
For done service, and to come:
    And that this so accepted sum,
Or dispensed in books, or bread,
(For with both the muse was fed)
Hath drawn on me, from the times,
All the envy of the rhymes,
And the rattling pit-pat noise,
Of the less-poetic boys;
When their pot-guns aim to hit,
20 With their pellets of small wit,
Parts of me (they judged) decayed,
But we last out, still unlaid.
    Please your majesty to make
Of your grace, for goodness sake,
Those your father's marks, your pounds;
Let their spite (which now abounds)
Then go on, and do its worst;
This would all their envy burst:

And so warm the poet's tongue
30 You'ld read a snake, in his next song.

LXXVII *To the Right Honourable, the Lord Treasurer of England. An Epigram*

If to my mind, great lord, I had a state,
I would present you now with curious plate
Of Nuremberg, or Turkey; hang your rooms
Not with the Arras, but the Persian looms.
I would, if price, or prayer could them get,
Send in, what or Romano, Tintaret,
Titian, or Raphael, Michael Angelo
Have left in fame to equal, or outgo
The old Greek hands in picture, or in stone.
10 This I would do, could I think Weston one
Catched with these arts, wherein the judge is wise
As far as sense, and only by the eyes.
But you, I know, my lord; and know you can
Discern between a statue, and a man;
Can do the things that statues do deserve,
And act the business, which they paint, or carve.
What you have studied are the arts of life;
To compose men, and manners; stint the strife
Of murmuring subjects; make the nations know
20 What worlds of blessings to good kings they owe:
And mightiest monarchs feel what large increase
Of sweets, and safeties, they possess by peace.
These I look up at, with a reverent eye,
And strike religion in the standers-by;
Which, though I cannot as an architect
In glorious piles, or pyramids erect
Unto your honour: I can tune in song
Aloud; and (haply) it may last as long.

LXXVIII An Epigram to My Muse, the Lady Digby, on Her Husband, Sir Kenelm Digby

Though, happy muse, thou know my Digby well;
Yet read him in these lines: he doth excel
In honour, courtesy, and all the parts
Court can call hers, or man could call his arts.
He's prudent, valiant, just, and temperate;
In him all virtue is beheld in state:
And he is built like some imperial room
For that to dwell in, and be still at home.
His breast is a brave palace, a broad street,
10 Where all heroic ample thoughts do meet;
Where nature such a large survey hath ta'en,
As other souls to his dwelt in a lane:
Witness his action done at Scanderoon;
Upon my birthday the eleventh of June;
When the apostle Barnaby the bright
Unto our year doth give the longest light,
In sign the subject, and the song will live
Which I have vowed posterity to give.
Go, muse, in, and salute him. Say he be
20 Busy, or frown at first; when he sees thee,
He will clear up his forehead: think thou bring'st
Good omen to him, in the note thou sing'st,
For he doth love my verses, and will look
Upon them (next to Spenser's noble book)
And praise them too. O! what a fame 'twill be!
What reputation to my lines, and me,
When he shall read them at the Treasurer's board!
The knowing Weston, and that learnèd lord
Allows them! Then, what copies shall be had,
30 What transcripts begged! How cried up, and how glad
Wilt thou be, muse, when this shall them befall!
Being sent to one, they will be read of all.

LXXIX

New years, expect new gifts: sister, your harp,
  Lute, lyre, theorbo, all are called today,
Your change of notes, the flat, the mean, the sharp,
  To show the rites, and t'usher forth the way
Of the New Year, in a new silken warp,
  To fit the softness of our year's gift: when
  We sing the best of monarchs, masters, men;
For, had we here said less, we had sung nothing then.

A New Year's Gift Sung to King Charles. 1635

RECTOR
Today old Janus opens the new year,

CHOR.
10 And shuts the old. Haste, haste, all loyal swains,
That know the times, and seasons when to appear,
  And offer your just service on these plains;
Best kings expect first-fruits of your glad gains.

  1. Pan is the great preserver of our bounds.
  2. To him we owe all profits of our grounds.
  3. Our milk. 4. Our fells. 5. Our fleeces. 6. And first lambs.
  7. Our teeming ewes. 8. And lusty-mounting rams.
  9. See where he walks with Mira by his side.

CHOR.
Sound, sound his praises loud, and with his, hers divide.

SHEP.
20 Of Pan we sing, the best of hunters, Pan,
  That drives the hart to seek unusèd ways,
And in the chase, more than Sylvanus can,

CHOR.
  Hear, O you groves, and hills, resound his praise.

NYM.

Of brightest Mira, do we raise our song,
  Sister of Pan, and glory of the spring:
Who walks on earth as May still went along:

CHOR.

  Rivers, and valleys, echo what we sing.

SHEP.

Of Pan we sing, the chief of leaders, Pan,
  That leads our flocks and us, and calls both forth
30 To better pastures than great Pales can:

CHOR.

  Hear, O you groves, and hills, resound his worth.

NYMP.

Of brightest Mira, is our song; the grace
  Of all that nature, yet, to life did bring;
And were she lost, could best supply her place:

CHOR.

  Rivers, and valleys, echo what we sing.

  1. Where e'er they tread the enamoured ground,
      The fairest flowers are always found;
  2. As if the beauties of the year,
      Still waited on them where they were.
40 1. He is the father of our peace;
  2. She, to the crown, hath brought increase.
  1. We know no other power than his,
      Pan only our great shepherd is,

CHORUS

Our great, our good. Where one's so dressed
In truth of colours, both are best.

Haste, haste you hither, all you gentler swains,
That have a flock, or herd, upon these plains;
This is the great preserver of our bounds,
To whom you owe all duties of your grounds;

50 Your milks, your fells, your fleeces, and first lambs,
Your teeming ewes, as well as mounting rams;
Whose praises let's report unto the woods,
That they may take it echoed by the floods.
    'Tis he, 'tis he, in singing he,
    And hunting, Pan, exceedeth thee.
    He gives all plenty, and increase,
    He is the author of our peace.

Where e'er he goes upon the ground,
The better grass, and flowers are found.
60 To sweeter pastures lead he can,
Than ever Pales could, or Pan;
He drives diseases from our folds,
The thief from spoil, his presence holds.
Pan knows no other power than his,
This only the great shepherd is.
    'Tis he, 'tis he, etc.

LXXX

Fair friend, 'tis true, your beauties move
    My heart to a respect:
Too little to be paid with love,
    Too great for your neglect.

I neither love, nor yet am free,
    For though the flame I find
Be not intense in the degree,
    'Tis of the purest kind.

It little wants of love, but pain,
10   Your beauty takes my sense,
And lest you should that price disdain,
    My thoughts, too, feel the influence.

'Tis not a passion's first access
    Ready to multiply,

But like love's calmest state it is
    Possessed with victory.

It is like love to truth reduced,
    All the false values gone,
Which were created, and induced
20   By fond imagination.

'Tis either fancy, or 'tis fate,
    To love you more than I;
I love you at your beauty's rate,
    Less were an injury.

Like unstamped gold, I weigh each grace,
    So that you may collect
The intrinsic value of your face,
    Safely from my respect.

And this respect would merit love,
30   Were not so fair a sight
Payment enough; for, who dare move
    Reward for his delight?

LXXXI On the King's Birthday

Rouse up thyself, my gentle muse,
    Though now our green conceits be grey,
And yet once more do not refuse
    To take thy Phrygian harp, and play
    In honour of this cheerful day:
        Long may they both contend to prove,
        That best of crowns is such a love.

Make first a song of joy, and love,
    Which chastely flames in royal eyes,
10 Then tune it to the spheres above,
    When the benignest stars do rise,
    And sweet conjunctions grace the skies.
        Long may etc.

To this let all good hearts resound,
   Whilst diadems invest his head;
Long may he live, whose life doth bound
   More than his laws, and better led
   By high example, than by dread.
     Long may etc.

20 Long may he round about him see
   His roses, and his lilies blown:
Long may his only dear, and he
   Joy in ideas of their own,
   And kingdom's hopes so timely sown.
     Long may they both contend to prove,
     That best of crowns is such a love.

LXXXII To My L[ord] the King, on the Christening His Second Son James

That thou art loved of God, this work is done,
Great king, thy having of a second son:
And by thy blessing, may thy people see
How much they are beloved of God, in thee;
Would they would understand it! Princes are
Great aids to empire, as they are great care
To pious parents, who would have their blood
Should take first seisin of the public good,
As hath thy James; cleansed from original dross,
10 This day, by baptism, and his saviour's cross:
Grow up, sweet babe, as blessèd, in thy name,
As in renewing thy good grandsire's fame;
Methought, Great Britain in her sea, before,
Sat safe enough, but now securèd more.
At land she triumphs in the triple shade,
Her rose, and lily, intertwined, have made.

   Oceano secura meo, securior umbris.

LXXXIII *An Elegy on the Lady Jane Pawlet, Marchion[ess] of Winton*

What gentle ghost, besprent with April dew,
Hails me, so solemnly, to yonder yew?
And beckoning woos me, from the fatal tree
To pluck a garland, for herself, or me?
I do obey you, beauty! For in death,
You seem a fair one! O that you had breath,
To give your shade a name! Stay, stay, I feel
A horror in me! All my blood is steel!
Stiff! Stark! My joints 'gainst one another knock!
10 Whose daughter? Ha? Great Savage of the rock?
He's good, as great. I am almost a stone!
And ere I can ask more of her she's gone!
Alas, I am all marble! Write the rest
Thou wouldst have written, Fame, upon my breast:
It is a large fair table, and a true,
And the disposure will be something new,
When I, who would the poet have become,
At least may bear the inscription to her tomb.
She was the Lady Jane, and marchioness
20 Of Winchester; the heralds can tell this.
Earl Rivers's grandchild – serve not forms, good Fame,
Sound thou her virtues, give her soul a name.
Had I a thousand mouths, as many tongues,
And voice to raise them from my brazen lungs,
I durst not aim at that: the dotes were such
Thereof, no notion can express how much
Their carract was! I, or my trump must break,
But rather I, should I of that part speak –
It is too near of kin to heaven – the soul,
30 To be described! Fame's fingers are too foul
To touch these mysteries! We may admire
The blaze, and splendour, but not handle fire!
What she did here, by great example, well,
To enlive posterity, her Fame may tell!
And, calling truth to witness, make that good

From the inherent graces in her blood!
Else, who doth praise a person by a new,
But a feigned way, doth rob it of the true.
Her sweetness, softness, her fair courtesy,
40 Her wary guards, her wise simplicity,
Were like a ring of virtues, 'bout her set,
And piety the centre, where all met.
A reverend state she had, an awful eye,
A dazzling, yet inviting, majesty:
What nature, fortune, institution, fact
Could sum to a perfection, was her act!
How did she leave the world? With what contempt?
Just as she in it lived! And so exempt
From all affection! When they urged the cure
50 Of her disease, how did her soul assure
Her sufferings, as the body had been away!
And to the torturers (her doctors) say,
Stick on your cupping-glasses, fear not, put
Your hottest caustics to burn, lance, or cut:
'Tis but a body which you can torment,
And I, into the world, all soul, was sent!
Then comforted her lord! And blessed her son!
Cheered her fair sisters in her race to run!
With gladness tempered her sad parents' tears!
60 Made her friends joys, to get above their fears!
And, in her last act, taught the standers-by,
With admiration, and applause to die!
Let angels sing her glories, who did call
Her spirit home, to her original!
Who saw the way was made it! And were sent
To carry and conduct the complement
'Twixt death and life! Where her mortality
Became her birthday to eternity!
And now, through circumfusèd light, she looks
70 On nature's secrets, there, as her own books:
Speaks heaven's language, and discourses free
To every order, every hierarchy!
Beholds her Maker! And, in him, doth see

What the beginnings of all beauties be;
And all beatitudes, that thence do flow:
Which they that have the crown are sure to know!
Go now, her happy parents, and be sad
If you not understand, what child you had,
If you dare grudge at heaven, and repent
80 To have paid again a blessing was but lent,
And trusted so, as it deposited lay
At pleasure, to be called for, every day,
If you can envy your own daughter's bliss,
And wish her state less happy than it is,
If you can cast about your either eye,
And see all dead here, or about to die!
The stars, that are the jewels of the night,
And day, deceasing! With the prince of light,
The sun! Great kings! And mightiest kingdoms fall!
90 Whole nations! Nay, mankind! The world, with all
That ever had beginning there, to have end!
With what injustice should one soul pretend
To escape this common known necessity,
When we were all born, we began to die;
And, but for that contention, and brave strife
The Christian hath to enjoy the future life,
He were the wretchedest of the race of men:
But as he soars at that, he bruiseth then
The serpent's head: gets above death, and sin,
100 And, sure of heaven, rides triumphing in.

LXXXIV *Eupheme;*

OR THE FAIR FAME LEFT TO POSTERITY OF THAT
TRULY-NOBLE LADY, THE LADY VENETIA DIGBY, LATE
WIFE OF SIR KENELM DIGBY, KNIGHT: A
GENTLEMAN ABSOLUTE IN ALL NUMBERS;
CONSISTING OF THESE TEN PIECES:

The dedication of her cradle
The song of her descent

The picture of the body
Her mind
Her being chosen a muse
Her fair offices
Her happy match
Her hopeful issue
Her apotheosis, *or relation to the saints*
Her inscription, or crown

Vivam amare voluptas, defunctam religio. Stat.

1 The dedication of her cradle
Fair fame, who art ordained to crown
With ever green, and great renown,
Their heads, that envy would hold down
    With her, in shade

Of death, and darkness; and deprive
Their names of being kept alive,
By thee, and conscience, both who thrive
    By the just trade

Of goodness still: vouchsafe to take
10 This cradle, and for goodness' sake,
A dedicated ensign make
    Thereof, to time.

That all posterity, as we,
Who read what the crepundia be,
May something by that twilight see
    'Bove rattling rhyme.

For, though that rattles, timbrels, toys,
Take little infants with their noise,
As properest gifts, to girls, and boys,
20   Of light expense;

Their corals, whistles, and prime coats,
Their painted masks, their paper boats,
With sails of silk, as the first notes
    Surprise their sense:

Yet, here are no such trifles brought,
No cobweb cauls; no surcoats wrought
With gold, or clasps, which might be bought
    On every stall.

But, here's a song of her descent;
30 And call to the high parliament
Of heaven; where seraphim take tent
    Of ordering all.

This, uttered by an ancient bard,
Who claims (of reverence) to be heard,
As coming with his harp, prepared
    To chant her 'gree,

Is sung: as als' her getting up
By Jacob's ladder, to the top
Of that eternal port kept ope
40   For such as she.

  2 The song of her descent
I sing the just, and uncontrolled descent
    Of dame Venetia Digby, styled the fair:
    For mind, and body, the most excellent
That ever nature, or the later air
    Gave two such houses as Northumberland,
    And Stanley, to the which she was co-heir.
Speak it, you bold penates, you that stand
    At either stem, and know the veins of good
    Run from your roots; tell, testify the grand
10 Meeting of graces, that so swelled the flood
    Of virtues in her, as, in short, she grew
    The wonder of her sex, and of your blood.
And tell thou, Aldeleigh, none can tell more true
    Thy niece's line, than thou that gav'st thy name
    Into the kindred, whence thy Adam drew
Meschin's honour with the Cestrian fame
    Of the first Lupus, to the family
    By Ranulph ....

(*The rest of this song is lost*)

3 The picture of the body
Sitting, and ready to be drawn,
What makes these velvets, silks, and lawn,
Embroideries, feathers, fringes, lace,
Where every limb takes like a face?

Send these suspected helps, to aid
Some form defective, or decayed;
This beauty, without falsehood fair,
Needs naught to clothe it but the air,

Yet something, to the painter's view,
10 Were fitly interposed; so new
He shall, if he can understand,
Work with my fancy, his own hand.

Draw first a cloud: all save her neck;
And, out of that, make day to break;
Till, like her face, it do appear,
And men may think, all light rose there.

Then let the beams of that, disperse
The cloud, and show the universe;
But at such distance, as the eye
20 May rather yet adore, than spy.

The heaven designed, draw next a spring,
With all that youth, or it can bring:
Four rivers branching forth like seas,
And paradise confining these.

Last, draw the circles of this globe,
And let there be a starry robe
Of constellations 'bout her hurled;
And thou hast painted beauty's world.

But, painter, see thou do not sell
30 A copy of this piece; nor tell
Whose 'tis: but if it favour find,
Next sitting we will draw her mind.

4 *The mind*

Painter, you are come, but may be gone,
Now I have better thought thereon,
This work I can perform alone;
And give you reasons more than one.

Not, that your art I do refuse:
But here I may no colours use.
Beside, your hand will never hit,
To draw a thing that cannot sit.

You could make shift to paint an eye,
10   An eagle towering in the sky,
The sun, a sea, or soundless pit;
But these are like a mind, not it.

No, to express this mind to sense,
Would ask a heaven's intelligence;
Since nothing can report that flame,
But what's of kin to whence it came.

Sweet mind, then speak yourself, and say,
As you go on, by what brave way
Our sense you do with knowledge fill,
20   And yet remain our wonder still.

I call you muse; now make it true:
Henceforth may every line be you;
That all may say, that see the frame,
This is no picture, but the same.

A mind so pure, so perfect fine,
As 'tis not radiant, but divine:
And so disdaining any trier;
'Tis got where it can try the fire.

There, high exalted in the sphere,
30   As it another nature were,
It moveth all; and makes a flight
As circular, as infinite.

Whose notions when it would express
In speech, it is with that excess
Of grace, and music to the ear,
As what it spoke, it planted there.

The voice so sweet, the words so fair,
As some soft chime had stroked the air;
And, though the sound were parted thence,
40   Still left an echo in the sense.

But, that a mind so rapt, so high,
So swift, so pure, should yet apply
Itself to us, and come so nigh
Earth's grossness; there's the how, and why.

Is it because it sees us dull,
And stuck in clay here, it would pull
Us forth, by some celestial sleight
Up to her own sublimèd height?

Or hath she here, upon the ground,
50   Some paradise, or palace found
In all the bounds of beauty fit
For her to inhabit? There is it.

Thrice happy house, that hast receipt
For this so lofty form, so straight,
So polished, perfect, round, and even,
As it slid moulded off from heaven.

Not swelling like the ocean proud,
But stooping gently, as a cloud,
As smooth as oil poured forth, and calm
60   As showers; and sweet as drops of balm.

Smooth, soft, and sweet, in all a flood
Where it may run to any good;
And where it stays, it there becomes
A nest of odorous spice, and gums.

In action, wingèd as the wind,
In rest, like spirits left behind

Upon a bank, or field of flowers,
Begotten by that wind, and showers.

In thee, fair mansion, let it rest,
70 Yet know, with what thou art possessed,
Thou entertaining in thy breast,
But such a mind, mak'st God thy guest.

*A whole quaternion in the midst of this poem is lost, containing
entirely the three next pieces of it, and all of the fourth (which
in the order of the whole, is the eighth) excepting the very end:
which at the top of the next quaternion goeth on thus:*

8
But, for you (growing gentlemen) the happy branches of two
so illustrious houses as these, wherefrom your honoured
mother is in both lines descended; let me leave you this
last legacy of council; which so soon as you arrive at
years of mature understanding, open you (sir) that are
the eldest, and read it to your brethren, for it will
concern you all alike. Vowed by a faithful servant, and
client of your family, with his latest breath expiring it.
B.J.

To Kenelm, John, George
Boast not these titles of your ancestors;
(Brave youths) they are their possessions, none of yours:
When your own virtues, equalled have their names,
'Twill be but fair, to lean upon their fames;
For they are strong supporters: but, till then,
The greatest are but growing gentlemen.
It is a wretched thing to trust to reeds;
Which all men do, that urge not their own deeds
Up to their ancestors; the river's side,
10 By which you are planted, shows your fruit shall bide:
Hang all your rooms, with one large pedigree:
'Tis virtue alone, is true nobility.
Which virtue from your father, ripe, will fall;
Study illustrious him, and you have all.

9 Elegy on my muse
THE TRULY HONOURED LADY, THE LADY VENETIA
DIGBY; WHO LIVING, GAVE ME LEAVE TO CALL HER
SO. BEING HER *Apotheosis*, OR RELATION TO THE
SAINTS.
Sera quidem tanto struitur medicina dolori.

'Twere time that I died too, now she is dead,
Who was my muse, and life of all I said,
The spirit that I wrote with, and conceived.
All that was good, or great in me she weaved,
And set it forth; the rest were cobwebs fine,
Spun out in name of some of the old nine!
To hang a window, or make dark the room,
Till swept away, they were cancelled with a broom!
Nothing, that could remain, or yet can stir
10 A sorrow in me, fit to wait to her!
O! had I seen her laid out a fair corse,
By death, on earth, I should have had remorse
On nature, for her: who did let her lie,
And saw that portion of herself to die.
Sleepy, or stupid nature, couldst thou part
With such a rarity, and not rouse art
With all her aids, to save her from the seize
Of vulture death, and those relentless cleies?
Thou wouldst have lost the phoenix, had the kind
20 Been trusted to thee: not to itself assigned.
Look on thy sloth, and give thyself undone,
(For so thou art with me) now she is gone.
My wounded mind cannot sustain this stroke,
It rages, runs, flies, stands, and would provoke
The world to ruin with it; in her fall,
I sum up mine own breaking, and wish all.
Thou hast no more blows, Fate, to drive at one:
What's left a poet, when his muse is gone?
Sure, I am dead, and know it not! I feel
30 Nothing I do; but, like a heavy wheel,
Am turned with another's powers. My passion

Whirls me about, and to blaspheme in fashion!
I murmur against God, for having ta'en
Her blessèd soul, hence, forth this valley vain
Of tears, and dungeon of calamity!
I envy it the angels' amity!
The joy of saints! The crown for which it lives,
The glory, and gain of rest, which the place gives!
Dare I profane, so irreligious be
40   To greet, or grieve her soft euthánasee?
So sweetly taken to the court of bliss,
As spirits had stolen her spirit, in a kiss,
From off her pillow, and deluded bed;
And left her lovely body unthought dead!
Indeed, she is not dead! But laid to sleep
In earth, till the last trump awake the sheep
And goats together, whither they must come
To hear their judge, and his eternal doom;
To have that final retribution,
50   Expected with the flesh's restitution.
For, as there are three natures, schoolmen call
One corporal, only; the other spiritual,
Like single; so, there is a third, commixed,
Of body and spirit together, placed betwixt
Those other two; which must be judged, or crowned:
This as it guilty is, or guiltless found,
Must come to take a sentence, by the sense
Of that great evidence, the conscience,
Who will be there, against that day prepared,
60   To accuse, or quit all parties to be heard!
O day of joy, and surety to the just!
Who in that feast of resurrection trust!
That great eternal holiday of rest,
To body, and soul! Where love is all the guest!
And the whole banquet is full sight of God!
Of joy the circle, and sole period!
All other gladness, with the thought is barred;
Hope hath her end! And faith hath her reward!
This being thus: why should my tongue, or pen

70 Presume to interpell that fulness, when
Nothing can more adorn it, than the seat
That she is in, or, make it more complete?
Better be dumb, than superstitious!
Who violates the Godhead, is most vicious
Against the nature he would worship. He
Will honoured be in all simplicity!
Have all his actions wondered at, and viewed
With silence, and amazement! Not with rude,
Dull, and profane, weak, and imperfect eyes,
80 Have busy search made in his mysteries!
He knows, what work he hath done, to call this guest,
Out of her noble body, to this feast:
And give her place, according to her blood
Amongst her peers, those princes of all good!
Saints, martyrs, prophets, with those hierarchies,
Angels, archangels, principalities,
The dominations, virtues, and the powers,

The thrones, the cherub, and seraphic bowers,
That, planted round, there sing before the Lamb,
90 A new song to his praise, and great I AM:
And she doth know, out of the shade of death,
What 'tis to enjoy an everlasting breath!
To have her captived spirit freed from flesh,
And on her innocence, a garment fresh
And white as that, put on: and in her hand
With boughs of palm, a crownèd victrice stand!
And will you, worthy son, sir, knowing this,
Put black, and mourning on? And say you miss
A wife, a friend, a lady, or a love;
100 Whom her redeemer, honoured hath above
Her fellows, with the oil of gladness, bright
In heaven empire, and with a robe of light?
Thither, you hope to come; and there to find
That pure, that precious, and exalted mind
You once enjoyed: a short space severs ye,
Compared unto that long eternity,
That shall rejoin ye. Was she, then, so dear,

When she departed? You will meet her there,
Much more desired, and dearer than before,
110   By all the wealth of blessings, and the store
Accumulated on her, by the lord
Of life, and light, the son of God, the Word!
There, all the happy souls, that ever were,
Shall meet with gladness in one theatre;
And each shall know, there, one another's face:
By beatific virtue of the place.
There shall the brother, with the sister walk,
And sons, and daughters, with their parents talk;
But all of God; they still shall have to say,
120   But make him all in all, their theme, that day:
That happy day, that never shall see night!
Where he will be, all beauty to the sight;
Wine, or delicious fruits, unto the taste;
A music in the ears, will ever last;
Unto the scent, a spicery, or balm;
And to the touch, a flower, like soft as palm.
He will all glory, all perfection be,
God, in the union, and the Trinity!
That holy, great, and glorious mystery
130   Will there revealèd be in majesty!
By light, and comfort of spiritual grace;
The vision of our saviour, face, to face
In his humanity! To hear him preach
The price of our redemption, and to teach
Through his inherent righteousness, in death,
The safety of our souls, and forfeit breath!
What fulness of beatitude is here?
What love with mercy mixèd doth appear?
To style us friends, who were, by nature, foes?
140   Adopt us heirs, by grace, who were of those
Had lost ourselves? And prodigally spent
Our native portions, and possessèd rent;
Yet have all debts forgiven us, and advance
By imputed right to an inheritance
In his eternal kingdom, where we sit

Equal with angels, and co-heirs of it.
Nor dare we under blasphemy conceive
He that shall be our supreme judge, should leave
Himself so uninformed of his elect,
150   Who knows the hearts of all, and can dissect
The smallest fibre of our flesh; he can
Find all our atoms from a point to a span!
Our closest creeks, and corners, and can trace
Each line, as it were graphic, in the face.
And best he knew her noble character,
For 'twas himself who formed, and gave it her.
And to that form, lent two such veins of blood
As nature could not more increase the flood
Of title in her! All nobility
160   (But pride, that schism of incivility)
She had, and it became her! She was fit
To have known no envy, but by suffering it!
She had a mind as calm, as she was fair;
Not tossed or troubled with light lady-air;
But, kept an even gait, as some straight tree
Moved by the wind, so comely movèd she.
And by the awful manage of her eye
She swayed all business in the family!
To one she said, do this, he did it; so
170   To another, move; he went; to a third, go,
He run; and all did strive with diligence
To obey, and serve her sweet commandéments.
She was in one, a many parts of life;
A tender mother, a discreeter wife,
A solemn mistress, and so good a friend,
So charitable, to religious end,
In all her petite actions, so devote,
As her whole life was now become one note
Of piety, and private holiness.
180   She spent more time in tears herself to dress
For her devotions, and those sad essays
Of sorrow, than all pomp of gaudy days:
And came forth ever cheerèd, with the rod

Of divine comfort, when she had talked with God.
Her broken sighs did never miss whole sense:
Nor can the bruisèd heart want eloquence:
For, prayer is the incense most perfumes
The holy altars, when it least presumes.
And hers were all humility! They beat
190   The door of grace, and found the mercy-seat.
In frequent speaking by the pious psalms
Her solemn hours she spent, or giving alms,
Or doing other deeds of charity,
To clothe the naked, feed the hungry. She
Would sit in an infirmary, whole days
Poring, as on a map, to find the ways
To that eternal rest, where now she hath place
By sure election, and predestined grace!
She saw her saviour, by an early light,
200   Incarnate in the manger, shining bright
On all the world! She saw him on the cross
Suff'ring, and dying to redeem our loss!
She saw him rise, triumphing over death
To justify, and quicken us in breath!
She saw him too, in glory to ascend
For his designèd work the perfect end
Of raising, judging, and rewarding all
The kind of man, on whom his doom should fall!
All this by faith she saw, and framed a plea
210   In manner of a daily apostrophe,
To him should be her judge, true God, true man,
Jesus, the only gotten Christ! Who can
As being redeemer, and repairer too
(Of lapsèd nature) best know what to do,
In that great act of judgement: which the Father
Hath given wholly to the Son (the rather
As being the Son of man) to show his power,
His wisdom, and his justice, in that hour,
The last of hours, and shutter up of all;
220   Where first his power will appear, by call
Of all are dead to life! His wisdom show

In the discerning of each conscience, so!
And most his justice, in the fitting parts,
And giving dues to all mankind's deserts!
In this sweet ecstasy, she was rapt hence.
Who reads, will pardon my intelligence
That thus have ventured these true strains upon;
To publish her a saint. My muse is gone.

> *In pietatis memoriam*
> *quam praestas*
> *Venetiae tuae illustrissim:*
> *Marit: dign: Digbeie*

Hanc ἀποτηεοσιυ, tibi, tuisque sacro.

The tenth, being her inscription, or crown, is lost

LXXXV *The Praises of a Country Life*

HORACE, SECOND EPODE

Happy is he, that from all business clear,
    As the old race of mankind were,
With his own oxen tills his sire's left lands,
    And is not in the usurer's bands:
Nor soldier-like started with rough alarms,
    Nor dreads the sea's enragèd harms:
But flees the bar and courts, with the proud boards,
    And waiting chambers of great lords.
The poplar tall, he then doth marrying twine
10   With the grown issue of the vine;
And with his hook lops off the fruitless race,
    And sets more happy in the place:
Or in the bending vale beholds afar
    The lowing herds there grazing are:
Or the pressed honey in pure pots doth keep
    Of earth, and shears the tender sheep:
Or when that Autumn, through the fields lifts round
    His head, with mellow apples crowned,

How plucking pears, his own hand grafted had,
20   And purple-matching grapes, he's glad!
With which, Priapus, he may thank thy hands,
    And, Sylvan, thine that kept'st his lands!
Then now beneath some ancient oak he may,
    Now in the rooted grass him lay,
Whilst from the higher banks do slide the floods;
    The soft birds quarrel in the woods,
The fountains murmur as the streams do creep,
    And all invite to easy sleep.
Then when the thundering Jove his snow and showers
30   Are gathering by the wintry hours;
Or hence, or thence, he drives with many a hound
    Wild boars into his toils pitched round:
Or strains on his small fork his subtle nets
    For the eating thrush, or pitfalls sets:
And snares the fearful hare, and new-come crane,
    And 'counts them sweet rewards so ta'en.
Who (amongst these delights) would not forget
    Love's cares so evil, and so great?
But if, to boot with these, a chaste wife meet
40   For household aid, and children sweet;
Such as the Sabines, or a sun-burnt blowse,
    Some lusty quick Apulian's spouse,
To deck the hallowed hearth with old wood fired
    Against the husband comes home tired;
That penning the glad flock in hurdles by,
    Their swelling udders doth draw dry:
And from the sweet tub wine of this year takes,
    And unbought viands ready makes:
Nor Lucrine oysters I could then more prize,
50   Nor turbot, nor bright golden-eyes:
If with bright floods, the winter troubled much,
    Into our seas send any such:
The Ionian godwit, nor the guinea hen
    Could not go down my belly then
More sweet than olives, that new gathered be
    From fattest branches of the tree:

Or the herb sorrel, that loves meadows still,
    Or mallows loosing body's ill:
Or at the feast of bounds, the lamb then slain,
60   Or kid forced from the wolf again.
Among these cates how glad the sight doth come
    Of the fed flocks approaching home!
To view the weary oxen draw, with bare
    And fainting necks, the turnèd share!
The wealthy household swarm of bondmen met,
    And 'bout the steaming chimney set!
These thoughts when usurer Alphius, now about
    To turn mere farmer, had spoke out,
'Gainst the ides, his monies he gets in with pain,
70   At the calends, puts all out again.

LXXXVI (Horace). Ode the First. The Fourth Book. To Venus

Venus, again thou mov'st a war
Long intermitted, pray thee, pray thee spare:
    I am not such, as in the reign
Of the good Cynara I was: refrain,
    Sour mother of sweet loves, forbear
To bend a man now, at his fiftieth year,
    Too stubborn for commands, so slack:
Go where youth's soft entreaties call thee back.
    More timely hie thee to the house,
10 With thy bright swans, of Paulus Maximus:
    There jest, and feast, make him thine host,
If a fit liver thou dost seek to toast;
    For he's both noble, lovely, young,
And for the troubled client files his tongue;
    Child of a hundred arts, and far
Will he display the ensigns of thy war.
    And when he smiling finds his grace
With thee 'bove all his rivals' gifts take place,
    He will thee a marble statue make

20 Beneath a sweetwood roof, near Alba lake:
    There shall thy dainty nostril take
In many a gum, and for thy soft ear's sake
    Shall verse be set to harp and lute,
And Phrygian hautboy, not without the flute.
    There twice a day in sacred lays,
The youths and tender maids shall sing thy praise:
    And in the Salian manner meet
Thrice 'bout thy altar with their ivory feet.
    Me now, nor wench, nor wanton boy,
30 Delights, nor credulous hope of mutual joy,
    Nor care I now healths to propound;
Or with fresh flowers to girt my temple round.
    But, why, oh why, my Ligurine,
Flow my thin tears, down these pale cheeks of mine?
    Or why, my well-graced words among,
With an uncomely silence fails my tongue?
    Hard-hearted, I dream every night
I hold thee fast! But fled hence, with the light,
    Whether in Mars his field thou be,
40 Or Tiber's winding streams, I follow thee.

LXXXVII Ode IX, 3 Book, to Lydia. Dialogue of Horace and Lydia

HOR.

    Whilst, Lydia, I was loved of thee,
And ('bout thy ivory neck) no youth did fling
    His arms more acceptable free,
I thought me richer than the Persian king.

LYD.

    Whilst Horace loved no mistress more,
Nor after Chloe did his Lydia sound;
    In name I went all names before,
The Roman Ilia was not more renowned.

HOR.

'Tis true, I am Thracian Chloe's, I,
10 Who sings so sweet, and with such cunning plays,
As, for her, I'd not fear to die,
So Fate would give her life, and longer days.

LYD.

And I am mutually on fire
With gentle Calais, Thurine Orinth's son;
For whom I doubly would expire,
So Fates would let the boy a long thread run.

HOR.

But, say old love return should make,
And us disjoined force to her brazen yoke,
That I bright Chloe off should shake;
20 And to left-Lydia, now the gate stood ope.

LYD.

Though he be fairer than a star;
Thou lighter than the bark of any tree,
And than rough Adria, angrier, far;
Yet would I wish to love, live, die with thee.

LXXXVIII Fragmentum Petron. Arbitr. *The Same Translated*

Doing, a filthy pleasure is, and short;
And done, we straight repent us of the sport:
Let us not then rush blindly on unto it,
Like lustful beasts, that only know to do it:
For lust will languish, and that heat decay,
But thus, thus, keeping endless holiday,
Let us together closely lie, and kiss,
There is no labour, nor no shame in this;
This hath pleased, doth please, and long will please; never
10 Can this decay, but is beginning ever.

LXXXIX *Epigramma Martialis. Lib. VIII. lxxvii. The Same Translated*

Liber, of all thy friends, thou sweetest care,
Thou worthy in eternal flower to fare,
If thou be'st wise, with Syrian oil let shine
Thy locks, and rosy garlands crown thy head;
Dark thy clear glass with old Falernian wine;
And heat, with softest love, thy softer bed.
He, that but living half his days, dies such,
Makes his life longer than 'twas given him, much.

Miscellaneous Poems

I To Thomas Palmer

When late (grave Palmer) these thy graffs and flowers
(So well disposed by thy auspicious hand)
Were made the objects to my weaker powers;
I could not but in admiration stand.
First: thy success did strike my sense with wonder;
That 'mongst so many plants transplanted hither,
Not one but thrives; in spite of storms and thunder,
Unseasoned frosts, or the most envious weather.
Then I admired, the rare and precious use
10 Thy skill hath made of rank despisèd weeds;
Whilst other souls convert to base abuse
The sweetest simples, and most sovereign seeds.
Next, that which rapt me, was: I might behold
How like the carbuncle in Aaron's breast
The seven-fold flower of art (more rich than gold)
Did sparkle forth in centre of the rest:
Thus, as a ponderous thing in water cast
Extendeth circles into infinites,
Still making that the greatest that is last,
20 Till the one hath drowned the other in our sights,
So in my brain; the strong impression
Of thy rich labours worlds of thoughts created,
Which thoughts being circumvolved in gyre-like motion
Were spent with wonder as they were dilated,
Till giddy with amazement I fell down
In a deep trance; . . .
. . . When, lo, to crown thy worth
I struggled with this passion that did drown

My abler faculties; and thus brake forth:
30 Palmer, thy travails well become thy name,
And thou in them shalt live as long as fame.

Dignum laude virum Musa vetat mori.

II In Authorem

Thou, that wouldst find the habit of true passion,
    And see a mind attired in perfect strains;
Not wearing moods, as gallants do a fashion,
    In these pied times, only to show their brains,
Look here on Breton's work, the master print:
    Where, such perfections to the life do rise.
If they seem wry, to such as look asquint,
    The fault's not in the object, but their eyes.
For, as one coming with a lateral view,
10   Unto a cunning piece wrought pérspective,
Wants faculty to make a censure true:
    So with this author's readers will it thrive:
Which being eyed directly, I divine,
His proof their praise will meet, as in this line.

III Author ad Librum

Go little book, go little fable
Unto the bright, and amiable
Lucy of Bedford; she, that bounty
Appropriates still unto that county:
Tell her, his muse that did invent thee
To Cynthia's fairest nymph hath sent thee,
And sworn, that he will quite discard thee
If any way she do reward thee
But with a kiss (if thou canst dare it)
10 Of her white hand; or she can spare it.

IV *To the Author*

In picture, they which truly understand,
   Require (besides the likeness of the thing)
   Light, posture, heightening, shadow, colouring,
All which are parts commend the cunning hand;
And all your book (when it is th'roughly scanned)
   Will well confess; presenting, limiting,
   Each subtlest passion, with her source, and spring,
So bold, as shows your art you can command.
   But now, your work is done, if they that view
10 The several figures, languish in suspense,
     To judge which passion's false, and which is true,
      Between the doubtful sway of reason, and sense;
        'Tis not your fault, if they shall sense prefer,
        Being told there, reason cannot, sense may err.

V *To the Worthy Author M[r] John Fletcher*

The wise, and many-headed bench, that sits
Upon the life, and death of plays, and wits,
(Composed of gamester, captain, knight, knight's man,
Lady, or pucel, that wears mask, or fan,
Velvet, or taffeta cap, ranked in the dark
With the shop's foreman, or some such brave spark,
That may judge for his sixpence) had, before
They saw it half, damned thy whole play, and more;
Their motives were, since it had not to do
10 With vices, which they looked for, and came to.
I, that am glad, thy innocence was thy guilt,
And wish that all the muses' blood were spilt,
In such a martyrdom; to vex their eyes,
Do crown thy murdered poem: which shall rise
A glorified work to time, when fire,
Or moths shall eat, what all these fools admire.

VI To the Right Noble Tom, Tell-Troth of His Travels, the Coriat of Odcombe, and His Book Now Going to Travel

T ry and trust Roger, was the word, but now
H onest Tom Tell-troth puts down Roger: how?
O f travel he discourseth so at large,
M arry, he sets it out at his own charge;
A nd therein (which is worth his valour too)
S hows he dares more than Paul's churchyard durst do.
C ome forth, thou bonny bouncing book then, daughter
O f Tom of Odcombe, that odd jovial author,
R ather his son I should have called thee: why?
10 Y es, thou wert born out of his travelling thigh
A s well as from his brains, and claim'st thereby
T o be his Bacchus as his Pallas: be
E ver his thighs male then, and his brains she.

VII To the London Reader, on the Odcombian Writer, Polytopian Thomas the Traveller

Whoever he be, would write a story at
The height, let him learn of Mr Tom Coriat;
Who, because his matter in all should be meet,
To his strength, hath measured it out with his feet.
And that, say philosophers, is the best model.
Yet who could have hit on it but the wise noddle
Of our Odcombian, that literate elf?
To line out no stride, but paced by himself?
And allow you for each particular mile,
10 By the scale of his book, a yard of his style?
Which, unto all ages, for his will be known,
Since he treads in no other man's steps but his own.
And that you may see he most luckily meant
To write it with the self-same spirit he went,
He says to the world, let any man mend it,
In five months he went it, in five months he penned it.

But who will believe this, that chanceth to look
The map of his journey, and sees in his book,
France, Savoy, Italy, and Helvetia,
20 The Low Countries, Germany, and Rhetia,
There named to be travelled? For this our Tom saith:
Pies on it, you have his historical faith.
Each leaf of his journal, and line doth unlock
The truth of his heart there, and tells what o'clock
He went out at each place, and at what he came in,
How long he did stay, at what sign he did inn.
Besides, he tried ship, cart, wagon, and chair,
Horse, foot, and all but flying in the air:
And therefore however the travelling nation,
30 Or builders of story have oft imputation
Of lying, he fears so much the reproof
Of his foot, or his pen, his brain, or his hoof,
That he dares to inform you, but somewhat meticulous,
How scabbed, how ragged, and how pediculous
He was in his travel, how like to be beaten,
For grapes he had gathered, before they were eaten.
How fain for his venery he was to cry *Tergum O*,
And lay in straw with the horses at Bergamo,
How well, and how often his shoes too were mended,
40 That sacred to Odcombe are now there suspended,
I mean that one pair, wherewith he so hobbled
From Venice to Flushing, were not they well cobbled?
Yes. And thanks God in his 'pistle or his book
How many learned men he have drawn with his hook
Of Latin and Greek, to his friendship. And seven
He there doth protest he saw of the eleven.
Nay more in his wardrobe, if you will laugh at a
Jest, he says. *Item* one suit of black taffeta
Except a doublet, and bought of the Jews:
50 So that not them, his scabs, lice, or the stews,
Or anything else that another should hide,
Doth he once dissemble, but tells he did ride
In a cart 'twixt Montrell and Abbeville.
And being at Flushing enforcèd to feel

Some want, they say in a sort he did crave:
I writ he only his tail there did wave;
Which he not denies. Now being so free,
Poor Tom, have we cause to suspect just thee?
No: as I first said, who would write a story at
60 The height, let him learn of Mr Tom Coriat.

VIII To His Much and Worthily Esteemed Friend the Author

Who takes thy volume to his virtuous hand,
Must be intended still to understand:
Who bluntly doth but look upon the same,
May ask, 'What author would conceal his name?'
Who reads may rove, and call the passage dark,
Yet may as blind men sometimes hit the mark.
Who reads, who roves, who hopes to understand,
May take thy volume to his virtuous hand.
Who cannot read, but only doth desire
10 To understand, he may at length admire.

IX To the Worthy Author on The Husband

It fits not only him that makes a book,
To see his work be good; but that he look
Who are his test, and what their judgement is:
Lest a false praise do make their dotage his.
I do not feel that ever yet I had
The art of uttering wares, if they were bad;
Or skill of making matches in my life:
And therefore I commend unto the *Wife*,
That went before, a *Husband*. She, I'll swear,
10 Was worthy of a good one; and this, here,
I know for such, as (if my word will weigh)
She need not blush upon the marriage day.

X *To His Friend the Author upon His* Richard

When these, and such, their voices have employed;
What place is for my testimony void?
Or, to so many, and so broad seals had,
What can one witness, and a weak one, add
To such a work, as could not need theirs? Yet
If praises, when they are full, heaping admit,
My suffrage brings thee all increase, to crown
Thy *Richard*, raised in song, past pulling down.

XI *To My Truly-Beloved Friend, Mr Browne: on His Pastorals*

Some men of books or friends not speaking right,
May hurt them more with praise, than foes with spite.
But I have seen thy work, and I know thee:
And, if thou list thyself, what thou canst be.
For, though but early in these paths thou tread,
I find thee write most worthy to be read.
It must be thine own judgement, yet, that sends
This thy work forth: that judgement mine commends.
And, where the most read books, on authors' fames,
10 Or, like our money-brokers, take up names
On credit, and are cozened; see, that thou
By offering not more sureties, than enou',
Hold thine own worth unbroke: which is so good
Upon the Exchange of letters, as I would
More of our writers would like thee, not swell
With the 'how much' they set forth, but the 'how well'.

XII To My Worthy and Honoured Friend, Mr George Chapman, on His Translation of Hesiod's Works and Days

Whose work could this be, Chapman, to refine
Old Hesiod's ore, and give it us; but thine,
Who hadst before wrought in rich Homer's mine?

What treasure hast thou brought us! And what store
Still, still, dost thou arrive with, at our shore,
To make thy honour, and our wealth the more!

If all the vulgar tongues, that speak this day,
Were asked of thy discoveries; they must say,
To the Greek coast thine only knew the way.

10 Such passage hast thou found, such réturns made,
As, now, of all men, it is called thy trade:
And who make thither else, rob, or invade.

XIII On the Author, Work, and Translator

Who tracks this author's, or translator's pen,
Shall find, that either hath read books, and men:
To say but one, were single. Then it chimes,
When the old words do strike on the new times,
As in this Spanish Proteus; who, though writ
But in one tongue, was formed with the world's wit:
And hath the noblest mark of a good book,
That an ill man dares not securely look
Upon it, but will loathe, or let it pass,
10 As a deformed face doth a true glass.
Such books deserve translators, of like coat
As was the genius wherewith they were wrote;
And this hath met that one, that may be styled
More than the foster-father of this child;
For though Spain gave him his first air and vogue,
He would be called, henceforth, the *English Rogue*,

But that he's too well-suited, in a cloth,
Finer than was his Spanish, if my oath
Will be received in court; if not, would I
20 Had clothed him so. Here's all I can supply
To your desert, who have done it, friend. And this
Fair emulation, and no envy is;
When you behold me wish myself, the man
That would have done that which you only can.

XIV To the Reader

This figure, that thou here seest put,
It was for gentle Shakespeare cut;
Wherein the graver had a strife
With nature, to outdo the life:
O, could he but have drawn his wit
As well in brass, as he hath hit
His face; the print would then surpass
All, that was ever writ in brass.
But, since he cannot, reader, look
10 Not on his picture, but his book.

XV To the Memory of My Beloved, the Author Mr William Shakespeare: And What He Hath Left Us

To draw no envy (Shakespeare) on thy name,
Am I thus ample to thy book, and fame:
While I confess thy writings to be such,
As neither man, nor muse, can praise too much.
'Tis true, and all men's suffrage. But these ways
Were not the paths I meant unto thy praise:
For seeliest ignorance on these may light,
Which, when it sounds at best, but echoes right;
Or blind affection, which doth ne'er advance
10 The truth, but gropes, and urgeth all by chance;

Or crafty malice, might pretend this praise,
And think to ruin, where it seemed to raise.
These are, as some infamous bawd, or whore,
Should praise a matron. What could hurt her more?
But thou art proof against them, and indeed
Above the ill fortune of them, or the need.
I therefore will begin. Soul of the age!
The applause, delight, the wonder of our stage!
My Shakespeare, rise; I will not lodge thee by
20 Chaucer, or Spenser, or bid Beaumont lie
A little further, to make thee a room:
Thou art a monument, without a tomb,
And art alive still, while thy book doth live,
And we have wits to read, and praise to give.
That I not mix thee so, my brain excuses;
I mean with great, but disproportioned muses:
For, if I thought my judgement were of years,
I should commit thee surely with thy peers,
And tell, how far thou didst our Lyly outshine,
30 Or sporting Kyd, or Marlowe's mighty line.
And though thou hadst small Latin, and less Greek,
From thence to honour thee, I would not seek
For names; but call forth thundering Aeschylus,
Euripides, and Sophocles to us,
Pacuvius, Accius, him of Cordova dead,
To life again, to hear thy buskin tread,
And shake a stage: or, when thy socks were on,
Leave thee alone, for the comparison
Of all that insolent Greece, or haughty Rome
40 Sent forth, or since did from their ashes come.
Triumph, my Britain, thou hast one to show,
To whom all scenes of Europe homage owe.
He was not of an age, but for all time!
And all the muses still were in their prime,
When like Apollo he came forth to warm
Our ears, or like a Mercury to charm!
Nature herself was proud of his designs,
And joyed to wear the dressing of his lines!

Which were so richly spun, and woven so fit,
50 As, since, she will vouchsafe no other wit.
The merry Greek, tart Aristophanes,
Neat Terence, witty Plautus, now not please;
But antiquated, and deserted lie
As they were not of nature's family.
Yet must I not give nature all: thy art,
My gentle Shakespeare, must enjoy a part.
For though the poet's matter, nature be,
His art doth give the fashion. And, that he,
Who casts to write a living line, must sweat,
60 (Such as thine are) and strike the second heat
Upon the muses' anvil: turn the same,
(And himself with it) that he thinks to frame;
Or for the laurel, he may gain a scorn,
For a good poet's made, as well as born.
And such wert thou. Look how the father's face
Lives in his issue, even so, the race
Of Shakespeare's mind, and manners brightly shines
In his well-turnéd, and true-filéd lines:
In each of which, he seems to shake a lance,
70 As brandished at the eyes of ignorance.
Sweet swan of Avon, what a sight it were
To see thee in our waters yet appear,
And make those flights upon the banks of Thames,
That so did take Eliza, and our James!
But stay, I see thee in the hemisphere
Advanced, and made a constellation there!
Shine forth, thou star of poets, and with rage,
Or influence, chide, or cheer the drooping stage;
Which, since thy flight from hence, hath mourned like night.
80 And despairs day, but for thy volume's light.

XVI *From* The Touchstone of Truth

Truth is the trial of itself,
    And needs no other touch,
And purer than the purest gold,
    Refine it ne'er so much.
It is the life and light of love,
    The sun that ever shineth,
And spirit of that special grace,
    That faith and love defineth.
It is the warrant of the Word,
10   That yields a scent so sweet,
As gives a power to faith, to tread
    All falsehood under feet.
It is the sword that doth divide,
    The marrow from the bone,
And in effect of heavenly love
    Doth show the holy one.
This, blessèd Warre, thy blessèd book
    Unto the world doth prove.
A worthy work, and worthy well,
20   Of the most worthy love.

XVII *To My Chosen Friend the Learnèd Translator of Lucan, Thomas May, Esquire*

When, Rome, I read thee in thy mighty pair,
And see both climbing up the slippery stair
Of Fortune's wheel by Lucan driven about,
And the world in it, I begin to doubt,
At every line some pin thereof should slack
At least, if not the general engine crack.
But when again I view the parts so peized,
And those in number so, and measure raised,
As neither Pompey's popularity,
10 Caesar's ambition, Cato's liberty,
Calm Brutus' tenor start; but all along

Keep due proportion in the ample song,
It makes me, ravished with just wonder, cry
What muse, or rather god of harmony
Taught Lucan these true moods! Replies my sense,
What gods but those of arts, and eloquence?
Phoebus and Hermes? They whose tongue, or pen
Are still the interpreters 'twixt gods, and men!
But who hath them interpreted, and brought
20 Lucan's whole frame unto us, and so wrought,
As not the smallest joint, or gentlest word
In the great mass, or machine there is stirred?
The self-same genius! So the work will say.
The sun translated, or the son of May.

XVIII The Vision of Ben Jonson, on the Muses of His Friend M. Drayton

It hath been questioned, Michael, if I be
A friend at all; or, if at all, to thee:
Because, who make the question, have not seen
Those ambling visits, pass in verse, between
Thy muse, and mine, as they expect. 'Tis true:
You have not writ to me, nor I to you;
And, though I now begin, 'tis not to rub
Hanch against hanch, or raise a rhyming club
About the town: this reckoning I will pay,
10 Without conferring symbols. This is my day.
    It was no dream! I was awake, and saw!
Lend me thy voice, O Fame, that I may draw
Wonder to truth, and have my vision hurled,
Hot from the trumpet, round about the world.
    I saw a beauty from the sea to rise,
That all earth looked on; and that earth, all eyes!
It cast a beam as when the cheerful sun
Is fair got up, and day some hours begun,
And filled an orb as circular, as heaven!
20 The orb was cut forth into regions seven,

And those so sweet, and well-proportioned parts,
As it had been the circle of the arts!
When, by thy bright *Ideas* standing by,
I found it pure, and perfect poesy,
There read I, straight, thy learnèd *Legends* three,
Heard the soft airs, between our swains and thee,
Which made me think, the old Theocritus,
Or rural Virgil come, to pipe to us!
But then, thy epistolar *Heroic Songs*,
30   Their loves, their quarrels, jealousies, and wrongs,
Did all so strike me, as I cried, who can
With us be called, the Naso, but this man?
And looking up, I saw Minerva's fowl,
Perched overhead, the wise Athenian *Owl*:
I thought thee then our Orpheus, that wouldst try
Like him, to make the air, one volary:
And I had styled thee, Orpheus, but before
My lips could form the voice, I heard that roar,
And rouse, the marching of a mighty force,
40   Drums against drums, the neighing of the horse,
The fights, the cries; and wondering at the jars
I saw, and read, it was thy *Barons' Wars*!
O, how in those, dost thou instruct these times,
That rebels' actions, are but valiant crimes!
And carried, though with shout, and noise, confess
A wild, and an authorized wickedness!
Say'st thou so, Lucan? But thou scorn'st to stay
Under one title. Thou hast made thy way
And flight about the isle, well near, by this,
50   In thy admired periegesis,
Or universal circumduction
Of all that read thy *Poly-Olbion*.
That read it? That are ravished! Such was I
With every song, I swear, and so would die;
But that I hear, again, thy drum to beat
A better cause, and strike the bravest heat
That ever yet did fire the English blood!
Our right in France, if rightly understood:

There, thou art Homer! Pray thee, use the style
60 Thou hast deserved: and let me read the while
Thy catalogue of ships, exceeding his,
Thy list of aids, and force, for so it is:
The poet's act! And for his country's sake
Brave are the musters, that the muse will make.
And when he ships them where to use their arms,
How do his trumpets breathe! What loud alarms!
Look, how we read the Spartans were inflamed
With bold Tyrtaeus' verse, when thou art named,
So shall our English youth urge on, and cry
70 An *Agincourt*, an *Agincourt*, or die.
This book! It is a catechism to fight,
And will be bought of every lord, and knight,
That can but read; who cannot, may in prose
Get broken pieces, and fight well by those.
The miseries of Margaret the queen
Of tender eyes will more be wept, than seen:
I feel it by mine own, that overflow,
And stop my sight, in every line I go.
But then refreshèd, with thy *Fairy Court*,
80 I look on *Cynthia*, and *Sirena*'s sport,
As, on two flowery carpets, that did rise,
And with their grassy green restored mine eyes.
Yet give me leave, to wonder at the birth
Of thy strange *Moon Calf*, both thy strain of mirth,
And gossip-got acquaintance, as, to us
Thou hadst brought Lapland, or old Cobalus,
Empusa, Lamia, or some monster, more
Than Afric knew, or the full Grecian store!
I gratulate it to thee, and thy ends,
90 To all thy virtuous, and well-chosen friends,
Only my loss is, that I am not there:
And, till I worthy am to wish I were,
I call the world, that envies me, to see
If I can be a friend, and friend to thee.

XIX On the Honoured Poems of His Honoured Friend, Sir John Beaumont, Baronet

This book will live; it hath a genius: this
Above his reader, or his praiser, is.
Hence, then, profane: here needs no words' expense
In bulwarks, ravelins, ramparts, for defence,
Such, as the creeping common pioneers use
When they do sweat to fortify a muse.
Though I confess a Beaumont's book to be
The bound, and frontier of our poetry;
And doth deserve all muniments of praise,
10 That art, or engine, on the strength can raise.
Yet, who dares offer a redoubt to rear?
To cut a dike, or stick a stake up, here,
Before this work, where envy hath not cast
A trench against it, nor a battery placed?
Stay, till she make her vain approaches. Then
If, maimed, she come off, 'tis not of men
This fort of so impregnable access,
But higher power, as spite could not make less,
Nor flattery! But secured, by the author's name,
20 Defies, what's cross to piety, or good fame.
And like a hallowed temple, free from taint
Of ethnicism, makes his muse a saint.

XX To My Worthy Friend, Master Edward Filmer, on His Work Published

What charming peals are these,
That, while they bind the senses, do so please?
They are the marriage-rites
Of two, the choicest pair of man's delights,
Music and poesy:
French air, and English verse, here wedded lie.
Who did this knot compose,
Again hath brought the lily to the rose;

And, with their chainèd dance,
10 Recelebrates the joyful match with France.
     They are a school to win
The fair French daughter to learn English in;
     And, gracèd with her song,
To make the language sweet upon her tongue.

XXI To My Old Faithful Servant: And (by His Continued Virtue) My Loving Friend: the Author of this Work, Mr Rich[ard] Brome

I had you for a servant, once, Dick Brome;
     And you performed a servant's faithful parts:
Now, you are got into a nearer room,
     Of fellowship, professing my old arts.
And you do do them well, with good applause,
     Which you have justly gainèd from the stage,
By observation of those comic laws
     Which I, your master, first did teach the age.
You learned it well; and, for it, served your time,
10   A prenticeship: which few do nowadays.
Now each court hobby-horse will wince in rhyme;
     Both learnèd, and unlearnèd, all write plays.
It was not so of old: men took up trades
     That knew the crafts they had been bred in, right:
An honest Bilbo-smith would make good blades,
     And the physician teach men spew, or shite;
The cobbler kept him to his nall; but, now
He'll be a pilot, scarce can guide a plough.

XXII To Mrs Alice Sutcliffe, on Her Divine Meditations

When I had read your holy *Meditations*,
And in them viewed the uncertainty of life,
The motives, and true spurs to all good nations,

The peace of conscience, and the godly's strife,
The danger of delaying to repent,
And the deceit of pleasures, by consent,
The comfort of weak Christians, with their warning,
From fearful backslides; and the debt we are in,
To follow goodness, by our own discerning
10   Our great reward, the eternal crown to win,
I said, who had supped so deep of this sweet chalice,
Must Celia be, the anagram of Alice.

XXIII To My Dear Son, and Right-Learnèd Friend, Master Joseph Rutter

You look, my Joseph, I should something say
Unto the world, in praise of your first play:
And truly, so I would, could I be heard.
You know, I never was of truth afeared,
And less ashamed; not when I told the crowd
How well I loved truth: I was scarce allowed
By those deep-grounded, understanding men,
That sit to censure plays, yet know not when,
Or why to like; they found, it all was new,
10   And newer, than could please them, because true.
Such men I met withal, and so have you.
Now, for mine own part, and it is but due,
(You have deserved it from me) I have read,
And weighed your play: untwisted every thread,
And know the woof, and warp thereof; can tell
Where it runs round, and even: where so well,
So soft, and smooth it handles, the whole piece,
As it were spun by nature, off the fleece:
This is my censure. Now there is a new
20   Office of wit, a mint, and (this is true)
Cried up of late: whereto there must be first
A master-worker called, the old standard burst
Of wit, and a new made: a warden then,
And a comptroller, two most rigid men

For order, and for governing the pix,
A 'say-master, hath studied all the tricks
Of fineness, and alloy: follow his hint,
You have all the mysteries of wit's new mint,
The valuations, mixtures, and the same
30   Concluded from a carract to a dram.

Other Commendatory Poems

XXIV

Stay, view this stone: and, if thou beest not such,
Read here a little, that thou mayst know much.
It covers, first, a virgin; and then, one
That durst be that in court: a virtue alone
To fill an epitaph. But she had more.
She might have claimed to have made the Graces four;
Taught Pallas language; Cynthia modesty;
As fit to have increased the harmony
Of spheres, as light of stars; she was earth's eye:
10   The sole religious house, and votary,
With rites not bound, but conscience. Wouldst thou all?
She was 'Sell Boulstred. In which name, I call
Up so much truth, as could I it pursue
Might make the *Fable of Good Women* true.

XXV A Speech Presented unto King James at a Tilting in the Behalf of the Two Noble Brothers S[ir]Robert and S[ir] Henry Rich, now Earls of Warwick and Holland

Two noble knights, whom true desire and zeal,
Hath armed at all points, charge me humbly kneel
Unto thee, king of men; their noblest parts
To tender thus, their lives, their loves, their hearts!

The elder of these two, rich hope's increase,
Presents a royal altar of fair peace,
And as an everlasting sacrifice
His life, his love, his honour, which ne'er dies,
He freely brings; and on this altar lays
10   As true oblations; his brother's emblem says,
Except your gracious eye as through a glass
Made prospective, behold him, he must pass
Still that same little point he was; but when
Your royal eye which still creates new men
Shall look, and on him so, then art's a liar
If from a little spark he rise not fire.

XXVI To the Most Noble, and above His Titles, Robert, Earl of Somerset

They are not those, are present with their face,
And clothes, and gifts, that only do thee grace
At these thy nuptials; but, whose heart, and thought
Do wait upon thee: and their love not bought.
Such wear true wedding robes, and are true friends,
That bid, God give thee joy, and have no ends.
Which I do, early, virtuous Somerset,
And pray, thy joys as lasting be, as great.
Not only this, but every day of thine,
10   With the same look, or with a better, shine.
May she, whom thou for spouse, today, dost take,
Outbe that *Wife*, in worth, thy friend did make:
And thou to her, that *Husband*, may exalt
Hymen's amends, to make it worth his fault.
So, be there never discontent, or sorrow,
To rise with either of you, on the morrow.
So, be your concord, still, as deep, as mute;
And every joy, in marriage, turn a fruit.
So, may those marriage-pledges, comforts prove:
20   And every birth increase the heat of love.
So, in their number, may you never see

Mortality, till you immortal be.
And when your years rise more, than would be told,
Yet neither of you seem to the other old.
That all, that view you then, and late; may say,
Sure, this glad pair were married, but this day.

XXVII Charles Cavendish to His Posterity

Sons, seek not me among these polished stones;
These only hide part of my flesh, and bones:
Which, did they ne'er so neat, or proudly dwell,
Will all turn dust, and may not make me swell.
Let such as justly have outlived all praise,
Trust in the tombs, their careful friends do raise;
I made my life my monument, and yours:
To which there's no material that endures;
Nor yet in description like it. Write but that;
10   And teach your nephews it to emulate:
It will be matter loud enough to tell
Not when I died, but how I lived. Farewell.

XXVIII To the Memory of That Most Honoured Lady Jane, Eldest Daughter to Cuthbert, Lord Ogle: and Countess of Shrewsbury

I could begin with that grave form, 'Here lies',
And pray thee, reader, bring thy weeping eyes
To see who it is. A noble countess, great,
In blood, in birth, by match, and by her seat;
Religious, wise, chaste, loving, gracious, good;
And number attributes unto a flood:
But every table in this church can say,
A list of epithets: and praise this way.
No stone in any wall here, but can tell
10   Such things of every body, and as well.
Nay, they will venture one's descent to hit,

And Christian name too, with a herald's wit.
But, I would have thee to know something new,
Not usual in a lady; and yet true:
At least so great a lady. She was wife
But of one husband: and since he left life,
But sorrow, she desired no other friend:
And her, she made her inmate to the end,
To call on sickness still, to be her guest,
20 Whom she, with sorrow first did lodge, then feast,
Then entertain, and as death's harbinger;
So wooed at last, that he was won to her
Importune wish; and by her loved lord's side
To lay her here, enclosed, his second bride.
Where spite of death, next life, for her love's sake,
This second marriage, will eternal make.

XXIX Epitaph on Katherine, Lady Ogle

O Zeus kateide chronios eis tas diphtheras

'Tis a record in heaven. You, that were
Her children, and grand-children, read it here!
Transmit it to your nephews, friends, allies,
Tenants, and servants, have they hearts, and eyes,
To view the truth and own it. Do but look
With pause upon it; make this page your book;
Your book? Your volume! Nay, the state, and story!
Code, digests, pandects of all female glory!

Diphthera Jovis:
She was the light (without reflex
10 Upon her self) to all her sex!
The best of women, her whole life
Was the example of a wife!
Or of a parent, or a friend!
All circles had their spring and end
In her, and what could perfect be,
Or without angles, it was she!

All that was solid, in the name
Of virtue, precious in the frame:
Or else magnetic in the force,
20 Or sweet, or various, in the course!
What was proportion, or could be
By warrant called just symmetry,
In number, measure, or degree
Of weight, or fashion, it was she.
Her soul possessed her flesh's state
In fair freehold, not an inmate:
And when the flesh, here, shut up day,
Fame's heat upon the grave did stay;
And hourly brooding o'er the same,
30 Keeps warm the spice of her good name,
Until the dust returnèd be
Into a phoenix, which is she.

For this did Katherine, Lady Ogle, die
To gain the crown of immortality,
Eternity's great charter; which became
Her right, by gift, and purchase of the lamb:
Sealed, and delivered to her, in the sight
Of angels, and all witnesses of light,
Both saints, and martyrs, by her lovèd lord.
40 And this a copy is of the record.

XXX *An Epigram to My Jovial Good Friend Mr Robert Dover, on His Great Instauration of His Hunting and Dancing at Cotswold*

I cannot bring my muse to drop her vies
'Twixt Cotswold, and the Olympic exercise:
But I can tell thee, Dover, how thy games
Renew the glories of our blessèd James:
How they do keep alive his memory;
With the glad country, and posterity:
How they advance true love, and neighbourhood,

And do both Church, and commonwealth the good,
In spite of hypocrites, who are the worst
10 Of subjects; let such envy, till they burst.

Odes

XXXI Ode Enthusiastic

Splendour! O more than mortal,
For other forms come short all
Of her illustrate brightness,
As far as sin's from lightness.

Her wit as quick, and sprightful
As fire; and more delightful
Than the stol'n sports of lovers,
When night their meeting covers.

Judgement (adorned with learning)
10 Doth shine in her discerning,
Clear as a naked vestal
Closed in an orb of crystal.

Her breath for sweet exceeding
The phoenix place of breeding,
But mixed with sound, transcending
All nature of commending.

Alas: then whither wade I,
In thought to praise this lady;
When seeking her renowning,
20 Myself am so near drowning?

Retire, and say; her graces
Are deeper than their faces:
Yet she's nor nice to show them,
Nor takes she pride to know them.

XXXII Ode Allegoric

Who saith our times nor have, nor can
     Produce us a black swan?
     Behold, where one doth swim,
        Whose note, and hue,
Besides the other swans admiring him,
       Betray it true:
      A gentler bird, than this,
Did never dint the breast of Tamesis.

Mark, mark, but when his wing he takes,
10   How fair a flight he makes!
     How upward, and direct!
        Whilst pleased Apollo
Smiles in his sphere, to see the rest affect,
       In vain to follow:
      This swan is only his,
And Phoebus's love cause of his blackness is.

He showed him first the hoof-cleft spring,
     Near which, the Thespiads sing;
     The clear Dircaean fount
20   Where Pindar swam;
The pale Pyrene, and the forkèd mount:
       And, when they came
      To brooks, and broader streams,
From Zephyr's rape would close him with his beams.

This changed his down; till this, as white
     As the whole herd in sight,
     And still is in the breast:
       That part nor wind,
Nor sun could make to vary from the rest,
30   Or alter kind.
      So much doth virtue hate,
For style of rareness, to degenerate.

Be then both rare, and good; and long
     Continue thy sweet song.

Nor let one river boast
    Thy tunes alone;
But prove the air, and sail from coast to coast:
    Salute old Mone,
    But first to Cluid stoop low,
40   The vale, that bred thee pure, as her hills snow.

From thence, display thy wing again
    Over Iërna main,
    To the Eugenian dale;
    There charm the rout
With thy soft notes, and hold them within pale
    That late were out.
    Music hath power to draw,
Where neither force can bend, nor fear can awe.

Be proof, the glory of his hand,
50   (Charles Montjoy) whose command
    Hath all been harmony:
    And more hath won
Upon the kern, and wildest Irishry,
    Than time hath done,
    Whose strength is above strength;
And conquers all things, yea itself, at length.

Whoever sipped at Baphyre river,
    That heard but spite deliver
    His far-admiréd acts,
60   And is not rapt
With entheate rage, to publish their bright tracts?
    (But this more apt
    When him alone we sing)
Now must we ply our aim; our swan's on wing.

Who (see) already hath o'er-flown
    The Hebrid Isles, and known
    The scattered Orcades;
    From thence is gone
To utmost Thule: whence, he backs the seas
70   To Caledon,

And over Grampius' mountain,
To Lomond Lake, and Tweed's black-springing fountain.

Haste, haste, sweet singer: nor to Tyne,
  Humber, or Ouse, decline;
  But over land to Trent:
   There cool thy plumes,
And up again, in skies, and air to vent
   Their reeking fumes;
  Till thou at Thames alight,
80 From whose proud bosom, thou began'st thy flight.

Thames, proud of thee, and of his fate
  In entertaining late
  The choice of Europe's pride;
   The nimble French;
The Dutch whom wealth (not hatred) doth divide;
   The Danes that drench
  Their cares in wine; with sure
Though slower Spain; and Italy mature.

All which, when they but hear a strain
90   Of thine, shall think the main
  Hath sent her mermaids in,
   To hold them here:
Yet, looking in thy face, they shall begin
   To lose that fear;
  And (in the place) envy
So black a bird, so bright a quality.

But should they know (as I) that this,
  Who warbleth *Pancharis*,
  Were Cycnus, once high flying
100   With Cupid's wing;
Though, now by love transformed, and daily dying:
   (Which makes him sing
  With more delight, and grace)
Or thought they, Leda's white adulterer's place

Among the stars should be resigned
　　To him, and he there shrined;
　　Or Thames be rapt from us
　　　　To dim and drown
In Heaven the sign of old Eridanus:
110　　　How they would frown!
　　　But these are mysteries
Concealed from all but clear prophetic eyes.

It is enough, their grief shall know
　　At their return, nor Po,
　　Iberus, Tagus, Rhine,
　　　Scheldt, nor the Maas,
Slow Arar, nor swift Rhone; the Loire, nor Seine,
　　　With all the race
　　　Of Europe's waters can
120　Set out a like, or second to our swan.

XXXIII Ode to Himself

　　　Come leave the loathèd stage,
　　　And the more loathsome age,
Where pride and impudence in faction knit,
　　　Usurp the chair of wit:
Indicting and arraigning every day,
　　　Something they call a play.
　　　Let their fastidious, vain
　　　Commission of the brain,
Run on, and rage, sweat, censure, and condemn:
10　They were not made for thee, less thou for them.

　　　Say that thou pour'st them wheat,
　　　And they would acorns eat:
'Twere simple fury, still thyself to waste
　　　On such as have no taste:
To offer them a surfeit of pure bread,
　　　Whose appetites are dead:
　　　No, give them grains their fill,

      Husks, draff to drink, and swill:
      If they love lees, and leave the lusty wine,
20   Envy them not, their palate's with the swine.

         No doubt a mouldy tale,
         Like Pericles, and stale
      As the shrieve's crust, and nasty as his fish,
         Scraps out of every dish,
      Thrown forth and raked into the common tub,
         May keep up the play club.
         Broome's sweepings do as well
         There, as his master's meal:
      For who the relish of these guests will fit,
30   Needs set them but the alms-basket of wit.

         And much good do it ye then,
         Brave plush and velvet men
      Can feed on orts; and safe in your scene clothes,
         Dare quit upon your oaths
      The stagers, and the stage-wrights too; your peers,
         Of stuffing your large ears
         With rage of comic socks,
         Wrought upon twenty blocks;
      Which, if they're torn, and foul, and patched enough,
40   The gamesters share your gilt, and you their stuff.

         Leave things so prostitute,
         And take the Alcaic lute;
      Or thine own Horace, or Anacreon's lyre;
         Warm thee by Pindar's fire:
      And though thy nerves be shrunk, and blood be cold,
         Ere years have made thee old,
         Strike that disdainful heat
         Throughout, to their defeat:
      As curious fools, and envious of thy strain,
50   May blushing swear, no palsy's in thy brain.

         But when they hear thee sing
         The glories of thy king;
      His zeal to God, and his just awe of men,

They may be blood-shaken, then
Feel such a flesh-quake to possess their powers,
That no tuned harp like ours,
In sound of peace or wars,
Shall truly hit the stars
When they shall read the acts of Charles his reign,
60 And see his chariot triumph 'bove his wain.

XXXIV *Ode*

If men, and times were now
Of that true face
As when they both were great, and both knew how
That fortune to embrace,
By cherishing the spirits that gave their greatness grace:
I then could raise my notes
Loud to the wondering throng
And better blazon them, than all their coats,
That were the happy subject of my song.

10 But, clownish pride hath got
So much the start
Of civil virtue, that he now is not
Nor can be of desert,
That hath not country impudence enough to laugh at art,
Whilst like a blaze of straw,
He dies with an ill scent,
To every sense, and scorn to those that saw
How soon with a self-tickling he was spent.

Break then thy quills, blot out
20 Thy long watched verse
And rather to the fire, than to the rout
Their laboured tunes rehearse,
Whose air will sooner hell, than their dull senses pierce;
Thou that dost spend thy days
To get thee a lean face,

And come forth worthy ivy, or the bays,
And in this age, canst hope no other grace.

Yet since the bright, and wise,
　　Minerva deigns
30 Upon so humbled earth to cast her eyes:
　　We'll rip our richest veins
And once more strike the ear of time with those fresh
　　strains:
　　　As shall besides delight
　　　And cunning of their ground
Give cause to some of wonder, some despite,
But unto more despair to imitate their sound.

Throw, Holy Virgin, then,
　　Thy crystal shield
About this isle, and charm the round, as when
40　　Thou mad'st in open field
The rebel giants stoop, and Gorgon envy yield,
　　　Cause reverence, if not fear,
　　　Throughout their general breasts,
And by their taking, let it once appear
Who worthy win, who not, to be wise Pallas' guests.

Songs from Jonson's Plays

XXXV

Slow, slow, fresh fount, keep time with my salt tears;
　　Yet, slower, yet; O faintly, gentle springs:
List to the heavy part the music bears,
　　Woe weeps out her division, when she sings.
　　　　Droop herbs, and flowers,
　　　　Fall grief in showers,
　　　　Our beauties are not ours:
　　　　　O, I could still,
Like melting snow upon some craggy hill,

10   Drop, drop, drop, drop,
Since nature's pride is, now, a withered daffodil.

(from *Cynthia's Revels*)

XXXVI

O, that joy so soon should waste!
    Or so sweet a bliss
        As a kiss,
Might not forever last!
So sugared, so melting, so soft, so delicious,
    The dew that lies on roses,
    When the morn herself discloses,
        Is not so precious.
O, rather than I would it smother,
10 Were I to taste such another;
        It should be my wishing
        That I might die kissing.

(from *Cynthia's Revels*)

XXXVII

Thou more than most sweet glove,
Unto my more sweet love,
        Suffer me to store, with kisses
        This empty lodging, that now misses
            The pure rosy hand that ware thee,
            Whiter than the kid that bare thee:
Thou art soft, but that was softer;
Cupid's self hath kissed it ofter,
Than e'er he did his mother's doves,
10 Supposing her the queen of loves,
        That was thy mistress,
        Best of gloves.

(from *Cynthia's Revels*)

XXXVIII

Queen and huntress, chaste, and fair,
Now the sun is laid to sleep,
Seated, in thy silver chair,
State in wonted manner keep:
  Hesperus entreats thy light,
  Goddess, excellently bright.

Earth, let not thy envious shade
Dare itself to interpose;
Cynthia's shining orb was made
10 Heaven to clear, when day did close:
  Bless us then with wishèd sight,
  Goddess, excellently bright.

Lay thy bow of pearl apart,
And thy crystal-shining quiver;
Give unto the flying hart
Space to breathe, how short soever:
  Thou, that mak'st a day of night,
  Goddess, excellently bright.

(from *Cynthia's Revels*)

XXXIX

If I freely may discover
What would please me in my lover,
I would have her fair, and witty,
Savouring more of court, than city;
A little proud, but full of pity:
Light and humourous in her toying,
Oft building hopes, and soon destroying,
Long, but sweet in the enjoying;
Neither too easy, nor too hard:
10 All extremes I would have barred . . .
She should be allowed her passions,

So they were but used as fashions;
Sometimes froward, and then frowning,
Sometimes sickish and then swowning,
Every fit, with change, still crowning.
Purely jealous, I would have her,
Then only constant when I crave her:
'Tis a virtue should not save her.
Thus, nor her delicates would cloy me,
20 Neither her peevishness annoy me.

(from *Poetaster*)

XL

Swell me a bowl with lusty wine,
Till I may see the plump Lyaeus swim
            Above the brim:
I drink as I would write,
In flowing measure filled with flame and sprite.

(from *Poetaster*)

XLI

Love is blind, and a wanton;
In the whole world, there is scant one
            Such another:
            No, not his mother.
He hath plucked her doves, and sparrows,
To feather his sharp arrows,
            And alone prevaileth,
            While sick Venus waileth.
But if Cypris once recover
10 The wag; it shall behove her
            To look better to him;
            Or she will undo him.

(from *Poetaster*)

XLII

Blush, folly, blush: here's none that fears
The wagging of an ass's ears,
Although a wolvish case he wears.
Detraction is but baseness' varlet;
And apes are apes, though clothed in scarlet.

(from *Poetaster*)

XLIII

ALBIUS
Wake! Our mirth begins to die;
    Quicken it with tunes and wine.
Raise your notes; you're out; fie, fie!
      This drowsiness is an ill sign.
      We banish him the choir of gods,
        That droops again:
        Then all are men,
    For here's not one but nods. . . .

HERMOGENES
Then, in a free and lofty strain,
10   Our broken tunes we thus repair;

CRISPINUS
And we answer them again,
    Running division on the panting air;

BOTH
      To celebrate this feast of sense,
      As free from scandal as offence.

HERMOGENES
Here is beauty for the eye;

CRISPINUS
For the ear sweet melody;

HERMOGENES
Ambrosiac odours, for the smell;

CRISPINUS
Delicious nectar, for the taste;

BOTH
For the touch, a lady's waist;
20 Which doth all the rest excel.

(from *Poetaster*)

XLIV

Fools, they are the only nation
Worth men's envy, or admiration;
Free from care, or sorrow-taking,
Selves, and others merry making:
All they speak, or do, is sterling.
Your fool, he is your great man's darling,
And your lady's sport and pleasure;
Tongue and bauble are his treasure.
E'en his face begetteth laughter,
10 And he speaks truth free from slaughter;
He's the grace of every feast,
And, sometimes, the chiefest guest;
Hath his trencher, and his stool,
When wit waits upon the fool.
      O, who would not be
      He, he, he?

(from *Volpone*)

XLV

Had old Hippocrates, or Galen,
(That to their books put medicines all in)
But known this secret, they had never

    (Of which they will be guilty ever)
    Been murderers of so much paper,
    Or wasted many a hurtless taper:
    No Indian drug had e'er been famed,
    Tobacco, sassafras not named;
    Nor yet, of guacum one small stick, sir,
10 Nor Raymond Lully's great elixir.
    Ne had been known the Danish gonswort.
    Or Paracelsus, with his long-sword.

    (from *Volpone*)

XLVI

    You that would last long, list to my song,
    Make no more coil, but buy of this oil.
    Would you be ever fair and young?
    Stout of teeth and strong of tongue?
    Tart of palate, quick of ear?
    Sharp of sight, of nostril clear?
    Moist of hand and light of foot?
    (Or, I will come nearer to it)
    Would you live free from all diseases?
10 Do the act your mistress pleases;
    Yet fright all aches from your bones?
    Here's a medicine, for the nones.

    (from *Volpone*)

XLVII

    Still to be neat, still to be dressed,
    As you were going to a feast;
    Still to be powdered, still perfumed:
    Lady, it is to be presumed,
    Though art's hid causes are not found,
    All is not sweet, all is not sound.

Give me a look, give me a face,
That makes simplicity a grace;
Robes loosely flowing, hair as free:
10 Such sweet neglect more taketh me,
Than all the adulteries of art;
They strike mine eyes, but not my heart.

(from *Epicoene*)

XLVIII

Modest, and fair, for fair and good are near
     Neighbours, howe'er.
No noble virtue ever was alone,
     But two in one.
Then, when I praise sweet modesty, I praise
     Bright beauty's rays:
And having praised both beauty and modesty,
     I have praised thee.
Silence in woman, is like speech in man,
10   Deny it who can.
     Nor, is it a tale,
That female vice should be a virtue male,
Or masculine vice, a female virtue be:
     You shall it see
     Proved with increase,
I know to speak, and she to hold her peace.

(from *Epicoene*)

XLIX

My masters and friends, and good people draw near,
And look to your purses, for that I do say;
And though little money, in them you do bear,
It cost more to get, than to lose in a day.
     You oft have been told,

Both the young and the old;
And bidden beware of the cutpurse so bold;
Then if you take heed not, free me from the curse,
Who both give you warning for, and the cutpurse.
10 Youth, youth, thou hadst better been starved by thy nurse
Than live to be hanged for cutting a purse.

It hath been upbraided to men of my trade,
That oftentimes we are the cause of this crime.
Alack and for pity, why should it be said?
As if they regarded or places, or time.
      Examples have been
      Of some that were seen,
      In Westminster Hall, yea the pleaders between:
Then why should the judges be free from this curse,
20 More than my poor self, for cutting the purse?
Youth, youth, thou hadst better been starved by thy nurse,
Than live to be hanged for cutting a purse.

At Worcester 'tis known well, and even i' the gaol,
A knight of good worship did there show his face,
Against the foul sinners, in zeal for to rail.
And lost (*ipso facto*) his purse in the place.
      Nay, once from the seat
      Of judgment so great,
      A judge there did lose a fair pouch of velvet.
30 O Lord for thy mercy, how wicked or worse,
Are those that so venture their necks for a purse!
Youth, youth, thou hadst better be starved by thy nurse,
Than live to be hanged for cutting a purse.

At plays and at sermons, and at the sessions,
'Tis daily their practice such booty to make:
Yea, under the gallows, at executions,
They stick not the stareabouts' purses to take.
      Nay one without grace,
      At a far better place,
40   At court and in Christmas, before the King's face.
Alack then for pity, must I bear the curse,
That only belongs to the cunning cutpurse?

But O, you vile nation of cutpurses all,
Relent and repent, and amend and be sound,
And know that you ought not, by honest men's fall,
Advance your own fortunes, to die above ground,
   And though you go gay,
   In silks as you may,
   It is not the high way to heaven (as they say)
50 Repent then, repent you, for better, for worse:
And kiss not the gallows for cutting a purse.
Youth, youth, thou hadst better been starved by thy nurse,
Than live to be hanged for cutting a purse.

(from *Bartholomew Fair*)

L

It was a beauty that I saw,
So pure, so perfect, as the frame
Of all the universe was lame,
To that one figure, could I draw,
Or give least line of it a law!

A skein of silk without a knot,
A fair march made without a halt,
A curious form without a fault,
A printed book without a blot,
10 All beauty, and without a spot!

(from *The New Inn*)

LI

Though I am young, and cannot tell,
Either what Death or Love is, well,
Yet I have heard they both bear darts,
And both do aim at human hearts:
And then again, I have been told,

Love wounds with heat, as Death with cold;
So that I fear they do but bring
Extremes to touch, and mean one thing.

As in a ruin we it call
10 One thing to be blown up, or fall;
Or to our end, like way may have,
By flash of lightning, or a wave:
So Love's inflamèd shaft, or brand,
May kill as soon as Death's cold hand;
Except Love's fires the virtue have
To fright the frost out of the grave.

(from *The Sad Shepherd*)

*Songs from Jonson's Masques
and Entertainments*

LII

Sound, sound aloud
The welcome of the orient flood
Into the west;
Fair Niger, son to great Oceanus,
Now honoured thus,
With all his beauteous race,
Who, though but black in face,
Yet are they bright,
And full of life and light,
10 To prove that beauty best
Which not the colour but the feature
Assures unto the creature.

(from *The Masque of Blackness*)

LIII

Daughters of the subtle flood,
   Do not let earth longer entertain you.
1 ECHO Let earth longer entertain you.
2 ECHO Longer entertain you.
   'Tis to them enough of good
That you give this little hope to gain you.
1 ECHO Give this little hope to gain you.
2 ECHO Little hope to gain you.
   If thy love,
10   You shall quickly see;
   For when to flight you move,
They'll follow you, the more you flee.
1 ECHO Follow you, the more you flee.
2 ECHO The more you flee.
   If not, impute it each to other's matter;
They are but earth –
1 ECHO   But earth,
2 ECHO   Earth –
   And what you vowed was water.
20 1 ECHO And what you vowed was water.
    2 ECHO   You vowed was water.

(from *The Masque of Blackness*)

LIV

Now Dian, with her burning face,
   Declines apace,
  By which our waters know
  To ebb, that late did flow.
Back seas, back nymphs; but with a forward grace
   Keep, still, your reverence to the place;
And shout with joy of favour you have won
   In sight of Albion, Neptune's son.

(from *The Masque of Blackness*)

LV

When Love at first did move
From out of Chaos, brightened
So was the world, and lightened
As now!
1 ECHO As now!
2 ECHO   As now!
Yield, night, then, to the light,
As blackness hath to beauty,
Which is but the same duty.
It was for Beauty that the world was made,
And where she reigns, Love's lights admit no shade.
10 1 ECHO Love's lights admit no shade.
2 ECHO Admit no shade.

(from *The Masque of Beauty*)

LVI

So beauty on the waters stood
When Love had severed earth from flood!
So when he parted air from fire,
He did with concord all inspire!
And then a motion he them taught
That elder than himself was thought,
Which thought was, yet, the child of earth,
For Love is elder than his birth.

(from *The Masque of Beauty*)

LVII

If all these Cupids now were blind,
    As is their wanton brother,
Or play should put it in their mind
    To shoot at one another,

What pretty battle they would make
If they their objects should mistake,
   And each one wound his mother!

It was no polity of court,
   Albe the place were charmèd,
10 To let, in earnest or in sport,
     So many Loves in armèd;
For say the dames should, with their eyes,
Upon the hearts here mean surprise,
   Were not the men like harmèd?

Yes, were the Loves or false or straying,
Or beauties not their beauty weighing;
But here no such deceit is mixed,
Their flames are pure, their eyes are fixed;
They do not war with different darts,
20 But strike a music of like hearts.

(from *The Masque of Beauty*)

LVIII

Had those that dwell in error foul,
And hold that women have no soul,
But seen these move, they would have then
Said women were the souls of men.
   So they do move each heart and eye,
   With the world's soul, true harmony.

(from *The Masque of Beauty*)

LIX

Still turn, and imitate the heaven
   In motion swift and even,
   And as his planets go,
   Your brighter lights do so.

May youth and pleasure ever flow;
　But let your state, the while,
　Be fixèd as the isle.

CHORUS
So all that see your beauty's sphere
May know the Elysian fields are here.

10　1 ECHO The Elysian fields are here.

　2 ECHO Elysian fields are here.

(from *The Masque of Beauty*)

LX

Bid all profane away;
None here may stay
To view our mysteries
But who themselves have been,
Or will in time be seen,
The self-same sacrifice.
For Union, mistress of these rites
Will be observed with eyes
As simple as her nights.

CHORUS
10　Fly then, all profane, away,
Fly far off, as hath the day;
Night her curtain doth display,
And this is Hymen's holiday.

(from *Masque of Hymen*)

LXI

These, these are they,
Whom humour and affection must obey;
Who come to deck the genial bower,

And bring with them the grateful hour
That crowns such meetings, and excites
The married pair to fresh delights,
As courtings, kissings, coyings, oaths and vows,
Soft whisperings, embracements, all the joys
And melting toys
10   That chaster love allows.

CHORUS
Haste, haste, for Hesperus his head down bows.

(from *Masque of Hymen*)

LXII

Now, now begin to set
    Your spirits in active heat,
And since your hands are met,
    Instruct your nimble feet,
    In motions swift and meet,
The happy ground to beat:

CHORUS
Whilst all this roof doth ring,
And each discording string
With every varied voice
10   In union doth rejoice.

(from *Masque of Hymen*)

LXIII

Think yet how night doth waste,
    How much of time is past,
What more than wingèd haste
    Yourselves would take
If you were but to taste
The joy the night doth cast

(O might it ever last)
On this bright virgin, and her happy make.

(from *Masque of Hymen*)

LXIV

O know to end, as to begin;
A minute's loss in love is sin.
These humours will the night outwear
In their own pastimes here;
You do our rites much wrong
In seeking to prolong
These outward pleasures:
The night hath other treasures
Than these, though long concealed,
10   Ere day to be revealed.
Then know to end, as to begin;
A minute's loss in love is sin.

(from *Masque of Hymen*)

LXV *Epithalamion*

Glad time is at his point arrived,
For which love's hopes were so long-lived.
   Lead, Hymen, lead away;
   And let no object stay,
   Nor banquets, but sweet kisses,
   The turtles from their blisses.
   'Tis Cupid calls to arm;
   And this his last alarm.

Shrink not, soft virgin, you will love
10   Anon, what you so fear to prove.
   This is no killing war,
   To which you pressèd are;
   But fair and gentle strife
   Which lovers call their life.

'Tis Cupid cries to arm;
And this his last alarm.

Help, youths and virgins, help to sing
The prize, which Hymen here doth bring.
   And did so lately rap
20   From forth the mother's lap,
   To place her by that side
   Where she must long abide.
   On Hymen, Hymen call,
   This night is Hymen's all.

See! Hesperus is yet in view.
What star can so deserve of you?
   Whose light doth still adorn
   Your bride, that ere the morn,
   Shall far more perfect be,
30   And rise as bright as he;
   When, like to him, her name
   Is changed, but not her flame.

Haste, tender lady, and adventure;
The covetous house would have you enter,
   That it might wealthy be,
   And you, her mistress, see:
   Haste your own good to meet;
   And lift your golden feet
   Above the threshold high,
40   With prosperous augury.

Now, youths, let go your pretty arms;
The place within chants other charms.
   Whole showers of roses flow;
   And violets seem to grow,
   Strewed in the chamber there,
   As Venus' mead it were.
   On Hymen, Hymen call,
   This night is Hymen's all.

Good matrons, that so well are known
50   To agèd husbands of your own,
      Place you our bride tonight;
      And snatch away the light:
      That she not hide it dead
      Beneath her spouse's bed;
      Nor he reserve the same
      To help the funeral flame.

So! Now you may admit him in;
The act he covets is no sin,
      But chaste and holy love,
60   Which Hymen doth approve:
      Without whose hallowing fires
      All aims are base desires.
      On Hymen, Hymen call,
      This night is Hymen's all.

Now free from vulgar spite or noise,
May you enjoy your mutual joys;
      Now, you no fear controls,
      But lips may mingle souls;
      And soft embraces bind
70   To each the other's mind,
      Which may no power untie,
      Till one or both must die!

And look, before you yield to slumber,
That your delights be drawn past number;
      Joys, got with strife, increase.
      Affect no sleepy peace;
      But keep the bride's fair eyes
      Awake with her own cries,
      Which are but maiden fears:
80   And kisses dry such tears.

Then coin them 'twixt your lips so sweet,
And let not cockles closer meet;
      Nor may your murmuring loves
      Be drowned by Cypris' doves:

Let ivy not so bind
As when your arms are twined:
That you may both ere day
Rise perfect every way.

And, Juno, whose great powers protect
90 The marriage-bed, with good effect
The labour of this night
Bless thou for future light:
And thou, thy happy charge,
Glad Genius, enlarge;
That they may both ere day
Rise perfect every way,

And Venus, thou, with timely seed,
Which may their after-comforts breed,
Inform the gentle womb;
100 Nor let it prove a tomb:
But ere ten moons be wasted,
The birth by Cynthia hasted.
So may they both ere day
Rise perfect every way.

And when the babe to light is shown,
Let it be like each parent known;
Much of the father's face,
More of the mother's grace;
And either grandsire's spirit
110 And fame let it inherit.
That men may bless the embraces
That joinèd two such races.

Cease, youths and virgins, you have done;
Shut fast the door: and as they soon
To their perfection haste,
So may their ardours last.
So either's strength outlive
All loss that age can give:

And though full years be told,
120 Their forms grow slowly old.

(from *Masque of Hymen*)

LXVI *Epithalamion*

Up, youths and virgins, up, and praise
The god whose nights outshine his days;
   Hymen, whose hallowed rites
Could never boast of brighter lights;
   Whose bands pass liberty.
Two of your troop, that with the morn were free,
   Are now waged to his war.
     And what they are,
   If you'll perfection see,
10   Yourselves must be.
Shine, Hesperus, shine forth, thou wishèd star!

What joy or honours can compare
With holy nuptials, when they are
   Made out of equal parts
Of years, of states, of hands, of hearts!
   When in the happy choice
The spouse and spousèd have the foremost voice!
   Such, glad of Hymen's war,
     Live what they are,
20   And long perfection see:
     And such ours be.
Shine, Hesperus, shine forth, thou wishèd star!

The solemn state of this one night
Were fit to last an age's light;
   But there are rites behind
Have less of state, but more of kind:
   Love's wealthy crop of kisses,
And fruitful harvest of his mother's blisses.
   Sound then to Hymen's war:

30   That what these are,
            Who will perfection see,
                May haste to be.
        Shine, Hesperus, shine forth, thou wishèd star!

        Love's commonwealth consists of toys;
        His council are those antic boys,
            Games, laughter, sports, delights,
        That triumph with him on these nights;
            To whom we must give way,
        For now their reign begins, and lasts till day.
40   They sweeten Hymen's war,
                And in that jar,
            Make all that married be
                Perfection see.
        Shine, Hesperus, shine forth, thou wishèd star!

        Why stays the bridegroom to invade
        Her that would be a matron made?
            Goodnight whilst yet we may
        Goodnight to you a virgin say:
            Tomorrow rise the same
50   Your mother is, and use a nobler name.
            Speed well in Hymen's war,
                That, what you are,
            By your perfection we
                And all may see.
        Shine, Hesperus, shine forth, thou wishèd star!

        Tonight is Venus' vigil kept,
        This night no bridegroom ever slept;
            And if the fair bride do,
        The married say, 'tis his fault too.
60   Wake then, and let your lights
        Wake too; for they'll tell nothing of your nights,
            But that in Hymen's war
                You perfect are.
            And such perfection we
                Do pray should be.
        Shine, Hesperus, shine forth, thou wishèd star!

That ere the rosy-fingered morn
Behold nine moons, there may be born
    A babe, to uphold the fame
70 Of Ratcliffe's blood and Ramsey's name:
       That may, in his great seed,
Wear the long honours of his father's deed.
    Such fruits of Hymen's war
      Most perfect are;
    And all perfection we
      Wish you should see.
Shine, Hesperus, shine forth, thou wishèd star!

(from *The Haddington Masque*)

LXVII *Charm*

The owl is abroad, the bat, and the toad,
    And so is the cat-a-mountain,
The ant, and the mole sit both in a hole,
    The frog peeps out of the fountain;
The dogs, they do bay, and the timbrels play,
    The spindle is now a-turning;
The moon it is red, and the stars are fled,
    But all the sky is a-burning:
The ditch is made, and our nails the spade,
10 With pictures full, of wax, and of wool;
Their livers I stick, with needles quick;
There lacks but the blood, to make up the flood.
    Quickly, dame, then bring your part in,
Spur, spur, upon little Martin,
Merrily, merrily, make him sail,
A worm in his mouth, and a thorn in his tail,
Fire above, and fire below,
With a whip in your hand, to make him go.
      O, now she's come!
'20   Let all be dumb.

(from *The Masque of Queens*)

LXVIII

Help, help all tongues to celebrate this wonder:
The voice of Fame should be as loud as thunder.
    Her house is all of echo made
      Where never dies the sound,
    And as her brows the clouds invade,
      Her feet do strike the ground.
Sing then good Fame that's out of Virtue born,
For who doth Fame neglect doth Virtue scorn.

(from *The Masque of Queens*)

LXIX

Who, Virtue, can thy power forget
That sees these live and triumph yet?
The Assyrian pomp, the Persian pride,
Greeks' glory, and the Romans', died;
    And who yet imitate
Their noises, tarry the same fate.
    Force greatness all the glorious ways
      You can, it soon decays,
    But so good Fame shall never:
10 Her triumphs, as their causes, are forever.

(from *The Masque of Queens*)

LXX

Buzz, quoth the blue-fly,
  Hum, quoth the bee;
Buzz and hum they cry,
  And so do we.
In his ear, in his nose,
  Thus, do you see?

He ate the dormouse,
  Else it was he.

(from *Oberon*)

LXXI

Now, my cunning lady moon,
Can you leave the side so soon
  Of the boy you keep so hid?
Midwife Juno sure will say
This is not the proper way
  Of your paleness to be rid.
But perhaps it is your grace
To wear sickness in your face,
  That there might be wagers laid
10 Still, by fools, you are a maid.

Come, your changes overthrow
What your look would carry so;
  Moon, confess then what you are.
And be wise, and free to use
Pleasures that you now do lose:
  Let us satyrs have a share.
Though our forms be rough and rude,
Yet our acts may be endued
  With more virtue: everyone
20 Cannot be Endymion.

(from *Oberon*)

LXXII

Melt earth to sea, sea flow to air,
  And air fly into fire,
Whilst we in tunes to Arthur's chair
  Bear Oberon's desire,

Than which there nothing can be higher,
Save James, to whom it flies:
But he the wonder is of tongues, of ears, of eyes.

Who hath not heard, who hath not seen,
    Who hath not sung his name?
10 The soul that hath not, hath not been;
      But is the very same
      With buried sloth, and knows not fame;
Which doth him best comprise:
For he the wonder is of tongues, of ears, of eyes.

(from *Oberon*)

LXXIII

The solemn rites are well begun,
    And though but lighted by the moon,
They show as rich as if the sun
    Had made this night his noon.
But may none wonder that they are so bright;
The moon now borrows from a greater light.
    Then, princely Oberon,
    Go on,
This is not every night.

(from *Oberon*)

LXXIV

Nay, nay,
You must not stay,
Nor be weary yet;
This is no time to cast away,
Or for fays so to forget
The virtue of their feet.
Knotty legs and plants of clay

Seek for ease, or love delay,
But with you it still should fare
10 As with the air of which you are.

(from *Oberon*)

LXXV

1 FAY
Nor yet, nor yet, O you in this night blessed,
Must you have will or hope to rest.

2 FAY
If you use the smallest stay,
You'll be overta'en by day.

1 FAY
And these beauties will suspect
That their forms you do neglect

2 FAY
If you do not call them forth.
Or that you have no more worth
Than the coarse and country fairy
10 That doth haunt the hearth or dairy.

(from *Oberon*)

LXXVI

Gentle knights,
Know some measure of your nights.
Tell the high-graced Oberon
It is time that we were gone.
Here be forms so bright and airy,
And their motions so they vary
As they will enchant the fairy,
If you longer here should tarry.

(from *Oberon*)

LXXVII

O yet how early, and before her time,
The envious morning up doth climb,
   Though she not love her bed!
What haste the jealous sun doth make
His fiery horses up to take,
   And once more show his head!
Lest, taken with the brightness of this night,
The world should wish it last, and never miss his light.

(from *Oberon*)

LXXVIII

Gentle Love, be not dismayed.
  See the muses, pure and holy,
  By their priests have sent thee aid
  Against this brood of folly.
It is true that Sphinx, their dame,
  Had the sense first from the muses,
  Which in uttering she doth lame,
  Perplexeth, and abuses.
But they bid that thou should'st look
10 In the brightest face here shining,
  And the same, as would a book,
  Shall help thee in divining.

(from *Love Freed from Ignorance and Folly*)

LXXIX

A crown, a crown for Love's bright head,
  Without whose happy wit
All form and beauty had been dead,
  And we had died with it.

For what are all the graces
Without good forms and faces?
        Then, Love, receive the due reward
        Those Graces have prepared.

CHORUS
And may no hand, no tongue, no eye,
10 Thy merit, or their thanks envy.

(from *Love Freed from Ignorance and Folly*)

LXXX

What just excuse had agèd Time,
        His weary limbs now to have eased,
And sat him down without his crime,
        While every thought was so much pleased!
For he so greedy to devour
        His own, and all that he brings forth,
Is eating every piece of hour
        Some object of the rarest worth.
Yet this is rescued from his rage,
10   As not to die by time or age.
        For beauty hath a living name
        And will to heaven, from whence it came.

(from *Love Freed from Ignorance and Folly*)

LXXXI

O how came Love, that is himself a fire,
        To be so cold!
Yes, tyran' money quencheth all desire,
        Or makes it old.
  But here are beauties will revive
  Love's youth and keep his heat alive:
        As often as his torch here dies,
        He needs but light it at fresh eyes.

Joy, joy the more; for in all courts
10   If Love be cold, so are his sports.

(from *Love Restored*)

LXXXII

This motion was of love begot
    It was so airy, light and good,
His wings into their feet he shot,
    Or else himself into their blood.
But ask not how. The end will prove
That love's in them, or they're in love.

(from *Love Restored*)

LXXXIII

Have men beheld the graces dance,
    Or seen the upper orbs to move?
So did these turn, return, advance,
    Drawn back by doubt, put on by love.
And now, like earth, themselves they fix,
Till greater powers vouchsafe to mix
    Their motions with them. Do not fear,
    You brighter planets of this sphere;
        Not one male heart you see
10   But rather to his female eyes
            Would die a destined sacrifice
            Than live at home and free.

(from *Love Restored*)

LXXXIV

Give end unto thy pastimes, Love,
    Before thy labours prove:

A little rest between
Will make thy next shows better seen.
    Now let them close their eyes, and see
    If they can dream of thee,
Since morning hastes to come in view;
And all the morning dreams are true.

(from *Love Restored*)

LXXXV

Bow both your heads at once, and hearts;
    Obedience doth not well in parts.
It is but standing in his eye,
    You'll feel yourselves changed by and by.
Few live that know how quick a spring
    Works in the presence of a king:
'Tis done by this; your slough let fall,
    And come forth new-born creatures all.

(from *The Irish Masque*)

LXXXVI

So breaks the sun earth's rugged chains,
    Wherein rude winter bound her veins;
So grows both stream and source of price,
    That lately fettered were with ice.
So naked trees get crispèd heads,
    And coloured coats the roughest meads,
And all get vigour, youth, and spright,
    That are but looked on by his light.

(from *The Irish Masque*)

LXXXVII

Soft, subtle fire, thou soul of art,
    Now do thy part
On weaker nature, that through age is lamed.
    Take but thy time, now she is old,
    And the sun her friend grown cold,
She will no more, in strife with thee be named.

Look, but how few confess her now,
    In cheek or brow!
From every head, almost, how she is frighted!
10   That very age abhors her so,
    That it learns to speak and go
As if by art alone it could be righted.

(from *Mercury Vindicated*)

LXXXVIII

NATURE
    How young and fresh am I tonight,
    To see it kept day by so much light,
And twelve my sons stand in their maker's sight!
    Help, wise Prometheus, something must be done,
    To show they are the creatures of the sun;
        That each to other
        Is a brother,
And Nature here no step-dame, but a mother.

CHORUS
Come forth, come forth, prove all the numbers then,
10 That make perfection up, and may absolve you men.

NATURE
    But show thy winding ways and arts,
    Thy risings and thy timely starts,
Of stealing fire from ladies' eyes and hearts.
    Those softer circles are the young man's heaven,

And there more orbs and planets are than seven,
>To know whose motion
>Were a notion
As worthy of youth's study as devotion.

CHORUS
Come forth, come forth, prove all the time will gain,
20 For Nature bids the best, and never bade in vain.

(from *Mercury Vindicated*)

LXXXIX

Hum drum, sauce for a cony;
>No more of your martial music;
Even for the sake of the next new stake,
>For there I do mean to use it.

And now to ye, who in place are to see,
>With roll and farthingale hoopèd:
I pray you know, though he want his bow,
>By the wings that this is Cupid.

He might go back, for to cry 'What you lack?'
10 >But that were not so witty:
His cap and coat are enough to note,
>That he is the Love of the city.

And he leads on, though he now be gone,
>For that was only his rule:
But now comes in Tom of Bosom's Inn,
>And he presenteth misrule.

Which you may know by the very show,
>Albeit you never ask it:
For there you may see what his ensigns be,
20 >The rope, the cheese, and the basket.

This carol plays, and has been in his days
>A chirping boy and a kill-pot;

Kit–cobbler it is, I'm a father of his,
 And he dwells in the lane called Fill-pot.

But who is this? O, my daughter Cis
 Mince-pie; with her do not dally
On pain of your life: she's an honest cook's wife,
 And comes out of Scalding Alley.

Next in the trace comes Gambol in place;
30 And to make my tale the shorter,
My son Hercules, ta'en out of Distaff Lane,
 But an active man and a porter.

Now Post and Pair, old Christmas' heir,
 Doth make and a jingling sally;
And wot you who, 'tis one of my two
 Sons, card-makers in Pur Alley.

Next in a trice, with his box and his dice,
 MacPippin my son, but younger,
Brings Mumming in; and the knave will win,
40 For he is a costermonger.

But New Year's Gift of himself makes shift
 To tell you what his name is:
With orange on head and his gingerbread,
 Clem Wasp of Honey Lane 'tis.

This I tell you is our jolly wassail,
 And for Twelfth Night more meet, too:
She works by the ell, and her name is Nell,
 And she dwells in Threadneedle Street, too.

Then Offering, he, with his dish and his tree,
50 That in every great house keepeth,
Is by my son, young Littleworth, done,
 And in Penny-rich Street he sleepeth.

Last, Baby-cake, that an end doth make
 Of Christmas' merry, merry vein-a,
Is Child Rowlan, and a straight young man,
 Though he come out of Crooked Lane-a.

There should have been, and a dozen I ween,
   But I could find but one more
Child of Christmas, and a log it was,
60   When I them all had gone o'er.

I prayed him, in a time so trim,
   That he would make one to prance it:
And I myself would have been the twelfth,
   O, but Log was too heavy to dance it.

(from *Christmas His Masque*)

XC

Nor do you think that their legs is all
   The commendation of my sons,
For at the Artillery Garden they shall
   As well forsooth use their guns.

And march as fine as the muses nine,
   Along the streets of London:
And in their brave tires, to give their false fires,
   Especially Tom my son.

Now if the lanes and the alleys afford
10   Such an ac-ativity as this;
At Christmas next, if they keep their word,
   Can the children of Cheapside miss?

Though put the case, when they come in place,
   They should not dance, but hop;
Their very gold lace with their silk would'em grace,
   Having so many knights of the shop.

But were I so wise I might seem to advise
   So great a potentate as yourself,
They should, sir, I tell ye, spare it out of their belly,
20   And this way spend some of their pelf.

Aye, and come to the court for to make you some sport,
   At the least once every year:

As Christmas hath done, with his seventh or eighth son,
   And his couple of daughters dear.

(from *Christmas His Masque*)

XCI

Break, Fant'sy, from thy cave of cloud
   And spread thy purple wings;
Now all thy figures are allowed,
   And various shapes of things;
Create of airy forms a stream;
   It must have blood and nought of phlegm,
And though it be a waking dream,
     Yet let it like an odour rise
      To all the senses here,
10   And fall like sleep upon their eyes,
      Or music in their ear.

(from *The Vision of Delight*)

XCII Hymn

Room, room, make room for the bouncing belly,
First father of sauce, and deviser of jelly,
Prime master of arts, and the giver of wit,
That found out the excellent engine, the spit,
The plough, and the flail, the mill, and the hopper,
The hutch, and the boulter, the furnace, and copper,
The oven, the bavin, the mawkin, the peel,
The hearth, and the range, the dog and the wheel,
He, he first invented the hogshead and tun,
10 The gimlet and vice too, and taught 'em to run.
And since, with the funnel, an Hippocras bag
He's made of himself, that now he cries swag.
Which shows, though the pleasure be but of four inches,
Yet he is a weasel, the gullet that pinches,
Of any delight, and not spares from the back

Whatever to make of the belly a sack.
Hail, hail, plump paunch, O the founder of taste
For fresh meats, or powdered, or pickle, or paste;
Devourer of broiled, baked, roasted or sod,
20 And emptier of cups, be they even or odd;
All which have now made thee so wide in the waist
As scarce with no pudding thou art to be laced;
But eating and drinking until thou dost nod,
Thou break'st all thy girdles, and break'st forth a god.

(from *Pleasure Reconciled to Virtue*)

XCIII

Come on, come on! And where you go,
    So interweave the curious knot,
As even the observer scarce may know
    Which lines are Pleasure's, and which not.

First figure out the doubtful way,
    At which awhile all youth should stay,
Where she and Virtue did contend,
    Which should have Hercules to friend.

Then, as all actions of mankind
10   Are but a labyrinth or maze:
So let your dances be entwined,
    Yet not perplex men unto gaze.

But measured, and so numerous too,
    As men may read each act you do;
And when they see the graces meet
    Admire the wisdom of your feet.

For dancing is an exercise,
    Not only shows the mover's wit,
But maketh the beholder wise,
20   As he hath power to rise to it.

(from *Pleasure Reconciled to Virtue*)

XCIV

It follows now you are to prove
    The subtlest maze of all, that's love,
        And if you stay too long,
        The fair will think you do 'em wrong.

Go choose among – but with a mind
    As gentle as the stroking wind
        Runs o'er the gentler flowers.

And so let all your actions smile
    As if they meant not to beguile
10   The ladies, but the hours.

Grace, laughter and discourse may meet,
    And yet the beauty not go less:
For what is noble should be sweet,
    But not dissolved in wantonness.

Will you that I give the law
    To all your sport, and sum it?
It should be such should envy draw,
    But ever overcome it.

(from *Pleasure Reconciled to Virtue*)

XCV

An eye of looking back were well,
    Or any murmur that would tell
        Your thoughts, how you were sent
        And went,
To walk with pleasure, not to dwell.
These, these are hours by virtue spared
Herself, she being her own reward,
        But she will have you know
        That though
10 Her sports be soft, her life is hard.

You must return unto the hill,
And there advance
With labour, and inhabit still
That height and crown
From whence you ever may look down
Upon triumphèd Chance.
She, she it is, in darkness shines.
'Tis she that still herself refines,
By her own light, to every eye
20 More seen, more known when vice stands by.
And though a stranger here on earth,
In heaven she hath her right of birth.
There, there is virtue's seat,
Strive to keep her your own;
'Tis only she can make you great,
Though place here make you known.

(from *Pleasure Reconciled to Virtue*)

XCVI

Howe'er the brightness may amaze,
Move you, and stand not still at gaze,
As dazzled with the light:
But with your motions fill the place,
And let their fulness win your grace,
Till you collect your sight.

So while the warmth you do confess,
And temper of these rays, no less,
To quicken than refine,
10 You may by knowledge grow more bold,
And so more able to behold
The body whence they shine.

(from *News from the New World*)

XCVII

Now look and see in yonder throne,
How all those beams are cast from one!
    This is that orb so bright,
Has kept your wonder so awake;
Whence you as from a mirror take
    The sun's reflected light.

Read him as you would do the book
Of all perfection, and but look
    What his proportions be;
10 No measure that is thence contrived,
Or any motion thence derived,
    But is pure harmony.

(from *News from the New World*)

XCVIII

From the famous Peak of Derby,
And the Devil's Arse there hard by,
Where we yearly keep our musters,
Thus the Egyptians throng in clusters.

Be not frighted with our fashion,
Though we seem a tattered nation;
We account our rags our riches,
So our tricks exceed our stitches.

Give us bacon, rinds of walnuts,
10 Shells of cockles, and of small nuts,
Ribands, bells, and saffroned linen,
All the world is ours to win in.

Knacks we have that will delight you,
Slights of hand that will invite you
To endure our tawny faces,
And not cause you cut your laces.

All your fortunes we can tell ye,
Be they for the back or belly:
In the moods too, and the tenses,
20 That may fit your fine five senses.

Draw but then your gloves, we pray you,
And sit still, we will not fray you;
For though we be here at Burleigh,
We'd be loth to make a hurly.

(from *The Gypsies Metamorphosed*)

XCIX

The fairy beam upon you,
The stars to glister on you:
        A moon of light,
        In the noon of night,
Till the fire-drake hath o'er-gone you.

The wheel of fortune guide you,
The boy with the bow beside you
        Run aye in the way,
        Till the bird of day,
10 And the luckier lot betide you.

(from *The Gypsies Metamorphosed*)

C

To the old, long life and treasure;
To the young, all health and pleasure;
        To the fair, their face
        With eternal grace;
And the soul to be loved at leisure.
To the witty, all clear mirrors,
To the foolish, their dark errors;
To the loving sprite,

A secure delight:
10   To the jealous, his own false terrors.

(from *The Gypsies Metamorphosed*)

CI

Cocklorrel woulds needs have the devil his guest,
    And bade him once into the Peak to dinner,
Where never the fiend had such a feast
    Provided him yet at the charge of a sinner.

His stomach was queasy (he came hither coached)
    The jogging had caused some crudities rise;
To help it he called for a puritan poached,
    That used to turn up the eggs of his eyes.

And so recovered unto his wish,
10   He sat him down, and he fell to eat;
Promoter in plum broth was the first dish –
    His own privy kitchen had no such meat.

Yet though with this he much were taken,
    Upon a sudden he shifted his trencher,
As soon as he spied the bawd and the bacon,
    By which you may note the devil's a wencher.

Six pickled tailors sliced and cut,
    Sempsters and tirewomen, fit for his palate;
With feathermen and perfumers put
20   Some twelve in a charger to make a great sallet.

A rich fat usurer stewed in his marrow,
    And by him a lawyer's head and green sauce:
Both which his belly took up like a barrow,
    As if till then he had never seen sauce.

Then carbonadoed and cooked with pains,
    Was brought up a cloven sergeant's face:
The sauce was made of his yeoman's brains,
    That had been beaten out with his own mace.

Two roasted sherriffs came whole to the board;
30   (The feast had been nothing without 'em)
Both living and dead they were foxed and furred,
    Their chains like sausages hung about 'em.

The very next dish was the mayor of a town,
    With a pudding of maintenance thrust in his belly,
Like a goose in the feathers, dressed in his gown,
    And his couple of hinch-boys boiled to a jelly.

A London cuckold hot from the spit,
    And when the carver up had broken him,
The devil chopped up his head at a bit,
40   But the horns were very near like to choke him.

The chine of a lecher too there was roasted,
    With a plump harlot's haunch and garlic,
A pandar's pettitoes, that had boasted
    Himself for a captain, yet never was warlike.

A large fat pasty of a midwife hot;
    And for a cold baked meat into the story,
A reverend painted lady was brought,
    And coffined in crust till now she was hoary.

To these, an over-grown justice of peace,
50   With a clerk like a gizzard trussed under each arm;
And warrants for sippits, laid in his own grease,
    Set over a chafing dish to be kept warm.

The jowl of a gaoler served for fish,
    A constable soused with vinegar by;
Two aldermen lobsters asleep in a dish.
    A deputy tart, a churchwarden pie.

All which devoured, he then for a close
    Did for a full draught of Derby call;
He heaved the huge vessel up to his nose,
60   And left not till he had drunk up all.

Then from the table he gave a start,
    Where banquet and wine were nothing scarce,

All which he flirted away with a fart,
    From whence it was called the Devil's Arse.

(from *The Gypsies Metamorphosed*)

CII Ballad

Though it may seem rude
For me to intrude,
    With these my bears, by chance-a;
'Twere sport for a king,
If they could sing
    As well as they can dance-a.

Then to put you out
Of fear or doubt,
    We came from St Katherine-a;
10 These dancing three,
By the help of me,
    Who am the post of the sign-a.

We sell good ware,
And we need not care
    Though court and country knew it;
Our ale's of the best,
And each good guest
    Prays for the soul that brew it.

For any ale-house,
20 We care not a louse,
    Nor tavern in all the town-a;
Nor the Vintry Cranes,
Nor St Clement Danes,
    Nor the Devil can put us down-a.

Who has once there been,
Comes hither again,
    The liquor is so mighty;
Beer strong and stale,

And so is our ale,
30   And it burns like aqua-vitae.

To a stranger there,
If any appear,
        Where never before he has been:
We show the iron gate,
The wheel of St Kate,
        And the place where the priest fell in.

The wives of Wapping,
They trudge to our tapping,
        And there our ale desire:
40 And they sit and drink,
Till they spew and stink,
        And often piss out our fire.

From morning to night,
And about to daylight,
        They sit, and never grudge it;
Till the fishwives join
Their single coin,
        And the tinker pawns his budget.

If their brains be not well,
50 Or their bladders do swell,
        To ease them of their burden,
My lady will come
With a bowl and a broom,
        And her handmaid with a jordan.

From court we invite
Lord, lady, and knight,
        Squire, gentleman, yeoman, and groom;
And all our stiff drinkers,
Smiths, porters, and tinkers,
60   And the beggars shall give ye room.

(from *The Masque of Augurs*)

CIII

Which way and whence the lightning flew,
Or how it burnèd bright and blue,
Design and figure by your lights;
Then forth, and show the several flights
Your birds have made, or what the wing
Or voice in augury doth bring;
Which hand the crow cried on, how high
The vulture or the erne did fly,
What wing the swan made, and the dove,
10　The stork, and which did get above;
Show all the birds of food or prey,
But pass by the unlucky jay,
The night-crow, swallow, or the kite:
Let those have neither right,

CHORUS

　　　　　　　　　　　nor part

In this night's art.

(from *The Masque of Augurs*)

CIV

PROTEUS
Come, noble nymphs, and do not hide
The joys, for which you so provide:

SARON
If not to mingle with the men,
What do you here? Go home again.

PORTUNUS
　　Your dressings do confess
By what we see, so curious parts
Of Pallas' and Arachne's arts,
　　That you could mean no less.

PROTEUS
Why do you wear the silk-worm's toils,
10 Or glory in the shell-fish spoils,
Or strive to show the grains of ore
That you have gathered on the shore,
    Whereof to make a stock
To graft the greener emerald on,
Or any better-watered stone?

SARON
    Or ruby of the rock?

PROTEUS
Why do you smell of ambergris,
Of which was formèd Neptune's niece,
The queen of love; unless you can,
20 Like sea-born Venus, love a man?

SARON
    Try, put yourselves unto it.

CHORUS
Your looks, your smiles, and thoughts that meet,
Ambrosian hands and silver feet,
    Do promise you will do it.

(from *Neptune's Triumph*)

CV Euclia's Hymn

So Love, emergent out of chaos, brought
    The world to light!
And gently moving on the waters, wrought
    All form to sight!
    Love's appetite
    Did beauty first excite,
  And left imprinted in the air
  Those signatures of good and fair,

CHORUS

Which since have flowed, flowed forth upon the sense,
10   To wonder first, and then to excellence,
By virtue of divine intelligence!

The Ingemination
            And Neptune too
            Shows what his waves can do,
            To call the muses all to play
            And sing the birth of Venus' day,

CHORUS

Which from the sea flowed forth upon the sense,
To wonder first and next to excellence,
By virtue of divine intelligence!

(from *Love's Triumph through Callipolis*)

CVI

ZEPHYRUS

Come forth, come forth, the gentle Spring,
And carry the glad news I bring
        To earth, our common mother:
It is decreed by all the gods
The heaven of earth shall have no odds,
        But one shall love another.

Their glories they shall mutual make,
Earth look on heaven for heaven's sake;
        Their honours shall be even;
10   All emulation cease, and jars;
Jove will have earth to have her stars
        And lights, no less than heaven.

SPRING

It is already done, in flowers
As fresh and new as are the hours,
        By warmth of yonder sun;

But will be multiplied on us
If from the breath of Zephyrus
    Like favour we have won.

ZEPHYRUS
Give all to him: his is the dew,
20 The heat, the humour –

    SPRING

                      All the true –
    Belovèd of the Spring!

ZEPHYRUS
The sun, the wind, the verdure –

SPRING   All
That wisest nature cause can call
    Of quickening anything.

(from *Chloridia*)

Other Miscellaneous Poems

CVII A Song of Welcome to King Charles

Fresh as the day, and new as are the hours,
Our first of fruits, that is the prime of flowers
Bred by your breath, on this low bank of ours;
    Now, in a garland by the graces knit:
    Upon this obelisk, advanced for it,
    We offer as a circle the most fit
To crown the years, which you begin, great king,
And you, with them, as father of our Spring.

CVIII   *A Song of the Moon*

To the wonders of the Peak,
I am come to add, and speak,
Or as some would say to break
  My mind unto you,
And I swear by all the light
At my back, I am no sprite,
But a very merry wight
  Pressed in to see you.

I had somewhat else to say,
10 But have lost it by the way,
I shall think on't ere't be day.
  The moon commends her
To the merry beards in hall,
Those turned up, and those that fall,
Morts, and mirkins that wag all,
  Tough, foul, or tender.

And as either news of mirth
Rise or fall upon the earth
She desires of every birth
20   Some taste to send her.
Specially the news of Derby;
For if there or peace or war be,
To the Peak it is so hard by,
  She soon will hear it.

If there be a cuckold major,
That the wife heads for a wager
As the standard shall engage her,
  The moon will bear it.
Though she change as oft as she,
30 And of circle be as free,
Or her quarters lighter be,
  Yet do not fear it.

Or if any strife betide
For the breeches with the bride,

'Tis but the next neighbour ride
   And she is pleased.
Or if it be the gossips' hap
Each to pawn her husband's cap,
At Pem Walker's good ale tap,
40   Her mind is eased.

Or by chance if in their grease
Or their ale, they break the peace,
Forfeiting their drinking lease,
   She will not seize it.

CIX Proludium

An elegy? No, muse, it asks a strain
Too loose, and cap'ring, for thy stricter vein.
Thy thoughts did never melt in amorous fire
Like glass, blown up, and fashioned by desire.
The skilful mischief of a roving eye
Could ne'er make price of thy white chastity.
Then, leave these lighter numbers, to light brains,
In whom the flame of every beauty reigns,
Such, as in lust's wild forest love to range,
10 Only pursuing constancy, in change.
Let these in wanton feet dance out their souls:
A further fury my raised spirit controls,
Which raps me up to the true heaven of love;
And conjures all my faculties to approve
The glories of it. Now our muse takes wing,
And now an epode, to deep ears, we sing.

CX A Panegyre, on the Happy Entrance of James, Our Sovereign, to His First High Session of Parliament in This Kingdom, the 19 of March, 1603

Heaven now not strives, alone, our breasts to fill
With joys: but urgeth his full favours still.

Again, the glory of our western world
Unfolds himself: and from his eyes are hurled
(Today) a thousand radiant lights, that stream
To every nook and angle of his realm.
His former rays did only clear the sky;
But these his searching beams are cast, to pry
Into those dark and deep concealèd vaults,
10 Where men commit black incest with their faults;
And snore supinely in the stall of sin,
Where murder, rapine, lust, do sit within,
Carousing human blood in iron bowls,
And make their den the slaughter-house of souls:
From whose foul reeking caverns first arise
Those damps, that so offend all good men's eyes;
And would (if not dispersed) infect the crown,
And in their vapour her bright metal drown.
      To this so clear and sanctified an end,
20 I saw, when reverend Themis did descend
Upon his state; let down in that rich chain,
That fasteneth heavenly power to earthly reign:
Beside her, stooped on either hand, a maid,
Fair Dice, and Eunomia; who were said
To be her daughters: and but faintly known
On earth, till now they came to grace his throne.
Her third, Irene, helped to bear his train;
And in her office vowed she would remain,
Till foreign malice, or unnatural spite
30 (Which Fates avert) should force her from her right.
With these he passed, and with his people's hearts
Breathed in his way; and souls (their better parts)
Hasting to follow forth in shouts, and cries;
Upon his face all threw their covetous eyes,
As on a wonder: some amazèd stood,
As if they felt, but had not known their good:
Others would fain have shown it in their words:
But, when their speech so poor a help affords
Unto their zeal's expression; they are mute:
40 And only with red silence him salute.

Some cry from tops of houses; thinking noise
The fittest herald to proclaim true joys:
Others on ground run gazing by his side,
All, as unwearied, as unsatisfied:
And every window grieved it could not move
Along with him, and the same trouble prove.
They that had seen, but four short days before,
His gladding look, now longed to see it more.
And as of late, when he through London went,
50 The amorous city spared no ornament,
That might her beauties heighten; but so dressed,
As our ambitious dames, when they make feast,
And would be courted: so this town put on
Her brightest tire; and, in it, equal shone
To her great sister; save that modesty,
Her place, and years, gave her precedency.
    The joy of either was alike, and full;
No age, nor sex, so weak, or strongly dull,
That did not bear a part in this consent
60 Of hearts and voices. All the air was rent,
As with the murmur of a moving wood;
The ground beneath did seem a moving flood:
Walls, windows, roofs, towers, steeples, all were set
With several eyes, that in this object met.
Old men were glad, their fates till now did last;
And infants, that the hours had made such haste
To bring them forth: whilst riper aged, and apt
To understand the more, the more were rapt.
This was the people's love, with which did strive
70 The nobles' zeal, yet either kept alive
The other's flame, as doth the wick and wax,
That friendly tempered, one pure taper makes.
Meanwhile, the reverend Themis draws aside
The king's obeying will, from taking pride
In these vain stirs, and to his mind suggests
How he may triumph in his subjects' breasts,
With better pomp. She tells him first, that kings
Are here on earth the most conspicious things:

That they, by Heaven, are placed upon his throne,
80 To rule like Heaven; and have no more, their own,
As they are men, than men. That all they do
Though hid at home, abroad is searched into:
And, being once found out, discovered lies
Unto as many envies, there, as eyes.
That princes, since they know it is their fate,
Oft-times, to have the secrets of their state
Betrayed to fame, should take more care, and fear
In public acts what form and face they bear.
She then remembered to his thought the place
90 Where he was going; and the upward race
Of kings, preceding him in that high court;
Their laws, their ends; the men she did report:
And all so justly, as his ear was joyed
To hear the truth, from spite, or flattery void.
She showed him, who made wise, who honest acts;
Who both, who neither: all the cunning tracts,
And thriving statutes she could promptly note;
The bloody, base, and barbarous she did quote;
Where laws were made to serve the tyrant will;
100 Where sleeping they could save, and waking kill;
Where acts gave licence to impetuous lust
To bury churches, in forgotten dust,
And with their ruins raise the pandar's bowers:
When, public justice borrowed all her powers
From private chambers; that could then create
Laws, judges, councillors, yea prince, and state.
All this she told, and more, with bleeding eyes;
For Right is as compassionate as wise.
Nor did he seem their vices so to love,
110 As once defend, what Themis did reprove.
For though by right, and benefit of times,
He owned their crowns, he would not so their crimes.
He knew that princes, who had sold their fame
To their voluptuous lusts, had lost their name;
And that no wretch was more unblessed than he,
Whose necessary good 'twas now to be

An evil king: and so must such be still,
Who once have got the habit to do ill.
One wickedness another must defend;
120 For vice is safe, while she hath vice to friend.
He knew, that those, who would, with love, command,
Must with a tender (yet a steadfast) hand
Sustain the reins, and in the check forbear
To offer cause of injury, or fear.
That kings, by their example, more do sway
Than by their power; and men do more obey
When they are led than when they are compelled.
   In all these knowing arts our prince excelled.
And now the dame had dried her dropping eyne,
130 When, like an April Iris, flew her shine
About the streets, as it would force a spring
From out the stones, to gratulate the king.
She blessed the people, that in shoals did swim
To hear her speech; which still began in him
And ceased in them. She told them, what a fate
Was gently fallen from heaven upon this state;
How dear a father they did now enjoy
That came to save, what discord would destroy:
And entering with the power of a king,
140 The temperance of a private man did bring,
That won affections, ere his steps won ground;
And was not hot, or covetous to be crowned
Before men's hearts had crowned him. Who (unlike
Those greater bodies of the sky, that strike
The lesser fires dim) in his access
Brighter than all, hath yet made no one less;
Though many greater: and the most, the best.
Wherein his choice was happy with the rest
Of his great actions, first to see, and do
150 What all men's wishes did aspire unto.
   Hereat, the people could no longer hold
Their bursting joys; but through the air was rolled
The lengthened shout, as when the artillery
Of heaven is discharged along the sky:

And this confession flew from every voice:
'Never had land more reason to rejoice.
Nor to her bliss, could aught now added be,
Save, that she might the same perpetual see.'
Which when Time, Nature, and the Fates denied,
160   With a twice louder shout again they cried,
'Yet, let blessèd Britain ask (without your wrong)
Still to have such a king, and this king long.'

Solus Rex, et Poeta non quotannis nascitur.

CXI

(a) *Murder*
Those that in blood such violent pleasure have,
Seldom descend but bleeding to their grave.

(b) *Peace*
War's greatest woes, and misery's increase,
Flows from the surfeits which we take in peace.

(c) *The Power of Gold*
Gold is a suitor, never took repulse,
It carries palm with it, (where e'er it goes)
Respect, and observation; it uncovers
The knotty heads of the most surly grooms,
Enforcing iron heads to yield it way,
Were they as strong rammed up as Etna gates.
It bends the hams of Gossip Vigilance,
And makes her supple feet, as swift as wind.
It thaws the frostiest, and most stiff disdain:
10   Muffles the clearness of election,
Strains fancy unto foul apostasy,
And strikes the quickest-sighted judgement blind.
Then why should we despair? Despair away:
Where gold's the motive, women have no nay.

CXII *The Phoenix Analysed*

Now, after all, let no man
   Receive it for a fable,
   If a bird so amiable,
Do turn into a woman.

Or (by our turtle's augur)
   That Nature's fairest creature,
   Prove of his mistress' feature,
But a bare type and figure.

CXIII *Over the Door at the Entrance into the Apollo*

Welcome all that lead or follow,
To the oracle of Apollo –
Here he speaks out of his pottle,
Or the tripos, his tower bottle:
All his answers are divine,
Truth itself doth flow in wine.
Hang up all the poor hop-drinkers,
Cries old Sym, the king of skinkers;
He the half of life abuses,
10 That sits watering with the muses.
Those dull girls no good can mean us,
Wine, it is the milk of Venus,
And the poet's horse accounted:
Ply it, and you all are mounted.
'Tis the true Phoebian liquor,
Cheers the brains, makes wit the quicker,
Pays all debts, cures all diseases,
And at once three senses pleases.
Welcome, all that lead or follow,
20 To the oracle of Apollo.

CXIV *An Epistle to a Friend*

Censure not sharply then, but me advise
Before I write more verse, to be more wise.

So ended your epistle, mine begins,
He that so censureth, or adviseth sins,
The empty carper, scorn, not credit wins.

I have, with strict advantage of free time
O'er-read, examined, tried, and proved your rhyme
As clear, and distant, as yourself from crime;

10   And though your virtue (as becomes it) still
Deigns mine the power to find, yet want I will
Or malice to make faults, which now is skill.

Little know they that prófess amity
And seek to scant her comely liberty,
How much they lame her, in her property:

And less they know, that being free to use
That friendship, which no chance, but love did choose,
Will unto licence, that free leave abuse:

It is an act of tyranny, not love,
20   In course of friendship, wholly to reprove:
And flattery, with friends' humours still to move.

From each of which, I labour to be free,
Yet, if with either's vice, I tainted be,
Forgive it as my frailty, and not me.

For no man lives, so out of passion's sway,
But sometimes shall be tempted to obey
Her fury, though no friendship he betray.

CXV Here Follow Certain Other Verses, as Charms, to Unlock the Mystery of the Crudities

A

Here, like Arion, our Coriat doth draw
   All sorts of fish with music of his maw.

B

Here, not up Holborn, but down a steep hill,
   He's carried 'twixt Montrell and Abbeville.

C

A horse here is saddled, but no Tom him to back,
   It should rather have been Tom that a horse did lack.

D

Here, up the Alps (not so plain as to Dunstable)
   He's carried like a cripple, from constable to constable.

E

A punk here pelts him with eggs. How so?
10   For he did but kiss her, and so let her go.

F

Religiously here he bids, row from the stews,
   He will expiate this sin with converting the Jews.

G

And there, while he gives the zealous bravado,
   A rabbin confutes him with the bastinado.

H

Here, by a boor too, he's like to be beaten
   For grapes he had gathered before they were eaten.

I

Old hat here, torn hose, with shoes full of gravel,
   And louse-dropping case, are the arms of his travel.

K

Here, finer than coming from his punk you him see,
20   F. shows what he was, K. what he will be.

L

Here France, and Italy both to him shed
  Their horns, and Germany pukes on his head.

M

And here he disdained not, in a foreign land
  To lie at livery, while the horses did stand.

N

But here, neither trusting his hands, nor his legs,
  Being in fear to be robbed, he most learnedly begs.

CXVI *Ben Jonson's Grace before King James*

Our royal king and queen, God bless,
The Palsgrave and the Lady Bess;
God bless Pembroke, and the state,
And Buckingham the fortunate;
God bless the council and keep them safe
And God bless me, and God bless Rafe.

CXVII *(To Mr Ben Jonson in His Journey, by Mr Craven)*

When wit, and learning are so hardly set
That from their needful means they must be barred,
Unless by going hard they maintenance get,
Well may Ben Jonson say the world goes hard.

This was Mr Ben Jonson's Answer of the Sudden
Ill may Ben Jonson slander so his feet,
For when the profit with the pain doth meet,
Although the gait were hard, the gain is sweet.

CXVIII An Expostulation with Inigo Jones

Master Surveyor, you that first began
From thirty pound in pipkins, to the man
You are; from them leapt forth an architect,
Able to talk of Euclid, and correct
Both him and Archimede; damn Architas,
The noblest engineer that ever was!
Control Ctesibius: overbearing us
With mistook names out of Vitruvius!
Drawn Aristotle on us! And thence shown
10 How much architectonic is your own !
Whether the building of the stage or scene,
Or making of the properties it mean!
Visors or antics! Or it comprehend
Something your sir-ship doth not yet intend!
By all your titles, and whole style at once
Of tire-man, mountebank and Justice Jones,
I do salute you! Are you fitted yet?
Will any of these express your place or wit?
Or are you so ambitious 'bove your peers
20 You would be an asinigo, by your ears?
Why, much good do it you! Be what beast you will,
You'll be, as Langley said, an Inigo still.
    What makes your wretchedness to bray so loud
In town and court? Are you grown rich and proud?
Your trappings will not change you. Change your mind:
No velvet sheath you wear, will alter kind.
A wooden dagger, is a dagger of wood
Though gold or ivory hafts would make it good.
What is the cause you pomp it so? I ask,
30 And all men echo, you have made a masque.
I chime that too: and I have met with those
That cry up the machine, and the shows!
The majesty of Juno in the clouds,
And peering forth of Iris in the shrouds!
The ascent of Lady Fame which none could spy;
Not they that sided her, Dame Poetry,

Dame History, Dame Architecture too,
And Goody Sculpture, brought with much ado
To hold her up. O shows, shows, mighty shows!
40 The eloquence of masques! What need of prose,
Or verse, or sense to express immortal you?
You are the spectacles of state! 'Tis true
Court hieroglyphics, and all arts afford
In the mere perspective of an inch board!
You ask no more than certain politic eyes,
Eyes that can pierce into the mysteries
Of many colours, read them, and reveal
Mythology there painted on slit deal!
O, to make boards to speak! There is a task!
50 Painting and carpentry are the soul of masque!
Pack with your peddling poetry to the stage,
This is the money-get, mechanic age!
To plant the music where no ear can reach,
Attire the persons as no thought can teach
Sense what they are, which by a specious fine
Term of the architects is called design!
But in the practised truth destruction is
Of any art, beside what he calls his!
Whither, O whither will this tireman grow?
60 His name is *Skeuopoios* we all know,
The maker of the properties; in sum
The scene, the engine! But he now is come
To be the music master, fabler too!
He is, or would be, the main dominus-do-
All in the work! And so shall still for Ben:
Be Inigo, the whistle, and his men!
He's warm on his feet now, he says, and can
Swim without cork! Why, thank the good Queen Anne.
I am too fat to envy him. He too lean
70 To be worth envy. Henceforth I do mean
To pity him, as smiling at his feat
Of lantern-lerry: with fuliginous heat
Whirling his whimsies, by a subtlety
Sucked from the veins of shop-philosophy.

What would he do now, giving his mind that way
In presentation of some puppet play!
Should but the king his justicehood employ
In setting forth of such a solemn toy!
How would he firk like Adam Overdo
80 Up and about! Dive into cellars too,
Disguised, and thence drag forth enormity,
Discover vice, commit absurdity,
Under the moral! Show he had a pate
Moulded or stroked up to survey a state!
O wise surveyor, wiser architect,
But wisest Inigo! Who can reflect
On the new priming of thy old sign posts
Reviving with fresh colours the pale ghosts
Of thy dead standards: or (with miracle) see
90 Thy twice conceived, thrice paid for imagery?
And not fall down before it and confess
Almighty architecture? Who no less
A goddess is, than painted cloth, deal boards,
Vermilion, lake, or cinnopar affords
Expression for, with that unbounded line
Aimed at in thy omnipotent design!
What poesy e'er was painted on a wall
That might compare with thee? What story shall
Of all the Worthies hope to outlast thy one,
100 So the materials be of Purbeck stone?
Live long the Feasting Room. And ere thou burn
Again, thy architect to ashes turn!
Whom not ten fires, nor a parliament can
With all remonstrance make an honest man.

CXIX To Inigo, Marquess Would Be, a Corollary

But cause thou hear'st the mighty king of Spain
Hath made his Inigo marquess, wouldst thou fain
Our Charles should make thee such? 'Twill not become

All kings to do the selfsame deeds with some!
Besides, his man may merit it, and be
A noble honest soul! What's this to thee?
He may have skill and judgement to design
Cities and temples: thou a cave for wine,
Or ale! He build a palace: thou a shop
10 With sliding windows, and false lights atop!
He draw a forum, with quadrivial streets:
Thou paint a lane, where Thumb the pigmy meets!
He some Colossus to bestride the seas,
From the famed pillars of old Hercules:
Thy canvas giant, at some channel aims,
Or Dowgate torrent falling into Thames,
And straddling shows the boys' brown paper fleet,
Yearly set out there, to sail down the street!
Your works thus differing, troth let so your style:
20 Content thee to be Pancridge earl the while;
An earl of show: for all thy work is show:
But when thou turn'st a real Inigo;
Or canst of truth the least entrenchment pitch,
We'll have thee styled the marquess of Newditch.

CXX To a Friend, an Epigram of Him

Sir Inigo doth fear it as I hear
(And labours to seem worthy of that fear)
That I should write upon him some sharp verse,
Able to eat into his bones and pierce
The marrow! Wretch, I 'quit thee of thy pain.
Th'art too ambitious: and dost fear in vain!
The Lybian lion hunts no butterflies,
He makes the camel and dull ass his prize.
If thou be so desirous to be read,
10 Seek out some hungry painter, that for bread,
With rotten chalk, or coal upon a wall,
Will well design thee, to be viewed of all

That sit upon the common draught: or Strand!
Thy forehead is too narrow for my brand.

CXXI (To Mr Jonson upon these Verses)

Your verses were commended, as 'tis true,
That they were very good; I mean to you:
For they returned you, Ben, I have been told,
The seld seen sum of forty pound in gold.
These verses then, being rightly understood,
His lordship, not Ben Jonson, made them good.

To My Detractor

My verses were commended, thou didst say,
And they were *very good*, yet thou think'st nay.
For thou objectest, as thou hast been told,
The envied return of forty pound in gold.
Fool, do not rate my rhymes; I have found thy vice
Is to make cheap the lord, the lines, the price:
But bark thou on; I pity thee, poor cur,
That thou shouldst lose thy noise, thy foam, thy stir,
To be known what thou art, a blatant beast;
10 By writing against me, thou look'st at least,
I now would write on thee: no, wretch, thy name
Shall not work out unto it, such a fame:
No man will tarry by thee, as he goes,
To ask thy name, if he have half his nose;
But fly thee like the pest! Walk not the street
Out in the dog days, lest the killer meet
Thy noddle with his club; and dashing forth
Thy dirty brains, men smell thy want of worth.

CXXII (On The Magnetic Lady)

... But to advise thee, Ben, in this strict age,
A brick-kiln's better for thee than a stage.
Thou better know'st a groundsill for to lay,

Than lay the plot or groundwork of a play,
And better canst direct to cap a chimney,
Than to converse with Clio or Polyhimny.
 Fall then to work in thy old age again,
Take up thy trudge and trowel, gentle Ben,
Let plays alone: or if thou needs will write,
10 And thrust thy feeble muse into the light;
Let Lowen cease, and Taylor scorn to touch
The loathèd stage, for thou hast made it such.

Ben Jonson's Answer
Shall the prosperity of a pardon still
Secure thy railing rhymes, infamous Gill,
At libelling? Shall no Star Chamber peers,
Pillory, nor whip, nor want of ears,
All which thou hast incurred deservedly;
Nor degradation from the ministry,
To be the Denis of thy father's school,
Keep in thy barking wit, thou bawling fool?
Thinking to stir me, thou hast lost thy end;
10 I'll laugh at thee, poor wretched tyke; go send
Thy blatant muse abroad, and teach it rather
A tune to drown the ballads of thy father:
For thou hast naught in thee to cure his fame,
But tune and noise, the echo of his shame.
A rogue by statute, censured to be whipped,
Cropped, branded, slit, neck-stocked; go, you are stripped.

CXXIII *The Garland of the Blessèd Virgin Mary*

Here, are five letters in this blessed name,
 Which, changed, a five-fold mystery design,
The M. the myrtle, A. the almond's claim,
 R. rose, I. ivy, E. sweet eglantine.

These form thy garland. Whereof myrtle green,
 The gladdest ground to all the numbered five,

Is so implexèd, and laid in, between,
    As love here studied to keep grace alive.

The second string is the sweet almond bloom
10   Ymounted high upon Selinis' crest:
As it, alone, (and only it) had room,
    To knit thy crown, and glorify the rest.

The third, is from the garden called, the rose,
    The eye of flowers, worthy, for his scent,
To top the fairest lily, now, that grows,
    With wonder on the thorny regiment.

The fourth is humble ivy, intersert,
    But lowly laid, as on the earth asleep,
Preservèd, in her antique bed of vert,
20   No faith's more firm, or flat, than, where't doth creep.

But, that which sums all, is the eglantine,
    Which, of the field is cleped the sweetest briar,
Inflamed with ardour to that mystic shine,
    In Moses' bush, unwasted in the fire.

Thus, love, and hope, and burning charity,
    (Divinest graces) are so intermixed,
With odorous sweets and soft humility,
    As if they adored the head, whereon they're fixed.

CXXIV *The Reverse on the Back Side*

These mysteries do point to three more great,
    On the reverse of this your circling crown,
    All pouring their full shower of graces down,
The glorious Trinity in union met.

Daughter, and mother, and the spouse of God,
    Alike of kin, to that most blessèd trine,
    Of persons, yet in union (one) divine.
How are thy gifts, and graces blazed abroad!

Most holy, and pure Virgin, blessèd Maid,
10   Sweet Tree of life, King David's strength and tower,
      The House of gold, the Gate of heaven's power,
The Morning star, whose light our fall hath stayed,

Great Queen of Queens, most mild, most meek, most wise,
      Most venerable, cause of all our joy;
      Whose cheerful look our sadness doth destroy,
And art the spotless mirror to man's eyes.

The seat of sapience, the most lovely mother,
      And most to be admirèd of thy sex,
      Who mad'st us happy all, in thy reflex,
20 By bringing forth God's only Son, no other.

Thou Throne of glory, beauteous as the moon,
      The rosy morning, or the rising sun,
      Who like a giant hastes his course to run,
Till he hath reached his two-fold point of noon,

How are thy gifts and graces blazed abroad,
      Through all the lines of this circumference,
      To imprint in all purged hearts this virgin sense,
Of being daughter, mother, spouse of God.

CXXV Martial. Epigram XLVII, Book X

The things that make the happier life, are these,
Most pleasant Martial; substance got with ease,
Not laboured for, but left thee by thy sire;
A soil, not barren; a continual fire;
Never at law; seldom in office gowned;
A quiet mind; free powers; and body sound;
A wise simplicity; friends alike-stated;
Thy table without art, and easy-rated:
Thy night not drunken, but from cares laid waste;
10 No sour, or sullen bed-mate, yet a chaste;
Sleep, that will make the darkest hours swift-paced;

Will to be, what thou art; and nothing more:
Nor fear thy latest day, nor wish therefore.

CXXVI A Speech out of Lucan

Just and fit actions, Ptolemey (he saith)
Make many, hurt themselves; a praisèd faith
Is her own scourge, when it sustains their states
Whom fortune hath depressed; come near the fates
And the immortal gods; love only those
Whom thou see'st happy; wretches flee as foes:
Look how the stars from earth, or seas from flames
Are distant, so is profit from just aims.
The main command of sceptres, soon doth perish
10 If it begin religious thoughts to cherish;
Whole armies fall swayed by those nice respects.
It is a licence to do ill, protects
Even states most hated, when no laws resist
The sword, but that it acteth what it list.
Yet ware: thou may'st do all things cruelly:
Not safe; but when thou dost them thoroughly:
He that will honest be, may quit the court,
Virtue and sovereignty, they not consort.
That prince that shames a tyrant's name to bear,
20 Shall never dare do anything but fear.

Horace, of the Art of Poetry

If to a woman's head a painter would
Set a horse-neck, and diverse feathers fold
On every limb, ta'en from a several creature,
Presenting upwards, a fair female feature,
Which in some swarthy fish uncomely ends:
Admitted to the sight, although his friends,
Could you contain your laughter? Credit me,
This piece, my Pisos, and that book agree,
Whose shapes, like sick men's dreams, are feigned so vain,
10 As neither head, nor foot, one form retain.
But equal power, to painter, and to poet,
Of daring all, hath still been given; we know it:
And both do crave, and give again, this leave.
Yet, not as therefore wild and tame should cleave
Together: not that we should serpents see
With doves; or lambs, with tigers coupled be.
  In grave beginnings, and great things professed,
Ye have ofttimes, that may o'er-shine the rest,
A scarlet piece, or two, stitched in: when or
20 Diana's grove, or altar, with the bor-
Dering circles of swift waters that entwine
The pleasant grounds, or when the river Rhine,
Or rainbow is described. But here was now
No place for these. And, painter, haply, thou
Know'st only well to paint a cypress tree.
What's this? If he whose money hireth thee
To paint him, hath by swimming, hopeless, scaped,
The whole fleet wrecked? A great jar to be shaped,
Was meant at first. Why, forcing still about
30 Thy labouring wheel, comes scarce a pitcher out?
In short; I bid, let what thou work'st upon,
Be simple, quite throughout, and wholly one.
  Most writers, noble sire, and either son,
Are, with the likeness of the truth, undone.
Myself for shortness labour; and I grow
Obscure. This, striving to run smooth, and flow,

Hath neither soul, nor sinews. Lofty he
Professing greatness, swells: that, low by lee
Creeps on the ground; too safe, too afraid of storm.
40 This, seeking in a various kind, to form
One thing prodigiously, paints in the woods
A dolphin, and a boar amid the floods.
So, shunning faults, to greater fault doth lead,
When in a wrong, and artless way we tread.
The worst of statuaries, here about
The Aemelian school, in brass can fashion out
The nails, and every curlèd hair disclose;
But in the main work hapless: since he knows
Not to design the whole. Should I aspire
50 To form a work, I would no more desire
To be that smith; than live, marked one of those,
With fair black eyes, and hair; and a wry nose.

    Take, therefore, you that write, still, matter fit
Unto your strength, and long examine it,
Upon your shoulders. Prove what they will bear,
And what they will not. Him, whose choice doth rear
His matter to his power, in all he makes,
Nor language, nor clear order e'er forsakes.
The virtue of which order, and true grace,
60 Or I am much deceived, shall be to place
Invention. Now, to speak; and then differ
Much, that mought now be spoke: omitted here
Till fitter season. Now, to like of this,
Lay that aside, the epic's office is.

    In using also of new words, to be
Right spare, and wary: then thou speak'st to me
Most worthy praise, when words that common grew,
Are, by thy cunning placing, made mere new.
Yet, if by chance, in uttering things abstruse,
70 Thou need new terms; thou may'st without excuse,
Feign words, unheard of to the well-trussed race
Of the Cethegi; and all men will grace,
And give, being taken modestly, this leave,
And those thy new, and late-coined words receive,

So they fall gently from the Grecian spring,
And come not too much wrested. What's that thing,
A Roman to Caecilius will allow,
Or Plautus, and in Virgil disavow,
Or Varius? Why am I now envied so,
80   If I can give some small increase? When, lo,
Cato's and Ennius' tongues have lent much worth,
And wealth unto our language; and brought forth
New names of things. It hath been ever free,
And ever will, to utter terms that be
Stamped to the time. As woods whose change appears
Still in their leaves, throughout the sliding years,
The first-born dying; so the agèd state
Of words decay, and phrases born but late
Like tender buds shoot up, and freshly grow.
90   Ourselves, and all that's ours, to death we owe:
Whether the sea received into the shore,
That from the north, the navy safe doth store,
A kingly work; or that long-barren fen
Once rowable, but now doth nourish men
In neighbour towns, and feels the weighty plough;
Or the wild river, who hath changèd now
His course so hurtful both to grain, and seeds,
Being taught a better way. All mortal deeds
Shall perish: so far off it is, the state,
100 Or grace of speech, should hope a lasting date.
Much phrase that now is dead, shall be revived;
And much shall die, that now is nobly lived,
If custom please; at whose disposing will
The power, and rule of speaking resteth still.
    The gests of kings, great captains, and sad wars,
What number best can fit, Homer declares.
In verse unequal matched, first sour laments,
After, men's wishes, crowned in their events,
Were also closed: but, who the man should be,
110 That first sent forth the dapper elegy,
All the grammarians strive; and yet in court
Before the judge, it hangs, and waits report.

Unto the lyric strings, the muse gave grace
To chant the gods, and all their god-like race,
The conquering champion, the prime horse in course,
Fresh lovers' business, and the wine's free source.
The iambic armed Archilochus to rave,
This foot the socks took up, and buskins grave,
As fit to exchange discourse; a verse to win
120 On popular noise with, and do business in.
    The comic matter will not be expressed
In tragic verse; no less Thyestes' feast
Abhors low numbers, and the private strain
Fit for the sock: each subject should retain
The place allotted it, with decent thews:
If now the turns, the colours, and right hues
Of poems here described, I can, nor use,
Nor know to observe: why (in the muse's name)
Am I called poet? Wherefore with wrong shame,
130 Perversely modest, had I rather owe
To ignorance still, than either learn, or know?
Yet, sometime, doth the comedy excite
Her voice, and angry Chremes chafes outright
With swelling throat: and, oft, the tragic wight
Complains in humble phrase. Both Telephus,
And Peleus, if they seek to heart-strike us
That are spectators, with their misery,
When they are poor, and banished, must throw by
Their bombard-phrase, and foot-and-half-foot words.
140 'Tis not enough, the elaborate muse affords
Her poems beauty, but a sweet delight
To work the hearers' minds, still, to their plight.
Men's faces, still, with such as laugh, are prone
To laughter; so they grieve with those that moan.
If thou wouldst have me weep, be thou first drowned
Thyself in tears, then me thy loss will wound,
Peleus, or Telephus. If you speak vile
And ill-penned things, I shall or sleep, or smile.
Sad language fits sad looks; stuffed menacings,
150 The angry brow; the sportive, wanton things;

And the severe, speech ever serious.
For Nature, first, within doth fashion us
To every state of fortune; she helps on,
Or urgeth us to anger; and anon
With weighty sorrow hurls us all along,
And tortures us: and, after, by the tongue
Her truch-man, she reports the mind's each throe.
If now the phrase of him that speaks, shall flow,
In sound, quite from his fortune; both the rout,
160 And Roman gentry, jeering, will laugh out.
It much will differ, if a God speak, then,
Or a hero; if a ripe old man,
Or some hot youth, yet in his flourishing course;
Where some great lady, or her diligent nurse;
A venturing merchant, or the farmer free
Of some small thankful land: whether he be
Of Colchis born; or in Assyria bred;
Or, with the milk of Thebes or Argus, fed.
Or follow fame, thou that dost write, or feign
170 Things in themselves agreeing: if again
Honoured Achilles chance by thee be seized,
Keep him still active, angry, unappeased;
Sharp, and contemning laws, at him should aim,
Be naught so above him but his sword let claim.
Medea make brave with impetuous scorn;
Ino bewailed; Ixion false, forsworn;
Poor Io wandering; wild Orestes mad:
If something strange, that never yet was had
Unto the scene thou bring'st, and dar'st create
180 A mere new person, look he keep his state
Unto the last, as when he first went forth,
Still to be like himself, and hold his worth.
    'Tis hard, to speak things common, properly:
And thou mayst better bring a rhapsody
Of Homer's forth in acts, than of thine own
First publish things unspoken, and unknown.
Yet common matter thou thine own mayst make,
If thou the vile, broad-trodden ring forsake.

For, being a poet, thou mayst feign, create,
190 Not care, as thou wouldst faithfully translate,
To render word for word: nor with thy sleight
Of imitation, leap into a strait,
From whence thy modesty, or poem's law
Forbids thee forth again thy foot to draw.
Nor so begin, as did that circler late,
'I sing a noble war, and Priam's fate.'
What doth this promiser such gaping worth
Afford? The mountains travailed, and brought forth
A scornèd mouse! O, how much better this,
200 Who naught essays unaptly, or amiss?
Speak to me, muse, the man, who, after Troy was sacked,
Saw many towns, and men, and could their manners tract.
He thinks not, how to give you smoke from light,
But light from smoke; that he may draw his bright
Wonders forth after: as Antiphates,
Scylla, Charybdis, Polypheme, with these.
Nor from the brand, with which the life did burn
Of Meleager, brings he the return
Of Diomede; nor Troy's sad war begins
210 From the two eggs, that did disclose the twins.
He ever hastens to the end, and so
(As if he knew it) raps his hearer to
The middle of his matter: letting go
What he despairs, being handled, might not show.
And so well feigns, so mixeth cunningly
Falsehood with truth, as no man can espy
Where the midst differs from the first: or where
The last doth from the midst disjoined appear.
Hear, what it is the people, and I desire:
220 If such a one's applause thou dost require,
That tarries till the hangings be ta'en down,
And sits, till the epilogue says clap, or crown;
The customs of each age thou must observe,
And give their years, and natures, as they swerve,
Fit rites. The child, that now knows how to say,
And can tread firm, longs with like lads to play;

Soon angry, and soon pleased, is sweet, or sour,
He knows not why, and changeth every hour.
    The unbearded youth, his guardian once being gone,
230 Loves dogs, and horses; and is ever one
In the open field; is wax like to be wrought
To every vice, as hardly to be brought
To endure council: a provider slow
For his own good, a careless letter-go
Of money, haughty, to desire soon moved,
And then as swift to leave what he hath loved.
    These studies alter now, in one, grown man;
His bettered mind seeks wealth, and friendship: then
Looks after honours, and bewares to act
240 What straightway he must labour to retract.
    The old man many evils do girt round;
Either because he seeks, and, having found,
Doth wretchedly the use of things forbear,
Or does all business coldly, and with fear;
A great deferrer, long in hope, grown numb
With sloth, yet greedy still of what's to come:
Froward, complaining, a commender glad
Of the times past, when he was a young lad;
And still correcting youth, and censuring.
250   Man's coming years much good with them do bring:
At his departing take much thence: lest, then,
The parts of age to youth be given; or men
To children; we must always dwell, and stay
In fitting proper adjuncts to each day.
    The business either on the stage is done,
Or acted told. But, ever, things that run
In at the ear, do stir the mind more slow
Than those the faithful eyes take in by show,
And the beholder to himself doth render.
260   Yet, to the stage, at all thou mayst not tender
Things worthy to be done within, but take
Much from the sight, which fair report will make
Present anon: Medea must not kill
Her sons before the people; nor the ill-

Natured, and wicked Atreus cook, to the eye,
His nephew's entrails; nor must Progne fly
Into a swallow there; nor Cadmus take,
Upon the stage, the figure of a snake.
What so is shown, I not believe, and hate.
270   Nor must the fable, that would hope the fate,
Once seen, to be again called for, and played,
Have more or less than just five acts: nor laid,
To have a god come in; except a knot
Worth his untying happen there: and not
Any fourth man, to speak at all, aspire.
    An actor's parts, and office too, the choir
Must maintain manly; not be heard to sing,
Between the acts, a quite clean other thing
Than to the purpose leads, and fitly 'grees.
280   It still must favour good men, and to these
Be won a friend; it must both sway, and bend
The angry, and love those that fear to offend.
Praise the spare diet, wholesome justice, laws,
Peace, and the open ports, that peace doth cause.
Hide faults, pray to the gods, and wish aloud
Fortune would love the poor, and leave the proud.
    The hautboy, not as now with latten bound,
And rival with the trumpet for his sound,
But soft, and simple, at few holes breathed time
290   And tune too, fitted to the chorus' rhyme,
As loud enough to fill the seats, not yet
So over-thick, but, where the people met,
They might with ease be numbered, being a few
Chaste, thrifty, modest folk, that came to view.
But, as they conquered, and enlarged their bound,
That wider walls embraced their city round,
And the uncensured might at feasts, and plays
Steep the glad genius in the wine, whole days,
Both in their tunes, the licence greater grew,
300   And in their numbers; for, alas, what knew
The idiot, keeping holiday, or drudge,
Clown, townsman, base, and noble, mixed, to judge?

Thus, to his ancient art the piper lent
Gesture, and riot, whilst he swooping went
In his trained gown about the stage: so grew
In time to tragedy, a music new.
The rash, and headlong eloquence brought forth
Unwonted language; and that sense of worth
That found out profit, and foretold each thing,
310 Now differed not from Delphic riddling.
    Thespis is said to be the first found out
The tragedy, and carried it about,
Till then unknown, in carts, wherein did ride
Those that did sing, and act: their faces dyed
With lees of wine. Next Aeschylus, more late,
Brought in the visor, and the robe of state,
Built a small-timbered stage, and taught them talk
Lofty, and grave; and in the buskin stalk.
He too, that did in tragic verse contend
320 For the vile goat, soon after, forth did send
The rough rude satyrs naked; and would try,
Though sour, with safety of his gravity,
How he could jest, because he marked and saw,
The free spectators, subject to no law,
Having well ate, and drunk (the rites being done)
Were to be stayed with softnesses, and won
With something that was acceptably new.
Yet so the scoffing satyrs to men's view,
And so their prating to present was best,
330 And so to turn all earnest into jest,
As neither any god were brought in there,
Or semi-god, that late was seen to wear
A royal crown, and purple, be made hop,
With poor base terms, through every baser shop:
Or, whilst he shuns the earth, to catch at air
And empty clouds. For tragedy is fair,
And far unworthy to blurt out light rhymes;
But, as a matron drawn at solemn times
To dance, so she should, shamefaced, differ far
340 From what the obscene, and petulant satyrs are.

Nor I, when I write satires, will so love
Plain phrase, my Pisos, as alone, to approve
Mere reigning words: nor will I labour so
Quite from all face of tragedy to go,
As not make difference, whether Davus speak,
And the bold Pythias, having cheated weak
Simo; and of a talent wiped his purse;
Or old Silenus, Bacchus' guard, and nurse.
    I can out of known gear, a fable frame,
350 And so, as every man may hope the same;
Yet he that offers at it may sweat much,
And toil in vain: the excellence is such
Of order, and connection; so much grace
There comes sometimes to things of meanest place.
But, let the fauns, drawn from their groves, beware,
Be I their judge, they do at no time dare
Like men street-born, and near the hall, rehearse
Their youthful tricks in over-wanton verse;
Or crack out bawdy speeches, and unclean.
360 The Roman gentry, men of birth, and mean,
Will take offence, at this: nor, though it strike
Him that buys chiches blanched, or chance to like
The nut-crackers throughout, will they therefore
Receive, or give it an applause, the more.
    To these succeeded the old comedy,
And not without much praise; till liberty
Fell into fault so far, as now they saw
Her licence fit to be restrained by law:
Which law received, the chorus held his peace,
370 His power of foully hurting made to cease.
    Two rests, a short and long, the Iambic frame;
A foot, whose swiftness gave the verse the name
Of trimeter, when yet it was six-paced,
But mere iambics all, from first to last.
Nor is it long since they did with patience take
Into their birth-right, and for fitness' sake,
The steady spondees; so themselves to bear
More slow, and come more weighty to the ear:

Provided, ne'er to yield, in any case
380 Of fellowship, the fourth, or second place.
This foot yet, in the famous trimeters
Of Accius, and Ennius, rare appears:
So rare, as with some tax it doth engage
Those heavy verses, sent so to the stage,
Of too much haste, and negligence in part,
Or a worse crime, the ignorance of art.
But every judge hath not the faculty
To note, in poems, breach of harmony;
And there is given too unworthy leave
390 To Roman poets. Shall I therefore weave
My verse at random, and licentiously?
Or rather, thinking all my faults may spy,
Grow a safe writer, and be wary-driven
Within the hope of having all forgiven?
'Tis clear, this way I have got off from blame,
But, in conclusion, merited no fame.
Take you the Greek examples, for your light,
In hand, and turn them over, day, and night.
    Our ancestors did Plautus' numbers praise,
400 And jests; and both to admiration raise
Too patiently, that I not fondly say;
If either you, or I, know the right way
To part scurrility from wit; or can
A lawful verse, by the ear, or finger scan.
    Our poets, too, left naught unprovèd here;
Nor did they merit the less crown to wear,
In daring to forsake the Grecian tracts,
And celebrating our own home-born facts;
Whether the guarded tragedy they wrought,
410 Or 'twere the gownèd comedy they taught.
    Nor had our Italy more glorious been
In virtue, and renown of arms, than in
Her language, if the stay, and care to have mended,
Had not our every poet like offended.
But you, Pompilius' offspring, spare you not
To tax that verse, which many a day, and blot

Have not kept in; and (lest perfection fail)
Not, ten times o'er, corrected to the nail.
Because Democritus believes a wit
420 Happier than wretchèd art, and doth, by it,
Exclude all sober poets, from their share
In Helicon; a great sort will not pare
Their nails, nor shave their beards, but to by-paths
Retire themselves, avoid the public baths;
For so, they shall not only gain the worth,
But fame of poets, they think, if they come forth,
And from the barber Licinus conceal
Their heads, which three Anticyras cannot heal.
O, I left-witted, that purge every spring
430 For choler! If I did not, who could bring
Out better poems? But I cannot buy
My title, at their rate: I had rather, I,
Be like a whetstone, that an edge can put
On steel, though itself be dull, and cannot cut.
I, writing naught myself, will teach them yet
Their charge, and office, whence their wealth to fet,
What nourisheth, what formèd, what begot
The poet, what becometh, and what not:
Whether truth may, and whether error bring.
440   The very root of writing well, and spring
Is to be wise; thy matter first to know;
Which the Socratic writings best can show:
And, where the matter is provided still,
There words will follow, not against their will.
He, that hath studied well the debt, and knows
What to his country, what his friends he owes,
What height of love, a parent will fit best,
What brethren, what a stranger, and his guest,
Can tell a statesman's duty, what the arts
450 And office of a judge are, what the parts
Of a brave chief sent to the wars: he can,
Indeed, give fitting dues to every man.
And I still bid the learnèd maker look
On life, and manners, and make those his book,

Thence draw forth true expressions. For, sometimes,
A poem, of no grace, weight, art, in rhymes,
With specious places, and being humoured right,
More strongly takes the people with delight,
And better stays them there, than all fine noise
460 Of verse mere matterless, and tinkling toys.
  The muse not only gave the Greeks a wit,
But a well-compassed mouth to utter it;
Being men were covetous of naught, but praise.
Our Roman youths they learn the subtle ways
How to divide, into a hundred parts,
A pound, or piece, by their long counting arts:
There's Albin's son will say, subtract an ounce
From the five ounces; what remains? Pronounce
A third of twelve, you may: four ounces. Glad,
470 He cries, good boy, thou'lt keep thine own. Now, add
An ounce, what makes it then? The half pound just;
Six ounces. O, when once the cankered rust,
And care of getting, thus, our minds hath stained,
Think we, or hope, there can be verses feigned
In juice of cedar worthy to be steeped,
And in smooth Cypress boxes to be kept?
Poets would either profit, or delight,
Or mixing sweet, and fit, teach life the right.
  Orpheus, a priest, and speaker for the gods,
480 First frighted men, that wildly lived, at odds,
From slaughters, and foul life; and for the same
Was tigers said, and lions fierce, to tame.
Amphion, too, that built the Theban towers,
Was said to move the stones, by his lute's powers,
And lead them with soft songs, where that he would.
This was the wisdom, that they had of old,
Things sacred, from profane to separate;
The public, from the private; to abate
Wild ranging lusts; prescribe the marriage good;
490 Build towns, and carve the laws in leaves of wood.
And thus, at first, an honour, and a name
To divine poets, and their verses came.

Next these great Homer and Tyrtaeus set
On edge the masculine spirits, and did whet
Their minds to wars, with rhymes they did rehearse;
The oracles, too, were given out in verse;
All way of life was shown; the grace of kings
Attempted by the muse's tunes, and strings;
Plays were found out; and rest, the end, and crown
500   Of their long labours, was in verse set down:
All which I tell, lest when Apollo's named,
Or muse, upon the lyre, thou chance be ashamed.

    Be brief, in what thou wouldst command, that so
The docile mind may soon thy precepts know,
And hold them faithfully; for nothing rests,
But flows out, that o'er-swelleth in full breasts.

    Let what thou feign'st for pleasure's sake, be near
The truth; nor let thy fable think, whate'er
It would, must be: lest it alive would draw
510   The child, when Lamia has dined, out of her maw.
The poems void of profit, our grave men
Cast out by voices; want they pleasure, then
Our gallants give them none, but pass them by:
But he hath every sufferage, can apply
Sweet mixed with sour, to his reader, so
As doctrine, and delight together go.
This book will get the Sosii money; this
Will pass the seas, and long as nature is,
With honour make the far-known author live.

520   There are yet faults, which we would well forgive,
For, neither doth the string still yield that sound
The hand, and mind would, but it will resound
Oft times a sharp, when we require a flat:
Nor always doth the loosèd bow hit that
Which it doth threaten. Therefore, where I see
Much in the poem shine, I will not be
Offended with few spots, which negligence
Hath shed, or human frailty not kept thence.
How then? Why, as a scrivener, if he offend
530   Still in the same, and warnèd will not mend,

Deserves no pardon; or who'd play, and sing
Is laughed at, that still jarreth on one string:
So he that flaggeth much, becomes to me
A Choerilus, in whom if I but see
Twice, or thrice good, I wonder: but am more
Angry. Sometimes, I hear good Homer snore.
But, I confess, that, in a long work, sleep
May, with some right, upon an author creep.
 As painting, so is poesy. Some man's hand
540 Will take you more, the nearer that you stand;
As some the farther off: this loves the dark;
This, fearing not the subtlest judge's mark,
Will in the light be viewed: this, once, the sight
Doth please: this, ten times over will delight.
 You, sir, the elder brother, though you are
Informèd rightly, by your father's care,
And, of yourself too, understand; yet mind
This saying: to some things there is assigned
A mean, and toleration, which does well:
550 There may a lawyer be, may not excel;
Or pleader at the bar, that may come short
Of eloquent Messalla's power in court,
Or knows not what Cassellius Aulus can;
Yet, there's a value given to this man.
But neither, men, nor gods, nor pillars meant,
Poets should ever be indifferent.
 As jarring music doth, at jolly feasts,
Or thick gross ointment, but offend the guests:
As poppy, and Sardane honey; 'cause without
560 These, the free meal might have been well drawn out:
So, any poem, fancied, or forth-brought
To bettering of the mind of man, in aught,
If ne'er so little it depart the first,
And highest; sinketh to the lowest, and worst.
 He, that not knows the games, nor how to use
His arms in Mars his field, he doth refuse;
Or, who's unskilful at the quoit, or ball,
Or trundling wheel, he can sit still, from all;

Lest the thronged heaps should on a laughter take:
570 Yet who's most ignorant, dares verses make.
Why not? I'm gentle, and free-born, do hate
Vice, and, am known to have a knight's estate.
Thou, such thy judgement is, thy knowledge too,
Wilt nothing against nature speak, or do:
But, if hereafter thou shalt write, not fear
To send it to be judged by Metius' ear,
And, to your father's, and to mine; though it be
Nine years kept in, your papers by, you are free
To change, and mend, what you not forth do set.
580 The writ, once out, never returnèd yet.
      'Tis now inquired, which makes the nobler verse,
Nature, or art. My judgement will not pierce
Into the profits, what a mere rude brain
Can; or all toil, without a wealthy vein:
So doth the one, the other's help require,
And friendly should unto one end conspire.
      He, that's ambitious in the race to touch
The wishèd goal, both did, and suffered much
While he was young; he sweat; and freezed again:
590 And both from wine, and women did abstain.
Who, since, to sing the Pythian rites is heard,
Did learn them first, and once a master feared.
But, now, it is enough to say; I make
An admirable verse. The great scurf take
Him that is last, I scorn to come behind,
Or, of the things that ne'er came in my mind,
To say, I'm ignorant. Just as a crier
That to the sale of wares calls every buyer;
So doth the poet, who is rich in land,
600 Or great in monies out at use, command
His flatterers to their gain. But say, he can
Make a great supper; or for some poor man
Will be a surety; or can help him out
Of an entangling suit; and bring it about:
I wonder how this happy man should know,
Whether his soothing friend speak truth, or no.

But you, my Piso, carefully beware,
(Whether you are given to, or giver are)
You do not bring, to judge your verses, one,
610   With joy of what is given him, over-gone:
For he'll cry 'Good, brave, better, excellent!'
Look pale, distil a shower (was never meant)
Out at his friendly eyes, leap, beat the groun'.
As those that hired to weep at funerals, swoon,
Cry, and do more than the true mourners: so
The scoffer, the true praiser doth outgo.

Rich men are said with many cups to ply,
And rack, with wine, the man whom they would try,
If of their friendship he be worthy, or no:
620   When you write verses, with your judge do so:
Look through him, and be sure, you take not mocks
For praises, where the mind conceals a fox.

If to Quintilius, you recited aught;
He'd say, 'Mend this, good friend, and this; 'tis naught.'
If you denied, you had no better strain,
And twice, or thrice, had 'ssayed it, still in vain:
He'll bid, blot all: and to the anvil bring
Those ill-turned verses, to new hammering.
Then: if your fault you rather had defend
630   Than change; no word, or work, more would he spend
In vain, but you, and yours, you should love still
Alone, without a rival, by his will.

A wise, and honest man will cry out shame
On artless verse; the hard ones he will blame;
Blot out the careless, with his turnèd pen;
Cut off superfluous ornaments; and when
They're dark, bid clear this: all that's doubtful wrote
Reprove; and, what is to be changèd, note:
Become an Aristarchus. And, not say,
640   Why should I grieve my friend this trifling way?
These trifles into serious mischiefs lead
The man once mocked, and suffered wrong to tread.

Wise, sober folk, a frantic poet fear,
And shun to touch him, as a man that were

Infected with the leprosy or had
The yellow jaundice, or were furious mad
According to the moon. But, then the boys
They vex, and follow him with shouts, and noise;
The while he belcheth lofty verses out,
650 And stalketh, like a fowler, round about,
Busy to catch a blackbird; if he fall
Into a pit, or hole; although he call,
And cry aloud, 'Help, gentle countrymen',
There's none will take the care, to help him then;
For, if one should, and with a rope make haste
To let it down, who knows, if he did cast
Himself there purposely, or no; and would
Not thence be saved, although indeed he could?
I'll tell you but the death, and the disease
660 Of the Sicilian poet Empedocles,
He, while he laboured to be thought a god
Immortal, took a melancholic, odd
Conceit, and into burning Etna leaped.
Let poets perish, that will not be kept.
He that preserves a man, against his will,
Doth the same thing with him, that would him kill.
Nor did he do this once; for if you can
Recall him yet, he'd be no more a man:
Or love of this so famous death lay by.
670 His cause of making verses none knows why:
Whether he pissed upon his father's grave;
Or the sad thunder-strucken thing he have
(Defilèd) touched; but certain he was mad,
And, as a bear, if he the strength but had
To force the grates, that hold him in, would fright
All; so this grievous writer puts to flight

Learned and unlearned; holding whom once he takes;
And, there an end of him, reciting makes;
Not letting go his hold, where he draws food,
680 Till he drop off, a horse-leech, full of blood.

Timber : or Discoveries;

made upon men and matter: as they have flowed out of his daily readings; or had their reflux to his peculiar notion of the times.

SYLVA

Rerum, & sententiarum, quasi $Y^\smile \lambda \eta$ dicta a multiplici materia, & varietate, in iis contenta. Quemadmodum enim vulgo solemus infinitam arborum nascentium indiscriminatim multitudinem *Sylvam* dicere: ita etiam libros suos in quibus variae, & diversae materiae opuscula temere congesta erant, *Sylvas* appellabant Antiqui: Timber-trees.

Explorata: or Discoveries

Fortuna

Ill fortune never crushed that man, whom good fortune deceived not. I therefore have councilled my friends, never to trust to her fairer side, though she seemed to make peace with them: but to place all things she gave them so, as she might ask them again without their trouble; she might take them from them, not pull them: to keep always a distance between her, and themselves. He knows not his own strength, that hath not met adversity. Heaven prepares good men with crosses; but no ill can happen to a good man. Contraries are not mixed. Yet, that which happens to any man, may to every man. But it is in his reason what he accounts it, and will make it.

Casus

Change into extremity is very frequent, and easy. As when a beggar suddenly grows rich, he commonly becomes a prodigal; for, to obscure his former obscurity, he puts on riot and excess.

Consilia

No man is so foolish, but may give another good council sometimes; and no man is so wise, but may easily err, if he will take no other's council, but his own. But very few men are wise by their own council; or learned by their own teaching. For he that was only taught by himself, had a fool to his master.

Fama

A fame that is wounded to the world, would be better cured by another's apology, than its own: for few can apply medicines well themselves. Besides, the man that is once hated, both his good, and his evil deeds oppress him: he is not easily emergent.

Negotia

In great affairs it is a work of difficulty to please all. And ofttimes we lose the occasion of carrying a business well, and thoroughly, by our too much haste. For passions are spiritual rebels, and raise sedition against the understanding.

Amor patriae

There is a necessity all men should love their country: he that professeth the contrary,

may be delighted with his words, but his heart
is there.

Ingenia

Natures that are hardened to evil, you shall
sooner break than make straight; they are like
poles that are crooked, and dry: there is no
attempting them.

Applausus

We praise the things we hear, with much
more willingness, than those we see: because we
envy the present, and reverence the past;
50   thinking ourselves instructed by the one, and
overlaid by the other.

Opinio

Opinion is a light, vain, crude, and imperfect
thing, settled in the imagination; but never
arriving at the understanding, there, to obtain
the tincture of reason. We labour with it more
than truth. There is much more holds us, than
presseth us. An ill fact is one thing, an ill
fortune is another: yet both often-times sway
us like, by the error of our thinking.

60 *Impostura*

Many men believe not themselves, what they
would persuade others; and less do the things,
which they would impose on others: but least
of all, know what they themselves most
confidently boast. Only they set the sign of the
cross over their outer doors, and sacrifice to
their gut, and their groin in their inner
closets.

Iactura vitae

What a deal of cold business doth a man
misspend the better part of life in! In
70   scattering compliments, tendering visits,
gathering and venting news, following feasts
and plays, making a little winter-love in a dark
corner.

Hypocrita

Puritanus hypocrita est haereticus, quem
opinio propriae perspicaciae, qua sibi videtur,
cum paucis, in ecclesiae dogmatibus errores
quosdam animadvertisse, de statu mentis
deturbavit: unde sacro furore percitus, phrenetice
pugnat contra magistratus, sic ratus, obedientiam
80   *praestare Deo.*

Mutua auxilia

Learning needs rest: sovereignty gives it.
Sovereignty needs council: learning affords it.

There is such a consociation of offices, between the prince, and whom his favour breeds, that they may help to sustain his power, as he their knowledge. It is the greatest part of his liberality, his favour: and from whom doth he hear discipline more willingly, or the arts discoursed more gladly, than from those, whom his own bounty, and benefits have made able and faithful?

Cognit universi

In being able to council others, a man must be furnished with an universal store in himself, to the knowledge of all nature: that is the matter, and seed plot; there are the seats of all argument, and invention. But, especially, you must be cunning in the nature of man: there is the variety of things, which are as the elements, and letters, which his art and wisdom must rank, and order to the present occasion. For we see not all letters in single words; nor all places in particular discourses. That cause seldom happens, wherein a man will use all arguments.

Consiliarii adjunct. Probitas. Sapientia

The two chief things that give a man reputation in council, are the opinion of his honesty; and the opinion of his wisdom: the authority of those two will persuade, when the same councils, uttered by other persons less qualified, are of no efficacy, or working.

Wisdom without honesty is mere craft, and cozenage. And therefore the reputation of honesty must first be gotten; which cannot

Vita recta

be, but by living well. A good life is a main argument.

Obsequentia

Next a good life, to beget love in the persons we council, by dissembling our knowledge of ability in ourselves, and avoiding all suspicion of arrogance; ascribing all to their instruction; as an ambassador to his master, or a subject to

Humanitas. Sollicitudo

his sovereign; seasoning all with humanity and sweetness, only expressing care and solicitude. And not to council rashly, or on the sudden, but with advice and meditation: (*Dat nox consilium*). For many foolish things fall from wise men, if they speak in haste, or be extemporal. It therefore behoves the giver of council to be circumspect; especially to beware of those with whom he is not thoroughly acquainted, lest any spice of rashness, folly, or self-love appear, which will be marked by new persons, and men of experience in affairs.

Modestia.
Parrhesia

And to the prince, or his superior, to behave himself modestly, and with respect. Yet free from flattery, or empire. Not with insolence, or precept; but as the prince were already furnished with the parts he should have, especially in affairs of state. For in other things they will more easily suffer themselves to be taught, or reprehended: they will not willingly contend. But hear (with Alexander) the answer the musician gave him, *Absit, o rex, ut tu melius haec scias, quam ego.*

Plutarc. in vita
Alex.
Perspicuitas
Elegantia.

A man should so deliver himself to the nature of the subject, whereof he speaks, that his hearer may take knowledge of his discipline with some delight: and so apparel fair and good matter, that the studious of elegancy be not defrauded; redeem arts from their rough, and braky seats, where they lay hid, and overgrown with thorns, to a pure, open, and flowery light: where they may take the eye, and be taken by the hand.

Natura non
effoeta

I cannot think nature is so spent, and decayed, that she can bring forth nothing worth her former years. She is always the same, like herself: and when she collects her strength, is abler still. Men are decayed, and studies: she is not.

Non nimium
credendum
antiquitati

I know nothing can conduce more to letters, than to examine the writings of the ancients, and not to rest in their sole authority, or take all upon trust from them; provided the plagues of judging, and pronouncing against them, be away; such as are envy, bitterness, precipitation, impudence, and scurrile scoffing. For to all the

130

140

150

160

observations of the ancients, we have our own
experience: which, if we will use, and apply,
we have better means to pronounce. It is true
they opened the gates, and made the way, that
went before us; but as guides, not commanders:
Non domini nostri, sed duces fuere. Truth lies
open to all; it is no man's several. *Patet
omnibus veritas; nondum est occupata. Multum
ex illa, etiam futuris relictum est.*

Dissentire licet

If in some things I dissent from others,
wit, industry, diligence, and judgement I look
up at, and admire: let me not therefore hear
presently of ingratitude, and rashness. For I
thank those, that have taught me, and will ever:
but yet dare not think the scope of their
labour, and inquiry, was to envy their
posterity, what they also could add, and find
out.

Sed cum
ratione

Non mihi
cedendum

If I err, pardon me: *Nulla ars simul &
inventa est, & absoluta.* I do not desire to be
equal to those that went before; but to have
my reason examined with theirs, and so much
faith to be given them, or me, as those shall
evict. I am neither author, or fautor of any sect.
I will have no man addict himself to me; but
if I have anything right, defend it as truth's,
not mine (save as it conduceth to a common
good). It profits not me to have any man fence,
or fight for me, to flourish, or take a side.

Sed veritati.
Scientiae
liberales

Stand for truth, and 'tis enough.

Arts that respect the mind, were ever
reputed nobler, than those that serve the body:
though we less can be without them. As tillage,
spinning, weaving, building, etc. without
which we could scarce sustain life a day. But
these were the works of every hand; the other
of the brain only, and those the most generous,
and exalted wits, and spirits that cannot rest,
or acquiesce. The mind of man is still fed with
labour: *Opere pascitur.*

Non vulgi
sunt

There is a more secret cause: and the power
of liberal studies lies more hid, than that it can

210

be wrought out by profane wits. It is not every man's way to hit. They are men (I confess) that set the carat, and value upon things, as they love them; but science is not every man's mistress. It is as great a spite to be praised in the wrong place, and by a wrong person, as can be done to a noble nature.

Honesta.
Ambitio

If diverse men seek fame, or honour, by diverse ways; so both be honest, neither is to be blamed: but they that seek immortality, are not only worthy of leave, but of praise.

220 Maritus
improbus

He hath a delicate wife, a fair fortune, and family to go to (to) be welcome; yet he had rather be drunk with mine host, and the fiddlers of such a town, than go home.

Afflictio pia
Magistra.

Affliction teacheth a wicked person sometime to pray: prosperity never.

Deploratis
facilis descensus
Averni.
The devil take
230 all.

Many might go to heaven with half the labour they go to hell, if they would venture their industry the right way: but the devil take all (quoth he) that was choked in the mill dam, with his four last words in his mouth.

Aegidius cursu
superat.

A cripple in the way out-travels a footman, or a post out of the way.

Prodigo nummi
nauci.

Bags of money to a prodigal person, are the same that cherry stones are with some boys, and so thrown away.

Munda et
sordida

A woman, the more curious she is about her face, is commonly the more careless about her house.

Debitum
240 deploratum.

Of this spilt water, there is little to be gathered up: it is a desperate debt.

Latro
sesquipedalis

The thief (with a great belly) that had a longing at the gallows to commit one robbery more, before he was hanged.

Com. de
Schortenhein

And like the German lord, when he went out of Newgate into the cart, took order to have his arms set up in the last herborough: said he was taken, and committed upon suspicion of treason; no witness appearing against him: but the judges entertained him most civilly,

250   discoursed with him, offered him the courtesy
of the rack; but he confessed etc.

Calumniae
fructus
       I am beholden to calumny, that she hath so
endeavoured and taken pains to belie me. It
shall make me set a surer guard on myself, and
keep a better watch upon my actions.

Impertinens
       A tedious person is one a man would leap a
steeple from; gallop down any steep hill to
avoid him; forsake his meat, sleep, nature
itself, with all her benefits, to shun him.

260   A mere impertinent: one that touched neither
heaven nor earth in his discourse. He opened an
entry into a fair room; but shut it again
presently. I spake to him of garlic, he answered
asparagus: consulted him of marriage, he tells
me of hanging; as if they went one by one, and
the same destiny.

Bellum
scribentium
       What a sight it is, to see writers committed
together by the ears, for ceremonies, syllables,
points, colons, commas, hyphens, and the like!

270 Fighting, as for their fires, and their altars;
and angry that none are frighted at their
noises, and loud brayings under their asses'
skins!

       There is hope of getting a fortune without
digging in these quarries. *Sed meliore (in omne)*
ingenio, animoque, quam fortuna, sum usus.
       Pingue solum lassat: sed iuvat ipse labor.

Differentia inter
doctos et sciolos
       Wits made out their several expeditions
then, for the discovery of truth, to find out

280 great and profitable knowledges; had their
several instruments for the disquisition of arts.
Now, there are certain *scioli*, or smatterers, that
are busy in the skirts, and outsides of learning,
and have scarce anything of solid literature to
commend them. They may have some edge, or
trimming of a scholar, a welt, or so: but it is no
more.

Impostorum
fucus
       Imposture is a specious thing; yet never
worse, than when it feigns to be best, and to

290 none discovered sooner, than the simplest. For

truth and goodness are plain, and open: but
imposture is ever ashamed of the light.

Icuncularum
motio

A puppet-play must be shadowed, and seen
in the dark: for draw the curtain, *Et sordet*
gesticulatio.

Principes, et
administri

There is a great difference in the
understanding of some princes, as in the
quality of their ministers about them. Some
would dress their masters in gold, pearl, and
300   all true jewels of majesty: others furnish
them with feathers, bells, and ribbands; and
are therefore esteemed the fitter servants. But
if they are ever good men, that must make good
the times: if the men be naught, the times will
be such. *Finis expectandus est in unoquoque*
hominum; animali, ad mutationem promptissimo.

Scitum
Hispanicum

It is a quick saying with the Spaniards:
artes inter haeredes non dividi. Yet these have
inherited their fathers' lying, and they brag of
310   it. He is a narrow-minded man, that affects a
triumph in any glorious study: but to triumph
in a lie, and a lie themselves have forged is
frontless. Folly often goes beyond her bounds,
but impudence knows none.

Non nova res
livor

Envy is no new thing, nor was it born only
in our times. The ages past have brought it
forth, and the coming ages will. So long as there
are men fit for it, *quorum odium virtute relicta*
placet, it will never be wanting. It is a barbarous
320   envy, to take from those men's virtues,
which because thou canst not arrive at, thou
impotently despairest to imitate. Is it a crime
in me that I know that, which others had not
known, but from me? Or that I am the author
of many things, which would never have come
in thy thought, but that I taught them? It is
a new, but foolish way you have found out,
that whom you cannot equal, or come near in
doing, you would destroy, or ruin with evil
330   speaking: as if you had bound both your wits,
and nature's prentices to slander, and then

came forth the best artificers, when you could form the foulest calumnies.

Nil gratius.
protervo lib

Indeed, nothing is of more credit, or request now, than a petulant paper, or scoffing verses; and it is but convenient to the times and manners we live with, to have then the worst writings, and studies flourish, when the best begin to be despised. Ill arts begin, where good end.

340

The time was, when men would learn, and study good things; not envy those that had them. Then men were had in price for learning:

Iam litterae
sordent

now letters only make men vile. He is upbraidingly called a poet, as if it were a most contemptible nickname. But the professors (indeed) have made the learning cheap. Railing, and tinkling rhymers, whose writings

Pastus hodier
Ingenu

the vulgar more greedily read; as being taken with the scurrility, and petulancy of such wits.

350

He shall not have a reader now, unless he jeer and lie. It is the food of men's natures: the diet of the times! Gallants cannot sleep else. The writer must lie, and the gentle reader rests happy, to hear the worthiest works misinterpreted; the clearest actions obscured; the innocentest life traduced; and in such a licence of lying, a field so fruitful of slanders, how can there be matter wanting to his

360

laughter? Hence comes the epidemical infection. For how can they escape the contagion of the writings, whom the virulency of the calumnies hath not staved off from reading?

Sed seculi
morbus

Nothing doth more invite a greedy reader, than an unlooked-for subject. And what more unlooked-for, than to see a person of an unblamed life, made ridiculous, or odious by the artifice of lying? But it is the disease of the

370

age: and no wonder if the world, growing old, begin to be infirm: old age itself is a disease. It is long since the sick world began to dote, and talk idly: would she had but doted still;

but her dotage is now broke forth into a
madness, and become a mere frenzy.

*Alastoris
malitia*

This Alastor, who hath left nothing
unsearched, or unassailed, by his impudent,
and licentious lying in his aguish writings (for
he was in his cold quaking fit all the while):
what hath he done more, than a troublesome
base cur? Barked, and made a noise afar off:
had a fool, or two to spit in his mouth, and
cherish him with a musty bone? But they are
rather enemies of my fame, than me, these
barkers.

*Mali choragi
fuere*

It is an art to have so much judgement, as
to apparel a lie well, to give it a good dressing;
that though the nakedness would show
deformed and odious, the suiting of it might
draw the readers. Some love any strumpet (be
she never so shop-like, or meritorious) in good
clothes. But these, nature could not have
formed them better to destroy their own
testimony; and over-throw their calumny.

Hearsay news

That an elephant, 630, came hither
ambassador from the great mogul (who could
both write and read) and was every day
allowed twelve cast of bread, twenty quarts of
Canary sack; besides nuts and almonds the
citizens' wives sent him. That he had a
Spanish boy to his interpreter, and his chief
negotiation was, to confer or practice with
Archy, the principal fool of state, about
stealing hence Windsor Castle, and carrying
it away on his back if he can.

*Lingua
sapientis,
potius quam
loquentis,
optanda*

A wise tongue should not be licentious, and
wandering; but moved, and (as it were)
governed with certain reins from the heart,
and bottom of the breast: and it was excellently
said of that philosopher; that there was a wall,
or parapet of teeth set in our mouth, to restrain
the petulancy of our words: that the rashness
of talking should not only be retarded by the
guard, and watch of our heart; but be fenced
in, and defended by certain strengths, placed

in the mouth itself, and within the lips. But you shall see some, so abound with words without any seasoning or taste of matter, in so profound a security, as while they are speaking, for the most part, they confess to speak they know not what.

Of the two (if either were to be wished) I would rather have a plain downright wisdom, than a foolish and affected eloquence. For what is so furious, and Bethlem-like, as a vain sound of chosen and excellent words, without any subject of sentence, or science mixed?

Whom the disease of talking still once possesseth, he can never hold his peace. Nay, rather than he will not discourse, he will hire men to hear him. And so heard, not hearkened unto, he comes off most times like a mountebank, that when he hath praised his medicines, finds none will take them, or trust him. He is like Homer's Thersites, *Aʼμετροεπὴς, Aʼκριτόμυθος*: speaking without judgement, or measure. *Loquax magis, quam facundus. Satis loquentiae sapientiae parum.*

Γλώσσης τοι θησαυρὸς ἐν ἀνθρώποισιν ἄριστος Φειδωλῆς, πλείστη δὲ χάρις κατὰ μέτρον ἰούσης. Optimus est homini linguae thesaurus, et ingens Gratia, quae parcis mensurat singula verbis.

Ulysses, in Homer, is made a long-thinking man, before he speaks; and Epaminondas is celebrated by Pindar, to be a man, that though he knew much, yet he spoke but little. Demaratus, when on the bench he was long silent, and said nothing; one asking him, if it were folly in him, or want of language, he answered: 'A fool could never hold his peace.' For too much talking is ever the indice of a fool. *Dum tacet indoctus, poterit cordatus haberi; Is morbos animi namque, tacendo tegit.*

Nor is that worthy speech of Zeno the philosopher to be passed over, without the

420

430

Thersites
Homeri.
Sallust.
Hesiodus

440

Homeri
Ulysses.
Pindari
Epaminond.
Demaratus
Plutarchi

450

Vid. Zeuxidis
pict. serm.
ad Megabizum.
Plutarch.

note of ignorance: who being invited to a feast in Athens, where a great Prince's ambassadors were entertained, and was the only person had said nothing at the table; one of them with courtesy asked him; 'What shall we return from thee, Zeno, to the prince our master, if he ask us of thee?' 'Nothing,' he replied, 'more, but that you found an old man in Athens, that knew to be silent amongst his cups.' It was near a miracle, to see an old man silent; since talking is the disease of age: but amongst cups makes it fully a wonder.

Argute dictum

It was wittily said upon one that was taken for a great and grave man, so long as he held his peace: this man might have been a councillor of state, till he spoke: but having spoken, not a beadle of the ward. Ἐχεμυθία *Pythagorae quam laudabilis!* γωσσῆς πρὸ τῶν spoken, not a beadle of the ward. Ἐχεμυθία *Pythagorae quam laudabilis!* γλώσσῆς πρὸ τῶν ἄλλων κράτει θεοῖς ἑπόμενος. *Linguam cohibe, prae, aliis omnibus, ad deorum exemplum.* *Digito compesce labellum.*

*Vide Apuleium. *Iuvenal.*

Acutius cernuntur vitia quam virtutes

There is almost no man, but he sees clearlier, and sharper, the vices in a speaker, than the virtues. And there are many, that with more ease, will find fault with what is spoken foolishly, than that can give allowance to that wherein you are wise silently. The treasure of a fool is always in his tongue (says the witty comic poet) and it appears not in anything more, than in that nation; whereof one, when he had got the inheritance of an unlucky old grange, would needs sell it; and to draw buyers, proclaimed the virtues of it. Nothing ever thrived on it (saith he). No owner of it ever died in his bed; some hung, some drowned themselves; some were banished, some starved; the trees were all blasted; the swine died of the measels, the cattle of the murrain, the sheep of the rot; they that stood were ragged, bare, and bald as your hand; nothing was ever reared there; not a duckling,

Plautus

Trin. Act. 2. Scaen. 6.

Sim. Mart. lib. I. ep. 85.	or a goose. *Hospitium fuerat calamitatis.* Was not this man like to sell it?
500 Vulgi expectatio	Expectation of the vulgar is more drawn, and held with newness, than goodness; we see it in fencers, in players, in poets, in preachers, in all, where fame promiseth anything; so it be new, though never so naught, and depraved, they run to it, and are taken. Which shows, that the only decay, or hurt of the best men's reputation with the people, is, their wits have outlived the people's palates. They have been too much, or too long a feast.
510 Claritas Patria	Greatness of name, in the father, ofttimes helps not forth, but overwhelms the son: they stand too near one another. The shadow kills the growth; so much, that we see the grandchild come more, and oftener to be the heir of the first, than doth the second: he dies between; the possession is the third's.
Eloquentia	Eloquence is a great, and diverse thing: nor did she yet ever favour any man so much, as to become wholly his. He is happy, that can arrive to any degree of her grace. Yet there are, who prove themselves masters of her, and absolute lords: but I believe, they may mistake their evidence: for it is one thing to be eloquent in the schools, or in the hall; another at the bar, or in the pulpit. There is a difference between mooting, and pleading; between fencing, and fighting. To make arguments in my study, and confute them, is easy; where I answer myself, not an adversary. So, I can see whole volumes dispatched by the umbratical doctors on all sides: but draw these forth into the just lists; let them appear *sub dio,* and they are changed with the place, like bodies bred in the shade; they cannot suffer the sun, or a shower; nor bear the open air: they scarce can find themselves, they that were wont to domineer so among their auditors; but indeed I would no more choose a rhetorician, for

Line numbers: 520 appears beside "arrive to any degree of her grace. Yet there are," and 530 appears beside "easy; where I answer myself, not an adversary."

540

reigning in a school; than I would a pilot, for
rowing in a pond.

Amor et
odium

Love, that is ignorant, and hatred, have
almost the same ends: many foolish lovers wish
the same to their friends, which their enemies
would: as to wish a friend banished, that they
might accompany him in exile: or some great
want, that they might relieve him: or a disease,
that they might sit by him. They make a
causeway to their courtesy by injury; as if it

550

were not honester to do nothing, than to seek
a way to do good by a mischief.

Injuriae

Injuries do not extinguish courtesies: they
only suffer them not to appear fair. For a man
that doth me an injury after a courtesy, takes
not away the courtesy, but defaces it: as he
that writes other verses upon my verses, takes
not away the first letters, but hides them.

Beneficia

Nothing is a courtesy, unless it be meant us;
and that friendly, and lovingly. We owe no

560

thanks to rivers, that they carry our boats; or
winds, that they be favouring, and fill our sails;
or meats, that they be nourishing. For these are,
what they are necessarily. Horses carry us,
trees shade us; but they know it not. It is
true, some man may receive a courtesy, and not
know it; but never any man received it from
him, that knew it not. Many men have been
cured of diseases by accidents; but they were
not remedies. I myself have known one helped

570

of an ague, by falling into a water; another
whipped out of a fever: but no man would
ever use these for medicines. It is the mind,
and not the event, that distinguish the courtesy
from wrong. My adversary may offend the
judge with his pride, and impertinences, and
I may win my cause: but he meant it not me
as a courtesy. I 'scaped pirates, by being
ship-wrecked: was the wreck a benefit
therefore? No: the doing of courtesies aright,

580

is the mixing of the respects for his own sake,
and for mine. He that doth them merely for his

own sake, is like one that feeds his cattle to
sell them: he hath his horse well-dressed for
Smithfield.

Valor rerum

The price of many things is far above, what
they are bought and sold for. Life, and health,
which are both inestimable, we have of the
physician: as learning, and knowledge, the
true tillage of the mind, from our schoolmasters.
But the fees of the one, or the salary of the
other, never answer the value of what we
received; but serve to gratify their labours.

Memoria

Memory, of all the powers of the mind, is the
most delicate, frail: it is the first of our
faculties, that age invades. Seneca, the father,
the rhetorician, confesseth of himself, he had a
miraculous one; not only to receive, but to
hold. I myself could, in my youth, have
repeated all, that ever I had made; and so
continued, till I was past forty: since, it is
much decayed in me. Yet I can repeat whole
books that I have read, and poems, of some
selected friends, which I have liked to charge
my memory with. It was wont to be faithful
to me, but shaken with age now, and sloth
(which weakens the strongest abilities) it may
perform somewhat, but cannot promise much.
By exercise it is to be made better, and
serviceable. Whatsoever I pawned with it,
while I was young, and a boy, it offers me
readily, and without stops: but what I trust
to it now, or have done of later years, it lays
up more negligently, and oftentimes loses;
so that I receive mine own (though frequently
called for) as if it were new, and borrowed.
Nor do I always find presently from it, what I
do seek; but while I am doing another thing,
that I laboured for, will come: and what I
sought with trouble, will offer itself, when I
am quiet. Now in some men I have found it as
happy as nature, who, whatsoever they read, or
pen, they can say without book presently; as
if they did then write in their mind. And it is

more a wonder in such, as have a swift style;
for their memories are commonly slowest:
such as torture their writings, and go into
council for every word, must needs fix
somewhat, and make it their own at last,
though but through their own vexation.

630 Comit.
    Suffragia

Suffrages in Parliament are numbered, not
weighed: nor can it be otherwise in these
public councils, where nothing is so unequal,
as the equality: for there, how odd soever
men's brains, or wisdoms are, their power is
always even, and the same.

Stare a
partibus

Some actions, be they never so beautiful
and generous, are often obscured by base, and
vile misconstructions; either out of envy, or ill
nature, that judgeth of others, as of itself.

640

Nay, the times are so wholly grown, to be
either partial, or malicious; that, if he be a
friend, all sits well about him; his very vices
shall be virtues: if an enemy, or of the
contrary faction; nothing is good, or tolerable
in him: insomuch, that we care not to
discredit, and shame our judgements, to
soothe our passions.

Deus in
creaturis

650

Man is read in his face: God in his creatures:
but not as the philosopher, the creature of
glory, reads him: but, as the divine, the
servant of humility: yet even he must take care,
not to be too curious. For to utter truth of
God (but as he thinks only) may be dangerous;
who is best known, by our not knowing.
Some things of him, so much as he hath
revealed, or commanded, it is not only lawful,
but necessary for us to know: for therein our
ignorance was the first cause of our wickedness.

Veritas
660 proprium
    hominis

Truth is man's proper good; and the only
immortal thing, was given to our mortality
to use. No good Christian, or Ethnic, if he be
honest, can miss it: no statesman, or patriot
should. For without truth all the actions of
mankind, are craft, malice, or what you will,
rather than wisdom. Homer says, he hates him

worse than hell-mouth, that utters one thing
with his tongue, and keeps another in his breast.
Which high expression was grounded on
divine reason. For a lying mouth is a stinking
670   pit, and murders with the contagion it venteth.
Beside, nothing is lasting that is feigned; it will
have another face than it had, ere long: as
Euripides saith, 'No lie ever grows old.'

Nullum   It is strange, there should be no vice without
vitium sine   his patronage, that (when we have no other
patrocinio   excuse) we will say, we love it; we cannot
                forsake it: as if that made it not more a fault.
                We cannot, because we think we cannot: and
                we love it, because we will defend it. We will
680   rather excuse it, than be rid of it. That we
                cannot, is pretended; but that we will not, is
                the true reason. How many have I known, that
                would not have their vices hid? Nay, and to be
                noted, live like Antipodes to others in the
                same city; never see the sun rise, or set, in so
                many years; but be as they were watching a
                corpse by torchlight; would not sin the common
                way; but held that a kind of rusticity; they
                would do it new, or contrary, for the infamy?
690   They were ambitious of living backward;
                and at last arrived at that, as they would love
                nothing but the vices; not the vicious customs.
                It was impossible to reform these natures; they
                were dried, and hardened in their ill. They
                may say, they desired to leave it; but do not
                trust them: and they may think they desired
                it, but they may lie for all that; they are a little
                angry with their follies, now and then; marry
                they come into grace with them as quickly.
700   They will confess, they are offended with their
                manner of living: like enough, who is not?
                When they can put me in security, that they are
                more than offended; that they hate it: then I'll
                hearken to them; and perhaps, believe them:
                but many, nowadays, love and hate their ill
                together.

De vere
Argutis

710

I do hear them say often: some men are not witty; because they are not everywhere witty; than which nothing is more foolish. If an eye or a nose be an excellent part in the face, therefore, be all eye or nose? I think the eye-brow, the forehead, the cheek, chin, lip, or any part else, are as necessary, and natural in the place. But now nothing is good that is natural: right and natural language seems to have least of the wit in it; that which is writhed and tortured, is counted the more exquisite. Cloth of bodkin, or tissue, must be embroidered; as if no face were fair, that were

720

not powdered, or painted! No beauty to be had, but in wresting, and writhing our own tongue! Nothing is fashionable, till it be deformed; and this is to write like a gentleman. All must be as affected, and preposterous as our gallants' clothes, sweet bags, and night-dressings: in which you would think our men lay in, like ladies: it is so curious.

Censura de
Poetis

730

Nothing in our age, I have observed, is more preposterous, than the running judgements upon poetry, and poets; when we shall hear those things commended, and cried up for the best writings, which a man would scarce vouchsafe, to wrap any wholesome drug in; he would never light his tobacco with them. And those men almost named for miracles. who yet are so vile, that if a man should go about, to examine, and correct them, he must make all they have done, but one blot. Their good is so entangled with their bad, as

740

forcibly one must draw on the other's death with it. A sponge dipped in ink will do all:

Mart. 14.
epig. 10

– *Comitetur punica librum*
Spongia. –
Et paulo post,
Non possunt . . . multae, una litura potest.

Yet their vices have not hurt them: nay, a great many they have profited; for they have

been loved for nothing else. And this false
opinion grows strong against the best men: if
once it take root with the ignorant. Cestius, in
his time, was preferred to Cicero; so far as the
ignorant durst: they learned him without book,
and had him often in their mouths. But a man
cannot imagine that thing so foolish, or rude,
but will find, and enjoy an admirer; at least, a
reader, or spectator. The puppets are seen now
in despite of the players: Heath's epigrams,
and the sculler's poems have their applause.
There are never wanting, that dare prefer the
worst preachers, the worst pleaders, the worst
poets: not that the better have left to write, or
speak better, but that they that hear them
judge worse; *Non illi pejus dicunt, sed hi
corruptius judicant.* Nay, if it were put to the
question of the water-rhymer's works, against
Spenser's; I doubt not, but they would find
more suffrages; because the most favour
common vices, out of a prerogative the vulgar
have, to lose their judgements, and like that
which is naught.

Poetry, in this latter age, hath proved but a
mean mistress, to such as have wholly addicted
themselves to her, or given their names up to
her family. They who have but saluted her on
the by, and now and then tendered their
visits, she hath done much for, and advanced
in the way of their own professions (both the
Law, and the Gospel) beyond all they could
have hoped, or done for themselves, without
her favour. Wherein she doth emulate the
judicious but preposterous bounty of the
time's grandees: who accumulate all they can
upon the parasite, or freshman in their
friendship; but think an old client, or honest
servant, bound by his place to write, and
starve.

Indeed, the multitude commend writers, as
they do fencers, or wrestlers; who if they come
in robustiously, and put for it, with a deal of

750 Cestius
      Cicero

      Heath
      Taylor

760

      Spenser

770

780

790 violence, are received for the braver fellows:
when many times their own rudeness is a cause
of their disgrace; and a slight touch of their
adversary, gives all that boisterous force the
foil. But in these things, the unskilful are
naturally deceived, and judging wholly by the
bulk, think rude things greater than polished;
and scattered more numerous, than composed:
nor think this only to be true in the sordid
multitude, but the neater sort of our gallants:
800 for all are the multitude; only they differ in
clothes, not in judgement or understanding.

De Shakespeare   I remember, the players have often
nostrat.   mentioned it as an honour to Shakespeare, that
in his writing (whatsoever he penned) he never
blotted out line. My answer hath been, would
he had blotted a thousand. Which they thought
a malevolent speech. I had not told posterity
this, but for their ignorance, who choose that
circumstance to commend their friend by,
810 wherein he most faulted. And to justify mine
own candour (for I loved the man, and do
honour his memory – on this side idolatry – as
much as any). He was (indeed) honest, and of
an open, and free nature: had an excellent
fancy; brave notions, and gentle expressions:
wherein he flowed with that facility, that
sometime it was necessary he should be
Augustus in   stopped: *sufflaminandus erat*; as Augustus said
Hat.   of Haterius. His wit was in his own power;
820 would the rule of it had been so too. Many
times he fell into those things, could not escape
laughter: as when he said in the person of
Caesar, one speaking to him; 'Caesar, thou
dost me wrong'. He replied: 'Caesar did never
wrong, but with just cause': and such like;
which were ridiculous. But he redeemed his
vices, with his virtues. There was ever more in
him to be praised, than to be pardoned.

Ingeniorum   In the difference of wits, I have observed;
830 discrimina.   there are many notes: and it is a little
Not. 1   mastery to know them: to discern, what every

nature, every disposition will bear: for, before
we sow our land, we should plough it. There
are no fewer forms of minds, than of bodies
amongst us. The variety is incredible; and
therefore we must search. Some are fit to make
divines, some poets, some lawyers, some
physicians; some to be sent to the plough, and
trades.

840   There is no doctrine will do good, where
nature is wanting. Some wits are swelling, and
high; others low and still: some hot and fiery;
others cold and dull: one must have a bridle,
the other a spur.

Not. 2   There be some that are forward, and bold;
and these do every little thing easily: I mean,
that is hard by, and next them; which they will
utter, unretarded, without any shamefastness.
These never perform much, but quickly. They

850 are what they are on the sudden; they show
presently, like grain, that, scattered on the top
of the ground, shoots up, but takes no root; has
a yellow blade, but the ear empty. They are
wits of good promise at first, but there is an

*A wit-stand.   *ingeni-stitium: they stand still at sixteen, they
get no higher.

Not. 3   You have others, that labour only to
ostentation; and are ever more busy about the
colours, and surface of a work, than in the

860 matter, and foundation: for that is hid, the
other is seen.

Not. 4.   Others, that in composition are nothing, but
Martial. lib. 11. what is rough and broken: *Quae per salebras,*
epig. 9   *altaque saxa cadunt.* And if it would come
gently, they trouble it of purpose. They would
not have it run without rubs, as if that style
were more strong and manly, that struck the
ear with a kind of unevenness. These men err
not by chance, but knowingly, and willingly;

870 they are like men that affect a fashion by
themselves, have some singularity in a ruff,
cloak, or hatband; or their beards, specially
cut to provoke beholders, and set a mark upon

themselves. They would be reprehended, while they are looked on. And this vice, one that is in authority with the rest, loving, delivers over to them to be imitated: so that ofttimes the faults which he fell into, the others seek for: this is the danger, when vice becomes a precedent.

880 Not. 5

Others there are, that have no composition at all; but a kind of tuning, and rhyming fall, in what they write. It runs and slides, and only makes a sound. Women's poets they are called: as you have women's tailors.

They write a verse, as smooth, as soft, as cream;
In which there is no torrent, nor scarce stream.

You may sound these wits, and find the depth of them, with your middle finger. They are cream-bowl, or but puddle deep.

890 Not. 6

Some, that turn over all books, and are equally searching in all papers, that write out of what they presently find or meet, without choice; by which means it happens, that what they have discredited, and impugned in one work, they have before, or after, extolled the same in another. Such are all the essayists,

Mic. de
Montaigne

even their master Montaigne. These, in all they write, confess still what books they have read last; and therein their own folly, so much,

900

that they bring it to the stake raw, and undigested: not that the place did need it neither; but that they thought themselves furnished, and would vent it.

Not. 7

Some again, who (after they have got authority, or, which is less, opinion, by their writings, to have read much) dare presently to feign whole books, and authors, and lie safely. For what never was, will not easily be found; not by the most curious.

910 Not. 8

And some, by a cunning protestation against all reading, and false venditation of their own naturals, think to divert the sagacity of their readers from themselves, and cool the scent of their own fox-like thefts; when yet they are so rank, as a man may find whole pages together usurped from one author, their necessities compelling them to read for present use, which could not be in many books; and so come forth more ridiculously, and palpably guilty, than those, who, because they cannot trace, they yet would slander their industry.

Not. 9   But the wretcheder are the obstinate contemners of all helps and arts: such as presuming on their own naturals (which perhaps are excellent) dare deride all diligence, and seem to mock at the terms, when they understand not the things; thinking that way to get off wittily, with their ignorance. These are imitated often by such as are their peers in negligence, though they cannot be in nature: and they utter all they can think, with a kind of violence, and indisposition; unexamined, without relation, either to person, place, or any fitness else; and the more wilful, and stubborn, they are in it, the more learned they are esteemed of the multitude, through their excellent vice of judgement: who think those things the stronger, that have no art: as if to break, were better than to open; or to rent asunder, gentler than to loose.

Not. 10   It cannot but come to pass, that these men, who commonly seek to do more than enough, may sometimes happen on something that is good and great; but very seldom: and when it comes, it doth not recompense the rest of their ill. For their jests, and their sentences (which they only, and ambitiously seek for) stick out, and are more eminent; because all is sordid, and vile about them; as lights are more discerned in a thick darkness, than a faint shadow. Now because they speak all they can (however unfitly) they are thought to have the greater copy; where the learned use ever election, and a mean; they look back to what they intended at first, and make all an even, and proportioned body. The true artificer will not run away from nature, as he were afraid of her; or depart from life, and the likeness of truth; but speak to the capacity of his hearers. And though his

960 language differ from the vulgar somewhat; it shall not fly from all humanity, with the Tamerlanes, and Tamarchams of the late age, which had nothing in them but the scenical strutting, and furious vociferation, to warrant them to the ignorant gapers. He knows it is his only art, so to carry it, as none but artificers perceive it. In the meantime perhaps he is called barren, dull, lean, a poor writer (or by what contumelious word can come into their

970 cheeks) by these men, who without labour, judgement, knowledge, or almost sense, are received, or preferred before him. He gratulates them, and their fortune. Another age, or juster men, will acknowledge the virtues of his studies: his wisdom, in dividing: his subtlety, in arguing: with what strength he doth inspire his readers; with what sweetness he strokes them: in inveighing, what sharpness; in jest, what urbanity he uses. How he doth

980 reign in men's affections; how invade, and break in upon them; and makes their minds like the thing he writes. Then in his elocution to behold, what word is proper: which hath ornament: which height: what is beautifully translated: where figures are fit: which gentle, which strong to show the composition manly. And how he hath avoided faint, obscure, obscene, sordid, humble, improper, or effeminate phrase; which is not only praised

990 of the most, but commended (which is worse) especially for that it is naught.

Ignorantia   I know no disease of the soul, but ignorance;
animae   not of the arts and sciences, but of itself: yet relating to those, it is a pernicious evil: the darkener of man's life: the disturber of his reason, and common confounder of truth: with which a man goes groping in the dark, no otherwise than if he were blind. Great

understandings are most racked and troubled
with it: nay, sometimes they will rather
choose to die, than not to know the things they
study for. Think then what an evil it is; and
what good the contrary.

1000

Scientia

Knowledge is the action of the soul; and is
perfect without the senses, as having the seeds
of all science, and virtue in itself; but not
without the service of the senses: by those
organs, the soul works: she is a perpetual
agent, prompt and subtle; but often flexible,
and erring; entangling herself like a silkworm:
but her reason is a weapon with two edges,
and cuts through. In her indagations ofttimes
new scents put her by; and she takes in errors
into her, by the same conduits she doth truths.

1010

Otium
Studiorum

Ease, and relaxation, are profitable to all
studies. The mind is like a bow, the stronger
by being unbent. But the temper in spirits is
all, when to command a man's wit; when to
favour it. I have known a man vehement on
both sides; that knew no mean, either to
intermit his studies, or call upon them again.
When he hath set himself to writing, he would
join night to day; press upon himself without
release, not minding it, till he fainted: and
when he left off, resolve himself into all sports,
and looseness again; that it was almost a
despair to draw him to his book: but once got
to it, he grew stronger, and more earnest by
the ease. His whole powers were renewed: he
would work out of himself, what he desired;
but with such excess, as his study could not be
ruled: he knew not how to dispose his own
abilities, or husband them, he was of that
immoderate power against himself. Nor was
he only a strong, but an absolute speaker, and
writer: but his subtlety did not show itself; his
judgement thought that a vice. For the ambush
hurts more that is hid; he never forced his
language, nor went out of the highway of
speaking; but for some great necessary, or

1020

1030

Studiorum

1040

apparent profit. For he denied figures to be invented for ornament, but for aid; and still thought it an extreme madness to bend, or wrest that which ought to be right.

Et stili eminentia. Virgil. Tully. Sallust. Plato

1050

It is no wonder, men's eminence appears but in their own way: Virgil's felicity left him in prose, as Tully's forsook him in verse. Sallust's orations are read in the honour of story: yet the most eloquent Plato's speech, which he made for Socrates, is neither worthy of the patron, or the person defended. Nay, in the same kind of oratory, and where the matter is one, you shall have him that reasons strongly, open negligently: another that prepares well, not fit so well: and this happens, not only to brains, but to bodies. One can wrestle well; another run well; a third leap, or throw the bar; a fourth lift, or stop a cart going: each hath his way of strength. So in other creatures; some

1060

dogs are for the deer; some for the wild boar; some are foxhounds: some otter-hounds. Nor are all horses for the coach, or saddle: some are for the cart, and panniers.

De claris Oratoribus

I have known many excellent men, that would speak suddenly, to the admiration of their hearers; who upon study and premeditation have been forsaken by their own wits; and no way answered their fame: their eloquence was greater, than their reading: and

1070

the things they uttered, better than those they knew. Their fortune deserved better of them, than their care. For men of present spirits, and of greater wits, than study, do please more in the things they invent, than in those they bring. And I have heard some of them compelled to speak, out of necessity, that have so infinitely exceeded themselves, as it was better, both for them, and their auditory, that they were so surprised, not prepared. Nor was it safe then

1080

to cross them, for their adversary; their anger made them more eloquent. Yet these men I could not but love, and admire, that they

returned to their studies. They left not
diligence (as many do) when their rashness
prospered. For diligence is a great aid, even to
an indifferent wit; when we are not contented
with the examples of our own age, but would
know the face of the former. Indeed, the more
we confer with, the more we profit by, if the
persons be chosen.

1090

Dominus
Verulanus

One, though he be excellent, and the chief,
is not to be imitated alone. For never no
imitator, ever grew up to his author; likeness
is always on this side truth: yet there happened,
in my time, one noble speaker, who was full of
gravity in his speaking. His language (where
he could spare, or pass by a jest) was nobly
censorious. No man ever spake more neatly,
more pressly, more weightily, or suffered less
emptiness, less idleness, in what he uttered.
No member of his speech, but consisted of the
own graces: his hearers could not cough, or
look aside from him, without loss. He
commanded where he spoke; and had his
judges angry, and pleased at his devotion. No
man had their affections more in his power.
The fear of every man that heard him was
lest he should make an end.

1100

Scriptorum
Catalogus. Sir
Thomas More.
Sir Thomas
Wyatt. Hen:
Earl of Surrey.
Sir Thomas
Chaloner. Sir
Thomas Smith.
Sir Thomas
Elyot.
B. Gardiner.
Sir Nic.
Bacon, L.K.
Sir Philip
Sidney.

1110

1120

Cicero is said to be the only wit, that the
people of Rome had equalled to their empire.
Ingenium par imperio. We have had many, and
in their several ages (to take in but the former
seculum) Sir Thomas More, the elder Wyatt;
Henry, Earl of Surrey; Chaloner, Smith,
Elyot, B. Gardiner, were for their times
admirable: and the more, because they began
eloquence with us. Sir Nicho[las] Bacon was
singular, and almost alone, in the beginning of
Queen Elizabeth's time. Sir Philip Sidney,
and Mr Hooker (in different matter) grew
great masters of wit, and language; and in
whom all vigour of invention, and strength
of judgement met. The Earl of Essex, noble
and high; and Sir Walter Raleigh, not to be

Mr Richard
Hooker. Rob.,
Earl of Essex.
Sir Walter
Raleigh. Sir
1130 Henry Savile.
Sir Edwin
Sandys.
Sir Thomas
Egerton, L.C.
Sir Francis
Bacon, L.C.

contemned, either for judgement, or style.
Sir Henry Savile grave, and truly lettered; Sir
Edwin Sandys, excellent in both; Lo[rd]
Egerton, the Chancellor, a grave, and great
orator; and best, when he was provoked. But
his learned, and able (though unfortunate)
successor is he, who hath filled up all numbers;
and performed that in our tongue, which may
be compared, or preferred, either to insolent
Greece, or haughty Rome. In short, within his
view, and about his times, were all the wits
born, that could honour a language, or help
study. Now things daily fall: wits grow
downward, and eloquence grows backward:
so he may be named, and stand as the mark, and

1140 ἀκμὴ of our language.

De Augmentis
scientiarum

I have ever observed it, to have been the
office of a wise patriot, among the greatest
affairs of the state, to take care of the
commonwealth of learning. For schools, they
are the seminaries of state: and nothing is
worthier the study of a statesman, than that
part of the republic, which we call the
advancement of letters. Witness the care of

Julius Caesar

Julius Caesar; who, in the heat of the civil war,
1150 writ his books of *Analogy*, and dedicated them

Lord St
Albans

to Tully. This made the late Lord St Albans
entitle his work *Novum Organum*. Which
though by the most of superficial men, who
cannot get beyond the title of nominals, it is
not penetrated, nor understood: it really
openeth all defects of learning, whatsoever;
and it is a book,

Horat: de art:
Poetica

Qui longum noto scriptori porriget aevum.

1160

My conceit of his person was never increased
toward him, by his place, or honours. But I
have, and do reverence him for the greatness,
that was only proper to himself, in that he
seemed to me ever, by his work, one of the
greatest men, and most worthy of
admiration, that had been in many ages. In his
adversity I ever prayed that God would give

him strength: for greatness he could not want.
Neither could I condole in a word, or syllable
for him; as knowing no accident could do
harm to virtue; but rather help to make it
manifest.

De corruptela
morum

There cannot be one colour of the mind;
another of the wit. If the mind be staid, grave,
and composed, the wit is so; that vitiated, the
other is blown, and deflowered. Do we not
see, if the mind languish, the members are dull?
Look upon an effeminate person: his very gait
confesseth him. If a man be fiery, his motion is
so: if angry, 'tis troubled, and violent. So that
we may conclude: wheresoever manners, and
fashions are corrupted, language is. It imitates
the public riot. The excess of feasts, and
apparel, are the notes of a sick state; and the
wantonness of language, of a sick mind.

De rebus
mundanis

If we would consider, what our affairs are
indeed; not what they are called; we should
find more evils belong us, than happen to us.
How often doth that, which was called a
calamity, prove the beginning, and cause of a
man's happiness? And on the contrary: that
which happened, or came to another with
great gratulation, and applause, how it hath
lifted him, but a step higher to his ruin! As if
he stood before, where he might fall safely.

Do but ask of nature, why all living creatures
are less delighted with meat, and drink, that
sustains them, than with venery, that wastes
them. And she will tell thee, the first respects
but a private; the other, a common good,
propagation.

Vulgi mores

The vulgar are commonly ill-natured; and
always against their governors: which makes,
that a prince has more business, and trouble
with them, than ever Hercules had with the
bull, or any other beast: by how much they
have more heads, than will be reined with one
bridle. There was not that variety of beasts in
the ark; as is of beastly natures in the

1170

1180

1190

1200

multitude; especially when they come to that iniquity, to censure their sovereign's actions. Then all the councils are made good or bad by the events. And it falleth out, that the same facts receive from them the names; now, of diligence; now, of vanity; now, of majesty; now, of fury: where they ought wholly to hang on his mouth; as he to consist of himself, and not others' councils.

After God, nothing is to be loved of man like the prince: he violates nature, that doth it not with his whole heart. For when he hath put on the care of the public good, and common safety; I am a wretch, and put off man, if I do not reverence, and honour him: in whose charge all things divine and human are placed.

He is the arbiter of life, and death: when he finds no other subject for his mercy, he should spare himself. All his punishments are rather to correct, than to destroy. Why are prayers with Orpheus said to be the daughters of Jupiter; but that princes are thereby admonished, that the petitions of the wretched, ought to have more weight with them, than the laws themselves?

It was a great accumulation to his majesty's deserved praise; that men might openly visit, and pity those, whom his greatest prisons had at any time received, or his laws condemned.

Wise, is rather the attribute of a prince, than learned, or good. The learned man profits others, rather than himself: the good man, rather himself than others: but the prince commands others, and doth himself. The wise Lycurgus gave no law, but what himself kept. Sylla and Lysander did not so: the one, living extremely dissolute himself, enforced frugality by the laws: the other permitted those licences to others, which himself abstained from. But the prince's prudence is his chief art and safety. In his councils and deliberations he foresees the future times. In the equity of his

---

Marginal notes (left column):

1210 — Morbus Comitialis

Princeps

1220

De eodem

Orpheus, 1230 hymn

De opt. Rege Iacobo

De Prince: adjunctis. 1240 — Sed vere prudens haud concipi possit Princeps, nisi simul & bonus. Lycurgus. Sylla. Lysander

1250

judgement, he hath remembrance of the past;
and knowledge of what is to be done, or
avoided for the present. Hence the Persians

Cyrus

gave out their Cyrus, to have been nursed by
a bitch, a creature to encounter ill, as of
sagacity to seek out good; showing that
wisdom may accompany fortitude, or it leaves
to be, and puts on the name of rashness.

De malign:
1260 studentium

There be some men are born only to suck
out the poison of books: *habent venenum pro
victu: imo, pro deliciis.* And such are they that
only relish the obscene, and foul things in
poets: which makes the profession taxed. But
by whom? Men, that watch for it, and (had they
not had this hint) are so unjust valuers of
letters; as they think no learning good, but what
brings in gain. It shows, they themselves would
never have been of the professions they are;
but for the profits and fees. But, if another

1270

learning, well used, can instruct to good life,
inform manners; no less persuade, and lead
men, than they threaten, and compel; and have
no reward: is it therefore the worse study? I
could never think the study of wisdom confined
only to the philosopher: or of piety to the
divine: or of state to the politic. But that he
which can feign a commonwealth (which is the
poet) can govern it with councils, strengthen
it with laws, correct it with judgements,

1280

inform it with religion, and morals; is all these.
We do not require in him mere elocution; or
an excellent faculty in verse; but the exact
knowledge of all virtues, and their contraries;
with ability to render the one loved, the other
hated, by his proper embattling them. The
philosophers did insolently, to challenge only
to themselves that which the greatest generals,
and gravest councillors never durst. For such
had rather do, than promise the best things.

1290 Controvers
scriptores

Some controverters in divinity are like
swaggerers in a tavern, that catch that which
stands next them, the candlestick or pots;

More
Andabatarum,
qui clausis
oculis pugnant

1300

turn everything into a weapon: ofttimes they fight blindfold; and both beat the air. The one milks a he-goat, the other holds under a sieve. Their arguments are as fluxive as liquor spilt upon a table; which with your finger you may drain as you will. Such controversies, or disputations, (carried with more labour, than profit) are odious: where most times the truth is lost in the midst; or left untouched. And the fruit of their fight is that they spit one upon another, and are both defiled. These fencers, in religion, I like not.

Morbi

1310

The body hath certain diseases, that are with less evil tolerated, than removed. As if to cure a leprosy, a man should bathe himself with the warm blood of a murdered child: so in the church, some errors may be dissimuled with less inconvenience, than can be discovered.

Iactantia
intempestiva

Men that talk of their benefits, are not believed to talk of them, because they have done them: but to have done them, because they might talk of them. That which had been great, if another had reported it of them, vanisheth; and is nothing, if he that did it speak of it. For men, when they destroy the deed, will yet be glad to take advantage of the boasting, and lessen it.

1320 *Adulatio*

1330

I have seen, that poverty makes men do unfit things; but honest men should not do them: they should gain otherwise. Though a man be hungry, he should not play the parasite. That hour, wherein I would repent me to be honest: there were ways enough open for me to be rich. But flattery is a fine pick-lock of tender ears: especially of those, whom fortune hath borne high upon their wings, that submit their dignity, and authority to it, by a soothing of themselves. For indeed men could never be taken, in that abundance, with the springes of others' flattery, if they began not there; if they did but remember, how much more profitable the bitterness of truth were, than all the honey distilling from a whorish voice; which is not praise, but poison. But now it is come to that extreme folly, or rather madness, with some: that he that flatters them modestly, or sparingly is thought to malign them. If their friend consent not to their vices, though he do not contradict them; he is nevertheless an enemy. When they do all things the worst way, even then they look for praise. Nay, they will hire fellows to flatter them, with suits, and suppers, and to prostitute their judgements. They have livery-friends, friends of the dish, and of the spit, that wait their turns, as my lord has his feasts, and guests.

1340

De vita
1350 humana

I have considered, our whole life is like a play: wherein every man, forgetful of himself, is in travail with expression of another. Nay, we so insist in imitating others, as we cannot (when it is necessary) return to ourselves: like children, that imitate the vices of stammerers so long, till at last they become such; and make the habit to another nature, as it is never forgotten.

De piis &
probis
1360

Good men are the stars, the planets of the ages wherein they live, and illustrate the times. God did never let them be wanting to the world: as Abel, for an example, of innocency; Enoch of purity, Noah of trust in God's mercies, Abraham of faith, and so of the rest. These, sensual men thought mad, because they would not be partakers, or practisers of their madness. But they, placed high on the top of all virtue, looked down on the stage of the world, and contemned the play of fortune. For though the most be players, some must be spectators.

1370 Mores Aulici

I have discovered, that a feigned familiarity in great ones, is a note of certain usurpation on the less. For great and popular men, feign themselves to be servants to others, to make those slaves to them. So the fisher provides baits for the trout, roach, dace etc. that they may be food to him.

Impiorum
querela.
Augustus.
1380 Varus. Tiberius

The complaint of Caligula, was most wicked, of the condition of his times: when he said; they were not famous by any public calamity, as the reign of Augustus was, by the defeat of Varus, and the legions; and that of Tiberius, by the falling of the theatre at Fidenae: whilst his oblivion was imminent, through the prosperity of his affairs. As that other voice of his, was worthier a headsman, than a head; when he wished the people of Rome had but one neck. But he found (when he fell) they had many hands. A tyrant, how great and mighty soever he may seem to cowards and sluggards; but is one creature, one animal.

1390

Nobilium
Ingenia

I have marked among the nobility, some are so addicted to the service of the prince, and commonwealth, as they look not for spoil; such are to be honoured, and loved. There are others, which no obligation will fasten on; and they are of two sorts. The first are such as love their own ease: or, out of vice of nature, or self-direction, avoid business and care. Yet, these the prince may use with safety. The other remove themselves upon craft, and design (as the architects say) with a premeditated thought to their own, rather than their prince's profit. Such let the prince take heed of, and not doubt to reckon in the list of his open enemies.

1400

Principum
varia. –
Firmissima
1410 vero omnium
basis jus
haereditarium
Principis

There is a great variation between him, that is raised to the sovereignty, by the favour of his peers; and him that comes to it by the suffrage of the people. The first holds with more difficulty; because he hath to do with many, that think themselves his equals; and raised him for their own greatness, and oppression of the rest. The latter hath no upbraiders; but was raised by them, that sought to be defended from oppression: whose end is both the easier, and the honester to satisfy. Beside, while he hath the people to friend, who are a multitude,

he hath the less fear of the nobility, who are
but few. Nor let the common proverb of 'He
that builds on the people, builds on the dirt'
discredit my opinion: for that hath only
place, where an ambitious, and private person,
for some popular end, trusts in them against
the public justice, and magistrate. There they
will leave him. But when a prince governs
them, so as they have still need of his
administration (for that is his art) he shall
ever make, and hold them faithful.

1430 Clementia   A prince should exercise his cruelty, not by
himself, but by his ministers: so he may save
himself, and his dignity with his people, by
sacrificing those, when he list, saith the great
Machiavel   doctor of state, Machiavel. But I say, he puts
off man, and goes into a beast, that is cruel. No
virtue is a prince's own; or becomes him more,
than his clemency: and no glory is greater,
than to be able to save with his power. Many
punishments sometimes, and in some cases,
as much discredit a prince, as many funerals
a physician. The state of things is secured by
clemency; severity represseth a few, but it
*Haud infima   irritates more. *The lopping of trees makes the
ars in Principe,   boughs shoot out thicker; and the taking away
ubi lenitas, ubi   of some kind of enemies, increaseth the
severitas, plus   number. It is then, most gracious in a prince
polleat in   to pardon, when many about him would make
commune   him cruel; to think then, how much he can
bonum callere.   save, when others tell him, how much he can
1450 Clementia   destroy: not to consider, what the impotence
tutela optima   of others hath demolished; but what his own
greatness can sustain. These are a prince's
virtues; and they that give him other councils,
are but the hangman's factors.

St Nicolas   He that is cruel to halves (saith the said
St Nicolas) loseth no less the opportunity of his
cruelty, than of his benefits: for then to use his
cruelty, is too late; and to use his favours will
be interpreted fear and necessity; and so he
loseth the thanks. Still the council is cruelty.

But princes, by harkening to cruel councils, become in time obnoxious to the authors, their flatterers, and ministers; and are brought to that, that when they would, they dare not change them: they must go on, and defend cruelty with cruelty: they cannot alter the habit. It is then grown necessary, they must be as ill, as those have made them: and in the end, they will grow more hateful to themselves, than to their subjects. Whereas, on the contrary, the merciful prince is safe in love, not in fear. He needs no emissaries, spies, intelligencers, to entrap true subjects. He fears no libels, no treasons. His people speak, what they think; and talk openly, what they do in secret. They have nothing in their breasts, that they need a cypher for. He is guarded with his own benefits.

Religio.

1480 Palladium
Homeri

The strength of empire is in religion. What else is the Palladium (with Homer) that kept Troy so long from sacking? Nothing more commends the sovereign to the subject, than it. For he that is religious, must be merciful and just necessarily. And they are two strong ties upon mankind. Justice is the virtue, that innocence rejoiceth in. Yet even that is not always so safe; but it may love to stand in the sight of mercy. For sometimes misfortune is made a crime, and then innocence is succoured, no less than virtue. Nay, oftentimes virtue is made capital: and through the condition of the times, it may happen, that that may be punished with our praise. Let no man therefore murmur at the actions of the prince, who is placed so far above him. If he offend, he hath his discoverer. God hath a height beyond him. But where the prince is good, Euripides saith: God is a guest in a human body.

Euripides

1500 Tyranni

There is nothing with some princes sacred above their majesty; or profane, but what violates their sceptres. But a prince, with such

1470

1490

council, is like the God Terminus, of stone, his own landmark; or (as it is in the fable) a crowned lion. It is dangerous offending such a one; who, being angry, knows not how to forgive. That cares not to do anything, for maintaining, or enlarging of empire; kills not men or subjects, but destroyeth whole countries, armies, mankind, male and female; guilty or not guilty, holy or profane: yea, some that have not seen the light. All is under the law of their spoil, and licence. But princes that neglect their proper office thus, their fortune

Sejanus

is oftentimes to draw a Sejanus, to be near about them; who will at last affect to get above them, and put them in a worthy fear, of rooting both them out, and their family. For no men hate an evil prince more than they that helped to make him such. And none more boastingly weep his ruin than they that procured and practised it. The same path leads to ruin which did to rule when men profess a licence in governing. A good king is a public servant.

Illiteratus princeps

A prince without letters, is a pilot without eyes. All his government is groping. In sovereignty it is a most happy thing, not to be compelled; but so it is the most miserable not to be councilled. And how can he be councilled that cannot see to read the best councillors (which are books) for they neither flatter us, nor hide from us? He may hear, you will say. But how shall he always be sure to hear truth, or be councilled the best things, not the sweetest? They say princes learn no art truly, but the art of horsemanship. The reason is, the brave beast is no flatterer. He will throw a prince as soon as his groom. Which is an argument, that the good councillors to princes are the best instruments of a good age. For though the prince himself be of the most prompt inclination to all virtue: yet the best pilots have need of mariners, beside sails, anchor, and other tackle.

Character
principis

1550

Alexander
magnus

1560

1570

1580

If men did know, what shining fetters,
gilded miseries, and painted happiness, thrones
and sceptres were, there would not be so
frequent strife about the getting, or holding of
them. There would be more principalities,
than princes. For a prince is the pastor of the
people. He ought to shear, not to flea his sheep;
to take their fleeces, not their fells. Who were
his enemies before, being a private man,
become his children, now he is public. He is
the soul of the commonwealth; and ought to
cherish it, as his own body. Alexander the
Great was wont to say: he hated that gardener,
that plucked his herbs, or flowers up by the
roots. A man may milk a beast, till the blood
come: churn milk, and it yieldeth butter:
but wring the nose, and the blood followeth.
He is an ill prince, that so pulls his subjects'
feathers, as he would not have them grow
again: that makes his exchequer a receipt for
the spoils of those he governs. No, let him keep
his own, not affect his subjects': strive rather
to be called just, than powerful. Not, like the
Roman tyrants, affect the surnames that grow
by human slaughters: neither to seek war in
peace, or peace in war; but to observe faith
given, though to an enemy. Study piety
toward the subject: show care to defend him.
Be slow to punish in diverse cases; but be a
sharp and severe revenger of open crimes.
Break no decrees, or dissolve no orders, to
slacken the strength of laws. Choose neither
magistrates civil, or ecclesiastic by favour or
price: but with long disquisition, and report of
their worth, by all suffrages. Sell no honours,
nor give them hastily; but bestow them with
council, and for reward; if he do,
acknowledge it (though late) and mend it. For
princes are easy to be deceived. And what
wisdom can escape it; where so many
court-arts are studied? But above all, the
prince is to remember that when the great

day of account comes, which neither magistrate
nor prince can shun, there will be required of
him a reckoning for those whom he hath

1590   trusted; as for himself; which he must provide.
And if piety be wanting in the priests, equity
in the judges, or the magistrate be found
rated at a price; what justice or religion is to
be expected? Which are the only two attributes
make kings akin to gods; and is the delphic
sword, both to kill sacrifices, and to chastise
offenders.

De Gratiosis   When a virtuous man is raised, it brings
gladness to his friends; grief to his enemies,

1600   and glory to his posterity. Nay, his honours are
a great part of the honour of the times: when
by this means he is grown to active men an
example; to the slothful a spur; to the
envious a punishment.

Divites   He which is sole heir to many rich men,
having (beside his father's and uncles') the
states of diverse his kindred come to him by
accession; must needs be richer than father, or

Haeredes   grand-father: so they which are left heirs
1610 ex asse   *ex asse*, of all their ancestors' vices; and by
their good husbandry improve the old, and
daily purchase new; must needs be wealthier
in vice, and have a greater revenue, or stock
of ill to spend on.

Fures publici   The great thieves of a state are lightly the
officers of the crown; they hang the less still;
play the pikes in the pond; eat whom they list.
The net was never spread for the hawk or
buzzard that hurt us, but the harmless birds,

1620   they are good meat.

Juvenalis.   *Dat veniam corvis, vexat censura columbas.*
Plautus   *Non rete accipitri tenditur, neque miluo.*

But they are not always safe, though,
especially, when they meet with wise masters.
They can take down all the huff and swelling
of their looks; and like dexterous auditors,
place the counter, where he shall value nothing.

Louis XI

1630

Let them but remember Louis the eleventh, who to a clerk of the Exchequer, that came to be Lord Treasurer, and had (for his device) represented himself sitting upon Fortune's wheel: told him, he might do well to fasten it with a good strong nail, lest, turning about, it might bring him where he was again. As indeed it did.

De bonis et
malis

1640

De innocentia

1650

1660

A good man will avoid the spot of any sin. The very aspersion is grievous: which makes him choose his way in his life, as he would in his journey. The ill man rides through all confidently; he is coated, and booted for it. The oftener he offends, the more openly; and the fouler, the fitter in fashion. His modesty, like a riding coat, the more it is worn, is the less cared for. It is good enough for the dirt still; and the ways he travels in. An innocent man needs no eloquence: his innocence is instead of it: else I had never come off so many times from these precipices, whither men's malice hath pursued me. It is true, I have been accused to the Lords, to the king; and by great ones: but it happened my accusers had not thought of the accusation with themselves; and so were driven, for want of crimes, to use invention, which was found slander: or too late (being entered so far) to seek starting-holes for their rashness, which were not given them. And then they may think, what accusation that was like to prove, when they, that were the engineers, feared to be the authors. Nor were they content to feign things against me, but to urge things, feigned by the ignorant, against my profession: which though from their hired and mercenary impudence I might have passed by, as granted to a nation of barkers, that let out their tongues to lick others' sores; yet I durst not leave myself undefended, having a pair of ears unskilful to hear lies; or have those things said of me, which I could truly prove of them.

1670

They objected, making of verses to me, when I
could object to most of them, their not being
able to read them, but as worthy of scorn. Nay,
they would offer to urge mine own writings
against me; but by pieces (which was an
excellent way of malice) as if any man's
context, might not seem dangerous, and
offensive, if that which was knit, to what went
before, were defrauded of his beginning; or
that things, by themselves uttered, might not

1680

seem subject to calumny, which read entire
would appear most free. At last they
upbraided my poverty; I confess, she is my
domestic; sober of diet, simple of habit; frugal,
painful; a good councillor to me; that keeps
me from cruelty, pride, or other more delicate
impertinences, which are the nurse-children
of riches. But let them look over all the great
and monstrous wickednesses, they shall never
find those in poor families. They are the issue

1690

of the wealthy giants and the mighty hunters:
whereas no great work, or worthy of praise, or
memory, but came out of poor cradles. It
was the ancient poverty that founded
commonwealths; built cities, invented arts,
made wholesome laws; armed men against
vices; rewarded them with their own virtues;
and preserved the honour and state of nations,
till they betrayed themselves to riches.

Amor nummi

1700

Money never made any man rich, but his
mind. He that can order himself to the law of
nature, is not only without the sense, but the
fear of poverty. O, but to strike blind the people
with our wealth, and pomp, is the thing! What
a wretchedness is this, to thrust all our riches
outward, and be beggars within: to contemplate
nothing but the little, vile and sordid things of
the world; not the great, noble and precious!
We serve our avarice, and not content with the
good of the earth, that is offered us; we search

1710

and dig for the evil that is hidden. God offered
us those things, and placed them at hand, and

near us, that he knew were profitable for us;
but the hurtful he laid deep, and hid. Yet do
we seek only the things, whereby we may
perish; and bring them forth, when God and
nature hath buried them. We covet superfluous
things; when it were more honour for us, if we
could contemn necessary. What need hath
nature of silver dishes, multitudes of waiters,
1720   delicate pages, perfumed napkins? She
requires meat only, and hunger is not
ambitious. Can we think no wealth enough,
but such a state, for which a man may be
brought into a praemunire, begged, proscribed,
or poisoned? O! If a man could restrain the
fury of his gullet, and groin, and think how
many fires, how many kitchens, cooks,
pastures, and ploughed lands; what orchards,
stews, ponds, and parks, coops, and garners he
1730   could spare: what velvets, tissues, embroideries,
laces he could lack; and then how short, and
uncertain his life is; he were in a better way to
happiness, than to live the emperor of these
delights; and be the dictator of fashions! But
we make ourselves slaves to our pleasures;
and we serve fame and ambition, which is an
equal slavery. Have I not seen the pomp of a
whole kingdom, and what a foreign king could
bring hither also to make himself gazed, and
1740   wondered at, laid forth as it were to the show,
and vanish all away in a day? And shall that
which could not fill the expectation of few
hours, entertain, and take up our whole lives,
when even it appeared as superfluous to the
possessors, as to me that was a spectator? The
bravery was shown, it was not possessed;
while it boasted itself, it perished. It is vile, and
a poor thing to place our happiness on these
desires. Say we wanted them all: famine ends
1750   famine.

De mollibus &   There is nothing valiant, or solid to be hoped
effoeminatis   for from such, as are always kempt and
perfumed; and every day smell of the tailor:

the exceedingly curious, that are wholly in
mending such an imperfection in the face, in
taking away the morphew in the neck; or
bleaching their hands at midnight, gumming,
and bridling their beards; or making the waist
small, binding it with hoops, while the mind
1760   runs at waste: too much pickedness is not
manly. Nor from those that will jest at their
own outward imperfections, but hide their
ulcers within, their pride, lust, envy, ill nature,
with all the art and authority they can. These
persons are in danger; for whilst they think to
justify their ignorance by impudence, and their
persons by clothes and outward ornaments;
they use but a commission to deceive
themselves. Where, if we will look with our
1770   understanding, and not our senses, we may
behold virtue and beauty (though covered with
rags) in their brightness; and vice, and
deformity so much the fouler, in having all the
splendour of riches to gild them, or the false
light of honour and power to help them. Yet
this is that, wherewith the world is taken, and
runs mad to gaze on: clothes and titles, the
birdlime of fools.

De stultitia   What petty things they are, we wonder at!
1780   Like children, that esteem every trifle; and
prefer a fairing before their fathers: what a
difference is between us and them, but that we
are dearer fools, coxcombs, at a higher rate?
They are pleased with cockleshells, whistles,
hobby-horses, and such like: we with statues,
marble pillars, pictures, gilded roofs, where
underneath is lath, and lime; perhaps loam.
Yet, we take pleasure in the lie, and are glad,
we can cozen ourselves. Nor is it only in our
1790   walls and ceilings; but all that we call happiness
is mere painting, and gilt: and all for money:
what a membrane of honour that is! And how
hath all true reputation fallen, since money
began to have any! Yet the great herd, the
multitude; that in all other things are divided;

in this alone conspire, and agree: to love
money. They wish for it, they embrace it, they
adore it; while yet it is possessed with greater
stir, and torment, than it is gotten.

1800 De sibi molestis   Some men, what losses soever they have, they
make them greater: and if they have none, even
all that is not gotten is a loss. Can there be
creatures of more wretched condition, than
these; that continually labour under their own
misery, and others' envy? A man should study
other things, not to covet, not to fear, not to
repent him: to make his base such, as no
tempest shall shake him: to be secure of all
opinion; and pleasing to himself, even for that,
1810   wherein he displeaseth others. For the worst
opinion gotten for doing well, should delight
us: would'st not thou be just, but for fame;
thou ought'st to be it with infamy: he that
would have his virtue published, is not the
servant of virtue, but glory.

Periculosa   It is a dangerous thing, when men's minds
melancholia   come to sojourn with their affections, and their
diseases eat into their strength: that when too
much desire, and greediness of vice, hath made
1820   the body unfit, or unprofitable; it is yet
gladded with the sight, and spectacle of it in
others: and for want of ability to be an actor;
is content to be a witness. It enjoys the pleasure
of sinning, in beholding others sin; as in
dicing, drinking, drabbing, etc. Nay, when it
cannot do all these, it is offended with his own
narrowness, that excludes it from the universal
delights of mankind; and ofttimes dies of a
melancholy, that it cannot be vicious enough.

1830 Falsae species   I am glad, when I see any man avoid the
fugiendae   infamy of a vice; but to shun the vice itself
were better. Till he do that, he is but like the
prentice, who being loath to be spied by his
master, coming forth of Black Lucy's, went in
again; to whom his master cried; the more
thou runnest that way to hide thyself, the more
thou art in the place. So are those, that keep a

tavern all day, that they may not be seen at
night. I have known lawyers, divines, yea,
great ones, of this heresy.

1840

Decipimur
specie

There is a greater reverence had of things
remote, or strange to us, than of much better,
if they be nearer, and fall under our sense. Men,
and almost all sort of creatures, have their
reputation by distance. Rivers, the farther
they run, and more from their spring, the
broader they are, and greater. And where our
original is known, we are the less confident:
among strangers we trust fortune. Yet a man
may live as renowned at home, in his own
country, or a private village, as in the whole
world. For it is virtue that gives glory: that will
endenisen a man everywhere. It is only that
can naturalize him. A native, if he be vicious,
deserves to be a stranger, and cast out of the
commonwealth, as an alien.

1850

Dejectio Aulic.

A dejected countenance, and mean clothes,
beget often a contempt; but it is with the
shallowest creatures: courtiers commonly:
look up even with them in a new suit; you get
above them straight. Nothing is more
short-lived than their pride: it is but while their
clothes last; stay but while these are worn out,
you cannot wish the thing more wretched, or
dejected.

1860

Poesis, et
pictura.
Plutarch

Poetry, and picture, are arts of a like nature;
and both are busy about imitation. It was
excellently said of Plutarch, poetry was a
speaking picture, and picture a mute poesy. For
they both invent, feign, and devise many
things, and accommodate all they invent to the
use, and service of nature. Yet of the two, the
pen is more noble than the pencil. For that
can speak to the understanding; the other,
but to the sense. They both behold pleasure,
and profit, as their common object; but should
abstain from all base pleasures, lest they
should err from their end; and while they seek
to better men's minds, destroy their manners.

1870

1880

They both are born artificers, not made. Nature is more powerful in them than study.

De pictura

Whosoever loves not picture, is injurious to truth: and all the wisdom of poetry. Picture is the invention of heaven: the most ancient, and most akin to nature. It is itself a silent work: and always of one and the same habit: yet it doth so enter, and penetrate the inmost affection (being done by an excellent artificer) as sometimes it o'ercomes the power of speech

1890

and oratory. There are diverse graces in it; so are there in the artificers. One excels in care, another in reason, a third in easiness, a fourth in nature and grace. Some have diligence, and comeliness: but they want majesty. They can express a human form in all the graces, sweetness, and elegancy; but they miss the authority. They can hit nothing but smooth cheeks; they cannot express roughness, or gravity. Others aspire to truth so much, as they

1900

are rather lovers of likeness, than beauty. Zeuxis, and Parrhasius, are said to be contemporaries: the first, found out the reason of lights, and shadows in picture: the other, more subtly examined the lines.

De stylo

In picture, light is required no less than shadow: so in style, height as well as humbleness. But beware they be not too

Pliny

humble; as Pliny pronounced of Regulus' writings: you would think them written, not

1910

on a child, but by a child. Many, out of their own obscene apprehensions, refuse proper and fit words; as 'occupy', 'nature', and the like: so the curious industry in some of having all alike good, hath come nearer a vice, than a virtue.

De progress.
Picturae.
Parrhasius

Picture took her feigning from poetry: from geometry her rule, compass, lines, proportion, and the whole symmetry. Parrhasius was the first won reputation, by adding symmetry to

1920

picture: he added subtlety to the countenance, elegancy to the hair, loveliness to the face; and, by the public voice of all artificers, deserved honour in the outer lines. Eupompus gave it splendour by numbers, and other elegancies. From the optics it drew reasons; by which it considered, how things placed at distance, and afar off, should appear less; how above, or beneath the head, should deceive the eye, etc. So from thence it took shadows, recessor, light, and heightenings. From moral philosophy it took the soul, the expression of senses, perturbations, manners, when they would paint an angry person, a proud, an inconstant, an ambitious, a brave, an humble, a dejected, a base, and the like. They made all heightenings bright, all shadows dark, all swellings from a plane; all solids from breaking. See *where he complains of their painting chimeras, by the vulgar unaptly called grotesques: saying, that men who were born truly to study, and emulate nature, did nothing but make monsters against nature; which [1]Horace so laughed at. The art plastic was moulding in clay, or potters' earth anciently. This is the parent of statuary: sculpture, graving and picture, cutting in brass, and marble, all serve under her. [2]Socrates taught Parrhasius, and Clito (two noble statuaries) first to express manners by their looks in imagery. [3]Polygnotus, and Aglaophon were ancienter. After them [4]Zeuxis, who was the lawgiver to all painters, after [5]Parrhasius. They were contemporaries, and lived both about Philip's time, the father of Alexander the Great.

There lived in this latter age six famous painters in Italy: who were excellent, and emulous of the ancients: [6]Raphael de Urbino, Michaelangelo Buonarota, Titian, Antonio of Correggio, Sebastian of Venice, Julio Romano, and Andrea Sartorio.

*There are flatterers for their bread, that praise all my oraculous lord does or says, be

Eupompus

1930

Plin. lib. 35. c.
2. 5. 6 & 7

*Vitruv.
li. 8 & 7

1940

1. Horat. in
arte poet.

2. Socrates.
Parrhasius.
1950 Clito.
3. Polygnotus.
Aglaophon.
4. Zeuxis.
5. Parrhasius

6. Raphael de
Urbino. Mich.
Ange.
Buonarota.
1960 Titian. Antonio
de Correg.
Sebast. de
Venet. Julio

Romano. Andrea
Sartorio

*Parasiti ad
mensam

1970

1980

it true or false: invent tales that shall please:
make baits for his lordship's ears: and if they
be not received in what they offer at, they shift
a point of the compass, and turn their tale,
presently tack about; deny what they
confessed, and confess what they denied; fit
their discourse to the persons, and occasions.
What they snatch up, and devour at one table,
utter at another: and grow suspected of the
master, hated of the servants, while they
inquire, and reprehend, and compound, and
delate business of the house they have nothing
to do with: they praise my lord's wine, and the
sauce he likes; observe the cook, and
bottleman, while they stand in my lord's
favour, speak for a pension for them: but
pound them to dust upon my lord's least
distaste, or change of his palate.

How much better is it, to be silent; or at
least, to speak sparingly! For it is not
enough to speak good, but timely things. If a
man be asked a question, to answer; but to
repeat the question, before he answer, is well,
that he be sure to understand it, to avoid
absurdity. For it is less dishonour, to hear
imperfectly, than to speak imperfectly. The
ears are excused, the understanding is not.
And in things unknown to a man, not to give
his opinion, lest by affectation of knowing too
much, he lose the credit he hath by speaking,
or knowing the wrong way, what he utters.
Nor seek to get his patron's favour, by
embarking himself in the factions of the family:
to enquire after domestic simulties, their
sports, or affections. They are an odious, and
vile kind of creatures, that fly about the house
all day; and picking up the filth of the house,
like pies or swallows, carry it to their nest (the
lord's ears) and oftentimes report the lies they
have feigned, for what they have seen and
heard.

1990

2000

Imo serviles

These are called instruments of grace, and

power, with great persons; but they are indeed
the organs of their impotency, and marks of
weakness. For sufficient lords are able to these
discoveries themselves. Neither will an
2010   honourable person inquire, who eats, and
drinks together, what that man plays, whom this
man loves; with whom such a one walks; what
discourse they held; who sleeps with whom.
They are base, and servile natures, that busy
themselves about these disquisitions. How
often have I seen (and worthily) these censors
of the family, undertaken by some honest
rustic, and cudgelled thriftily? These are
commonly the off-scouring, and dregs of men,
2020   that do these things, or calumniate others: yet I
know not truly which is worse; he that
maligns all, or that praises all. There is as great
a vice in praising, and as frequent, as in
detracting.

De liberis   It pleased your lordship of late, to ask my
educandis   opinion, touching the education of your sons,
and especially to the advancement of their
studies. To which, though I returned somewhat
for the present; which rather manifested a will
2030   in me, than gave any just resolution to the
thing propounded: I have upon better
cogitation called those aids about me, both of
mind, and memory; which shall venter my
thoughts clearer, if not fuller, to your
lordship's demand. I confess, my lord, they
will seem but petty, and minute things I shall
offer to you, being writ for children, and of
them. But studies have their infancy, as well
as creatures. We see in men, even the strongest
2040   compositions had their beginnings from milk,
and the cradle; and the wisest tarried sometimes
about apting their mouths to letters, and
syllables. In their education, therefore, the
care must be the greater had of their beginning,
to know, examine, and weigh their natures:
which though they be proner in some children
to some disciplines; yet are they naturally

prompt to taste all by degrees, and with
change. For change is a kind of refreshing in
2050 studies, and infuseth knowledge by way of
recreation. Thence the school itself is called a
play, or game: and all letters are so best taught
to scholars. They should not be affrighted, or
deterred in their entry, but drawn on with
exercise, and emulation. A youth should not
be made to hate study, before he know the
causes to love it: or taste the bitterness before
the sweet; but called on, and allured, entreated,
and praised: yea, when he deserves it not. For
2060 which cause I wish them sent to the best
school, and a public; which I think the best.
Your lordship, I fear, hardly hears of that,
as willing to breed them in your eye, and at
home; and doubting their manners may be
corrupted abroad. They are in more danger in
your own family, among ill servants (allowing,
they be safe in their school-master) than
amongst a thousand boys, however immodest:
would we did not spoil our own children,
2070 and overthrow their manners ourselves by too
much indulgence! To breed them at home, is
to breed them in a shade; where in a school
they have the light, and heat of the sun. They
are used, and accustomed to things and men.
When they come forth into the commonwealth,
they find nothing new, or to seek. They have
made their friendships and aids; some to last
till their age. They hear what is commanded
to others, as well as themselves, much approved,
2080 much corrected; all which they bring to their
own store, and use; and learn as much as they
hear. Eloquence would be but a poor thing, if we
should only converse with singulars; speak
but man and man together. Therefore I like
no private breeding. I would send them where
their industry should be daily increased by
praise; and that kindled by emulation. It is a
good thing to inflame the mind: and though
ambition itself be a vice, it is often the cause of

2090

great virtue. Give me that wit, whom praise
excites, glory puts on, or disgrace grieves: he is
to be nourished with ambition, pricked forward
with honour; checked with reprehension;
and never to be suspected of sloth. Though he
be given to play, it is a sign of spirit, and
liveliness; so there be a mean had of their
sports, and relaxations. And from the rod, or
ferrule, I would have them free, as from the
menace of them: for it is both deformed, and

2100

servile.

De stylo, et
optimo scribendi
genere

For a man to write well, there are required
three necessaries. To read the best authors,
observe the best speakers: and much exercise
of his own style. In style to consider, what
ought to be written; and after what manner;
he must first think, and excogitate his matter;
then choose his words, and examine the weight
of either. Then take care in placing, and ranking
both matter, and words, that the composition

2110

be comely; and to do this with diligence, and
often. No matter how slow the style be at first,
so it be laboured, and accurate: seek the best,
and be not glad of the forward conceits, or first
words, that offer themselves to us, but judge
of what we invent; and order what we approve.
Repeat often, what we have formerly written;
which beside, that it helps the consequence,
and makes the juncture better, it quickens the
heat of imagination, that often cools in the time

2120

of setting down, and gives it new strength, as if
it grew lustier, by the going back. As we see in
the contention of leaping, they jump farthest,
that fetch their race largest: or, as in throwing a
dart, or javelin, we force back our arms, to make
our loose the stronger. Yet, if we have a fair
gale of wind, I forbid not the steering out of
our sail, so the favour of the gale deceive us not.
For all that we invent doth please us in the
conception, or birth; else we would never set

2130

it down. But the safest is to return to our
judgement, and handle over again those

things, the easiness of which might make them
justly suspected. So did the best writers in
their beginnings; they imposed upon themselves
care, and industry. They did nothing rashly.
They obtained first to write well, and then
custom made it easy, and a habit. By little and
little, their matter showed itself to them more
plentifully; their words answered, their
2140   composition followed; and all, as in a
well-ordered family, presented itself in the
place. So that the sum of all is: ready writing
makes not good writing; but good writing
brings on ready writing: yet when we think we
have got the facu ty, it is even then good to
resist it: as to give a horse a check sometimes
with a bit, which doth not so much stop his
course, as stir his mettle. Again, whither a
man's genius is best able to reach, thither
2150   should more and more contend, lift and dilate
itself, as men of low stature, raise themselves
on their toes; and so ofttimes get even, if not
eminent. Besides, as it is fit for grown and able
writers to stand of themselves, and work with
their own strength, to trust and endeavour by
their own faculties: so it is fit for the beginner,
and learner, to study others, and the best. For
the mind, and memory are more sharply
exercised in comprehending another man's
2160   things, than our own; and such as accustom
themselves, and are familiar with the best
authors, shall ever and anon find somewhat
of them in themselves, and in the expression
of their minds, even when they feel it not, be
able to utter something like theirs, which hath
an authority above their own. Nay, sometimes
it is the reward of a man's study, the praise of
quoting another man fitly: and though a man
be more prone, and able for one kind of
2170   writing, than another, yet he must exercise all.
For as in an instrument, so in style, there must
be a harmony, and consent of parts.

Praecipiendi
modi

I take this labour in teaching others, that
they should not be always to be taught; and I
would bring my precepts into practice. For
rules are ever of less force, and value, than
experiments. Yet with this purpose, rather to
show the right way to those that come after,
than to detect any that have slipped before by
2180 error, and I hope it will be more profitable.
For men do more willingly listen, and with
more favour, to precept, than reprehension.
Among diverse opinions of an art, and most of
them contrary in themselves, it is hard to make
election; and therefore, though a man cannot
invent new things after so many, he may do a
welcome work yet to help posterity to judge
rightly of the old. But arts and precepts avail
nothing, except nature be beneficial, and
2190 aiding. And therefore these things are no more
written to a dull disposition, than rules of
husbandry to a barren soil. No precepts will
profit a fool; no more than beauty will the
blind, or music the deaf. As we should take
care, that our style in writing, be neither dry,
nor empty: we should look again it be not
winding, or wanton with far-fetched
descriptions; either is a vice. But that is worse
which proceeds out of want, than that which
2200 riots out of plenty. The remedy of fruitfulness
is easy, but no labour will help the contrary:
I will like, and praise some things in a young
writer; which yet if he continue in, I cannot but
justly hate him for the same. There is a time
to be given all things for maturity; and that
even your country husbandman can teach;
who to a young plant will not put the pruning
knife, because it seems to fear the iron, as not
able to admit the scar. No more would I tell
2210 a green writer all his faults, lest I should make
him grieve and faint, and at last despair. For
nothing doth more hurt, than to make him so
afraid of all things, as he can endeavour
nothing. Therefore youth ought to be

instructed betimes, and in the best things: for
we hold those longest, we take soonest; as the
first scent of a vessel lasts: and that tinct the
wool first receives. Therefore a master should
temper his own powers, and descend to the
2220   other's infirmity. If you pour a glut of water
upon a bottle, it receives little of it; but with a
funnel, and by degrees, you shall fill many of
them, and spill little of your own; to their
capacity they will all receive, and be full.
And as it is fit to read the best authors to youth
first, so let them be of the openest, and

Livy. Sallust.   clearest. As Livy before Sallust, Sidney before
Sidney. Donne.   Donne: and beware of letting them taste
Gower. Chaucer   Gower, or Chaucer at first, lest falling too
2230   much in love with antiquity, and not
apprehending the weight, they grow rough and
barren in language only. When their judgements
are firm, and out of danger, let them read both,
the old and the new: but no less take heed, that
their new flowers, and sweetness do not as
much corrupt, as the other's dryness and

Spenser   squalor, if they choose not carefully. Spenser,
in affecting the ancients, writ no language: yet
I would have him read for his matter; but as
2240 Virgil. Ennius.   Virgil read Ennius. The reading of Homer and
Homer. Virgil.   Virgil is councilled by Quintilian, as the best
Quintilian   way of informing youth, and confirming man.
For besides that the mind is raised with the
height, and sublimity of such a verse, it takes
spirit from the greatness of the matter, and is
tincted with the best things. Tragic, and lyric
poetry is good too: and comic with the best,
if the manners of the reader be once in safety.

Plautus   In the Greek poets, as also in Plautus, we shall
2250   see the economy, and disposition of poems,
Terence   better observed than in Terence, and the later:
who thought the sole grace, and virtue of their
fable the sticking in of sentences, as ours do the
forcing in of jests.

Fals. querel.   We should not protect our sloth with the
fugiend.   patronage of difficulty. It is a false quarrel

against nature, that she helps understanding,
but in a few; when the most part of mankind are
inclined by her thither, if they would take the
pains; no less than birds to fly, horses to run,
etc. Which if they lose, it is through their own
sluggishness, and by that means they become
her prodigies, not her children. I confess,
nature in children is more patient of labour in
study, than in age; for the sense of the pain,
the judgment of the labour is absent, they do
not measure what they have done. And it is the
thought, and consideration, that affects us
more, than the weariness itself. Plato was not
content with the learning that Athens could
give him, but sailed into Italy for Pythagoras'
knowledge: and yet not thinking himself
sufficiently informed, went into Egypt to the
priests, and learned their mysteries. He
laboured, so must we. Many things may be
learned together, and performed in one point
of time; as musicians exercise their memory,
their voice, their fingers, and sometime their
head, and feet at once. And so a preacher, in
the invention of matter, election of words,
composition of gesture, look, pronunciation,
motion, useth all these faculties at once. And
if we can express this variety together, why
should not diverse studies, at diverse hours,
delight, when the variety is able alone to refresh
and repair us? As when a man is weary of
writing, to read; and then again of reading, to
write. Wherein, howsoever we do many things,
yet are we (in a sort) still fresh to what we begin:
we are recreated with change, as the stomach is
with meats. But some will say, this variety
breeds confusion, and makes, that either we
lose all, or hold no more than the last. Why do
we not then persuade husbandmen, that they
should not till land, help it with marl, lime,
and compost, plant hop-gardens, prune trees,
look to bee-hives, rear sheep, and all other
cattle at once? It is easier to do many things,

2260

Platonis
2270 Peregrinatio
in Italiam

2280

2290

and continue, than to do one thing long.

2300 Praecept.
Element.

It is not the passing through these learnings that hurts us, but the dwelling and sticking about them. To descend to those extreme anxieties, and foolish cavils of grammarians, is able to break a wit in pieces: being a work of manifold misery, and vainness, to be *elementarii senes*. Yet even letters are, as it were, the bank of words, and restore themselves to an author, as the pawns of language. But talking and eloquence are not the same: to speak, and

2310

to speak well are two things. A fool may talk, but a wise man speaks, and out of the observation, knowledge, and use of things. Many writers perplex their readers, and hearers with mere nonsense. Their writings need sunshine. Pure and neat language I love, yet plain and customary. A barbarous phrase hath often made me out of love with a good sense; and doubtful writing hath racked me beyond my patience. The reason why a poet is said,

2320

that he ought to have all knowledges, is that he should not be ignorant of the most, especially of those he will handle. And indeed, when the attaining of them is possible, it were a sluggish, and base thing to despair. For frequent imitation of anything, becomes a habit quickly. If a man should prosecute as much, as could be said of everything; his work would find no end.

De orationis
dignitate

2330

Speech is the only benefit man hath to express his excellency of mind above other creatures. It is the instrument of society. Therefore Mercury, who is the president of language, is called *deorum hominumque interpres*. In all speech, words and sense are as the body, and the soul. The sense is as the life and soul of language, without which all words are dead. Sense is wrought out of experience, the knowledge of human life, and actions, or of the liberal arts, which the Greeks

Ε'γκυκλοπαιδέιαν

2340

called *Ε'γκυκλοπαιδέιαν*. Words are the people's; yet there is a choice of them to

Julius Caesar.
Of words see
Hor. de Art.
Poetic. Quintil.
1. 8. Ludov.
Vives, pag. 6
& 7. Metaphora

be made. For *verborum delectus, origo est eloquentiae.* They are to be chose according to the persons we make speak, or the things we speak of. Some are of the camp, some of the sheepcote, some of the pulpit, some of the bar etc. And herein is seen their elegance, and propriety, when we use them fitly, and draw them forth to their just strength and nature, by way of translation, or metaphor. But in this

2350

translation we must only serve necessity (*nam temere nihil transfertur a prudenti*) or commodity, which is a kind of necessity; that is, when we either absolutely want a word to express by, and that is necessity; or when we have not so fit a word, and that is commodity. As when we avoid loss by it, and escape obsceneness, and gain in the grace and property, which helps significance. Metaphors farfet hinder to be understood, and affected,

2360

lose their grace. Or when the person fetcheth his translation from a wrong place. As if a privy councillor should at the table take his metaphor from a dicing house, or ordinary, or a vintner's vault; or a justice of peace, draw his similitudes from the mathematics; or a divine from a bawdy-house, or taverns; or a gentleman of Northamptonshire, Warwickshire, or the midland, should fetch all his illustrations to his country neighbours from shipping, and tell

2370

them of the main sheet, and the boulin. Metaphors are thus many times deformed, as in him that said, *castratam morte aphricani rempublicam.* And another, *stercus curiae glauciam.* And *cana nive conspuit Alpes.* All attempts that are new in this kind are dangerous, and somewhat hard, before they be softened with use. A man coins not a new word without some peril, and less fruit; for if it happen to be received, the praise is but

2380

moderate; if refused, the scorn is assured. Yet we must adventure, for things, at first hard and rough, are by use made tender and gentle. It is an honest error that is committed, following great chiefs.

Consuetudo

Custom is the most certain mistress of language, as the public stamp makes the current money. But we must not be too frequent with the mint, every day coining. Nor fetch words from the extreme and utmost ages; since the

2390 Perspicuitas.
Venustas

chief virtue of a style is perspicuity, and nothing so vicious in it, as to need an interpreter. Words borrowed of antiquity, do lend a kind of majesty to style, and are not without their delight sometimes. For they have

Authoritas

the authority of years, and out of their intermission do win to themselves a kind of grace like newness. But the eldest of the present, and newest of the past language is the best. For what was the ancient language, which some

2400

men so dote upon, but the ancient custom? Yet when I name custom, I understand not the vulgar custom: for that were a precept no less dangerous to language, than life, if we should speak or live after the manners of the vulgar: but that I call custom of speech, which is the consent of the learned; as custom of life, which

Virgil

is the consent of the good. Virgil was most loving of antiquity; yet how rarely doth he

Lucretius
2410

insert *aquai*, and *pictai*! Lucretius is scabrous and rough in these; he seeks them: as some do

Chaucerisme

Chaucerisms with us, which were better expunged and banished. Some words are to be culled out for ornament and colour, as we gather flowers to strew houses, or make garlands; but they are better when they grow to our style; as in a meadow, where though the mere grass and greenness delights, yet the variety of flowers doth heighten and beautify. Marry, we must not play, or riot too much with them, as

2420 Paranomasia

in paranomasies: nor use too swelling, or ill-sounding words; *quae per salebras, altaque, saxa cadunt.* It is true, there is no sound but shall find some lovers, as the bitterest confections are grateful to some palates. Our composition

must be more accurate in the beginning and
end, than in the midst; and in the end more
than in the beginning; for through the midst the
stream bears us. And this is attained by
custom more than care, or diligence. We must
2430　　　　express readily, and fully, not profusely. There
is difference between a liberal, and a prodigal
hand. As it is a great point of art, when our
matter requires it, to enlarge, and veer out of
sail; so to take it in, and contract it, is of no less
praise when the argument doth ask it. Either of
them hath their fitness in the place. A good man
always profits by his endeavour, by his help;
yea, when he is absent; nay, when he is dead,
by his example and memory. So good authors
2440　De stylo.　　　in their style: a strict and succinct style is that,
　　　Tacitus　　　where you can take away nothing without loss,
　　　　　　　　　and that loss to be manifest. The brief style is
　　　The laconic.　　that which expresseth much in little. The
　　　Suetonius　　　concise style, which expresseth not enough,
　　　　　　　　　but leaves somewhat to be understood. The
　　　　　　　　　abrupt style, which hath many breaches, and
　　　Seneca &　　　doth not seem to end, but fall. The congruent,
　　　Fabianus　　　and harmonious fitting of parts in a sentence,
　　　　　　　　　hath almost the fastening, and force of
2450　　　　knitting, and connection: as in stones
　　　　　　　　　well-squared, which will rise strong a great way
　　　　　　　　　without mortar.
　　　Periodi　　　　Periods are beautiful when they are not too
long; for so they have their strength too, as in a
pike or javelin. As we must take the care that
our words and sense be clear; so, if the obscurity
happen through the hearers', or readers' want
of understanding, I am not to answer for them;
no more than for their not listening or marking;
2460　　　　I must neither find them ears, nor mind. But
a man cannot put a word so in sense, but
something about it will illustrate it, if the
writer understand himself. For order helps
much to perspicuity, as confusion hurts.
*Rectitudo lucem adfert; obliquitas et
circumductio offuscat.* We should therefore

2470

Obscuritas
offundit
tenebras.

speak what we can, the nearest way, so as we
keep our gait, not leap; for too short may as well
be not let into the memory, as too long not kept
in. Whatsoever loseth the grace, and clearness,
converts into a riddle; the obscurity is marked,
but not the value. That perisheth, and is
passed by, like the pearl in the fable. Our style
should be like a skein of silk, to be carried, and
found by the right thread, not ravelled, and
perplexed; then all is a knot, a heap. There are
words, that do as much raise a style, as others

Superlatio

can depress it. Superlation, and overmuchness
amplifies. It may be above faith, but never

2480 Cestius

Virgil

above a mean. It was ridiculous in Cestius,
when he said of Alexander: *Fremit oceanus,
quasi indignetur, quod terras relinquas*; but
propitiously from Virgil:

> *Credas innare revulsas*
> *Cycladas.*

2490 Caesar comment:
circa fin

Quintilian

2500

He doth not say it was so, but seemed to be so.
Although it be somewhat incredible, that is
excused before it be spoken. But there are
hyperboles, which will become one language,
that will by no means admit another. As *eos esse
P.R. exercitus, qui coelum possint perrumpere*:
who would say this with us, but a mad man?
Therefore we must consider in every tongue
what is used, what received. Quintilian warns
us, that in no kind of translation, or metaphor,
or allegory, we make a turn from what we
began; as if we fetch the original of our
metaphor from sea, and billows; we end not in
flames and ashes; it is a most foul
inconsequence. Neither must we draw out our
allegory too long, lest either we make ourselves
obscure, or fall into affectation, which is
childish. But why do men depart at all from
the right, and natural ways of speaking?
Sometimes for necessity, when we are driven,
or think it fitter to speak that in obscure words,
or by circumstance, which uttered plainly

would offend the hearers. Or to avoid
obsceneness, or sometimes for pleasure, and
2510   variety; as travellers turn out of the highway,
drawn, either by the commodity of a foot-path,
or, the delicacy, or freshness of the fields. And
all this is called ἐσχηματισμένη, or figured
language.

Oratio imago animi   Language most shows a man: speak that I
may see thee. It springs out of the most
retired, and inmost parts of us, and is the image
of the parent of it, the mind. No glass renders
a man's form, or likeness, so true as his speech.
2520   Nay, it is likened to a man: and as we consider
feature, and composition in a man; so words
in language: in the greatness, aptness, sound,

Structura, & statura, sublimis, humilis, pumila.   structure, and harmony of it. Some men are tall,
and big, so some language is high and great.
Then the words are chosen, their sound
ample, the composition full, the absolution
plenteous, and poured out, all grave, sinewy
and strong. Some are little and dwarfs: so of
speech it is humble, and low, the words poor
and flat; the members and periods, thin and
2530   weak, without knitting, or number. The middle

Mediocris, plana & placida. Vitiosa oratio, vasta, tumens, enormis, affectata, abjecta.   are of a just stature. There the language is
plain, and pleasing: even without stopping,
round without swelling; all well-turned,
composed, elegant, and accurate. The vicious
language is vast, and gaping, full of rock,
mountain, and pointedness: as it affects to be
low, it is abject, and creeps, full of bogs, and
holes. And according to their subject, these
2540   styles vary, and lose their names: for that which
is high and lofty, declaring excellent matter,
becomes vast and tumorous, speaking of petty
and inferior things: so that which was even, and
apt in a mean and plain subject, will appear
most poor and humble in a high argument.
Would you not laugh, to meet a great councillor
of state in a flat cap, with his trunk-hose, and a
hobby-horse cloak, his gloves under his girdle,
and yond haberdasher in a velvet gown,

2550

Figura

Cutis sive
Cortex.
Compositio

2560

Carnosa.
Adipata

2570

Redundans

Jejuna,
macilenta,
2580 strigosa.

Ossea &
nervosa.
Notae Domini
St Albani de
2590 doctrin:
intemper.

furred with sables? There is a certain latitude
in these things, by which we find the degrees.
The next thing to the stature, is the figure and
feature in language: that is, whether it be
round, and straight, which consists of short and
succinct periods, numerous, and polished; or
square and firm, which is to have equal and
strong parts everywhere answerable, and
weighed. The third is the skin, and coat,
which rests in the well-joining, cementing, and
coagmentation of words; when as it is smooth,
gentle and sweet; like a table, upon which you
may run your finger without rubs, and your nail
cannot find a joint; not horrid, rough, wrinkled,
gaping, or chapped. After these the flesh, blood,
and bones come in question. We say it is a
fleshy style, when there is much periphrasis,
and circuit of words; and when with more than
enough, it grows fat and corpulent; *arvina
orationis*, full of suet and tallow. It hath blood,
and juice, when the words are proper and apt,
their sound sweet, and the phrase neat and
picked. *Oratio uncta, & bene pasta.* But where
there is redundancy, both the blood and juice
are faulty, and vicious. *Redundat sanguine,
quae multo plus dicit, quam necesse est.* Juice in
language is somewhat less than blood; for if
words be but becoming, and signifying, and
the sense gentle, there is juice: but where that
wanteth, the language is thin, flagging, poor,
starved, scarce covering the bone; and shows
like stones in a sack. Some men, to avoid
redundancy, run into that; and while they
strive to have no ill blood, or juice, they lose
their good. There be some styles, again, that
have not less blood, but less flesh, and
corpulence. These are bony and sinewy: *ossa
habent, et nervos.*

It was well noted by the late L[ord] St
Albans, that the study of words is the first
distemper of learning: vain matter the second:
and a third distemper is deceit, or the likeness

Dictator.
Aristoteles

of truth; imposture held up by credulity. All
these are the cobwebs of learning, and to let
them grow in us, is either sluttish or foolish.
Nothing is more ridiculous, than to make an
author a dictator, as the Schools have
done Aristotle. The damage is infinite
knowledge receives by it. For to many things a
man should owe but a temporary belief, and a
2600   suspension of his own judgement, not an
absolute resignation of himself, or a perpetual
captivity. Let Aristotle, and others have their
dues; but if we can make further discoveries of
truth and fitness than they, why are we envied?
Let us beware, while we strive to add, we do not
diminish, or deface; we may improve, but not
augment. By discrediting falsehood, truth
grows in request. We must not go about like
men anguished, and perplexed, for vicious
2610   affectations of praise: but calmly study the
separation of opinions, find the errors have
intervened, awake antiquity, call former times
into question; but make no parties with the
present, nor follow any fierce undertakers,
mingle no matter of doubtful credit, with the
simplicity of truth, but gently stir the mould
about the root of the question, and avoid all
digladations, facility of credit, or superstitious
simplicity; seek the consonancy, and
2620   concatenation of truth; stoop only to point of
necessity, and what leads to convenience.
Then make exact animadversion where style
hath degenerated, where flourished, and thrived
in choiceness of phrase, round and clean
composition of sentence, sweet falling of the
clause, varying an illustration by tropes and
figures, weight of matter, worth of subject,
soundness of argument, life of invention, and
depth of judgement. This is *monte potiri*, to get
2630   the hill. For no perfect discovery can be made
upon a flat or a level.

De optimo
scriptore

Now, that I have informed you in the knowing
these things; let me lead you by the hand a

little farther in the direction of the use; and
make you an able writer by practice. The
conceits of the mind are pictures of things, and
the tongue is the interpreter of those pictures.
The order of God's creatures in themselves, is
not only admirable, and glorious, but eloquent:
2640   then he who could apprehend the consequence
of things in their truth, and utter his
apprehensions as truly, were the best writer, or
Cicero   speaker. Therefore Cicero said much when he
said, *dicere recte nemo potest, nisi qui prudentur
intelligit*. The shame of speaking unskilfully
were small, if the tongue only thereby were
disgraced: but as the image of a king, in his seal
ill-represented, is not so much a blemish to the
wax, or the signet that sealed it, as to the prince
2650   it representeth; so disordered speech is not so
much injury to the lips that give it forth, as to
the disproportion, and incoherence of things in
themselves, so negligently expressed. Neither
can his mind be thought to be in tune, whose
words do jar; nor his reason in frame, whose
sentence is preposterous; nor his elocution clear
and perfect, whose utterance breaks itself into
fragments and uncertainties: were it not a
dishonour to a mighty prince, to have the
2660   majesty of his embassage spoiled by a careless
ambassador? And is it not as great an indignity,
that an excellent conceit and capacity, by the
indiligence of an idle tongue, should be
disgraced? Negligent speech doth not only
discredit the person of the speaker, but it
discrediteth the opinion of his reason and
judgement; it discrediteth the force and
uniformity of the matter, and substance. If it
be so then in words, which fly and escape
2670   censure, and where one good phrase begs pardon
for many incongruities, and faults; how shall he
then be thought wise, whose penning is thin
and shallow? How shall you look for wit from
him, whose leisure and head, assisted with the

examination of his eyes, yield you no life, or
sharpness in his writing?

De stylo
epistolari.
Inventio

2680

In writing of letters there is to be regarded
the invention, and the fashion. For the
invention, that ariseth upon your business;
whereof there can be no rules of more
certainty, or precepts of better direction given,
than conjecture can lay down, from the several
occasions of men's particular lives, and
vocations: but sometimes men make business
of kindness: as 'I could not satisfy myself, till
I had discharged my remembrance, and
charged my letter with commendations to you',
or 'My business is no other than to testify my
love to you, and to put you in mind of my

2690

willingness to do you all kind offices', or 'Sir,
have you leisure to descend to the remembering
of that assurance you have long possessed in
your servant; and upon your next opportunity,
make him happy with some commands from
you?' Or, the like; that go a-begging for some
meaning, and labour to be delivered of the
great burthen of nothing. When you have
invented, and that your business be matter,
and not bare form, or mere ceremony, but

2700

some earnest: then you are to proceed to the
ordering of it, and digesting the parts, which is
had out of two circumstances. One is the
understanding of the persons, to whom you are
to write; the other is the coherence of your
sentence. For men's capacity, you are to weigh,
what will be apprehended with greatest
attention, or leisure; what next regarded, and
longed for especially; and what last will leave
most satisfaction, and as it were the sweetest

2710

memorial, and brief of all that is past in his
understanding, whom you write to. For the
consequence of sentences, you must be sure,
that every clause do give the cue one to the
other, and be spoken ere it come. So much for
invention and order.

Modus. 1.
Brevitas

2720

2730

2740

2750

Now for fashion, it consists in four things, which are qualities of your style. The first is brevity. For they must not be treatises, or discourses (your letters) except it be to learned men. And even among them, there is a kind of thrift, and saving of words. Therefore you are to examine the clearest passages of your understanding, and through them to convey the sweetest, and most significant words you can devise; that you may the easier teach them the readiest way to another man's apprehension, and open their meaning fully, roundly, and distinctly. So as the reader may not think a second view cast away upon your letter. And though respect be a part following this; yet now here, and still I must remember it. If you write to a man, whose estate and cense you are familiar with, you may the bolder (to set a task to his brain) venture on a knot. But if to your superior, you are bound to measure him in three farther points: first, your interest in him: secondly, his capacity in your letters: thirdly, his leisure to peruse them. For your interest, or favour with him, you are to be the shorter, or longer, more familiar, or submiss, as he will afford you time. For his capacity, you are to be quicker, and fuller of those reaches, and glances of wit, or learning, as he is able to entertain them. For his leisure, you are commanded to the greater briefness, as his place is of greater discharges, and cares. But, with your betters, you are not to put riddles of wit, by being too scarce of words; nor to cause the trouble of making breviates, by writing too riotous, and wastingly. Brevity is attained in matter, by avoiding idle compliments, prefaces, protestations, parentheses, superfluous circuit of figures, and digressions: in the composition, by omitting conjunctions, 'not only; but also', 'both the one, and the other', 'whereby it cometh to pass', and such like idle particles, that have no great business in a serious letter,

but breaking of sentences; as oftentimes a short
journey is made long, by unnecessary baits.

2760 Quintilian

But, as Quintilian saith, there is a briefness
of the parts sometimes, that makes the whole
long, as 'I came to the stairs, I took a pair of
oars, they launched out, rowed apace, I
landed at the court gate, I paid my fare, went up
to the presence, asked for my lord, I was
admitted'. All this is but 'I went to the court,
and spake with my lord'. This is the fault of
some Latin writers, within these last hundred
years, of my reading, and perhaps Seneca may

2770 be appeached of it; I accuse him not.

2. Perspicuitas

The next property of epistolary style is
perspicuity, and is oftentimes endangered by
the former quality (brevity), oftentimes by
affectation of some wit ill-angled for, or
ostentation of some hidden terms of art. Few
words they darken speech, and so do too many:
as well too much light hurteth the eyes, as too
little; and a long Bill of Chancery confounds
the understanding, as much as the shortest

2780 note. Therefore, let not your letters be penned
like English statutes, and this is obtained.
These vices are eschewed by pondering your
business well, and distinctly conceiving
yourself, which is much furthered by
uttering your thoughts, and letting them as
well come forth to the light, and judgement of
your own outward senses, as to the censure of
other men's ears: for that is the reason why
many good scholars speak but fumblingly;

2790 like a rich man, that, for want of particular note
and difference, can bring you no certain ware
readily out of his shop. Hence it is, that talkative
shallow men do often content the hearers,
more than the wise. But this may find a
speedier redress in writing; where all comes
under the last examination of the eyes. First
mind it well, then pen it, then examine it, then
amend it. Under this virtue may come
plainness, which is not to be curious in the

2800 order, as to answer a letter, as if you were to
answer to interrogatories: as to the first, first;
and to the second, secondly, etc. But both in
method and words to use (as ladies do in their
attire) a diligent kind of negligence, and their
sportive freedom; though with some men you
are not to jest, or practise tricks: yet the delivery
of the most important things, may be carried
with such a grace, as that it may yield a pleasure
to the conceit of the reader. There must be
2810 store, though no excess of terms; as if you are to
name 'store', sometimes you may call it
'choice', sometimes 'plenty'; sometimes
'copiousness', or 'variety': but ever so, that the
word which comes in lieu, have not such
difference of meaning, as that it may put the
sense of the first in hazard to be mistaken.
You are not to cast a ring for the perfumed
terms of the time, as 'accommodation',
'compliment', 'spirit' etc. But use them
2820 properly in their place, as others.

3. Vigor   There followeth life, and quickness, which is
the strength and sinews (as it were) of your
penning by pithy sayings, similitudes, and
conceits, allusions to some known history, or
other common place, such as are in the
Courtier, and the second book of Cicero *De
Oratore*.

4. Discretio   The last is; respect to discern what fits
yourself; him to whom you write; and that
2830 which you handle, which is a quality fit to
conclude the rest, because it doth include all.
And that must proceed from ripeness of
judgement, which, as one truly saith, is gotten
by four means, God, nature, diligence, and
conversation. Serve the first well, and the rest
will serve you.

De Poetica   We have spoken sufficiently of oratory; let
us now make a diversion to poetry. Poetry, in
the primogeniture, had many peccant humours,
2840 and is made to have more now, through the
levity, and inconstancy of men's judgements.

Whereas, indeed, it is the most prevailing
eloquence, and of the most exalted charact.
Now the discredits and disgraces are many it
hath received, through men's study of
depravation or calumny: their practice being
to give it diminution of credit, by lessening the
professors' estimation, and making the age
afraid of their liberty: and the age is grown so

2850   tender of her fame, as she calls all writings
aspersions. That is the state-word, the phrase
of court (Placentia College) which some call
Parasites' Place, the Inn of Ignorance.

    Whilst I name no persons, but deride follies;
why should any man confess, or betray himself?

D. Hieronimus   Why doth not that of S. Hierome come into
their mind; *Ubi generalis est de vitiis
disputatio, ibi nullius esse personae injuriam?* Is it
such an inexpiable crime in poets, to tax vices

2860   generally; and no offence in them who, by
their exception, confess they have committed
them particularly? Are we fallen into those
times that we must not

Pers. Sat. 1   *Auriculas teneras mordaci rodere vero?*

Livius   *Remedii votum semper verius erat, quam spes.*
If men may by no means write freely, or speak
truth, but when it offends not; why do
physicians cure with sharp medicines, or
corrosives? Is not the same equally lawful in the

2870   cure of the mind, that is in the cure of the body?
Some vices (you will say) are so foul, that it is
better they should be done, than spoken.
But they that take offence where no name,
character, or signature doth blazon them,
seem to me like affected as women; who, if
they hear anything ill spoken of the ill of their
sex, are presently moved, as if the contumely

Sexus foemin':   respected their particular: and, on the
contrary, when they hear good of good

2880   women, conclude, that it belongs to them all.
If I see anything that toucheth me, shall I come
forth a betrayer of myself, presently? No; if

ʳ be wise, I'll dissemble it; if honest, I'll avoid
ᵗ: lest I publish that on my own forehead,
ᵛhich I saw there noted without a title. A man,
tnat is on the mending hand, will either
ingenuously confess or wisely dissemble his
disease. And, the wise, and virtuous, will never
think anything belongs to themselves that is
2890 written, but rejoice that the good are warned
not to be such; and the ill to leave to be such.
The person offended hath no reason to be
offended with the writer, but with himself;
and so to declare that properly to belong to him,
which was so spoken of all men, as it could be no
man's several, but his that would wilfully and
desperately claim it. It sufficeth I know, what
kind of persons I displease, men bred in the
declining, and decay of virtue, betrothed to
2900 their own vices; that have abandoned, or
prostituted their good names; hungry and
ambitious of infamy, invested in all deformity,
enthralled to ignorance and malice, of a hidden
and concealed malignity, and that hold a
concomitancy with all evil.

What is a poet?

Poeta   A poet is that, which by the Greeks is called
κατ᾽ εξοχὴν, ὁ Ποιητὴς, a maker, or a feigner:
his art, an art of imitation, or feigning;
2910 expressing the life of man in fit measure,
numbers, and harmony, according to Aristotle:
from the word ποιετυ, which signifies to make,
or feign. Hence, he is called a poet, not he
which writeth in measure only; but that
feigneth and formeth a fable, and writes things
like the truth. For, the fable and fiction is (as
it were) the form and soul of any poetical
work, or poem.

What mean you by a poem?

2920 Poema   A poem is not alone any work, or composition
of the poet's in many, or few verses; but even
one alone verse sometimes makes a perfect
poem. As, when Aeneas hangs up, and

Virgilius. Aeneid lib. 3	consecrates the arms of Abas, with this inscription:

Aeneas haec de Danais victoribus arma.

Martial. lib. 8 epigr. 19	And calls it a poem, or *carmen.* Such are those in Martial:

*Omnia, Castor, emis: sic fiet, ut omnia
2930   vendas.*

And

Pauper videri Cinna vult , & est pauper.

Horatius. Lucretius	So were Horace his odes called *Carmina*; his lyric songs. And Lucretius designs a whole book, in his sixth:

Quod in primo quoque carmine claret.

Epicum. Dramaticum. Lyricum. 2940 Elegiacum. Epigrammat:	And anciently, all the oracles were called *carmina*; or, whatever sentence was expressed, were it much, or little, it was called, an epic, dramatic, lyric, elegiac, or epigrammatic poem.

Poesis   *But, how differs a poem from what we call poesy?*
A poem, as I have told you, is the work of the
poet; the end, and fruit of his labour, and
study. Poesy is his skill, or craft of making: the
very fiction itself, the reason, or form of the
work. And these three voices differ, as the
thing done, the doing, and the doer; the thing
feigned, the feigning, and the feigner: so the
2950   poem, the poesy, and the poet. Now, the poesy
Artium Regina   is the habit, or the art: nay, rather the queen
of arts: which had her original from heaven,
received thence from the Hebrews, and had in
prime estimation with the Greeks, transmitted
to the Latins, and all nations, that professed
civility. The study of it (if we will trust
Aristotle   Aristotle) offers to mankind a certain rule, and
pattern of living well, and happily; disposing
M. T. Cicero   us to all civil offices of society. If we will
2960   believe Tully, it nourisheth, and instructeth

our youth; delights our age; adorns our prosperity; comforts our adversity; entertains us at home; keeps us company abroad; travels with us; watches; divides the times of our earnest, and sports; shares in our country recesses, and recreations; insomuch as the wisest and best learned have thought her the absolute mistress of manners, and nearest of kin to virtue. And, whereas they entitle 2970 philosophy to be a rigid, and austere poesy: they have (on the contrary) styled poesy, a dulcet, and gentle philosophy, which leads on, and guides us by the hand to action, with a ravishing delight, and incredible sweetness. But, before we handle the kinds of poems, with their special differences; or make court to the art itself, as a mistress, I would lead you to the knowledge of our poet, by a perfect information, what he is, or should be by 2980 nature, by exercise, by imitation, by study; and so bring him down through the disciplines of grammar, logic, rhetoric, and the ethics, adding somewhat, out of all, peculiar to himself, and worthy of your admittance, or reception.

Poet: differentiae

1. *Ingenium*

First, we require in our poet, or maker, (for that title our language affords him, elegantly, with the Greek) a goodness of natural wit. For, whereas all other arts consist of doctrine, and precepts: the poet must be 2990 able by nature, and instinct, to pour out the treasure of his mind; and as Seneca saith, *Aliquando secundum Anacreontem insanire, iucundum esse*: by which he understands, the poetical rapture. And according to that of Plato; *Frustra poeticas fores sui compos pulsavit*: and of Aristotle; *Nullum magnum ingenium sine mixtura demeniae fuit. Nec potest grande aliquid, & supra caeteros loqui, nisi mota mens.* Then it riseth higher, as by a divine instinct, 3000 when it contemns common, and known conceptions. It utters somewhat above a mortal mouth. Then it gets aloft, and flies away with

Seneca

Plato.
Aristotle

his rider, whither, before, it was doubtful to
ascend. This the poets understood by their

Helicon. Pegasus. Helicon, Pegasus, or Parnassus; and this made
Parnassus. Ovid to boast:
Ovidius.

Est, deus in nobis; agitante calescimus illo:
Sedibus aetheris spiritus ille venit.

Lipsius And Lipsius, to affirm; *Scio, poetam neminem*
3010 *praestantem fuisse, sine parte quadam uberiore*
divinae aurae. And, hence it is, that the coming
up of good poets (for I mind not mediocres, or
imos) is so thin and rare among us; every
Petron. in beggarly corporation affords the state a mayor,
fragm. or two bailiffs, yearly: but *solus rex, aut poeta,*
2. Exercitatio *non quotannis nascitur.* To this perfection of
nature in our poet, we require exercise of those
parts, and frequent. If his wit will not arrive
suddenly at the dignity of the ancients, let him
3020 not yet fall out with it, quarrel, or be over-
hastily angry; offer, to turn it away from study,
in a humour; but come to it again upon better
cogitation; try another time, with labour. If
then it succeed not, cast not away the quills,
yet: nor scratch the wainscot, beat not the poor
desk; but bring all to the forge, and file, again;
turn it anew. There is no statute law of the
kingdom bids you be a poet, against your will;
or the first quarter. If it come, in a year, or
3030 two, it is well. The common rhymers pour forth
verses, such as they are, extempore, but there
never comes from them one sense, worth the
life of a day. A rhymer, and a poet, are two
Virgil things. It is said of the incomparable Virgil,
that he brought forth his verses like a bear, and
Scaliger after formed them with licking. Scaliger, the
father, writes it of him, that he made a quantity
of verses in the morning, which afore night he
reduced to a less number. But, that which
3040 *Valerius* Valerius Maximus hath left recorded of
Maximus. Euripides, the tragic poet, his answer to
Euripides. Alcestis, another poet, is as memorable, as
Alcestis. modest: who, when it was told to Alcestis, that

Euripides had in three days brought forth but
three verses, and those with some difficulty,
and throes; Alcestis, glorying he could with
ease have sent forth a hundred in the space;
Euripides roundly replied, 'Like enough. But
here is the difference; thy verses will not last
3050 these three days; mine will to all time.' Which
was, as to tell him, he could not write a verse.
I have met many of these rattles, that made a
noise, and buzzed. They had their hum; and no
more. Indeed, things, wrote with labour,
deserve so to be read, and will last their age.

3. Imitatio   The third requisite in our poet, or maker, is
imitation, to be able to convert the substance,
or riches of another poet, to his own use. To
make choice of one excellent man above the
3060 rest, and so to follow him, as the copy may be
mistaken for the principal. Not, as a creature,
that swallows, what it takes in, crude, raw, or
indigested; but, that feeds with an appetite,
and hath a stomach to concoct, divide, and
turn all into nourishment. Not, to imitate

Horatius   servilely, as Horace saith, and catch at vices, for
virtue: but, to draw forth out of the best, and
choicest flowers, with the bee, and turn all into
honey, work it into one relish, and savour:
3070   make our imitation sweet: observe how the best
Virgilius.   writers have imitated, and follow them. How
Statius. Homer.   Virgil, and Statius have imitated Homer; how
Horat. Archil.   Horace, Archilochus; how Alcaeus, and the
Alcaeus. etc.   other lyrics: and so of the rest. But, that, which
we especially require in him is an exactness of
study, and multiplicity of reading, which
maketh a full man, not alone enabling him to
4. Lectio   know the history, or argument of a poem, and
to report it: but so to master the matter, and
3080   style, as to show he knows how to handle,
place, or dispose of either, with elegancy, when
need shall be. And not think he can leap forth
suddenly a poet, by dreaming he hath been in
Parnassus.   Parnassus, or having washed his lips in
Helicon. Ars   Helicon. There goes more to his making, than

coron.

M. T. Cicero

Simylus. Stob.

Horatius.
Aristoteles

so. For to nature, exercise, imitation, and study,
art must be added, to make all these perfect.
And, though these challenge to themselves
much, in the making up of our maker, it is art
only can lead him to perfection, and leave him
there in possession, as planted by her hand. It
is the assertion of Tully, if to an excellent
nature, there happen an accession, or
conformation of learning, and discipline, there
will then remain somewhat noble, and
singular. For, as Simylus saith in Stobaeus;

Οὔτε φύσις ἱκανὴ γίνεται τέχνης ἄτερ
οὔτε πάν τέχνη μὴ φύσιν κεκτημένη

without art, nature can never be perfect; &,
without nature, art can claim no being. But,
our poet must beware, that his study be not
only to learn of himself; for, he that shall
affect to do that, confesseth his ever having a
fool to his master. He must read many; but,
ever the best and choicest: those, that teach
him anything, he must ever account his
masters, and reverence: among whom Horace,
and (he that taught him) Aristotle, deserve to
be the first in estimation. Aristotle was the
first accurate critic, and truest judge; nay, the
greatest philosopher, the world ever had: for,
he noted the vices of all knowledges, in all
creatures, and out of many men's perfections
in a science, he formed still one art. So he
taught us two offices together, how we ought
to judge rightly of others, and what we ought
to imitate specially in ourselves. But all this in
vain, without a natural wit, and a poetical
nature in chief. For, no man, so soon as he
knows this, or reads it, shall be able to write the
better; but as he is adapted to it by nature, he
shall grow the perfect writer. He must have
civil prudence, and eloquence, & that whole;
not taken up by snatches, or pieces, in sentences,
or remnants, when he will handle business, or
carry councils, as if he came then out of the

Virorum schola
3130 Respub.

declaimers' gallery, or shadow, but furnished
out of the body of the state, which commonly
is the school of men. The poet is the nearest
borderer upon the orator, and expresseth all his
virtues, though he be tied more to numbers; is
his equal in ornament, and above him in his
strengths. And (of the kind) the comic comes
nearest: because, in moving the minds of men,
and stirring of affections (in which oratory
shows, and especially approves her eminence)
he chiefly excels. What figure of a body was

Lysippus.
Apelles
3140

Lysippus ever able to form with his graver, or
Apelles to paint with his pencil, as the comedy
to life expresseth so many, and various
affections of the mind? There shall the spectator
see some, insulting with joy; others, fretting
with melancholy; raging with anger; mad with
love; boiling with avarice; undone with riot;
tortured with expectation; consumed with
fear: no perturbation in common life, but the
orator finds an example of it in the scene. And
then, for the elegancy of language, read but

Naevius

this inscription on the grave of a comic poet:

3150

Immortales mortales, si fas esset, flere,
Flerent divae Camoenae Naevium poetam;
Itaque postquam est Orcino traditus thesauro,
Obliti sunt Romae, lingua loqui Latina.

L. Aelius
Stilo. Plautus

Or, that modester testimony given by Lucius
Aelius Stilo upon Plautus; who affirmed,
Musas, si latine loqui voluissent, Plautino
sermone fuisse loquuturas. And that illustrious

M. Varro

judgement by the most learned M. Varro of
him; who pronounced him the prince of
3160 letters, and elegancy, in the Roman language.
I am not of that opinion to conclude a poet's
liberty within the narrow limits of laws, which
either the grammarians, or philosophers
prescribe. For, before they found out those
laws, there were many excellent poets, that
fulfilled them. Amongst whom none more

Sophocles

Demosthenes.
3170 Pericles

Alcibiades

perfect than Sophocles, who lived a little before
Aristotle. Which of the Greeklings durst ever
give precepts to Demosthenes? Or to Pericles,
whom the age surnamed heavenly, because
he seemed to thunder, and lighten, with his
language? Or to Alcibiades, who had rather
nature for his guide, than art for his master?

But, whatsoever nature at any time dictated
to the most happy, or long exercise to the most
laborious; that the wisdom, and learning of
Aristotle, hath brought into an art: because, he
understood the causes of things: and what
other men did by chance or custom, he doth by
reason; and not only found out the way not to
err, but the short way we should take, not to
err.

Aristotle

3180

Euripides.
Aristophanes

Many things in Euripides hath Aristophanes
wittily reprehended; not out of art, but out of
truth. For, Euripides is sometimes peccant, as
he is most times perfect. But judgement when
it is greatest, if reason doth not accompany it, is
not ever absolute.

Cens: Scal: in
3190 Lil. Gre. Senec:
de brev: vit:
cap. 13 &
epist. 88

To judge of poets is only the faculty of
poets; and not of all poets, but the best. *Nemo
infaelicius de poetis judicavit, quam qui de
poetis scripsit*. But, some will say, critics are a
kind of tinkers; that make more faults, than
they mend ordinarily. See their diseases, and
those of grammarians. It is true, many bodies
are the worse for the meddling with: and the
multitude of physicians hath destroyed many
sound patients, with their wrong practice. But
the office of a true critic, or censor, is, not to
3200 throw by a letter anywhere, or damn an
innocent syllable, but lay the words together,
and amend them; judge sincerely of the author,
and his matter, which is the sign of solid, and
perfect learning in a man. Such was Horace,
an author of much civility; and (if any one
among the heathen can be) the best master,
both of virtue and wisdom; an excellent, and
true judge upon cause, and reason; not because

Horace

he thought so; but because he knew so, out of
3210   use and experience.

Heins: de   Cato, the Grammarian, a defender of
Sat: 265   Lucilius.

Cato Grammaticus, Latina syren,
Qui solus legit, & facit poetas.

Pag. 267.   Quintilian of the same heresy, but rejected.
Pag. 270. 271.   Horace his judgement of Chaerilus,
Pag. 273 & seq.   defended against Joseph Scaliger. And, of
Pag. in comm.   Laberius, against Julius.
153 & seq.   But chiefly his opinion of Plautus,
3220   vindicated against many, that are offended, and
say, it is a hard censure upon the parent of all
conceipt, and sharpness. And, they wish it had
not fallen from so great a master, and censor in
the art: whose bondmen knew better how to
judge of Plautus, than any that dare patronize
the family of learning in this age; who could
not be ignorant of the judgement of the times,
in which he lived, when poetry, and the Latin
language were at the height; especially, being
3230   a man so conversant, and inwardly familiar
with the censures of great men, that did
discourse of these things daily amongst
themselves. Again, a man so gracious, and in
high favour with the emperor, as Augustus
often called him his witty manling (for the
littleness of his stature); and (if we may trust
antiquity) had designed him for a secretary
of estate; and invited him to the palace, which
he modestly prayed off, and refused.
3240 Terence.   Horace did so highly esteem Terence his
Menander   comedies, as he ascribes the art in comedy to
him alone, among the Latins, and joins him
with Menander.
Now, let us see what may be said for either,
to defend Horace his judgement to posterity;
and not wholly to condemn Plautus.
The parts of a   The parts of a comedy are the same with a
comedy and   tragedy, and the end is partly the same. For,
tragedy.   they both delight, and teach: the comics are

3250

called, διδάσχαλοι, of the Greeks; no less than the tragics.

Nor, is the moving of laughter always the end of comedy, that is rather a fooling for the people's delight, or their fooling. For, as Aristotle says rightly, the moving of laughter is a fault in comedy, a kind of turpitude, that depraves some part of a man's nature without a disease. As a wry face without pain moves laughter, or a deformed vizard, or a rude

Aristotle

3260

clown, dressed in a lady's habit, and using her actions, we dislike, and scorn such representations; which made the ancient philosophers ever think laughter unfitting in a

Plato.

wise man. And this induced Plato to esteem of

Homer

Homer, as a sacrilegious person; because he presented the gods sometimes laughing. As, also, it is divinely said of Aristotle, that to seem ridiculous is a part of dishonesty, and foolish.

3270 The wit of the old comedy

So that, what either in the words, or sense of an author, or in the language, or actions of men, is awry, or depraved, doth strangely stir mean affections, and provoke for the most part to laughter. And therefore it was clear that all insolent, and obscene speeches; jests upon the best men; injuries to particular persons; perverse and sinister sayings (and the rather unexpected) in the old comedy, did move laughter; especially, where it did imitate any

3280

dishonesty; and scurrility came forth in the place of wit: which who understands the nature and genius of laughter, cannot but perfectly know.

Aristophanes.
Plautus

Of which Aristophanes affords an ample harvest, having not only outgone Plautus, or any other in that kind; but expressed all the moods, and figures of what is ridiculous, oddly. In short, as vinegar is not accounted good, until the wine is corrupted: so jests that are true and

3290

natural, seldom raise laughter, with the beast, the multitude. They love nothing, that is right, and proper. The farther it runs from reason, or possibility with them, the better it is. What could have made them laugh, like to see Socrates presented, that example of all good life, honesty, and virtue, to have him hoisted up with a pulley, and there play the philosopher, in a basket? Measure, how many foot a flea could skip geometrically, but a just scale, and edify the people from the engine? This was theatrical wit, right stage-jesting, and relishing a play-house, invented for scorn, and laughter; whereas, if it had savoured of equity, truth, perspicuity, and candour, to have tasten a wise, or a learned palate, spit it out presently; this is bitter and profitable, this instructs, and would inform us: what need we know anything, that are nobly born, more than a horse-race, or a hunting-match, our day to break with citizens, and such innate mysteries? This is truly leaping from the stage to the tumbril again, reducing all wit to the original dungcart.

Socrates

3300 *Theatrical wit*

3310

Of the magnitude and compass of any fable, epic or dramatic

To the resolving of this question, we must first agree in the definition of the fable. The fable is called the imitation of one entire, and perfect action; whose parts are so joined, and knit together, as nothing in the structure can be changed, or taken away, without impairing, or troubling the whole; of which there is a proportionable magnitude in the members. As for example; if a man, would build a house, he would first appoint a place to build it in, which he would define within certain bounds; so in the constitution of a poem, the action is aimed at by the poet, which answers place in a building; and that action hath his largeness, compass, and proportion. But, as a court or king's palace, requires other dimensions than a private house: so the epic asks a magnitude,

What the measure of a fable is. The fable or **3320** *plot of a poem, defined*

3330

The epic fable

from other poems. Since, what is place in the one, is action in the other, the difference is in space. So that by this definition we conclude the fable to be the imitation of one perfect, and entire action; as one perfect, and entire place is required to a building. By perfect, we understand that to which nothing is wanting; as place to the building, that is raised, and action to the fable, that is formed. It is perfect, perhaps, not for a court, or king's palace, which requires a greater ground; but for the structure we would raise. So the space of the action, may not prove large enough for the epic fable, yet be perfect for the dramatic, and whole.

Differing from the dramatic (marginal note)

Whole, we call that, and perfect, which hath a beginning, a midst, and an end. So the place of any building may be whole, and entire, for that work; though too little for a palace. As, to a tragedy or a comedy, the action may be convenient, and perfect, that would not fit an epic poem in magnitude. So a lion is a perfect creature in himself, though it be less than an elephant. The head of a lion is a whole, though it be less than that of a buffalo, or a rhinocerote. They differ; but in specie: either in the kind is absolute. Both have their parts, and either the whole. Therefore, as in every body; so in every action, which is the subject of a just work, there is required a certain proportionable greatness, neither too vast, nor too minute. For that which happens to the eyes, when we behold a body, the same happens to the memory, when we contemplate an action. I look upon a monstrous giant, as Tityus, whose body covered nine acres of land, and mine eye sticks upon every part; the whole that consists of those parts, will never be taken in at one entire view. So in a fable, if the action be too great, we can never comprehend the whole together in our imagination. Again, if it be too little, there ariseth no pleasure out of the

What we understand by whole (marginal note)

3340 3350 3360 3370

object, it affords the view no stay: it is beheld
and vanisheth at once. As if we should look
upon an ant or pismire, the parts fly the sight,
and the whole considered is almost nothing.
The same happens in action, which is the
object of memory, as the body is of sight. Too
vast oppresseth the eyes, and exceeds the
memory: too little scarce admits either.

3380

What the
utmost bound
of a fable

Now, in every action it behoves the poet to
know which is his utmost bound, how far with
fitness, and a necessary proportion, he may
produce, and determine it. That is, till either
good fortune change into the worse, or the
worse into the better. For, as a body without
proportion cannot be goodly, no more can the
action, either the comedy, or tragedy, without
his fit bounds. And every bound, for the
nature of the subject, is esteemed the best that
is largest, till it can increase no more: so it
behoves the action in tragedy, or comedy, to be
let grow, till the necessity ask a conclusion:
wherein two things are to be considered; first
that it exceed not the compass of one day: next,
that there be place left for digression, and art.
For the episodes, and digressions in a fable,
are the same that household stuff, and other
furniture are in a house. And so far for the
measure, and extent of a fable dramatic.

3390

3400

What by one
and entire

Now, that it should be one, and entire. One
is considerable two ways: either, as it is only
separate, and by itself: or as being composed
of many parts, it begins to be one, as those
parts grow, or are wrought together. That it
should be one the first way alone, and by itself,
no man that hath tasted letters ever would say,
especially having required before a just
magnitude, and equal proportion of the parts
in themselves. Neither of which can possibly
be, if the action be single and separate, not
composed of parts, which laid together in
themselves, with an equal and fitting proportion,
tend to the same end; which thing out of

3410

antiquity itself, hath deceived many; and more
this day it doth deceive.

So many there be of old, that have thought
the action of one man to be one: as of Hercules,
Theseus, Achilles, Ulysses, and other heroes;
which is both foolish and false; since by one
and the same person many things may be
severally done, which cannot fitly be referred,
or joined to the same end: which not only the
excellent tragic poets, but the best masters of
the epic, Homer, and Virgil saw. For, though
the argument of an epic poem be far more
diffused, and poured out, than that of tragedy;
yet Virgil, writing of Aeneas, hath
pretermitted many things. He neither tells how
he was born, how brought up; how he fought
with Achilles; how he was snatched out of the
battle by Venus; but that one thing, how he
came into Italy, he prosecutes in twelve books.
The rest of his journey, his error by sea, the
sack of Troy, are put not as the argument of
the work, but episodes of the argument. So
Homer laid by many things of Ulysses and
handled no more, than he saw tended to one
and the same end.

Contrary to which and foolishly those
poets did, whom the philosopher taxeth; of
whom one gathered all the actions of Theseus;
another put all the labours of Hercules in one
work. So did he, whom Juvenal mentions in the
beginning, hoarse Codrus, that recited a
volume compiled, which he called his
Theseide, not yet finished, to the great trouble
both of his hearers and himself: amongst
which there were many parts had no coherence,
nor kindred one with another, so far they
were from being one action, one fable. For as a
house, consisting of diverse materials, becomes
one structure, and one dwelling; so an action,
composed of diverse parts, may become one
fable epic, or dramatic. For example, in a
tragedy, look upon Sophocles his *Ajax*:

3420 Hercules.
Theseus.
Achilles.
Ulysses

Homer and
Virgil

3430 Aeneas

Homer
3440

Theseus.
Hercules.
Juvenal. Codrus

3450

Sophocles. Ajax   Ajax deprived of Achilles' armour, which he
3460   hoped from the suffrage of the Greeks,
disdains; and, growing impatient of the injury,
rageth, and turns mad. In that humour he
doth many senseless things; and at last falls
upon the Grecian flocks, and kills a great ram

Ulysses   for Ulysses: returning to his senses, he grows
ashamed of the scorn, and kills himself; and
is by the chiefs of the Greeks forbidden
burial. These things agree, and hang together,
not as they were done; but as seeming to be
3470   done; which made the action whole, entire,
and absolute.

The conclusion   For the whole, as it consisteth of parts; so
concerning the   without all the parts it is not the whole; and to
whole and the   make it absolute, is required, not only the parts,
parts   but such parts as are true. For a part of the
whole was true; which if you take away, you
either change the whole, or it is not the whole.
For, if it be such a part, as being present or
absent, nothing concerns the whole, it cannot
3480   be called a part of the whole: and such are the
Which are ·   episodes, of which hereafter. For the present,
episodes. Ajax,   here is one example; the single combat of Ajax
and Hector.   with Hector, as it is at large described in
Homer   Homer, nothing belongs to this *Ajax* of
Sophocles.

You admire no poems, but such as run like
a brewer's-cart upon the stones, hobbling,

Martial.   *Et, quae per salebras, altaque saxa cadunt.*
lib. 11.   *Actius, & quidquid Pacuviusque vomunt.*
3490 epigr. 91   *Attonitusque legis terrai, frugiferai.*

FINIS

Ben Jonson's
Conversations with William Drummond
of Hawthornden

Ben Ionsiana: informations by Ben Jonson to W. D. when he came to Scotland upon foot, 1619.
Certain informations and manners of Ben Jonson's to W. Drummond.

1. That he had an intention to perfect an epic poem entitled *Herologia*, of the worthies of his country, roused by fame, and was to dedicate it to his country, it is all in couplets, for he detesteth all other rhymes. Said he had written a discourse of poesy both against Campion and Daniel, especially this last, where he proves couplets to be the bravest sort of verses, especially when they are broken, like hexameters; and that cross-rhymes and stanzas (because the purpose would lead him beyond eight lines to conclude) were all forced.

10 2. He recommended to my reading Quintilian (who – he said – would tell me all the faults of my verses as if he had lived with me) and Horace, Plinius secundus, *Epistles*, Tacitus, Juvenal, Martial; whose epigram 'Vitam quae faciunt beatiorem' etc., he hath translated.

3. His censure of the English poets was this, that Sidney did not keep a decorum in making everyone speak as well as himself.

Spenser's stanzas pleased him not, nor his matter, the meaning of which allegory he had delivered in papers to
20 Sir Walter Raleigh.

Samuel Daniel was a good honest man, had no children: but no poet.

That Michael Drayton's *Poly-Olbion* (if he had performed what he promised to write, the deeds of all the worthies) had been excellent: his long verses pleased him not.

That Sylvester's translation of Du Bartas was not well done, and that he wrote his verses before it ere he understood to confer. Nor that of Fairfax his.

That the translations of Homer and Virgil in long Alex-
30 andrines were but prose.

That John Harington's Ariosto, under all translations, was the worst. That when Sir John Harington desired him to tell the truth of his epigrams, he answered him, that he loved not the truth, for they were narrations, and not epigrams.

That Warner, since the king's coming to England, had marred all his *Albion's England*.

That Donne's *Anniversary* was profane and full of blasphemies: that he told Mr Donne, if it had been written of the Virgin Mary it had been something; to which he answered, that he described the idea of a woman, and not as she was.

That Donne, for not keeping of accent, deserved hanging.

That next himself only Fletcher and Chapman could make a masque.

That Shakespeare wanted art.

That Sharpham, Day, Dekker, were all rogues and that Minshew was one.

That Abram Francis in his English hexameters was a fool.

4. His judgement of stranger poets was that he thought not Bartas a poet but a verser, because he wrote not fiction.

He cursed Petrarch for redacting verses to sonnets, which he said were alike that tyrant's bed, where some who were too short were racked, others too long cut short.

That Guarini, in his *Pastor Fido*, kept not decorum, in making shepherds speak as well as himself could.

That Lucan, taken in parts, was good divided, read altogether merited not the name of a poet.

That Bonefonius' *Virgilium Veneris* was excellent.

That he told Cardinal de Perron, at his being in France, anno 1613, who shew him his translations of Virgil, that they were nought.

That the best pieces of Ronsard were his odes.

All this was to no purpose for he neither doth understand French nor Italian.

5. He read his translation of that ode of Horace,
'Beatus ille qui procul negotiis' etc.
and admired it.
Of an epigram of Petronius,
'Foeda et brevis est Veneris voluptas',

70 concluding it was better to lie still and kiss than . . . .

To me he read the preface of his *Art of Poesy*, upon Horace *Art of Poesy*, where he hath an apology of a play of his, *St Bartholomee's Fair*, by Criticus is understood Donne. There is an epigram of Sir Edward Herbert's before it, the [translation] he said he had done in my Lord Aubigny's house ten years since anno 1604.

The most common piece of his repetition was a dialogue pastoral between a shepherd and shepherdess about singing, another Ferrabosco's pavane with his letter, that epigram of
80 gut, my Lady Bedford's buck, his verses of drinking, 'Drink to me but with thine eyes', 'Swell me a bowl' etc., his verses of a kiss,

But kiss me once and faith I will be gone;
And I will touch as harmless as the bee
That doth but taste the flower and flee away.
That is but half a one;
What should be done but once should be done long.

He read a satire of a lady come from the bath; verses on the pucelle of the court, Mistress Bulstrode, whose epitaph
90 Donne made; a satire, telling there was no abuses to write a satire of and in which he repeateth all the abuses in England and the world. He insisted in that of Martial's 'Vitam quae faciunt beatiorem'.

6. His censure of my verses was that they were all good, especially my epitaph of the prince, save that they smelled too much of the Schools, and were not after the fancy of the time; for a child, says he, may write after the fashion of the Greeks and Latin verses in running; yet that he wished, to please the king, that piece of 'Forth Feasting' had been his
100 own.

7. He esteemeth Donne the first poet in the world, in some things: his verses of the lost chain he hath by heart; and that passage of 'The Calm', that dust and feathers do not stir, all was so quiet. Affirmeth Donne to have written all his best pieces ere he was twenty-five years old.

Sir Henry Wotton's verses of a happy life he hath by heart, and a piece of Chapman's translation of the thirteen of the *Iliads*, which he thinketh well done.

That Donne said to him he wrote that epitaph on Prince
110 Henry, 'Look to me, faith', to match Sir Ed: Herbert in obscureness.

He hath by heart some verses of Spenser's *Calendar*, about wine, between Colin and Percy.

8. The conceit of Donne's 'Transformation' or 'μετεμψυ-χοσις' was, that he sought the soul of that apple which Eva pulled, and thereafter made it the soul of a bitch, then of a she wolf, and so of a woman. His general purpose was to have brought in all the bodies of the heretics from the soul of Cain, and at last left it in the body of Calvin. Of this he
120 never wrote but one sheet, and now, since he was made doctor, repenteth highly, and seeketh to destroy all his poems.

9. That Petronius, Plinius secundus, Tacitus, spoke best Latin; that Quintilian's 6, 7, 8 books were not only to be read, but altogether digested. Juvenal, Perse, Horace, Martial, for delight and so was Pindar. For health Hippocrates.

Of their nation, Hooker's *Ecclesiastical History* (whose children are now beggars) for church matters. Selden's
130 *Titles of Honour* for antiquities here; and one book of the *Gods of the Gentiles*, whose names are in the scripture, of Selden's.

Tacitus, he said, wrote the secrets of the council and senate, as Suetonius did those of the cabinet and court.

10. For a heroic poem, he said, there was no such ground as King Arthur's fiction and that S[ir] P. Sidney had an intention to have transformed all his *Arcadia* to the stories of King Arthur.

11. His acquaintance and behaviour with poets living with
140 him.

Daniel was at jealousies with him.

Drayton feared him, and he esteemed not of him.

That Francis Beaumont loved too much himself and his own verses.

That Sir John Roe loved him; and when they two were ushered by my Lord Suffolk from a masque, Roe wrote a moral epistle to him, which began 'That next to plays, the court and the state were the best. God threateneth kings, kings lords, and lords do us'.

150 He beat Marston, and took his pistol from him.

Sir W. Alexander was not half kind unto him, and neglected him, because a friend to Drayton.

That Sir R. Ayton loved him dearly.

Ned Field was his scholar, and he had read to him the satires of Horace, and some epigrams of Martial.

That Markham (who added his *English Arcadia*) was not of the number of the faithful, i.e. poets, and but a base fellow.

That such were Day and Middleton.

That Chapman and Fletcher were loved of him.

160 Overbury was first his friend, then turned his mortal enemy.

12. Particulars of the actions of other poets, and apothegms. That the Irish, having robbed Spenser's goods and burnt his house and a little child new-born, he and his wife escaped, and after he died for lack of bread in King Street, and refused 20 pieces sent to him by my Lord of Essex, and said he was sorry he had no time to spend them.

That in that paper S[ir] W. Raleigh had of the allegories of his *Faerie Queene*, by the blating beast the puritans were

170 understood; by the false Duessa the Q[ueen] of Scots.

That Southwell was hanged; yet so he had written that piece of his 'The burning babe', he would have been content to destroy many of his.

Franc[is] Beaumont died ere he was thirty years of age.

Sir John Roe was an infinite spender, and used to say, when he had no more to spend he could die. He died in his arms of the pest, and he furnished his charges, £20; which was given him back.

That Drayton was challenged for entitling one book
180 *Mortimuriados*.

That S[ir] J. Davies played in an epigram on Drayton,
who in a sonnet concluded his mistress might been the
ninth Worthy; and said, he used a phrase like Dametas in
Arcadia, who said, 'For wit his mistress might be a giant'.

Donne's grandfather, on the mother side, was Heywood
the epigrammatist.

That Donne himself, for not being understood, would
perish.

That Sir W. Raleigh esteemed more of fame than con-
190 science.

The best wits of England were employed for making of his
History. Ben himself had written a piece to him of the Punic
War, which he altered and set in his book. S[ir] W. hath
written the life of Queen Elizabeth, of which there is copies
extant.

Sir P. Sidney had translated some of the psalms, which
went abroad under the name of the Countess of Pembroke.

Marston wrote his father-in-law's preachings, and his
father-in-law his comedies.
200 Shakespeare, in a play, brought in a number of men
saying they had suffered shipwreck in Bohemia, where there
is no sea near by some 100 miles.

Daniel wrote *Civil Wars*, and yet hath not one battle in
all his book.

The Countess of Rutland was nothing inferior to her
father, S[ir] P. Sidney, in poesy. Sir Th. Overbury was in
love with her, and caused Ben to read his 'Wife' to her,
which he, with an excellent grace, did, and praised the
author. That the morn thereafter he discorded with Over-
210 bury, who would have him to intend a suit that was unlawful.
The lines my lady kept in remembrance, 'He comes too
near, who comes to be denied'. Beaumont wrote that elegy
on the death of the Countess of Rutland, and in effect her
husband wanted the half of his in his travels.

Owen is a poor pedantic schoolmaster, sweeping his living

from the posteriors of little children, and hath nothing good in him, his epigrams being mere narrations.

Chapman hath translated Musaeus in his verses, like his Homer.

220 Fletcher and Beaumont, ten years since, hath written *The Faithful Shepherdess*, a tragicomedy, well done.

Dyer died unmarried.

Sir P. Sidney was no pleasant man in countenance, his face being spoiled with pimples, and of high blood, and long: that my lord Lisle, now Earl of Leicester, his eldest son resembleth him.

13. Of his own life, education, birth, actions. His grandfather came from Carlisle, and he thought from Annandale to it, he served Henry VIII, and was a gentleman. His 230 father lost all his estate under Queen Mary, having been cast in prison and forfeited, at last turned minister: so he was a minister's son. He himself was posthumous born, a month after his father's decease, brought up poorly, put to school by a friend (his master Camden), after taken from it, and put to another craft (I think was to be a wright or bricklayer), which he could not endure, then went he to the Low Countries, but returning soon he betook himself to his wonted studies. In his service in the Low Countries, he had, in the face of both the camps, killed an enemy and taken 240 *opima spolia* from him, and since his coming to England, being appealed to the fields, he had killed his adversary, which had hurt him in the arm, and whose sword was ten inches longer than his: for the which he was imprisoned, and almost at the gallows. Then took he his religion by trust, of a priest who visited him in prison. Thereafter he was twelve years a papist.

He was Master of Arts in both the universities, by their favour, not his study.

He married a wife who was a shrew yet honest, five years 250 he had not bedded with her, but remained with my lord Aubigny.

In the time of his close imprisonment, under Queen

Elizabeth, his judges could get nothing of him to all their demands but 'aye' and 'no'. They placed two damned villains to catch advantage of him, with him, but he was advertised by his keeper; of the spies he hath an epigram.

When the king came in England, at that time the pest was in London, he being in the country at S[i]r Robert Cotton's home with old Camden, he saw in a vision his
260 eldest son (then a child and at London) appear unto him with the mark of a bloody cross on his forehead, as if he had been cutted with a sword, at which amazed he prayed unto God, and in the morning he came to Mr Camden's chamber to tell him, who persuaded him it was but an apprehension of his fantasy at which he should not be disjected; in the meantime comes there letters from his wife of the death of that boy in the plague. He appeared to him (he said) of a manly shape, and of that growth that he thinks he shall be at the resurrection.

270 He was delated by Sir James Murray to the king for writing something against the Scots in a play, *Eastward Ho*, and voluntarily imprisoned himself with Chapman and Marston, who had written it amongst them. The report was, that they should then have their ears cut and noses. After their delivery, he banqueted all his friends; there was Camden, Selden and others. At the midst of the feast his old mother drank to him, and shew him a paper which she had (if the sentence had taken execution) to have mixed in the prison among his drink, which was full of lusty strong
280 poison, and that she was no churl, she told, she minded first to have drunk of it herself.

He had many quarrels with Marston, beat him, and took his pistol from him, wrote his *Poetaster* on him; the beginning of them were that Marston represented him in the stage.

In his youth given to venery. He thought the use of a maid nothing in comparison to the wantonness of a wife, and would never have another mistress. He said two accidents strange befell him: one, that a man made his own wife to court him, whom he enjoyed two years ere he knew of it,
290 and one day finding them by chance, was passingly de-

lighted with it; one other, lay diverse times with a woman, who shew him all that he wished, except the last act, which she would never agree unto.

S[ir] W. Raleigh sent him governor with his son, anno 1613, to France. This youth, being knavishly inclined, among other pastimes (as the setting of the favours of damsels on a cod-piece), caused him to be drunken, and dead drunk, so that he knew not where he was, thereafter laid him on a car, which he made to be drawn by pioneers through the streets, at every corner showing his governor stretched out, and telling them, that was a more lively image of the crucifix than any they had: at which sport young Raleigh's mother delighted much (saying, his father young was so inclined), though the father abhorred it.

He can set horoscopes, but trusts them not. He with the consent of a friend cozened a lady, with whom he had made an appointment to meet an old astrologer, in the suburbs, which she kept; and it was himself disguised in a long gown and a white beard at the light of dim-burning candles, up in a little cabinet reached unto by a ladder.

Every first day of the New Year he had £20 sent him from the Earl of Pembroke to buy books.

After he was reconciled with the church, and left off to be a recusant, at his first communion, in token of true reconciliation, he drank out all the full cup of wine.

Being at the end of my lord Salisbury's table with Inigo Jones, and demanded by my lord why he was not glad, said he 'You promised I should dine with you, but I do not', for he had none of his meat; he esteemed only that his meat which was of his own dish.

He hath consumed a whole night in lying looking to his great toe, about which he hath seen Tartars and Turks, Romans and Carthaginians, fight in his imagination.

Northampton was his mortal enemy for brawling, on a St George's Day, one of his attenders: he was called before the Council for his *Sejanus*, and accused both of popery and treason by him.

Sundry times he hath devoured his books, once sold them all for necessity.

330 He hath a mind to be a churchman, and so he might have favour to make one sermon to the king, he careth not what thereafter should befall him: for he would not flatter though he saw death.

At his hither coming, Sir Francis Bacon said to him, he loved not to see Poesy go on other feet than poetical dactilus and spondaius.

14. His narrations of great ones.

He never esteemed of a man for the name of a lord.

Queen Elizabeth never saw herself after she became old in 340 a true glass; they painted her, and sometimes would vermilion her nose. She had always about Christmas evens set dice that threw sixes or fives, and she knew not they were other, to make her win and esteem herself fortunate. That she had a membrana on her, which made her uncapable of man, though for her delight she tried many. At the coming over of Monsieur, there was a French surgeon who took in hand to cut it, yet fear stayed her, and his death. King Philip had intention by dispensation of the pope to have married her.

350 Sir P. Sidney's mother, Leicester's sister, after she had the little pox, never showed herself in court thereafter but masked.

The Earl of Leicester gave a bottle of liquor to his lady, which he willed her to use in any faintness, which she, after his return to court, not knowing it was poison, gave him, and so he died.

Salisbury never cared for any man longer nor he could make use of him.

My lord Lisle's daughter, my Lady Wroth, is unworthily 360 married on a jealous husband.

Ben one day being at table with my lady Rutland, her husband coming in, accused her that she kept table to poets, of which she wrote a letter to him, which he answered. My lord intercepted the letter, but never challenged him.

My Lord Chancellor of England wringeth his speeches from the strings of his band, and other councillors from the picking of their teeth.

Pembroke and his lady discoursing, the Earl said the women were men's shadows, and she maintained them. Both appealing to Jonson, he affirmed it true; for which my lady gave a penance to prove it in verse, hence his epigram.

Essex wrote that epistle or preface before the translation of the last part of Tacitus, which is A.B. The last book the gentleman durst not translate for the evil it contains of the Jews.

The king said Sir P. Sidney was no poet. Neither did he see ever any verses in England to the sculler's.

It were good that half of the preachers of England were plain ignorants, for that either in their sermons they flatter, or strive to show their own eloquence.

15. His opinion of verses.
That he wrote all his first in prose, for so his master Camden, had learned him.

That verses stood by sense without either colours or accent; which yet other times he denied.

A great many epigrams were ill, because they expressed in the end, what should have been understood by what was said, as that of Sir John Davies.

Some loved running verses, *plus mihi complacet.*

He imitated the description of a night from Bonifonius his *Virgilium Veneris.*

He scorned such verses as could be transposed:

Where is the man that never yet did hear
Of fair Penelope, Ulysses' queen?
Of fair Penelope, Ulysses' queen,
Where is the man that never yet did hear?

16. Of his works.
That the half of his comedies were not in print.

He hath a pastoral entitled *The May Lord.* His own name is Alkin, Ethra the Countess of Bedford's, Mogibell Overbury, the old Countess of Suffolk an enchantress, other names are given to Somerset's lady, Pembroke, the Countess of Rutland, Lady Wroth. In his first story, Alkin cometh in mending his broken pipe. Contrary to all other pastorals he bringeth the clowns making mirth and foolish sports.

He hath intention to write a fisher or pastoral play, and set the stage of it in the Lomond Lake.

410 That epithalamion that wants a name in his printed works was made at the Earl of Essex's marriage.

He is to write his foot pilgrimage hither, and to call it a discovery.

In a poem he calleth Edinburgh
'The heart of Scotland, Britain's other eye'.

A play of his, upon which he was accused, *The Devil is an Ass*; according to *comedia vetus*, in England the devil was brought in either with one vice or other: the play done the devil carried away the vice, he brings in the devil so over-come with the wickedness of this age that thought himself an 420 ass. Παρεργως is discoursed of the Duke of Drounland: the king desired him to conceal it.

He hath commented and translated Horace, *Art of Poesy*: it is in dialogue ways; by Criticus he understandeth Dr Donne. The old book that goes about, *The Art of English Poesy*, was done twenty years since, and kept long in writ as a secret.

He had an intention to have made a play like Plautus' *Amphitrio*, but left it off, for that he could never find two so like others that he could persuade the spectators they were 430 one.

17. Of his jests and apothegms.

At what time Henry the fourth turned catholic, Pasquil had in his hand a book, and was asked by Morphorius what it was. He told him it was grammar. 'Why do you study grammar, being so old?' asked Morphorius. 'Because,' answered he, 'I have found a positive that hath no super-lative, and a superlative that wants a positive: the King of Spain is Rex Catholicus, and is not Catholicissimus; and the French King Christianissimus, yet is not Christianus.'

440 When they drank on him he cited that of Pliny that they called him *ad prandium, non ad poenam et notam.*

And said of that panegyrist who wrote panegyrics in acrostics, windows, crosses, that he was *homo miserrimae patientiae.*

He scorned anagrams; and had ever in his mouth,

Turpe est difficiles amare nugas,
Et stultus labor est ineptiarum.

A cook who was of an evil life, when a minister told him he would go to hell; asked what torment was there. Being 450 answered 'Fire', 'Fire,' said he, 'that is my play-fellow.'

A lord playing at tennis, and having asked those in the gallery whether a stroke was chase or loss, a brother of my lord Northumberland's answered it was loss. The lord demanded if he did say it. 'I say it,' said he, 'what are you?' 'I have played your worth,' said the lord. 'Ye know not the worth of a gentleman!' replied the other. And it proved so, for ere he died he was greater than the other. Another English lord lost all his game, if he had seen a face that liked him not, he struck all his balls at that gallery.

460 An Englishman who had maintained Democritus' opinion of atoms, being old, wrote a book to his son (who was not then six years of age), in which he left him arguments to maintain, and answer objections, for all that was in his book; only, if they objected obscurity against his book, he bid him answer, that his father, above all names in the world, hated most the name of Lucifer, and all open writers were Luciferi.

Butler excommunicated from his table all reporters of long poems, wilful disputers, tedious discoursers: the best 470 banquets were those where they mustered no musicians to chase time.

The greatest sport he saw in France was the picture of our Saviour with the Apostles eating the paschal lamb that was all larded.

At a supper where a gentlewoman had given him un-savoury wild fowl, and thereafter, to wash, sweet water; he commended her that she gave him sweet water, because her flesh stinked.

He said to Prince Charles of Inigo Jones, that when he wanted words to express the greatest villain in the world, he would call him an Inigo.

Jones having accused him for naming him, behind his back, a fool: he denied it; but, says he, 'I said he was an arrant knave, and I avouch it.'

One who fired a tobacco pipe with a ballad the next day having a sore head, swore he had a great singing in his head, and he thought it was the ballad: a poet should detest a ballad maker.

He saw a picture painted by a bad painter, of Easter, Haman, and Assuerus; Haman courting Esther, in a bed after the fashion of ours, was only seen by one leg. Assuerus' back was turned, with this verse over him, 'And wilt thou, Haman, be so malicious as to lie with my own wife in mine house?'

He himself being once so taken, the goodman said, 'I would not believe ye would abuse my house so.'

In a profound contemplation a student of Oxford ran over a man in the fields, and walked twelve miles ere he knew what he was doing.

One who wore side hair being asked of another who was bald, why he suffered his hair to grow so long, answered it was to see if his hair would grow to seed, that he might sow of it on bald pates.

A painter who could paint nothing but a rose, when an inn-keeper had advised him about an ensign, said that a horse was a good one, so was a hare, but a rose was above them all.

A little man drinking Prince Henry's health between two tall fellows, said he made up the H.

Sir Henry Wotton, before his majesty's going to England, being disguised at Leith on Sunday, when all the rest were at church, being interrupted of his occupation by another wench who came in at the door, cried out, 'Pox on thee, for thou hast hindered the procreation of a child,' and betrayed himself.

A justice of peace would have commanded a captain to sit first at a table, because, says he, 'I am a justice of peace'; the other drawing his sword commanded him, for saith he, 'I am a justice of war.'

520   What is that, that the more you cut of it, groweth still the longer? – a ditch.

He used to say, that they who delight to fill men extraordinary full in their own houses, loved to have their meat again.

A certain puritan minister would not give the communion save unto thirteen at once (imitating, as he thought, our Master). Now, when they were set, and one bethinking himself that someone of them must represent Judas, that it should not be he returned, and so did all the rest, under-
530   standing his thought.

A gentlewoman fell in such a fantasy or frenzy with one Mr Dod, a puritan preacher, that she requested her husband that, for the procreation of an angel or saint, he might lie with her; which having obtained, it was but an ordinary birth.

Scaliger writes an epistle to Casaubon, where he scorns his English speaking of Latin, for he thought he had spoken English to him.

A gentleman reading a poem that began with

540   Where is that man that never yet did hear
Of fair Penelope, Ulysses' queen?

calling his cook, asked if he had ever heard of her, who answering 'No', demonstrate to him,

Lo, there the man that never yet did hear
Of fair Penelope, Ulysses' queen!

A waiting woman having cockered with muscadel and eggs her mistress' page, for a she meeting in the dark, his mistress invaded; of whom she would of such boldness have

a reason. 'Faith, lady,' (said he) 'I have no reason, save that
550 such was the good pleasure of muscadel and eggs.'

A judge coming along a hall, and being stopped by a
throng, cried 'Dominum cognoscite vestrum.' One of them
there said they would if he durst say the beginning of that
verse (for he had a fair wife): 'Actaeon ego sum,' cried he,
and went on.

A packet of letters which had fallen overboard was de-
voured of a fish that was ta'en at Flushing, and the letters
were safely delivered to him to whom they were written at
London.

560 He scorned that simplicity of Cardan about the pebble-
stone of Dover, which he thought had that virtue, kept
between one's teeth, as to save him from being sick.

A scholar expert in Latin and Greek, but nothing in the
English, said of hot broth, that he would make the danger of
it: for it could not be ill English that was bad Latin,
facere periculum.

A translator of the *Emperor's Lives*, translated Antonius
Pius, Anthony Pye.

The word 'harlot' was taken from 'Arlott', who was the
570 mother of William the Conqueror; a rogue from the Latin
'erro', by putting a 'g' to it.

Sir Geslaine Percy asked the mayor of Plymouth
whether it was his own beard or the town's beard that he
came to welcome my lord with, for, he thought, it was so
long that he thought everyone of the town had eked some
part to it.

That he struck at Sir Hierome Bowes' breast, and asked
him if he was within.

An epitaph was made upon one who had a long beard,
580 Here lies a man at a beard's end, etc.

He said to the king, his master M[r] G. Buchanan, had
corrupted his ear when young, and learned him to sing verses
when he should have read them.

Sir Francis Walsingham said of our king, when he was
ambassador in Scotland, 'Hic nunquam regnabit super nos.'

Of all his plays he never gained two hundred pounds.

He had oft this verse, though he scorned it:

So long as we may, let us enjoy this breath,
For nought doth kill a man so soon as death.

590   One Mr Guyse told the king of a man who, being con-
sumed, occupied his wife with a dildo, and she never knew
of it till one day he all sleppery had there left his.

Heywood the epigrammatist being apparelled in velvet
by Queen Mary, with his cap on in the presence, in spite of
all the gentlemen, till the queen herself asked him what he
meant, and then he asked her if he was Heywood, for she had
made him so brave that he almost had misknown himself.

His impresa was a compass with one foot in centre, the
other broken, the word, *Deest quod duceret orbem.*

600   Essex, after his brother's death, Mr Devereux, in France,
at tilt had a black shield void, the word, *Par nulla figura
dolori.* Another time, when the queen was offended at him, a
diamond with its own ashes, with which it is cut, about it the
word, *Dum formas minuis.*

He gave the prince, *Fax gloria mentis honestae.*

He said to me, that I was too good and simple, and that
oft a man's modesty made a fool of his wit.

His arms were three spindles or rhombi, his own word
about them, *Percunctator* or *Perscrutator.*

610   His epitaph, by a companion written, is

Here lies Benjamin Jonson dead, .
And hath no more wit than goose in his head,
That as he was wont, so doth he still
Live by his wit, and evermore will.

Another:

Here lies honest Ben
That had not a beard on his chin.

18. Miscellanies.
John Stow had monstrous observations in his *Chronicle*, and
620   was of his craft a tailor. 'He and I walking alone,' he asked

two cripples, 'What they would have to take him to their order.'

In his *Sejanus* he hath translated a whole oration of Tacitus: the first four books of Tacitus ignorantly done in English.

J. Selden liveth on his own, is the law-book of the judges of England, the bravest man in all languages; his book *Titles of Honour*, written to his chamber-fellow Heyward.

Taylor was sent along here to scorn him.

630   Camden wrote that book *Remains of Bretagne*.

Joseph Hall the harbinger to Donne's 'Anniversary'.

The epigram of Martial 'In Verpum' he vaunts to expone.

Lucan, Sidney, Guarini, make every man speak as well as themselves, forgetting decorum; for Dametas sometimes speaks grave sentences.

Lucan taken in parts excellent, altogether nought.

He dissuaded me from poetry, for that she had beggared him, when he might have been a rich lawyer, physician, or merchant.

640   Questioned about English 'them', 'they', 'those'. 'They' is still the nominative, 'those' accusative, 'them' neuter; collective not 'them' men, 'them' trees, but 'them' by itself referred to many. 'Which', 'who', be relatives, not 'that'. 'Floods', 'hills' he would have masculines.

He was better versed, and knew more in Greek and Latin, than all the poets in England, and quintessenceth their brains.

He made much of that epistle of Plinius, where *Ad prandium, non ad notam* is and that other of Marcellinus,
650   who Pliny made to be removed from the table, and of the gross turbot.

One wrote an epigram to his father, and vaunted he had slain ten, the quantity of 'decem' being false, another answered the epigram, telling them that 'decem' was false.

S[ir] J. Davies' epigram of the whore's C. compared to a coul.

Of all styles he loved most to be named honest, and hath

of that an hundred letters so naming him.
    He had this oft:

660 Thy flattering picture, Phrenee, is like thee
    Only in this, that ye both painted be.

    In his merry humour he was wont to name himself The
    Poet.

    He went from Leith homeward the 25 of January, 1619, in
    a pair of shoes which, he told, lasted him since he came from
    Darnton, which he minded to take back that far again; they
    were appearing like Coriat's: the first two days he was all
    excoriate.

    If he died by the way, he promised to send me his papers
670 of this country, hewen as they were.

    I have to send him descriptions of Edinburgh borough-
    laws, of the Lomond.

    That piece of the pucelle of the court was stolen out of
    his pocket by a gentleman who drank him drowsy, and given
    Mistress Bulstrode; which brought him great displeasure.

    19. He sent me this madrigal:

    [Printed as *Underwoods* VIII: for variants see notes to that
    poem].

    And this which is (as he said) a picture of himself:

680 [Printed as *Underwoods* IX: for variants see notes to that
    poem]

    He is a great lover and praiser of himself, a contemner and
    scorner of others, given rather to lose a friend than a jest,
    jealous of every word and action of those about him (especi-
    ally after drink, which is one of the elements in which he
    liveth), a dissembler of ill parts which reign in him, a bragger
    of some good that he wanteth, thinketh nothing well but
    what either he himself or some of his friends and country-
    men hath said or done, he is passionately kind and angry,
690 careless either to gain or keep, vindictive, but, if he be well
    answered, at himself.

For any religion, as being versed in both. Interpreteth best sayings and deeds often to the worst. Oppressed with fantasy, which hath over-mastered his reason, a general disease in many poets. His inventions are smooth and easy; but above all he excelleth in a translation.

When his play of a *Silent Woman* was first acted, there was found verses after on the stage against him, concluding that the play was well named *The Silent Woman*, there was never 700   one man to say 'plaudite' to it.

Notes

In these notes Jonson's works are given their full titles, with these exceptions:

Miscellaneous Poems – abbreviated to *MP*
Timber, or Discoveries – *Discoveries*
Ben Jonson's Conversations with William Drummond – *Conversations*
Every Man out of his Humour – *EMO*

The main edition of Jonson's works referred to is that of Herford and Simpson and this has been abbreviated to *H/S*. References to the plays are to this edition unless otherwise specified. References to the masques are to the Yale edition. Other Jonson editors are mentioned by surname only: for details of the editions of Hunter, Patterson and Schelling see Further Reading. *Gifford* refers to his edition of 1816; *Whalley* to his of 1756; *Cunningham* to his undated version of Gifford's edition.

Abbreviations of academic journals used are:

JCWI   *Journal of the Courtauld and Warburg Institutes*
JEGP   *Journal of English and Germanic Philology*
MLR   *Modern Language Review*
MP   *Modern Philology*
NQ   *Notes and Queries*
RES   *Review of English Studies*
RMS   *Renaissance and Modern Studies*
SEL   *Studies in English Literature*

All references to Martial are to his *Epigrams* and all quotations from the Bible are from the Authorized Version (*AV*). Wherever possible I have used Loeb texts for the classical quotations given.

The translations from Latin and Greek are my own (but see acknowledgements at end of Preface). The General Editor has kindly agreed to this departure from the series policy of using, where possible, translations that the author might have known, since, with Jonson, this would have been impossible in many cases and often misleading when possible. I have, however, used Jonson's version of Horace for translations from the *Ars Poetica*.

Epigrams

The arrangement of Jonson's epigrams and their publication in the *Works* of 1616 are referred to in the Preface. Jonson clearly valued these poems, calling them in his dedication 'the ripest of my studies', and he was well aware of what he was trying to do with this collection. In *Epigrams* XVIII, for example, he draws a distinction between his work and that of poets like Sir John Davies and John Weever, while in the *Conversations* he attacks Harington and Owen for writing 'narrations' rather than real epigrams. Jonson was aiming at achieving in English what Martial had achieved with the Latin epigram, and Jonson's collection is the first set of English epigrams showing genuine understanding of what Martial's poems were like. This is true in that Jonson makes much better use, for example, of the decisive closing line than any earlier English writer of epigrams and also in his awareness of the value of a varied arrangement of the poems. (The relationships between Martial and Jonson are discussed in T. K. Whipple's book *Martial and the English Epigram from Sir Thomas Wyatt to Ben Jonson*, 1925.)

DEDICATION

Heading William Herbert (1580–1630) was the third Earl of Pembroke. Jonson also dedicated *Catiline* to him and addresses him in *Epigrams* CII. See also *Conversations* 311.

12-13 *make a party for them* gather support for them.

20 *in all numbers* in all particulars.

32 *mountebank* charlatan, quack.

34 *vizards* visages, countenances.

35-6 *publish their faces ... without scandal* from Martial's letter to the reader before book I of his *Epigrams*: 'non intret Cato theatrum meum aut, si intraverit, spectet' ('do not let Cato enter my theatre, or if he does let him watch carefully').

II

3-5 These are characteristic features of Elizabethan formal satire: the association of epigram and satire is common at this time.

10 Martial VII. xii, 4: 'et mihi de nullo fama rubore placet' ('and fame gained by making another blush is not something which pleases me').

12 Horace, *Satires* I. iv, 82-3: 'solutos/qui captat risus hominum famamque dicacis' ('the person who seeks others' loud laughter and the name of a wit').

III

Originally intended for John Stepneth, the bookseller, in 1612.

1-2 Martial XIV. cxciv: 'Sunt quidam qui me dicant non esse poetam/ sed qui me vendit bybliopola putat' ('Some say I am no poet but the bookseller who sells me thinks I am').

7–8 The references are to common Elizabethan advertising practices. *H/S* (XI, 1–2) quote from West Heath and Campion, who share Jonson's attitude.
9 *termers* visitors to London during term-time at the Inns of Court.
12 *Bucklersbury* an area of London where grocers congregated: the sheets of the failed book would be used to wrap groceries. See Horace, *Epistles* II. i, 269–70. The basic idea is an Elizabethan commonplace (see Dekker, *Guls Horne Book*; Harvey, *Four Letters*). See also *Discoveries* 732–4.

IV

2 *best of poets* *His Maiesties Poeticall Exercises* was published in Edinburgh in 1591.
5 The reference is to James's *Essays of a Prentise . . .* (1584): James was then eighteen.
7–8 Pliny, *Panegyricus* XXVI. i: 'talis denique quales alii principes futuros se tantum pollicentur' ('such a prince in reality as others can only vow to be').

V

Title The union is that between England and Scotland: James spoke of the idea of a single nation in his first speech to the English parliament. The poem was written in 1604 and survives in several *MSS*.

1 *contract*] marriage *MS*.
2 *celebrated*] solemnized *MS*.
   truth of] royal *MS*.
4 *spousèd*] married *MSS*.
   realms] nations *MS*.

VII

Title *Hot-House* the poem is built on the double-meaning of this word: 'brothel' and 'bath-house'.
4 *synonima* synonyms.

VIII

1 *Ridway . . . Duncote* unidentified and quite possibly fictional: Jonson does not name those he satirizes in *Epigrams* except in CXXXIII.
2 *arraigned* formally accused.

XI

3 *statesman* a real or pretended expert in the nature and organization of states.

XII

Title Jonson also uses this name in *EMO*: the prose character-sketch given there resembles the figure of this poem.

1 *squires* pandars.

7 *quarter-day* rents were commonly payable on quarter-days.

9 *'ssays* tries on.

11 *ordinaries* gambling houses.

13 *takes up fresh commodity, for days* buys parcels of goods from a usurer on short-term credit to resell at a lower price to raise ready cash.

15 *essays* Florio's translation of Montaigne's *Essaies* was published in 1603 and the form soon became popular.

18 *Calls for his stool* the reference is to the habit, among real or would-be gentlemen, of paying extra to sit on a stool on the stage at a playhouse.

21 *cockatrice* whore.

24 *pocky* pox-riddled.

XIII

2 *Aesculape* Aesculapius, the god of medicine, was the son of Apollo and Coronis.

XIV

Title William Camden (1551–1623) was Jonson's master at Westminster and the author of *Britannia* (1586).

3 (*How nothing's that ?*) 'How little is that ?'

5–6 Pliny, *Epistles* IV. xvii, 4: 'Obversator oculis ille vir quo neminem aetas nostra graviorem sanctiorem subtiliorem tulit' ('I can see him now, the greatest influence, the finest character, and the most incisive intellect of our time').

7–9 Pliny, *Epistles* I. xxii, 2–3: 'Quam peritus ille et privati iuris et publici! quantum rerum, quantum exemplorum, quantum antiquitatis tenet! nihil est quod discere velis quod ille docere non possit. . . . Iam quanta sermonibus eius fides, quanta auctoritas' ('His legal experience, both civil and constitutional, his knowledge of human matters and history's lessons are such that there is nothing you might want to learn which he could not teach. . . . He is honest and authoritative in speech').

11–12 Claudian, *De Consulatu Stilichonis* II, 329: 'Tandem vince tuum, vincis cuncta, pudorem' ('At last conquer your modesty, which conquers everything').

XV

1 *Psalms* xxii, 6: 'But I am a worm, and no man'.

XVI

10 Plutarch, *Lysander* § 437: 'ὁ γὰρ ἐχθρὸν ὁμολογεῖ δεδιέναι, τοῦ δὲ θεπῦ καταφρονεῖν' ('he who overcomes his enemy by using an oath shows that he is afraid of that enemy, but despises God').

XVII

6 *the chaste tree* the laurel, into which Daphne was transformed to save her from rape by Apollo (see Ovid, *Metamorphoses* I).

XVIII

Title *Mere* wholly, absolutely (in the sense of someone whose horizons are completely parochial; specifically here someone who knows nothing about the nature of the classical epigram).

4 Sir John Davies's *Epigrams* were printed *c.* 1590, and John Weever's *Epigrams in the Oldest Cut* ... in 1599.

XIX

Title *Cod* perfume-bag (see also *Epigrams* L).

1 *can get no widow* widows were favourite targets for fortune-hunters because of money they might have inherited from their deceased husbands.
2 *scent*] *F3*; sent *F1*. The *F1* reading blurs the sense.
 ill sprite the point is in the double-meaning, (i) an evil spirit; (ii) stinking breath.

XXI

3 *off*] *F2*; of *F1*. 'Of' is defensible, but 'of' and 'off' were variant spellings at this time and 'off' gives the appropriate sense of 'out of date'.
4 *the Word* the Bible. The synonym is particularly characteristic of the puritans, who also – at times at least – favoured short hair. (Haller, *The Rise of Puritanism* (1957), 32, quotes the preacher Edward Topsell as attacking 'our gallant youths and proper servingmen, whose heads are hanged with hair, as if they would fright away both Christ and his ministers'.)
6 *bastinado* a stick used for beating the victim, usually on the soles of the feet (so there may be a pun – soul/sole – in l. 8).

XXII

The motifs of this epitaph are traditional Christian *consolatio* themes: some, for example, are to be found in the Middle English poem *Pearl* and in Dante, *Vita Nuova* XXVIII. Jonson uses the idea of 'heaven's gifts' (l. 3) elsewhere: see *Epigrams* XLV, CIX; *Underwoods* LXXIII.

Title This child may have been called Mary but nothing is known of the circumstances of her death.

11–12 Martial V. xxxiv: 'mollia non rigidus caespes tegat ossa nec illi, / terra, gravis fueris: non fuit illa tibi' ('may no hard earth cover her gentle bones: do not lie heavily on her, Earth; she was not a heavy weight on you').

XXIII

This tribute was printed with Donne's poems in editions of 1650, 1654 and 1669.

1 *Phoebus* Apollo, god of poetry.
2 *refuse* the syntax leading up to this verb is ambiguous, but the meaning seems to be 'Phoebus and each of the muses reject all brains in favour of yours'.

XXV

4 *Ganymede* a Trojan prince who became cupbearer to Zeus. Here, as commonly at this time, 'homosexual partner'.
   goat figuratively a goat is a licentious person, usually male but probably female here.
5 *cucqueen* female cuckold.
8 *haste*] *F2*; hast *F1*. The phrase 'woman's haste' refers to the conventional idea of woman as sexually untrustworthy.

XXVI

1 *know* in the sexual sense (thus the line means 'Although Beast now sleeps only with his chaste wife . . .').
1-2 Seneca, *De Constantia* II, vii, 4 'Si quis cum uxore sua tanquam aliena concumbat, adulter erit' ('If anyone sleeps with his wife as though she were someone else he is like an adulterer').

XXVII

Title *Sir John Roe* born 1581, son of a merchant tailor; travelled to Moscow; served in Ireland; minor poet; died ?1606 of the plague. See also *Epigrams* XXXII, XXXIII.

1 *scutcheons* 'funeral tablets, often containing the armorial bearings of the deceased' (*Hunter*).

XXVIII

Title See also *Epigrams* LXXXII. The name is used for a character in *The Alchemist*.

4 *rhinocerote's nose* sneeringly. Martial I. iii, 3-6: 'nescis, heu, nescis dominae fastidia Romae . . / maiores nusquam rhonchi: iuvenesque senesque / et pueri nasum rhinocerotis habent' ('louder sneers are nowhere to be heard; young and old men, boys even, have noses tilted up like that of a rhinoceros').
7 *tympanies* tumours.

XXIX

3 *device* a pictorial representation of an object or objects with a verbal motto, usually expressive of a person's principles or aspirations (see, for example, Marlowe, *Edward II* II. ii).

XXX

Title See also *Epigrams* XXXVIII.

XXXI

Title See also *Epigrams* XLIV.
2 *travel* the modern zation of the folio 'travaile' obscures the double-meaning, 'travel' / 'toil', 'work'.

XXXII

Title See *Epigrams* XXVII and note.

3 *self-divided Belgia* the Pacification of Ghent (1576) had united Holland and Belgium, but in 1579 Calvinist–Catholic tension again divided the Netherlands.
6 *change ... mind*) Horace, *Epistles* I. xi, 27: 'caelum, non animum, mutant qui trans mare currunt' ('they who rush across the sea change their climate, not their minds').
7 *repair* place of retreat.
10 *serenes* cool evening dampnesses.

XXXV

This poem was probably written in 1604.

7 *treasons* perhaps alluding to the Gowry affair of 1600 and the Cobham–Raleigh plot of 1603.

XXXVI

2 *Domitian* Emperor AD 81–96; son of Vespasian; brother and successor of Titus; Martial's patron.

XXXVII

Title *Cheveril* Chevrel, or kid-leather, is pliable. See also *Epigrams* LIV.
1 *leese* lose.

XXXVIII

Title See *Epigrams* XXX.

XXXIX
Title *Colt* the name implies sexual virility and promiscuity.

XL

Title   Sister of Sir John Ratcliffe; a maid of honour to Queen Elizabeth; died 1599. See *Epigrams* XCIII.

7   *Expresser truth ... truer*] Express her ... her *MS*.

XLI

Title   *Gypsy*   a cunning, deceitful woman; sometimes a whore.

2   *the college*   the College of Physicians.
3   *quaint*   pun: 'unusual'; 'cunt'.

XLII

This poem is an expansion of Martial VIII. xxxv: 'Cum sitis similes paresque vita, uxor pessima, pessimus maritus, / miror non bene convenire vobis' ('Since you are like each other, and make a pair in your behaviour, most beastly of husbands, vilest of wives, I wonder that you don't get on together').

2   *mood can*] matter *MS*.
5   *By ... free*] With ... good *MS*.
11   *long-yarned*   having a long thread of life. The root idea is of the three Fates who controlled human life in classical mythology.
16   *will, and nill   H/S* (XI, 8) refer to Sallust but the phrase is at least as old in English as the Old English translation of Boethius ('Som we willan, som we nillan'). So also Malory (*Works* 1966), ed. Vinaver, 13): 'for ye shal overcome hem all, whether they wille or nylle'.

XLIII

This poem was written in 1605. Robert Cecil (?1563-1605) was made Secretary of State in 1596 and created Earl of Salisbury in 1605. See *Epigrams* LXIII, LXIV and *Conversations* 316-20 and 357-8.

5   *'Tofore*] Of old *MS*.
8   *fame*] praise *MS*.
9   *book*] verse *MS*.
   Cecil's] Sarum's *MS*.
10-12   Pliny, *Panegyricus* I: 'tantumque a specie adulationis absit gratiarum actio mea quantum abest a necessitate' ('and may my vote of thanks be as far from showing a sign of flattery as it is from inhibition').

XLIV

Title   See *Epigrams* XXXI. *Chuff* means 'churl'.

XLV

This poem was written in 1603, the year of the child's death. Its motifs are traditional: see, for example, Drummond, *A Cypress Grove*, ed. Clegg (1919), 43-4, 68; D. L. Peterson, *The English Lyric from Wyatt to Donne* (1967), 62.

1 *child of my right hand* the boy's name was Benjamin, which in Hebrew means 'fortunate' or 'dexterous'. The latter has the root-meaning 'right-handed', so there is a kind of trilingual pun here, with the additional English sense of 'right-handed' meaning 'essential'.

5 *lose* the modern sense of the word conceals the double-meaning lose/loose ('abandon').

10 *best piece of poetry* Jonson is playing on two senses of 'maker': poet/father.

12 Martial VI. xxix, 8: 'quidquid ames; cupias non placuisse nimis' ('whatever you love, pray that you do not find it too pleasing').

XLVI

1 *waste* idle, worthless.
3 *band* bond.

XLIX

Title See also *Epigrams* LXVIII, C.

3 *salt* 'wit'. In the line as a whole Jonson is playing on the sense of 'salt' meaning 'salacious'.

L

Title See also *Epigrams* XIX, XX.

2 *clysters* pipes.

LI

Title (*Upon ... 1607*) there was a widely believed rumour in 1606 that James had died after being stabbed with a poisoned knife while hunting. Jonson has misdated his poem.

3 *panic* groundless.
6 *gratulate* express joy about.

LIII

2 *pilled* compiled (also, here, 'stolen').
8 *witness* the Puritan equivalent to a godparent.
9 *motley* the vari-coloured costume of the jester.

LIV

Title See *Epigrams* XXXVII and note.

2 Adapted from Horace, *Satires* II. i, 47: 'Cervius iratus leges minitatur et urnam' ('When he is angry Cervius threatens his enemies with the laws and the judge's urn').

LV

Title *Francis Beaumont* (*c*. 1584–1616); son of Francis Beaumont, a Justice of Common Pleas; Oxford and the Inner Temple; poet and playwright. Jonson's lines, which were printed with the first and second folios of the *Works* of Beaumont and John Fletcher, are a response to Beaumont's famous *Letter to Ben Jonson*.

2 *religion* faithfulness.

LVI

It is not known to whom this poem alludes (if indeed it has any specific target): there is a groundless tradition that Jonson is attacking Shakespeare.

2 *frippery* rubbish, old clothes.
3 *brocage* dealing in castoffs.
6 *Buy the reversion of old plays* have the use of the texts of plays when nobody else wants them. 'Reversals' were the granting of offices to someone on the incumbent's death, the grant being made before that death.

LVIII

6 *losing my points* misunderstanding my punctuation, and hence my meaning.

LIX

Title See *Conversations* 256.

LX

Title *William, Lord Mounteagle* William Parker (1575–1622), fourth Baron Mounteagle, received a letter giving a clue about the Gunpowder Plot and, although himself a Roman Catholic, informed the Government.

LXII

Title *Lady Would-Be* the name is also used in *Volpone*.

8–12 In one *MS* these lines form a separate epigram.
9 *What ... be?*] Why are you barren? *MS*.

LXIII

Title See *Epigrams* XLIII and note.

2–3 *With what ... fortune* Valerius Maximus, *Factorum et Dictorum* VIII. xv, 2: 'magisque suo merito quam fortunae beneficio magnum' ('and more by his merit than by the great benefit of fortune').
5–6 Pliny, *Epistles* I. xxii, 5: 'omnia ad conscientiam refert recteque facti non ex populi sermone mercedem, sed ex facto petit' ('refers all things to

conscience, looking for reward in the doing of a good deed and not in public opinion of it').

11 *his muse*] my voice *MS*.
    that could] if it *MS*.

LXIV

Title Salisbury became Treasurer on 6 May 1608.

11–12 Pliny, *Epistles* V. xiv, 6: 'His ex causis ut illi sic mihi gratulor, nec privatim magis quam publice, quod tandem homines non ad pericula, ut prius verum ad honores virtute perveniunt' ('So I congratulate myself as much as I do him, for public reasons as well as personal ones. Now finally men's merits produce official recognition instead of the dangers of the past').

LXV

4 *luxury* desire for comfort.

LXVI

Title *Sir Henry Cary* (*c.* 1575–1633); Comptroller of the Household (1618–22); Lord Deputy of Ireland (1622–9).

9–12 Cary was captured when Maurice of Nassau was defeated near the Ruhr–Rhine junction in October 1605.
12 Jonson himself gives a gloss on this line: 'The castle and river near where he was taken'.

LXVII

Title *Thomas, Earl of Suffolk* Thomas Howard (1561–1626); Earl of Suffolk (1603); Lord Chamberlain (1603–14); Lord High Treasurer (1614–19). *H/S* (XI, 12) suggest that this epigram is in thanks for Howard's help in obtaining the release of Jonson and Chapman from their incarceration over *Eastward Ho*.

1–2 *Since . . . flatteries* Pliny, *Epistles* III. xxi, 3: 'Nam postquam desimus facere laudanda, laudari quoque ineptum putamus' ('For now that we do nothing to earn a poet's tribute, it seems silly to receive one').
7–8, 11–12 Claudian, *De Consulatu Stilichonis* I, 49, 50: 'Taciti suffragia vulgi / iam tibi detulerant quidquid mox dedidit aula' ('The votes of the silent people had already granted you what, later, the palace yielded up').

LXVIII

Title See *Epigrams* XLIX, C.

LXIX

Title *Pertinax Cob* 'pertinax' (Latin) = 'obstinate'; 'Cob' here = 'ball', 'testicle'.

2 *weapon* penis (so Martial IX. lxiii, 2: 'mentula quem pascit' – 'he who lives by his prick').

LXX

Title *William Roe* (1585–1667); brother to Sir John Roe. See also *Epigrams* CXXVIII.

1–2 Seneca, *De Brevitate Vitae* III, 5: 'Quam serum est tunc vivere incipere, cum desinendum est' ('How late it is to start living just as we must cease to live').

5 Seneca, *De Brevitate Vitae* IX, 1: 'Maxima porro vitae iactura dilatio est ... Maximum vivendi impedimentum est expectatio, quae pendet ex crastino, perdit hodiernum' ('Procrastination is life's greatest waste ... Expectancy is living's biggest hindrance, for it waits on tomorrow and wastes today').

6 Virgil, *Georgics* III, 66–7: 'Optima quaeque dies miseris mortalibus aevi/prima fugit' ('All the best days of this wretched mortal life are the first to flee away').

LXXI

This epigram may be aimed at the minor epigrammatist Henry Parrot (see *H/S* XI, 13).

LXXIII

5 *In primis* in the first place.
9 *Babylonian* confused.
10 *posy* verses attached to, or inscribed on, a ring or similar object.
13 *partie per pale* divided by a perpendicular stripe (a heraldic term).
14 *cypress* black crape.
   cobweb lawn fine white linen.
15 *imprese* device, badge.
20 *vein* (1) 'style'; (2) 'vanity'.

LXXIV

Title *Thomas, Lord Chancellor* Thomas Egerton (?1540–1617); Solicitor General (1581); Attorney General (1592); Master of the Rolls (1594); Lord Keeper (1596); Lord Chancellor (1603). See also *Underwoods* XXXI, XXXII.

2 *not of one year* Horace, *Odes* IV. ix, 39: 'consul que non unius anni' ('and consul not just for one year'). Jonson's point, borne out by Egerton's long record of service to the government, is that he has the authority of experience.

5 *present to* intent on.

9–10 Astraea, virgin goddess of justice, fled the world at the beginning of the Age of Iron (Virgil, *Eclogues* IV, 6). It is a commonplace of the period that Elizabeth's reign represented Astraea's return to earth.

LXXV

Title *Lip* from Latin 'lippus' ('bleary').

3 *at Paul's* preaching at St Paul's Cathedral.

LXXVI

Title *Lucy, Countess of Bedford* daughter of John, first Baron Harington; married Edward, third Earl of Bedford, in 1594; patron of such men as Jonson, Donne, Drayton, Daniel, Florio; died 1627. See also *Epigrams* LXXXIV, XCIV.

9 *facile* affable.

10 Claudian, *De Consulatu Stilichonis* II, 160–62: 'Quin ipsa superbia longe / discessit, vitium rebus sollemne secundis / virtutumque ingrata comes' (Jonson's line follows the Latin quite closely.)

15–16 *The rock . . . spin* the reference is to the Fates and their emblems: Clotho spun the thread of life; Lachesis decided its length; Atropos cut the thread to end the life.

15 *rock* distaff.

LXXVIII

1 *stall* theatre.

LXXIX

Title *Elizabeth, Countess of Rutland* daughter of Sir Philip Sidney and wife of Roger Manners, fifth Earl of Rutland; died 1612.

3–4 Martial VIII. lxx, 3–4: 'cum siccare sacram largo Permessida posset / ore, verecundam maluit esse sitim' ('although he could have drained holy Parnassus with huge draughts, he chose to ease his thirst temperately').

6 *that most masculine issue* the *Arcadia*.

LXXX

1 *ports* gates.

2 *meeds* rewards, deserts.

5–8 These lines form a separate poem in one *MS*.

LXXXI

Title *Prowl* here someone who stealthily steals the writings of others. The poem is a development of Martial I. lxiii: 'Ut recitem tibi nostra rogas epigrammata. nolo. / non audire, Celer, sed recitare cupis' ('You ask me to recite you my epigrams. I don't wish to. You don't want to listen to them, Celer, but to recite them').

4 *wealthy* trustworthy.

LXXXII

Title *Cashiered* dismissed from service. See also *Epigrams* XXVIII.
2 *cast* dismissed.

LXXXIV

Title See *Epigrams* LXXVI and note.
3 *prevented* my request was anticipated (Latin 'praevenio').
9 *transfer* transport me poetically, and alter my circumstances.

LXXXV

Title *Sir Henry Goodyere* a gentleman of James's privy chamber; knighted in 1599; close friend to Donne; minor poet; died 1628.

4 Jonson again links Apollo with the hawk in his *Masque of Augurs* (see l. 353 and Jonson's own note).

LXXXVII

Title *Hazard* the name of a popular dice-game.
2 *his* that is, his 'false play'.
5 On reckoning profits up he realized that his whore's activities had become more profitable than his own.

LXXXVIII

6 *halfway tree* H/S (XI, 16) suggest that this must have been a well-known landmark between London and Dover.
10 *The French disease* syphilis.
15 *motion* here some sort of mechanically turning dummy.
16 People went to St Paul's churchyard to show off their fashionable clothing: it was thus a good place for tailors to tout for custom.

LXXXIX

Title *Edward Alleyn* (1566–1626); theatre impresario; partner and son-in-law of Philip Henslowe; founded Dulwich College in 1619. Here eulogized for his ability as an actor.

3 Horace, *Epistles* II. i, 82: 'quae gravis Aesopus, quae doctus Roscius egit' ('what stately Aesopus and learned Roscius acted once'). Roscius was famous as a comic actor and Aesopus for tragedy, and the pair are commonly linked

at this time as the models of what great acting could be. Latin 'gravis' and Jonson's *grave* = 'impressive', 'stately'.

6 *Than Cicero* in *De Oratore* I. xxviii, 129–30; lxi, 258; and *Pro Sestio* LVII, 121; LVIII, 123.

XC

17–18 *Milo ... bull* Milo of Crotona was a famous Greek athlete of the sixth century BC. *H/S* (XI, 17) refer to Petronius, *Satyricon* 25: 'Posse taurum tollere, qui vitulum sustulerit' ('He who has taken the weight of a calf can take that of a bull'). Jonson gives a sexual twist to his *bearing . . . bear*.

17 *wull*] *F1*; will *F2*. *Wull* is a variant form retained here to keep the rhyme.

XCI

Title *Sir Horace Vere* (1565–1635); a soldier who fought with distinction in the Netherlands, being made Baron Vere of Tilbury for his relief of the siege of Breda in 1625.

1–3 The point of these lines depends upon our linking Vere's Christian name with the Roman poet and his surname with Latin 'vere' ('truly').

8 *relish* grace (a musical term).

9 *prosecute* follow.

15–16 Seneca, *De Clementia* I. v, 4: 'Clementia in quamcumque domum pervenerit, eam felicem tranquillamque praestabit, sed in regio quo rarior, eo mirabilior' ('Mercy will bring peace and happiness to any house it comes to; but – so rarely does it appear – its presence in the palace is all the more wonderful').

18 Pliny, *Panegyricus* 46: 'Et quis terror valuisset efficere, quod reverentia tui effecit?' ('Could any terror have been powerful enough to effect what our regard for you has achieved?').

XCII

10 *chapmen* traders.

16 *gazetti* news sheets. *H/S* (XI, 18) suggest derivation from 'gazet' (a small Venetian coin) or 'gazzetta', diminutive of 'gazza' (magpie).

Gallo-Belgicus the reference is to the news register *Mercurii Gallo-Belgicus* published in Cologne between 1598 and 1630.

17 *locked*] *F2*; looked *F1* an obvious misprint.

19 *Star Chamber* a major secular prerogative court which became very unpopular in the 1630s (under Charles I) and was abolished in 1641.

21 *mart* market.

23 *Rimee's* James Rime had a bookshop in Blackfriars.

24 *Bills'* John Bills, a London bookseller.

25 *Porta* Giovanni Baptista Porta, author of *De Furtivis Literarum Notis* (1563).

30 *the States* the Netherlands.
35 *the Brethren* the puritans.

XCIII

Title *Sir John Radcliffe* brother of Margaret Radcliffe (*Epigrams* XL); knighted by Essex in Ireland in 1599; died 1627.

11 *a whiter soul* Horace, *Satires* I. v, 41–2: 'animae qualis candidiores / terra tulit, neque quis me sit devinctior alter' ('the whitest souls ever born, to whom no one can be more deeply attached than I am').

XCIV

See *Epigrams* LXXVI and note. Jonson's poem was printed with editions of Donne's poems in 1650, 1654, 1669. Donne's satires were not published until 1633 but were probably written in the 1590s.

1 *Lucy, you brightness* Jonson is playing on the connection between *Lucy* and Latin 'lux' ('light', 'brightness').

XCV

Title *Sir Henry Savile* (1549–1622); Warden of Merton (1585); Provost of Eton (1596); founded chairs of geometry and astronomy at Oxford; translated four books of Tacitus' *History*; edited Chrysostom. See *Conversations* 372–5 and *Discoveries* 1126.

2 *that ... doctrine* metempsychosis (transmigration of souls).
7–8 Savile added an original section on Nero and Galba to his *Tacitus*.
9 *proper* personal gift (Latin 'propria').
16 *Minerva's loom* Minerva was, among other things, goddess of weaving.
23 Sallust, the Roman historian, served in Africa with the army of Julius Caesar.
28 *apt* make fitting.
29–30 Pliny, *Epistles* I. xvi, 4: 'Idem tamen in historia magis satisfaciet vel brevitate vel luce vel suavitate vel splendore etiam et sublimitate narrandi' ('His histories will please you still more by their concision and clarity, by the beauty and brilliance of their style and force of expression').
31–6 Jonson here follows the Ciceronian ideal of history as expounded in *De Oratore* II. xv, 62–3.

XCVI

Title See *Epigrams* XXIII and note.

1 *where* whether.
8 *better stone* see Jonson's *King's Entertainment* 289 and his own note. Jonson there refers to Pliny, *Natural History* vii, 40. On this occasion Jonson uses the idea of the white or fortunate ('better') stone as a way of underlining Donne's authority. Jonson may also have in mind the white stone of *Revelation*

ii 17 which – according to the gloss in the Geneva Bible – is 'a token of God's favour and grace'. Interestingly, Joseph Conrad speaks of 'white stone days' in the sense of fortunate ones (*An Outcast of the Islands*).

10 *puisnees* juniors

12 Pliny, *Epistles* IV. xii, 7: 'Etenim nescio quo pacto vel magis homines iuvat gloria lata quam magna' ('For some reason it is widespread rather than durable fame that most men prefer').

XCVII

Title *Motion* puppet-play. The poem is one of Jonson's attacks on Inigo Jones (see also *Epigrams* CXV, CXXIX, *MP* CXVIII–CXX and *Conversations*, 479–84).

1 *fading* Irish dance.

10 *bawdy stock* brothels.

14 *neadd squires*] I follow *H/S* in accepting this folio reading and taking 'neadd' as a form of the past participle 'needed'. For full discussion see *H/S* XI, 20. A case could be made for Whalley's emendation to 'need o' squires' except that this makes the line metrically awkward.

15 The Danish king visited England in 1606.

XCVIII

Title *Sir Thomas Roe* (1581–1644); knighted in 1605; ambassador to the Great Mogul in 1614; Chancellor of the Garter in 1621.

3–5 Horace, *Satires* II. vii, 86–8: 'in se ipso totus, teres atque rotundus . . . / in quem manca ruit semper fortuna' ('. . . is, in himself a whole, smoothed and rounded . . . against whom Fortune is always injured when she attacks').

XCIX

3–4 Pliny, *Epistles* VI. xvi, 3: 'Equidem beatos puto, quibus deorum munere datum est aut facere scribenda aut scribere legenda, beatissimos vero quibus utrumque' ('In my view the fortunate man is the one to whom the gods have given the power either to achieve something worth recording or to write something worth reading: most fortunate of all is he who can do both').

7–9 Pliny, *Epistles* VI. xxiv, 1: 'Quam multum interest quid a quoque fiat! Eadem enim facta claritate vel obscuritate facientium aut tolluntur altissime aut humillime deprimuntur' ('How often we judge actions by their performers! Precisely the same actions are praised to the skies or let sink into oblivion simply according to whether the persons involved are or are not well known').

C

Title See *Epigrams* XLIX, LXVIII.

1 *toys* trifles.

4 *passed him a play* were enough to make a play out of, by his standards.

CI

1–5 For general analogues see Martial V. lxxviii; X. xlviii; XI. lii.

7–8 Martial V lxxviii, 16: 'vinum tu facies bonum bibendo' ('you will make the wine good by drinking it').

8 *cates* food, provisions.

9 *rectify* remove impurities from (a chemical term).

16 *think*] say *MS*.

17 *lie* this is clearly the best reading: the 'buy' of one *MS* is undermined by the classical phrase Jonson is using. This is Martial XI. lii, 13: 'mentiar, ut venias' ('I'll lie to make you come').

19–20 *and ... too*] And perhaps if we can / A duck and mallard *MS*.

19 *godwit* a marsh bird rather like a curlew.

20 *Knat* a bird of the snipe family (red-breasted sandpiper.)
    rail a bird of the species *Rallidae*.
    ruff a male bird of the sandpiper family.

21–2 For a general parallel see Juvenal, *Satires* xi, 179–81.

24 Martial XI. lii, 16: 'plus ego polliceor: nil recitabo tibi' ('I also promise I'll recite nothing to you').

30 *the Mermaid's* the Mermaid tavern was Jonson's favourite drinking place.

31 *Anacreon* sixth-century BC Greek lyric poet, noted it seems for his clarity of expression and rhythmical smoothness.

33 *the Thespian spring* Aganippe, on Mount Helicon.

34 *Luther's beer* clearly here a synonym for inferior drink. I have not found any helpful specific reference to Luther's views on alcohol and my guess is that Jonson is using a loose association of Luther's name with anti-joy living to make his amusingly hyperbolic point.

36 *no Pooly, or Parrot by*] fool, or parrot *one MS*. It seems clear that Jonson is making specific references. One Robert Pooly is known as a government spy who betrayed Babington in 1586 and Parrot is clearly of the same kind although he has not been positively identified.

37–42 Martial X. xlviii, 21–4: 'accedent sine felle ioci nec mane timenda / libertos et nil quod tacuisse velis: / de prasino conviva meus venetoque loquator, / nec faciunt quemquam pocula nostra reum' ('to crown these things there shall be jests without bitterness, and freedom not to be feared next morning, with nothing you would wish had been unsaid. Let my guests talk about the Green and the Blue – drinking with me will not make any man a defendant'). The Green and Blue to which Martial refers were factions among the charioteers in the Roman circus.

CII

Title See note to the Dedication to *Epigrams*.

3–4 Seneca, *De Tranquillitate Animi* VII, 5: 'utraque enim turba opus erat, ut Cato posset intellegi: habere debuit et bonos, quibus se approbaret, et malos, in quibus vim suam experiretur' ('for both classes were necessary so that Cato could be understood: he had to have good men so that he might gain their approval and bad ones to prove his strength').

9–10 Seneca, *Epistles* CXV, 10: 'ad mercedem pii sumus, ad mercedem impii, et honesta, quamdiu aliqua illis spes inest, sequimur, in contrarium transituri, si plus scelera promittent' ('if it pays we fulfil our duties, or if it pays we neglect them, and we pursue an honourable course so long as it suits our hopes, ready to change sides if dishonesty promises us more').

12 *discerns* distinguishes.

13 Seneca, *Epistles* LXXI. 8: 'Virtus autem non potest maior aut minor fieri; unius staturae est' ('Virtue, however, cannot be increased or decreased: its stature is unchanging').

CIII

Title *Mary, Lady Wroth* eldest daughter of Robert Dudley, first Earl of Leicester; niece of Sir Philip Sidney; married Sir Robert Wroth in 1604. See *Epigrams* CV, *The Forest* III, *Underwoods* XXVIII, *Conversations* 359.

2 *twilight* here, early morning light.

7 *imprese* see *Epigrams* LXXIII, 15 and note.

CIV

Title *Susan, Countess of Montgomery* Susan Vere (1587–1629), daughter of Edward de Vere, seventeenth Earl of Oxford, married Sir Philip Herbert in 1604. He was created Earl of Montgomery in 1605. She also had connections with Donne and Drayton.

CV

Title See *Epigrams* CIII and note.

2 *crossed* destroyed, cancelled.

7–8 *wheaten hat . . . Ceres* Ceres (Demeter) was the daughter of Chronos and Rhea and the elder sister of Zeus. She is the goddess of grain and of the growth of crops.

10 *Oenone* a nymph and wife of Paris.
    Flora Roman goddess of flowers.
    May Italian goddess, sometimes seen as an earth-goddess; often linked with Flora and Ops.

11 *the Idalian queen* Venus.

14 *Diana* (Artemis), daughter of Zeus and Leto; virgin goddess of hunting.

15 *stile* this is a reference to the Greek 'stylus' – writing implement – as a symbol of Pallas Athena's role as goddess of wisdom.

16 *Pallas' pluméd casque* Pallas Athena (Minerva) was born from the brow of Zeus. She is the goddess of wisdom but usually represented in armour (*casque* = 'helmet') since in early Greek mythology she is best known as a warrior.

18 *Juno . . . peacock* (Hera), daughter of Chronos and Rhea and wife of her brother Zeus. The peacock is her sacred bird.

CVI

Title *Sir Edward Herbert* (1583–1648), philosopher, poet, statesman; created Lord Herbert of Cherbury in 1629; elder brother of George Herbert.

CVII

For a general analogue see Martial IX. xxxv. Written about 1601.

6 *their two emperors* Ferdinand I (1558–62); Maximilian (1562–76).
8 *Moravian horse* Magyar horses were famous for quality.
   Venetian bull quite unidentifiable and quite possibly a fictional part of Jonson's mockery of Hungary's pretensions (see l.21 ff. and the treatment of a figure like Bobadill in *Every Man in his Humour*).
17 *hap* good fortune.
21 *Villeroys ... Silleries* Nicholas, Seigneur de Villeroy, was Secretary of State to Henri IV and Nicholas, Marquis de Sillery, was the same king's Chancellor.
22 *Janins* the best guess at identification is Newdigate's: he refers to Pierre Jeannin, a French statesman.
   nuncios papal representatives at a foreign court.
   Tuilleries part of the French palace, originally designed by Delorme in 1564.
23 *Beringhams* Hunter suggests that this is Pierre de Beringhen, who served both Henri IV and Louis XIII.
25-6 *Hanou ... Boutersheim* Hanou and Rotenberg are real towns (in Hesse-Nassau) while the other names are insulting coinages. Thus Shieter-Huissen means shit-house; Popenheim, puppet's house; Hans-spiegel, mirror of fools; Boutersheim, home of butter.

CVIII

This poem appears as ll. 131–40 pf the 'Apologetical Dialogue' for *Poetaster*, and thus must have been written before the winter of 1601.

5-7 Jonson had, by his own account, served in Flanders, but the period of his service remains largely conjectural. See *Conversations* 236ff.

CIX

Title *Sir Henry Nevil* (?1564–1615); a Member of Parliament (1584–1614); knighted (1599); ambassador to France; fined and imprisoned for complicity in the Essex rebellion-plot.

11 *lent life* see *Epigrams* XXII and note.

CX

Title *Clement Edmonds* (?1564–1622); Clerk of the Council (1609); knighted in 1617; Secretary of State (1622). His *Observations upon the Five First Books of Caesar's Commentaries* was published in 1600 and supplemented in 1604. Jonson's poem first reached print in an edition of Edmonds's work in 1609.

2 *these west parts* Gaul and Britain.
6 *stile* see note to *Epigrams* CV, 15.
13 *scarce one just age* Caesar lived from 100 to 44 BC, and fifty-six years is well short of the biblical three score years and ten, so it is difficult to see exactly Jonson's point but he probably means 'just' in the sense of 'full' or 'reasonable', with the idea that Caesar lived long enough to fulfil himself and, behind that, the belief (see, for example, *Underwoods* LXX, 65) that it is life's quality that counts and not duration.
14 *parts* factions.
17 *Promethean art* Prometheus was one of the Titans who defied Zeus. His consequent sufferings make him a symbol of endurance and undaunted effort.

CXI

Like CX this was first printed with the Edmonds edition of 1609.

4 *Beholding*] Beholden *1609*. The folio reading makes enough sense to be retained.
9 *grutch* grumble, grudge.
11 *deprave* distort, disfigure (Latin 'depravo').

CXII

See Martial XII. xciv for the basis of this poem.

4 *rank setting* excessive betting.
18-22 Jonson here uses several terms from the then popular card-game of primero: *pluck* = 'draw a card'; *never art encountered* = 'you never have the right colour or suit'; *rest* = 'remaining stake'; *prime* = 'winning hand'.

CXIII

Title *Sir Thomas Overbury* (1581–1613); poet and miscellaneous writer; a friend of Robert Carr, Earl of Somerset; knighted in 1608; lost favour with Carr and was put in the Tower in 1613, to be poisoned there at Lady Essex's instigation. See *Conversations* 160–61, 206–10.

CXIV

Title *Mrs Philip Sidney Mrs* is here the formal 'mistress' and not referring to a married person. This lady (1594–1620) was the daughter of Robert Sidney, first Earl of Leicester; *Philip* is the name she was given at baptism (see L. C. John, *JEGP* LV (1946), 214–17).

CXV

The poem is probably an attack on Inigo Jones. See also *Epigrams* XCVII, CXXIX; *MP* CXVIII–CXX.

5 Martial XI. xcii: 'non vitiosus homo es, Zoile, sed vitium' ('you are not a vicious person, Zoilus, but vice itself').

10 *sow out a long meal* since the folio *sow* makes sense it has been kept in spite of *H/S* view (XI, 26) that it is a corruption of 'strow'.

26 *dore* trick, disguise (Jonson uses the verb 'dors' in *Every Man in his Humour*, ed. Seymour-Smith, IV. vi, 130).

27 *Acts old Iniquity* punning on Jones's Christian name and the Vice of the miracle plays. (c.f. l.5).

31 *engineer* maker, creator.

CXVI

Title *Sir William Jephson* a friend of Jonson's; knighted in 1603.

7 *entailed* in law, entailing is the limitation of lands to certain members of a family. Here the phrase means 'not restricted to those with titles'.

9–10 Sallust, *Iugurtha* lxxxv, 15: 'Quanquam ego naturam unam et communem omnium existumo, sed fortissimum quemque generossumum' ('I myself believe that all men have one and the same nature, but that those born with the greatest moral strength are those who are best born').

16 *solecism* in rhetoric, the misuse of grammatical terms.

CXVII

2 *occupy* Groin occupies his whore sexually and thus still, figuratively, his land which he sold for her.

CXVIII

Title see *Underwoods* XLVII, 13; *Conversations* 79–80.

CXIX

Title *Sir Ra[l]ph Shelton* knighted in 1607. See *Epigrams* CXXXIII, where Shelton's contemporary reputation for being a buffoon is exploited, whereas this poem seems a standard piece of complimentary verse.

4 *prease* the press or crowd.

15–16 Martial VIII. lxxvii, 7–8: 'qui sic vel medio finitus vixit in aevo, / longior huic facta est quam data vita fuit' ('for whoever has lived like this, even if his end comes in middle age, life has been made by him longer than his allotted span').

CXX

Title *S.P.* Salomon Pavy, one of the Children of Queen Elizabeth's Revels; he acted in *Cynthia's Revels* and died in 1602.

3 *a tear you*] these tears are *MS*.

7 *seemed to*] both did *MS*.

11 *three filled*] thrice past *MS*.

13–15 *And . . . one*] *MS reads:*
And what we now do moan
He played old men so duly
The destinies thought him to be one . . .

14 *duly* aptly.

14–16 Martial X. liii: 'invida quem Lachesis raptum trieteride nona, / dum numerat palmas, credidit esse senem' ('jealous Lachesis snatched me away in my ninth span of three years because when he counted up my victories he thought I must be old').

15 *Parcae* the three Fates.

16 *played*] feigned *MS*.

17–18 *So . . . consented*] *MS reads:*
And in that error they consented
To his fatal death . . .

20–22 *They . . . him*] *MS reads:*
. . . since have repented
And would have given new breath.
Nay they desire (not able) to give birth
In charms to sleep him.

CXXI

Title *Benjamin Rudyerd* (1572–1658); friend of the third Earl of Pembroke; minor poet; knighted in 1618.

CXXII

3 *times* past times, and specifically Saturn's golden age.

CXXIV

Title *Elizabeth, L. H.* there are several *MSS* of this poem and they have differing titles: unfortunately none gives any clue to the seemingly deliberate anonymity of the folio title. James McKenzie (*NQ*, June 1962) suggests the person is Lady Elizabeth Hunsdon, a patron of poets, whose husband became Lord Chamberlain in 1597. He died in 1603 but the date of her death is unknown.

6 *virtue, than*] beauty than *one MS*.

7 *all*] most *two MSS*.

11 *where*] when *one MS*.

CXXV

Title *Sir William Uvedale* knighted in 1613; Treasurer of the Chamber (1618); Treasurer at Arms of the Northern Army (1639).

1 *piece of the first times* remnant from the golden age.

CXXVI

Title *His Lady* Lady Uvedale was the daughter of Sir Edward Carey.

2–8 *Phoebus . . . tree* Apollo (Phoebus) chased Daphne, who was turned into a laurel tree to save her from rape.

CXXVII

Title *Esmé, Lord Aubigny* (1574–1624); Seigneur d'Aubigny; Duke of Lennox (1583). See *The Forest* XIII; *Underwoods* LXXV. *Sejanus* is dedicated to him.

CXXVIII

Title See *Epigrams* LXX and note.

12 *Aeneas* the wandering hero of Virgil's *Aeneid* and supposed founder of the Roman race.

14 *travelled* again there is the double-meaning 'travelled'/'travailed'.

CXXIX

Probably another attack on Inigo Jones. See *Epigrams* XCVII, CXV; *MP* CXVIII–CXX.

4 *Brainford* Brentford.
   Bow Stratford-atte-Bow.
12 *babion* baboon.
   brave ruffian.

16–17 In *Bartholomew Fair* Cokely and Coriat are again used as examples of jesters and fools (III. 4) and again in a context which is apparently aimed at Jones. Pod (see *Bartholomew Fair* V.1.8) was, it seems, a master of puppets, while Gue is also mentioned in the Induction to Marston's *Antonio and Mellida*, ed. Hunter, 131, in a similarly unflattering way. For Coriat see also *Underwoods* XIII, 128; *MP* VI, VII, CXV.

CXXX

Title *Alphonso Ferrabosco* (d. 1628); lutenist and composer. This epigram was originally prefixed to *Airs: By Alfonso Ferrabosco* (1609). Ferrabosco set a number of Jonson's songs to music and wrote the music for *Hymenaei*.

2 See Horace, *Ars Poetica* 391–6.

11–14 Jonson draws on Pythagorean cosmology: eight concentric globes, revolving round the earth, produced a supreme melody ('the music of the spheres'). The ninth sphere was a crystalline one which organized the equinoxes.

CXXXI

This poem was first published in *Lessons for 1. 2. and 3. by Alfonso Ferrabosco* (1609).

13   Persius, *Satires* I, 7: 'nec te quaesiveris extra' ('look to nobody but yourself').

CXXXII

Title   *Joshua Sylvester* (1563–1618); a prolific translator from French. Jonson's epigram first appeared with the 1605 quarto of Sylvester's translation of Guillaume Du Bartas's *Semaine ou Creation du Monde*. This translation was remarkably popular, influencing, for example, Milton and, at a lower level, the colonial poetess Anne Bradstreet. Jonson's view of Sylvester had changed by the time he met Drummond (see *Conversations* 26–8).

6   *confer*   compare.

CXXXIII

Title   Written *c.* 1610.

2   *Hercules*   descended into Hades and captured Cerberus as the twelfth labour imposed on him by Eurystheus.
    Theseus   descended into Hades to help Perithous abduct Persephone.
3   *Orpheus*   descended into Hades to save his captured wife Eurydice and succeeded because his music charmed Persephone.
    Ulysses   in Homer's *Odyssey* XI Odysseus (Ulysses) sails to the land of the Cimmerians which has access to Hades and goes there to ask Tiresias how he can find his way home.
    the Latin muse   Virgil.
4   *Troy's just knight*   Aeneas. He visits Hades in *Aeneid* VI.
5   *Shelton ... Heyden*   for Shelton see *Epigrams* CXIX; Heyden has not been identified.
7–8   *Styx ... Phlegeton*   all rivers in Hades.
8   *onc*   the Fleet Ditch.
12   *Charon*   the boatman who ferried the souls of the dead to Hades.
14   *Cerberus*   the three-headed watchdog of Hades.
20   *adventer*   adventure: the thought seems to be that while earlier times had produced the definitive poets, this adventure by Shelton and Heyden surpasses those of which the earlier poets wrote.
21   *wights*   men (mildly archaic).
27–8   *gave ... His three for one*   paid a dividend of three to one in profits on investments for the voyage.
28   *lordings*   archaic form of 'lords' (part of the mock-heroic apparatus of Jonson's poem).
30   *shoon*   archaic plural ('shoes').
34   *embassage*   commission, message.
35   *backward went to Berwick*   H/S (XI, 30) quote from Rowley's *A Search*

for Money (1609) 'the fellow's going backward to Berwick', but the 'fellow' has not been identified.

36 *the famous Morris, unto Norwich,* Will Kemp, the actor, danced from London to Norwich in 1599.

39 *his to Bristo'* Richard Ferris rowed in a wherry from Tower Wharf to Bristol in 1590.

40 *his to Antwerp* who did this has not been identified, but *H/S* (XI, 30) quote from Samuel Rowlands: 'Another, with his oars and slender wherry / From London unto Antwerp o'er did ferry'.

41 *A dock* Bridewell Dock was the outlet of the Fleet Ditch.

Avernus a lake near Naples, close to which was the cave by which Aeneas descended into Hades.

48 *Sybil . . . golden bough* in *Aeneid* VI, 136ff. Aeneas plucks the golden bough before descending to Hades and this bough forces Cerberus to ferry him over Acheron. It was the Cumaean sibyl who instructed Aeneas to pluck the bough.

50–51 *Alcides* Hercules (see note to l. 2).

55 *Great club-fist* Hercules is often represented holding a large club.

62 *Ycleped* archaic past participle ('called').

74 *the ox in Livy* Livy XXXV. xxi: 'nuntiatum est . . . consulis Cn. Domitii bovem locutum, Roma cave tibi' ('it is said . . . that a cow belonging to the consul Gnaeus Domitius spoke, and said, Rome, beware for yourself').

75 *sink* drain, sewer.

77 *Castor . . . Pollux* twin sons of Leda and Zeus.

80 *Chimera* a monster, part lion, part goat, part snake.

81 *Briareus* a giant with a hundred hands, son of earth and sky (see *Iliad* I, 402–6).

83 *Hydra* a multiple-headed monster killed by Hercules as his second labour.

84 *the trull* 'Jonson has copied the Roman poets in confusing the sea-monster Scylla with Scylla the daughter of Nisus of Megara, who, to win the love of Minos, cut off her father's hair on which his life depended . . .' (*H/S* XI, 31).

85 *lighter* barge.

89 *How hight the place?* 'What is the place called?': *hight* is an archaic past tense, part of the mock-heroic context.

95 *ab excelsis* from on high.

96 *Paracelsus* (1493–1541); a famous alchemist.

100 *subtlety* fineness, refinement.

102 *Suppositories* medicines, shaped like cylinders, for insertion into vagina or rectum.

cataplasms plasters, poultices.

108 *grave fart* seems to refer to a famous fart by Henry Ludlow which – voluntarily or involuntarily – answered a message brought to him by the Sergeant of the House of Lords.

112–13 see *Odyssey* IX. 431–4.

115   *sough*   sigh.
   lurden   something heavy or useless.
117   *meat-boat of Bears' college*   in the early seventeenth century the Butchers'
Company used to send offal by boat for the King's bears.
118   *Kate Arden*   see *Underwoods* XLIII, 148 and note.
120   *foist*   barge, with a pun on 'foist' ('foul smell').
128   *Democrite ... Hill Nicholas*   Democritus (born *c.* 460 BC) was the
founder of the theory of atoms; Nicholas Hill (?1570–1610) was a follower
who wrote *Philosophia, Epicurea, Democritiana, Theophrastica, proposita
simpliciter, non edocta* (1601).
133   *nare*   nostril.
155   *Tiberts*   Tibert is the name of the cat in the fable of Reynard the fox:
here a generic name for cats.
156   *Banks*   exhibited his horse Morocco in the 1580s and 1590s: there are
several literary allusions to him, but he was not – as Jonson implies – dead in
1625.
166   *peason*   peas.
167   *meat*   food.
172   *the Fleet*   a famous Elizabethan prison.
173   *the plague-bill*   the list of the names of the dead published during
visitations of the plague.
177   *three sergeants' heads*   the Rhadamanthus, Minos, Aeacus of ll. 187–9.
The reference seems to be to a public-house sign.
180   *madam Caesar*   see *The Alchemist* V. 4; obviously well-known as a
brothel-keeper.
186   *the triple head without a sop*   the three-headed Cerberus could be
bribed with food to allow passage into Hades.
190   *purblind fletcher*   a completely blind maker of arrows.
196   *his, that sung A-JAX*   a reference to Sir John Harington (1561–1612),
writer of epigrams, translator of Ariosto, author of a witty treatise on water-
closets (= 'jakes', hence the A-JAX pun). On Harington, see also *Con-
versations* 31–5.

The Forest

On this collection see the Preface. These poems are also a kind of manifesto of
one of the ways in which early seventeenth-century poetry sought freedom
from sixteenth-century modes and conventions. The title is an English
equivalent to Latin 'silva' used, by Statius for example, for collections of
occasional poems (see Jonson's notes on pp. 122 and 373).

I

This poem was written around 1611–12.

II

Written before November 1612 (see l. 77: Prince Henry died in that November). On the general background to Jonson's poem see Maren-Sofie Røstvig, *The Happy Man* (1962) and G. R. Hibbard, 'The country-house poem of the seventeenth-century', *JCWI* XIX (1956).

1ff. . . . Jonson is clearly, in this opening description, aiming to establish the integrated, functional nature of Penshurst as against the more flamboyant building of some Elizabethan–Jacobean *nouveaux riches*. The poem is at pains to make this integration a matter of social and moral importance and it obviously touched a real contemporary nerve: James tried, by legislation, to make country nobles and gentry live in their country homes instead of succumbing to the pleasures of London, and this was because the social organization of England depended greatly upon regional authority exercised by great local families. At the same time Jonson, as Gayle Wilson argues (*SEL* VIII, (1969), underlays this contemporary analysis/eulogy by drawing upon the imagery of *1 Kings* vi and vii. Wilson relates the seemingly local and specific reference to a *lanthern* (l. 4) to *1 Kings* vii 5, and I have not been able to find a contemporary reference which makes a more particular point although I suspect that there was one.

2   *touch*   black marble.

10   *dryads*   tree nymphs.

11–12   see Martial IX. lxi, 11–16 for a general parallel.

14   *his great birth*   that of Sir Philip Sidney in 1554.

16   *Sylvan*   Silvanus was a Roman wood-spirit: by Jonson's time a sylvan was a common synonym for a rural lover. The *flames* are the flames of love.

17   *satyrs*   in Greek mythology satyrs were attendants on Dionysius and spirits of woods and hills. Grotesque mixtures of human and bestial elements, they were sometimes identified with the 'fauni' (Jonson's *faun*) who were also woodland spirits.

18   *thy lady's oak*   Gifford says that 'a Lady Leicester' went into labour under an oak at Penshurst and that this oak was thereafter called 'My Lady's Oak'.

19   *named of Gamage*   Barbara Gamage married Lord Sidney in 1584.

25   *conies*   rabbits.

29   *painted partridge*   Martial's 'picta perdix' (III. lviii, 15).

30   Juvenal, *Satires* IV, 68–9: 'et tua servatum consume in saecula rhombum / ipse capi voluit' ('and eat a turbot that has been kept to grace your reign. The fish himself was anxious to be caught'). The idea of this line and of the passage down to l. 36 becomes a popular *topos* (see, for example, Carew, *To Saxham* 21–8, and – for a debased version – Ashton (ed.) *Humour, Wit, and Satire of the Seventeenth Century* (1968), 36). Wilson, in the article cited above, also refers to *Genesis* ix, 1–3.

36   *Officiously*   dutifully (Latin 'officiose').

48–71   Jonson is here working from the basis of Martial III, lviii, 33–44, but the Latin has been thoroughly naturalized so that Jonson's lines are an epitome of that native hospitality which was an important part of English social organization at this time (see note to l. 1). An interesting example of how seriously the matter was regarded by the monarchy is that when James gave the Earl of Lincoln permission to lead a regiment to fight in Germany under Count Mansfeld in 1624 he ordered that Lady Lincoln should stay in the country to 'keep hospitality' and not come up to London (see E. W. White, *Anne Bradstreet* (1971), 73).

48 *clown* peasant.

73 *livery* here, provision.

79 *Penates* Roman household gods.

91 *thy great lord* Robert, brother of Sir Philip Sidney; knighted in 1586; Baron Sidney; Viscount Lisle (1605); Earl of Leicester (1618).

102 Martial XII. i, 8: 'Quam bene non habitas' ('How well you are, not housed'). The whole of Martial's epigram is relevant to Jonson's line.

III

Title *Sir Robert Wroth* (1576–1614); knighted in 1601; connected with the Sidney family by marriage. Jonson is writing of Wroth's estate of Durrants in Enfield. He is less flattering about Wroth at *Conversations* 359. For the background to this poem see Horace, *Epistles* II; Martial I. xlix and III. lviii; Virgil, *Georgics* II.

6 *sheriff's . . . mayor's*] sergeants . . . sheriffs *MSS*.

25 *heart*] heat *MSS*.

26 *Divid'st*] Dispend'st *MSS*.

28 *gladder*] welcome *MSS*

34 *greedy*] hungry *MSS*.

41 *ears . . . height*] ears cut down in their most height *MSS*.

43 *that . . . last*] and ploughed land upcast *MSS*.

44 *mast* acorn-eating.

47 *Sylvan* a Roman woodland deity, associated by Virgil with Pan.

48 *Comus* a god of revelry: not a genuine classical figure, but a pseudo-pagan one; found in a number of renaissance texts, including Jonson's *Pleasure Reconciled to Virtue*.

50 *Saturn's reign* the age of gold.

54–8 Statius, *Silvarum* I. vi, 43–5: 'Una vescitur omnis ordo mensa, / parvi femina plebs eques senatus; / libertas reverentiam remisit' ('Every class of man eats from the same table – children, women, commoners, knights, senators; freedom from restraint has made inroads into our sense of rank').

61 *leese* lose.

77 *Let . . . disinherit*] Then hardest let him more disinherit *MSS*.

84 An almost literal translation of a line from Pithou, *Epigrammata* (1590): 'Avarus, nisi cum moritur, nil recte facit' (quoted *H/S* XI, 36).

87 *glad*] proud *MSS*.

95–106 Juvenal, *Satires* X, 346–59: 'nil ergo optabunt homines? si consilium vis, / permittes ipsis expendere numinibus quid / conveniat nobis rebusque sit utile nostris. / nam pro iucundis aptissima quaeque dabunt di, / carior est illis homo quam sibi. nos animorum / inpulsu et caeca magnoque cupidine ducti / coniugium petimus partumque uxoris, at illis / notum qui pueri qualisque futura sit uxor. / ut tamen et poscas aliquid voveasque sacellis / exta et candiduli divina tenacula porci, / orandum est ut sit mens sana in corpore sano. / fortem posce animum mortis terrore carentem, / qui spatium vitae extremum inter munera ponat / naturae, qui ferre queat quoscumque labores' ('Is there nothing, then, worth praying for? My advice is to let the gods themselves decide what is right for us, and what is necessary in our various conditions. They will give what we need, not what we want: a man is more important to them than he is to himself. Pushed along by irrational impulses and strong, blind desires we seek marriage and children. But only the gods know what they will be like, these future wives and children. Still, if you do have to have something to pray for; if you are determined to offer the entrails and holy sausages from a white piglet to every shrine – ask for a sound mind in a sound body, a brave heart that thinks long life the least of Nature's gifts, that can endure all sorts of toil.')

105–6 See *Epigrams* XXII, LXXX.

IV

Title The gentlewoman of the subtitle has not been identified and may well be an imaginary figure.

24 *gyves* chains, fetters.
25–32 Horace, *Satires* II. vii, 68–71: 'Evasti: credo, metues doctusque cavebis; / quaeres, quando iterum paveas iterumque perire / possis, o totiens servus! quae belua ruptis, / cum semel effugit, reddit se prava catenis?' ('Imagine you have escaped: then, I suppose, you will be afraid and cautious after the lesson you have learnt. No, you will seek an opportunity to be in fear again, to face ruin once more. Oh, you many times over slave! What beast, even, having snapped its fetters and escaped, perversely goes back to them again?').
31 *wull* will.
36 *gins* traps.
56 *grutch* complain.

V

This poem appears in *Volpone* (1606), III. 7. 166–83 and is based on Catullus V ('Vivamus, mea Lesbia, atque amemus'), a poem which is translated, in whole or in part, by a number of English poets of this period (see, for example, Campion's *My Sweetest Lesbia*, Raleigh's *The Sun May Set and Rise*, Crashaw's *Come and Let Us Live My Dear*).

6–8 Catullus V, 4–6: 'Soles occidere et redire possunt: / nobis cum semel occidit brevis lux / nox est perpetua una dormienda'. Jonson's lines are a close translation.

VI

6–11 Catullus V, 7–11: 'Da mi basia mille, deinde centum, / dein mille altera, dein secunda centum, / deinde usque altera mille, deinde centum. / Dein, cum milia multa fecerimus, / conturbabimus illa . . .'. Jonson's lines are again a close translation. (The motif of thousands of kisses is often used in love poetry of this period – see, for example, Johannes Secundus, *Basia* and Thomas Stanley, *Imitatio Catulliana*).

12–22 Catullus VII: 'Quaeris, quot mihi basiationes / tuae, Lesbia, sint satis superque. / quam magnus numerus Libyssae harenae / lasarpiciferis iacet Cyrenis, / oraculum Iovis inter aestuosi / et Batti veteris sacrum sepulcrum, / aut quam sidera multa, cum tacet nox, / furtivos hominum vident amores; / tam te basia multa basiare / vesano satis et super Catullo est, / quae nec pernumerare curiosi / possint nec mala fascinare lingua.' ('Lesbia, you ask how many kisses are enough for me, and more than enough. As large as the number of the Libyan sands on the silphium-bearing Cyrene, between sultry Jove's oracle and old Battus' sacred tomb; or as many as the stars in the silent night which see men's stolen delights. To kiss you with that many kisses, Lesbia, is enough and more than enough for your maddened Catullus; kisses which shall not be counted by curious eyes nor bewitched by any evil tongue.') Jonson's lines appear in *Volpone* III. 7. 236–9.

15 *Thames*] streams *MS*.
16 *his streams*] the Thames *MS*.
22 *pined* pained.

VII

According to *Conversations* 368–71 this poem was written as a result of a dispute between the Earl of Pembroke and his wife on this topic. Jonson was asked his opinion and provided it by adapting Aneau's 'Mulier umbra Viri' (from *Picta Poesis*, 1552). *H/S* (XI, 38) print the full Aneau text.

VIII

3 *ynow* enough.
10 *Spittles* here, leper-hospitals.
    pest-house hospital for victims of the plague or small-pox.
11 *store*] score *MS*.
27 *price*] prize *MSS*.
31 *emp'rics* quacks, charlatans.
33 *oil of Talc* used as a cosmetic.
38 *stew* brothel.
39 *entail* bequeath.
48 *rest*] best *MS*.

IX

This lyric is a mosaic from the prose *Epistles* of Philostratus. A. D. Fitton
Brown (*MLR* LIV (1959), 554–7) suggests that Jonson's poem may have been
influenced by Bonfini's Latin translation of the Greek. The earliest surviving
setting of this song is sung by James Oswald (1753–4) but there have been many
later ones.

1–4 Philostratus XXXIII, 5–7: 'ἐμοὶ δὲ μόνοις πρόπινε τοῖς ὄμμασιν,
ὧν καὶ ὁ Ζεὺς γευσάμενος καλὸν οἰνοχόον παρεστήσατο. εἰ δὲ βούλει,
τὸν μὲν οἶνον μὴ παραπόλλυε, μόνον δ' ἐμβαλοῦσα ὕδατος καὶ τοῖς χείλεσι
προσφέρουσα πλήρου φιλημάτων τὸ ἔκπωμα καὶ οὕτως δίδου τοῖς
δεομένοις.' ('drink to me only with your eyes. . . . And, if you please, do
not waste the wine, but pour water in, and, bringing it to your lips, fill the
cup with kisses and pass it like this to the thirsty').

2 *I will pledge*] I'll pledge thee *M S S*.
3 *Or leave a kiss but in*] Leave but a kiss within *M S S*.
4 *not look for*] expect no *M S S*.

5–7 Philostratus XXXII, 8–12: 'πόσους ἱστᾷς ἐπειγομένους; πόσους
κατέχεις παρατρέχοντας, πόσους φθεγξαμένη καλεῖς; ἐγὼ πρῶτος,
ἐπειδὰν ἴδω σέ, διψῶ καί ἵσταμαι μή θέλων τὸ ἔκπωμα κατέχων. τὸ
μὲν οὐ προσάγω τοῖς χείλεσι, σου δ' οἶδα πίνων.' ('First of all, when I see
you, I feel thirsty, and stand still against my will, and hold back the cup; I do
not lift it to my lips but I know that I am drinking of you').

7 *Jove's*] Love's *M S*.

8–12 Philostratus II, 13–16: 'Πέπομφά σοι στέφανον ῥόδων, οὐ σὲ τιμῶν,
καὶ τοῦτο μὲν γάρ ἀλλ'αὐτοῖς τι χαριξόμενος τοῖς ῥόδοις, ἵνα μὴ
μαρανθῇ' ('I sent you a rose garland not to honour you – though I would wish
that as well – but to do the roses a favour so that they may not be withered').

10 *much honouring*] to honour *M S S*.
11 *As . . . there*] But being well assured that there *M S S*.

13–16 Philostratus XLVI, 8–9: 'εἰ δὲ βούλει τι φίλῳ χαρίζεσθαι, τὰ λείψανα
αὐτῶν ἀντίπεμψον μηκέτι πνέοντα ῥόδων μόνον ἀλλὰ καὶ σοῦ' ('send what
is left of them back, since their scent is not now just of roses but also of you').

15 *grows*] lives *M S S*.

X

This, together with the next poem and *MP* XXXI. CXII, was printed
among the 'Diverse Poetical Essays' in Robert Chester's *Love's Martyr*
(1601). *H/S* (XI, 40–42) give a long note on Chester and the circumstances
surrounding his volume.

1 *And . . . sing?* We must sing too? *Chester*.
   I choose?] We choose *Chester*.
3 *my*] our *Chester*.
4–5 The reference is to the twelve labours Eurystheus imposed on Hercules.
6 *I'll*] Lets *Chester*.

7 *cart* chariot.

8 *I*] we *Chester (and so at ll. 10, 13, 28, 30)*.

9 *foundered* exhausted.

   my] our *Chester (and so at ll. 11, 18, 28, 29)*.

13–16 Pallas was born from the head of Zeus. The birth was facilitated by Zeus' head being opened by an axe-blow from Hephaestus (the Greek fire-god). Vulcan, an early Roman god of fire is – like Hephaestus – also identified with smithying, and is sometimes merged with the Greek god. Since Hephaestus was the husband of Aphrodite (Venus) Jonson is obviously linking Vulcan and Hephaestus.

17 *tribade trine* (a) the three Graces; (b) lesbians.

19 *the old boy, your son* the idea that Cupid is both the youngest and the oldest god is a Platonic one.

22 *Hermes, the cheater* Hermes is, among other things, the god of rogues and thieves.

   shall not] cannot *Chester*.

23 *his sisters'* the muses.

24 *riffle* raffle.

   Petasus one of Hermes' identifying features is his broad-brimmed hat (Greek 'petasos').

25 *Thespian lake* Aganippe, on the Helicon.

28 *commission* command, instruction.

30 *epode* a lyric metre, invented by Archilochus, where a longer line is followed by a shortened one. The form is also used in Roman verse and Jonson adapts it in the following poem.

XI

1–4 This is based on Plato, *Gorgias* 478d.

9 *ports* gates.

19 *true*] fair *MSS*.

37–46 Lucian, *Demosthenis Encomium* XIII ('. . . the two kinds of human love, one grown from a desire like the sea, ontrageous, fierce, rocking the soul with storms; it is a real wave of the sea, which the earthly Aphrodite sets moving with the violent passions of youth; but the other is the steady pull of a gold thread from heaven; it does not burn and stab and leave festering wounds; it impels the pure and unsoiled ideal of absolute beauty . . .').

45 *far more gentle*] most gentile, and *MS*.

63–4 Matthew iv 5–6: 'Then the devil taketh him into the holy city; and he set him on the pinnacle of the temple / And saith unto him, If thou art the Son of God, cast thyself down . . .'.

67 *we*] I *MSS*.

68 *we*] I *MS*.

69 *luxury* lust.

73–4 Sparrows are associated with Venus and hence with sexuality, whereas turtle-doves are a common symbol of chaste love.

75 *ourselves*] myself *MSS*.

76 *We*] I *MSS.*

83 *we*] I *MSS.*

84 *filled*] graced *MSS.*

85 *we*] I *MSS.*

87–90 Horace, *Epistles* I. xvi, 52–4: 'Oderunt peccare boni virtutis amore / tu nihil admittes in te formidine poenae: / sit spes fallendi, miscebis sacra profanis' ('The good hate vice since they love virtue; you dare commit no crime because you are scared of punishment; you make no difference between the sacred and the profane').

88 *crown-worthy*] praiseworthy *MSS.*

91 *we propose*] I conceive *MSS.*

   our] my *MSS.*

115–16 Seneca, *Phaedra* 162–4: 'Quid poena praesens, consciae mentis pavor / animusque culpa plenus et semet timens? / Scelus aliqua tutum, nulla securum tulit' ('What of the price paid, the inner punishment, the great fear of the conscious heart, the soul that cannot face itself? Some people may have sinned safely, none with an untroubled conscience').

XII

See *Epigrams* LXXIX and note. This poem is a New Year's gift for 1600.

9 *huishers* ushers.

12 *peer*] prince *MS.*

22 *gilt* the folio reads 'guilt'. The main point here is the juxtaposition with 'golden' and as 'guilt' is a seventeenth-century alternative spelling of 'gilt' I have used the latter form, although I think that the modern sense of 'guilt' = 'guilty' is also suggested.

25 Horace, *Odes* III. iii, 49–50: 'aurum inrepertum et sic melius situm / cum terra celat' ('undiscovered gold – better so, while still hidden in the earth').

29 *Turn ... their quarter-face* turn almost completely away in aversion.

31 *your great father* Sir Philip Sidney.

42 *hold up, and*] there hold up *MSS.*

43 *glorious* boastful (Latin 'gloriosus').

43–57 Horace, *Odes* IV. viii, 11–32: 'gaudes carminibus: carmina possumus / donare et pretium dicere muneri. / non incisa notis marmora publicis, / per quae spiritus et vita redit bonis / post mortem ducibus, non celeres fugae / reiectaeque retrorsum Hannibalis minae, / non incendia Carthaginis impiae / eius, qui domita nomen ab Africa / lucratus rediit, clarius indicant / laudes quam Calabrae Pierides neque, / si chartae sileant quod bene feceris, / mercedem tuleris. quid foret Iliae / Mavortisque puer, si taciturnitas / obstaret meritus invida Romuli? / ereptum Stygiis fluctibus Aeacum / virtus et favor et lingua potentium / vatum divitibus consecrat insulis. / dignum laude virum Musa vetat mori. / caelo Musa beati sic Iovis interest / optatis epulis impiger Hercules, / clarum Tyndarides sidus ab infimis / quassas eripiunt aequoribus rates' ('you delight in songs, songs which we can give, and can rate the value

of such a tribute. Neither marble inscribed with public records, which bring
a return to life and breath to great heroes after their deaths; nor Hannibal's
rapid retreat and his self-recoiling threats; nor the burning of wicked Car-
thage, show more finely the fame of he who returned home from subjugating
Africa, than do the Calabrian muses; nor would you gain your just reward
should the parchment fail to announce your worthy deeds. What would the
child of Ilia and Mars be today if jealous silence had barred the path of Romu-
lus' deserts? The powers of talented singers, their favour and their verse save
Aeacus from the Stygian waves and gain him a sacred home in the Islands of
the Blessed. It is the muse that forbids the hero who is worthy of fame to be
forgotten. It is the muse which gives heaven's boon. It is thus that the untir-
ing Hercules shares the hoped-for table of Jove; thus that Tyndareus' sons,
gleaming fires, save storm-shaken ships from the abyss of the sea').

Also Horace, *Odes* IV. ix, 19–28: '... non pugnavit ingens / Idomeneus
Sthenelusve solus / dicenda Musis proelia; non ferox / Hector vel acer Dei-
phobus graves / excepit ictus pro pudicis / coniugibus pueribusque primus. /
vixere fortes ante Agamemnona / multi; sed omnes inlacrimabiles / urgentur
ignotique longa / nocte, carent quia vate sacro' ('not only have great
Idomeneus or Sthenelus fought battles worth the muses' songs. Nor were
strong Hector and keen Deiphobus the first to meet powerful blows to save
chaste wives and children. Many heroes lived before Agamemnon; but they
are all drowned in never-ending night because they lacked a sacred poet').

44 *touch* durable black marble.

49 *the Argive queen* Helen.

52 *Or, in an army's* Or, at the head of an army, encased in armour.

54 *Idomen* Idomeneus, Cretan captain at Troy.

57-8 *Who ... stars?* the exploits of Hercules are told, for example, in
Euripides' *Heracles*, Sophocles' *Trachinian Women* and Seneca's *Hercules
Furens* and *Hercules Octaeus*. Jonson's point with several of these questions
is rather that it was the poets who gave the relevant heroes immortality than
that they wrote specifically of their stellification.

58 *the Tyndarides* Castor and Pollux.

59 According to Hyginus (*Fabulae* 14) Minerva achieved this.

60 Dionysus did this (Ovid, *Metamorphoses* VIII, 177–9).

61 *Berenice's hair* Berenice was wife to Ptolemy III and the story of how
she dedicated a lock of her hair to his safe return from a journey was told in a
poem by Callimachus which was translated by Catullus (LXVI).

62 *Cassiopea* the mother of Andromeda; the story of Andromeda and
Perseus is told by Ovid (*Metamorphoses* V–VI).

63 *only*] holy *MSS*.
   rage] sense *MSS*.

66 *Lucina ... Lucy the bright* Queen Elizabeth ... Lucy, countess of
Bedford (in both cases Jonson is playing on the Latin 'lux', meaning 'light').

68-9 *H/S* (XI, 45) follow Short in taking this to refer to Drayton.

72 *sanguine* hopeful, cheerful.

76 *the notes*] *one MS*; to notes *one MS, F1*. I follow *H/S* in preferring the plural version. The *notes* in question refer to a projected celebration of the ladies of Britain which Jonson either never wrote or which has disappeared.

77 *act*] arts *one MS.*

78 According to tradition Orpheus' lyre-playing could even move trees and stones.

79 *muse*] verse *MSS.*

87 *tickling*] tinkling *MS.*

90 *ecstasies* rapturous thoughts.

92 *your brave friend* the Earl of Rutland.

93 *whereso'er he be* Jonson in the folio cancelled what follows, presumably because the marriage was not consummated. I follow *H/S* in completing the poem from the ending in the *MSS.*

99 *circled*] *one MS*; feathered *one MS.*

XIII

Title *Katherine, Lady Aubigny* daughter of Sir Gervase Clifton; married Esmé, Seigneur d'Aubigny in 1609 (see *Epigrams* CXXVII and note); died 1627.

25 *slightly* slightingly.

33 *taken up of* bought from.

39 *cozening farmer of the customs* a cheating tax-collector (who paid a set sum to his appointee for what he was able to collect and was allowed to keep the surplus).

72 *Maintain their liegers forth* 'have agents living abroad to supply the newest fashions' (*H/S* XI, 46).

86 Seneca, *Epistles* CXXII, 18: 'Nolunt solita peccare, quibus peccandi praemium infamia est' ('They are unwilling to be conventionally wicked because notoriety is what they gain from their special brand of wickedness').

102 *triple trine* nine months. A trine is a threefold unit.

XIV

Title *Sir William Sidney* son of Robert, Lord Sidney; born 1590; knighted 1610; died 1612. L. C. John (*MLR* LII (1957), 168f.) gives further biographical information, claiming that Sidney had achieved little when this poem was written and that it is serious advice rather than conventional eulogy.

11 *from the Thespian well* from the muses (the well presumably refers to the springs of Hippocrene and Aganippe on Helicon).

42 *Whose nephew, whose grand-child* Sir William was nephew to Sir Philip and grandchild of Sir Henry Sidney.

XV

5 *the reins* strictly the loins or kidneys, but – as these areas of the body were thought to be the seat of the passions – also used to denote these passions.

H/S (XI, 47) quote *Psalms* vii. 9: 'for the righteous God trieth the hearts and reins'.

21–2 Ovid, *Ex Ponto* II. vii, 41–2: 'sic ego continuo Fortunae vulneror ictu, / vixque habet in nobis iam nova plaga locum' ('so I am wounded by Fate's persistent blows until now I have hardly any room for a new wound').

23–5 *Romans* vii. 24: 'O wretched man, that I am: Who shall deliver me from the body of this death?'

Underwoods

On the publication and arrangement of these poems see the Preface.

TO THE READER

See the introductory note to *The Forest*.

I, I

10 *Psalms* li. 17: 'a broken and a contrite heart, O God, thou wilt not despise'.

11–12 *I Samuel* xv. 22: 'Behold, to obey is better than sacrifice: and to hearken than the fat of rams'.

34 *union*] unity *F1*. Gifford's emendation is obviously required by the rhyme scheme – the folio printer probably carried over 'unity' from l. 30.

42 *mediate*] meditate *F1*. Gifford's emendation is preferable.

48 *rest !*] *F3*; rest? *F1*. The question mark is often used in the sixteenth and seventeenth centuries for an exclamation mark, and it seems to me that this poem is meant to end confidently and not with a Donne-like doubt.

I, 2

H/S refer to a setting of this by William Crosse (1635) but Macdonald Emslie (*NQ* (November 1953), 466–8) argues that the relevant Egerton *MS* setting is anonymous and not necessarily by Crosse: he suggests Ferrabosco.

I, 3

10 *take* contain.

II, I

Title Written in 1623, whereas the other *Charis* lyrics were probably written considerably earlier, although the fact that II, 4 is used in *The Devil is an Ass* (1616) is proof only that that lyric had been written by that date.

23–4 The idea of the mistress as being the animator of the world is a conventional hyperbole of sixteenth-century love poetry.

II, 2

4 *then*] *F3*; than *F1*. 'Then' makes better sense and defends Jonson from being accused of 'vicious inversion' – at least on this occasion.
22 *with*] *Gifford*; which *F1 and 2*.

II, 3

21 *wreak* vengeance.

II, 4

Title Ll. 11–30 appear as II. 6. 94–113 of *The Devil is an Ass*.

21–4 Martial V. xxxvii, 6: 'nivesque primas liliumque non tactum' ('fresh snows and the untouched lily').
21–30 The final stanza of this poem was widely known and used by other poets. Thus *H/S* mention Suckling's song in IV. 3 of *The Sad One* and Carew's *Would you know what's soft? I dare* (*H/S* call this latter a variation by Carew of a song by James Shirley. Dunlap, *The Poems of Thomas Carew* (1964), 286, accepts it as Shirley's while pointing out that the text in the latter's *Poems* of 1646 – where Shirley complains of some of his poems being 'mingled with other men's . . . conceptions in print' – differs considerably from the version in Carew's *Poems* of 1640).
28 *nard* spikenard, an aromatic ointment.

II, 5

13 See *Iliad* XVII, 51.
14–17 The reference is to the graceful lyrics of the *Anacreontea*, a collection that may contain some examples of Anacreon's own poetry but is largely made up of imitations of this Greek poet of *c*. 550 BC.
16 *about*] *F1 and 2*; above *H/S*. The emendation is attractive but not strictly necessary. See *H/S* VIII, 136.
35 *proin* preen.
37–8 *Her . . . same* Charis was the wife of Hephaestus; Venus – Cupid's mother – was the wife of Vulcan. The Greek and Roman gods and goddesses of similiar function were often identified and Jonson makes use of this here.
41 *girdle 'bout her waist* in Homer the goddess of love has a magic girdle of aphrodisiac power.
45–8 Juno, Pallas and Venus competed before Paris, the apple being the prize for the greatest beauty.
53 *Juno . . . walks* Virgil, *Aeneid* I, 46: 'ast ego, quae divom incedo regina' ('yet I, queen of the divine, despite my stately walk . . .').
54 *Minerva . . . talks* Minerva is the goddess of wisdom and eloquence.

II, 7

2 *long*] beg *MS*.
    beg] ask *MSS*.

6 *touch*] suck *M S S.*
16 *sucks out*] I have preferred the reading in the *M S S.* The folio reads simply *suck others* and Gifford adds *the* to save the metre: *H/S* follow Gifford.

II, 8

17 *emissary eye* Plautus, *Aulularia* 41: 'circumspectatrix cum oculis emissiciis' ('you snooper, with your prying eyes').
23 *purl* lace or embroidery border.
25 *secretary Sis* confidential attendant.

II, 9

Title *Dictamen* statement, dictation.

13 *more slack* duller
18 *Front . . . of*] Forehead large, and white as *M S.*
32 *love's school*] love's art *M S.*
40 *set*] pent *M S.*
  brake framework.

III

'Pastoral dialogues' are quite common in poetry of this period (for some examples see *England's Helicon* (ed. Macdonald, 1949), 31, 82, 111 and Marvell, *Clorinda and Damon*). Jonson's poem, in some form, was written by 1618, since he quoted it to Drummond (see *Conversations* 77–8).

3 *each*] one *M S.*
8 *but must lose*] doth not want *M S.*
9 *then your*] we our *M S S.*
15 *No tunes are sweet*] No voice so sweet *one M S*; no voice is sweet *two M S S*; no ear hath sound *two M S S.*
  nor words have sting] no words have sting *three M S S*; no voice hath sting *one M S*; no voice hath sung *one M S.*
16 *those*] your *M S S.*
17 *They*] Some *M S S.*
  mark] view *M S S.*
19 *pleasure*] passion *M S S.*
20] On what they see or know *three M S S*; On which they see or know *one M S*; On that they see or know *one M S*; Themselves with what they know *one M S.*
21 *O . . . then*] Sing you no more then *three M S S*; Sing we no more then *two M S S.*
24 *earth*] hell *M S.*
25 *Nay*] Let *M S S.*
  souls] notes *M S S.*
27 *state*] seat *M S.*

IV

8 *spill* kill, destroy (Old English 'spillan').

V

Jonson here draws on a passage from Seneca, *Epistles* IX, 7: 'Attalus philo-sophus dicere solebat, iucundius esse amicum facere quam habere, quomodo artifici iucundius pingere est quam pinxisse ... Non aeque delectatur, qui ab opere perfecto removit manum. Iam fructu artis suae fruitur; ipsa fruebatur arte, cum pingeret' ('The philosopher Attalus would say, "It is pleasanter to make a friend than to keep one, as it is more pleasant for the artist to be painting than to have finished painting. ... But when one has taken one's hand away from the completed piece, the pleasure is less. From that time it is the results of his art which he enjoys: while he was painting it was the art itself"').

VIII

A copy of this poem was sent to Drummond (see *Conversations* 676). *H/S* (XI, 53) quote the Latin poem by Amaltei on which Jonson's poem is based.

1–2 A single line in Drummond, *Works* (1711) and in *MSS*.

2 *running*] moving *MS*.

4–5 A single line in Drummond, *Works* (1711) and *MSS*.

8 *Turned*] Burned *three MSS*; Was straightway turned *one MS, Drummond, Works (1711) and 1640 Benson quarto*.

9] Yes; as in life, so in their deaths unblest *Drummond, Works (1711) and 1640 quarto;* Whereby (in death, as life, unblest!) *MS*.

11] That lovers' ashes find no rest *one MS*; The ashes of lovers find no rest *one MS*; That lovers' ashes take no rest *two MSS*; A lover's ashes never can find rest *Drummond, Works (1711) and 1640 quarto*.

IX

Written in 1619. A *MS* was sent to Drummond (see *Conversations* 679).

5 *love*] suit *Drummond, Works (1611), 1640 quarto, MS*.

7 *close* in music, the conclusion of a strain or movement.

8 *sentence*] numbers *Drummond, Works (1611), MS*.

9 *youngest*] wisest *Drummond, Works (1611), 1640 quarto*.

13 *Tell*] Prompt *Drummond, Works (1611)*.

15 *seven*] six *Drummond, Works (1611), 1640 quarto, MS*.

X

16 Seneca, *De Ira* I. xii, 6: 'Abominandum remedii genus est samtatem debere morbe' ('It is a hateful sort of remedy to owe one's health to illness').

XII

Title *Vincent Corbet* Aubrey says that Corbet was a gardener, but he is called 'gentleman' and was a fairly substantial land-owner, so his gardening must have been by way of a hobby. Several contemporaries speak of his horticultural skill. He was the father of Richard Corbet, bishop and poet, and died in 1619.

1 *have*] hope *MSS*.

4 *Before me here*] And join in one *MS*.

the friend and son the friend has not been identified, but Richard Corbet's *Elegie upon the Death of His Own Father* is on p. 67 of Bennett and Trevor-Roper's edition (1955) of his poems.

14 *All*] At *MSS*.

17 *uncleanness*] maliciousness *MS*.

20 *specious*] spacious *MSS*. 'Specious' means 'splendid' (Latin 'speciosus').

26 *twice*] once *MS*.

28 Martial X. xxxiii, 10: 'parcere personis, dicere de vitiis' ('to spare the person, to denounce the vice').

34 *for . . . will*] these tears for me would *MS*.

XIII

Title *Sir Edward Sackville* (1591-1652); became fourth earl of Dorset in 1624.

1-4 Seneca, *De Beneficiis* I. i, 1-2: 'Beneficia nec dare scimus nec accipere. . . . Nec mirum est inter plurima maximoque vitia nullum esse frequentius quam ingrati animi' ('We neither know how to give favours nor how to accept them. . . . It is no wonder that, among so many serious failings, there is none more common than ingratitude').

5-6 Seneca, *De Beneficiis* I. i, 3, 8: 'Reddit enim beneficium qui libentur debet . . . Eodem animo beneficium debetur quo datur' ('For he who freely acknowledges a favour is doing a favour. . . . A favour is owed in the same spirit in which it is given').

9-12 Seneca, *De Beneficiis* II. i, 3: 'Gratissima sunt beneficia parata, facilia, occurentia, ubi nulla mora fuit nisi in accipientis verecundia. Optimum est antecedere desiderium cuiusque, proximum sequi. Illud melius, occupare ante quam rogemur, quia, cum homini probo ad rogandum os concurrat et suffundatur rubor, qui hoc tormentum remittit multiplicat munus suum' ('The benefits that produce most gratitude are those which are really and freely obtainable and which hurry to our hands, where – if there is any delay – it arises from the tact of the recipient. The best line of action is to anticipate each person's wish; the next best course is to indulge it. The first is better: to forestall the request since a decent man closes his lips and is suffused with blushes if he has to beg. He who spares him this pain multiplies the value of his gift').

18-22 Seneca, *De Beneficiis* I. xv, 4: 'Beneficia tu vocas, quorum auctorem fateri pudet? At illa quanto gratiora sunt quantoque in partem interiorem animi numquam exitura descendunt, cum delectant cogitantem magis a quo, quam quid acceperis?' ('Do you call those benefits when you are ashamed to admit the name of the giver? But how much more acceptable gifts are, how much deeper an impression they make on the mind, never to leave it, when the pleasure of them comes from thinking less of what you have received than of him who did the giving!').

24 Seneca, *De Beneficiis* I. i, 7: 'nemo autem libenter debet, quod non accepit, sed expressit' ('yet nobody is happy to be indebted for what he has extorted rather than received').

25-8 Seneca, *De Beneficiis* I. i, 6: 'in angusto vero compressus aut distulit, id est timide negavit, aut promisit, sed difficulter, sed subductis superciliis, sed malignis et vix exeuntibus verbis?'(' who, when really cornered, has not either delayed the favour – that is, has been too cowardly to refuse it – or promised it ungraciously, frowningly, and with unwilling and muttered words?').

34 .Seneca, *De Beneficiis* I. ii, 3: 'Nemo beneficia in calendario scribit nec avarus exactor ad horam et diem appellat' ('Nobody enters his givings in his account books, or – like a grasping tax-collector – calls for payment on a set day and a fixed hour').

37-8 Seneca, *De Beneficiis* II. xiii, 1: 'O superbia, magnae fortunae stultissimum malum! Ut a te nihil accipere iuvat! Ut omne beneficium in iniuriam convertis!' ('O pride, bane of good fortune and its most stupendous folly! How glad we are to receive nothing from you! How you transform all kinds of benefits into injuries!').

47-9 Seneca, *De Beneficiis* II. xxiii, 1, 2: 'Sunt quidam, qui nolunt nisi secreto accipere; testem beneficii et conscium vitant ... Quidam furtive agunt gratias et in angulo et ad aurem' ('There are some people who will not accept a gift unless it is given privately; they dislike having a witness of the donation or for anyone to know about it').

57 Seneca, *De Beneficiis* II. xxiv, 1: 'Alii pessime locuntur de optime meritis' ('Others speak most hostilely of those who have treated them best').

63 *was made* made knight.

67-72 Jonson here uses a fable of Phaedrus, II. iii. Text in *H/S* XI, 55-6.

74 *at still* nevertheless.

77-8 Seneca, *De Beneficiis* I. ii, 1-2: 'Beneficia in volgus cum largiri institueris / perdenda sunt multa, ut semel ponas bene' ('You love to pour bounty on the mob: you must lose many gifts for each one that is properly placed').

78 *place*] pace *Whalley, H/S*. The folio text makes quite adequate sense in the light of the Senecan loan.

101 *Rear-suppers* late meals – later than the usual evening meal.

105-8 Seneca, *Epistles* LXXXV, 28: 'Non dubitarent, quid conveniret forti viro, si scirent, quid esset fortitudo. Non est enim inconsulta temeritas nec periculorum amor nec formidabilium adpetitio: scientia est distinguendi, quid sit malum et quid non sit' ('If men knew what bravery was they would have no doubts about the proper conduct of a brave man. For bravery is not mindless rashness, nor a love of danger, nor the encouragement of awe-inspiring objects: it is knowing how to distinguish between what is evil and what is not').

120–34 Jonson here draws on a long passage from Plutarch, *Quomodo quis suos in virtute sentiat profectus* (text in *H/S* XI, 56).

128 *Coriat* see *Epigrams* CXXIX and note; *MP* VI, VII, CXV.

136 Seneca *Epistles* CXVIII, 16: 'Unus lapis facit fornicem, ille, qui latera inclinata cuneavit et interventu suo vinxit. Summa adiectio . . . non auget, sed implet' ('One stone makes an arch; the stone that wedges the inclining sides and holds the arch together by its medial position. The last stone added does not increase – it completes').

145–54 Jonson again uses Plutarch, *Quomodo quis suos in virtute sentiat profectus* (text in *H/S* XI, 57).

156 *indice* indicator.

XIV

Title *John Selden* (1584–1654); jurist and friend of Jonson; this poem (1614) was prefixed to Selden's *Titles of Honour*. See *Conversations* 276, 626–8.

2 Horace, *Ars Poetica* 25–6: 'brevis esse laboro, obscurus fio' ('Myself for shortness labour, and I grow / Obscure . . .' – Jonson's translation).

4 *Truth . . . naked*] Since, naked, best Truth, and the Graces *Selden*. The Graces are Greek goddesses (usually three) personifying beauty. Their full significance, especially in the pictorial arts, is discussed in Chapter II of Edgar Wind's *Pagan Mysteries in the Renaissance* (1967).

17 *far otherwise*] far from this fault *Selden*.

21 *terms* limits.

37 *To instruct*] To inform *MS, Selden*.

48 *act*] art *Selden (a reading adopted by H/S)*.

58 *colours* rhetorical figures.

72 *Thy learnèd chamber-fellow* Edward Hayward (1600–58), dedicatee of *Titles of Honour*.

76 *same*] rich *Selden*.

80 *comings in* benefits, income.

81 *grain* character, quality.

XV

Title *a Friend . . . to the Wars* the friend is named as Colby in l. 176 but is otherwise unidentified. The wars in question may well be, as *H/S* suggest, the religious wars on the Continent at this period.

1 *from . . . lethargy*] and find thyself; awake *MS*.

9 *but*] mere *MS*.

37 *capital* our most prominent concern; perhaps also 'deserving the greatest punishment'.

56 *leese* lose.

57–8 Juvenal, *Satires* xi, 176–8: 'Alea turpis, / turpe et adulterium mediocribus: haec eadem illi / omnia cum faciunt, hilares nitidique vocantur' ('If ordinary folk play dice or commit adultery it is thought disgraceful; but when such activities come from the well-to-do they are thought smart and sporty').

61-2 *If . . . would* Juvenal, *Satires* i, 79: 'Si natura negat, facit indignatio versum' ('Even if natural ability were lacking anger would make me write verse').

67 *pound a prick* excite the male organ sexually.

70 *pickardil* a large and fashionable collar.

71 *brise* gadfly.

76 *saut* salt, in the sense of salacious.

80 *Pitts, or Wright, or Modet* clearly contemporary whores of some reputation.

86 This refers to a commercial activity in which the borrower was forced to take part or all of a loan in merchandise: he could try to resell it, but the given material was usually unsellable.

96 *embrions* embryos.

97 *infamed* disgraced, defamed.

105 *the Counters, or the Fleet* both prisons, the Counters being specifically for debtors.

109 *where* whereas.

113 *O, friend*] the folio has a blank after 'O', which could indicate omission of a profanity, but the Newcastle MS has 'friend' which seems reasonable enough, although it does not explain the folio blank.

135-9 Horace, *Satires* II. vii, 15-18: 'scurra Volanerius, postquam illi iusta cheragra / contudit articulos, qui pro se tolleret atque / mitteret in phimum talos, mercede diurna / conductum pavit' ('the joker Volanerius, when his well-earned gout crippled his fingers, hired a man at a daily rate to pick the dice up for him and put them in the box').

138 *views*] *MS*; viewers *folio*. The folio reading is clearly an error since the rhyme demands 'views'.

160 *boot*] *MS*; both *folio*. The folio reading can be defended but looks suspiciously like a printer's slip in repeating the 'both' earlier in the line.

174 *muster-master* a person charged with taking account of troops.

176 *Colby . . . be*] which shall ever be *MS*.

196 *rise a star* achieve immortality (see *The Forest* XII, 57ff. and note).

XVI

Title *Philip Gray* perhaps the eldest son of Sir Edward Gray of Morpeth Castle.

XVII

Title *a Friend* not identified.

7 *protested be* have liability alleged against me.

9 *band* bond.

15 *Venter* venture, speculate.

XVIII

Like other writers of his time Jonson often uses 'elegy' in the Roman sense of a longish love poem in elegiac couplets (although the English poets do not always imitate the Latin form).

7-8 Seneca, *Epistles* LXXI, 24: 'Sic quaedam rectissima, cum in aquam demissa sunt, speciem curvi praefractique visentibus reddunt' ('So certain objects which are completely straight, seem – when put into water – to an onlooker to be crooked or broken').

8 *conceit* idea.

11 *Both these are blind* it is a commonplace in Renaissance art and thought that both Cupid and Fortune are blind.

13 *error* wandering, erratic (Latin 'erro').

XIX

3 *stand* a platform or standing-point for shooting at game.

4 *double bow* each of the mistress's eyebrows is seen as a bow of Cupid: the eyebrow–bow comparison is a commonplace of sixteenth-century love-poetry.

XX

Title *Shrub* this may be a quietly humorous extension of the imagery of *The Forest* and *Underwoods*. The critics and scholars who get upset by the tone of this poem should perhaps pay more attention to the riposte of the next piece and also remember that, like many other Renaissance poets, Jonson uses the dual medieval tradition of woman as Eve and woman as Virgin Mary.

17 *Do ... her*] Ask not to know this woman *MS*.

XXI

8 *the lay-stall* a place for dumping rubbish.

XXII

23 *acquit* reward, requite.

29 *offering*] Whalley; offspring *folio*. The folio reading can make sense, but only awkwardly, and the emendation is more in line with the thought-train of the surrounding lines.

XXIII

Jonson's other, more famous, ode to himself is printed as *MP* XXXIII. This one does not seem to spring from a specific incident as does that on the failure of *The New Inn* but to represent a more general irritation with the reception of his plays.

1-2 Ovid, *Amores* I. xv, 1: 'Quid mihi, Livor edax, ignavos obicis annos. /

ingeniique vocas carmen inertis opus?' ('Why, devouring Envy, do you accuse me of wasting my years and call a poem of genius an idler's work?').

3 Horace, *Odes* IV. ix, 29–30: 'paulum sepultae distat inertiae / celata virtus' ('in the tomb there is small difference between worthiness and cowardice').

4 *security* obscurity *MS*.

6 *oft*] *H/S*. I follow *H/S* in adding *oft* from the MSS to keep the metre.

7 *the Aonian springs* according to legend the Aonians were the ancient inhabitants of Boeotia, a country in north-west Greece, and associated – via the legend of Cadmus – with the origin of writing. Jonson's main point here, however, is that Boeotia was Pindar's birthplace.

8 *Thespia* Thespis was a semi-legendary Greek poet from Attica (*c*. 534 BC), specifically connected with tragedy.

9 *Clarius* Apollo.

12 *defaced*] displaced *MS*.

16 *great*] quick *MS*.

19 *fry* small fish.

23 *die*] drink *MS*.

27 *Japhet's line* Iapetus was a Titan and father to Prometheus, who stole fire from heaven for man's use.

aspire H/S gloss 'inspire', which is part of the sense, but the context also requires the sense 'aspire to'.

29 *give*] guide *MS*.

30 *the issue of Jove's brain* Minerva/Pallas (see *The Forest* X, 13–16 and note).

35–6 also used as the last two lines of the 'Apologetic Dialogue' to *Poetaster*.

XXIV

Title *to a Book* the book was Raleigh's *History of the World* (1614) and Jonson's lines describe Raleigh's frontispiece quite closely, so *mind* here probably carries the sense of 'explication'. See *Discoveries* 1124 and *Conversations* 191–3.

3 *or*] *Raleigh (1614)*; and *folio*.

5 *Wise*] *folio*; High *Raleigh (1614)*. The variant is attractive (cf. *Raising* in l. 3), but the folio version makes quite adequate sense.

8] And the reward, and punishment assured *Raleigh (1614)*.

9 *Which makes that (lighted*] This makes, that lighted *Raleigh (1614)*.

12 *mete* measure.

XXV

Title *James, Earl of Desmond* James Fitzgerald was the son of Gerald Fitzjames. The earldom of Desmond, which the father had lost through his rebellious behaviour in Ireland, was restored to the son in 1600. (*H/S* XI, 62 give a fuller account of his rather complicated history. See also G. Morton, *Elizabethan Ireland*, 1971).

3 *Pindar* the great master of the ode in Greek (fifth century BC).

8 *Cynthius* Apollo.

9 *bolder*] flowing *MS*.

12 With prophetic inspiration as from the shrine of Apollo at Delphi.

20 *holds*] *Whalley*; hold *folio*; curbs *MS*. The *Whalley* emendment brings the reading in line with *keeps* (l. 21).

26 *Palm grows straight* a commonplace of contemporary emblem books (*H/S* XI, 62 quote from Alciati's influential *Emblemata*, 1574).

29 *wries*] sways *MS*. *Wries* means 'twists away'.

37 *her dead*] thy white *MS*.

38 Surgeons' Hall was in Monkswell Street near Cripplegate.

39 *statist's* politician's, statesman's.
  read lecture on.
  phlebotomy the letting of blood.

40–42 *Brontes* ... *Steropes* ... *Pyracmon* the three cyclops who make Aeneas' shield in *Aeneid* VIII.

42] An hour will come they must affect their ease *MS*.

44 *the Etnean ire* the anger of the volcanic Mount Etna: Virgil, *Aeneid* VIII associates the cyclops with Etna.

48–50 *He* ... *hit* Seneca, *De Constantia Sapientis* III. iv, 3: 'Involnerabile est non quod feritur, sed quod non laeditur' ('He is undamaged who is not hurt, not he who is not struck').

58 *our fair Phoebe*] dread Cynthia's *MS*. The reference is to Queen Elizabeth.

XXVI

1 The friend has not been identified.

2 *corsives* used here with the sense of 'antiseptics'.

18 *husband* husbandman, conserver.

23 Ausonius, *Epistles* VIII, 7–8.

XXVII

1 *Helen* ... *Homer* Helen, daughter of Zeus and Leda, was married to Menelaus and abducted by Paris to Troy: hence the Trojan War, subject of Homer's *Iliad*.

3–7 Horace, *Odes* IV. ix, 9–12: 'nec siquid olim lusit Anacreon, / delevit aetas; / spirat adhuc amor / vivuntque commissi calores / Aeoliae fidibus puellae' ('and time has not obliterated what once Anacreon sang joyfully. The love of the Aeolian maiden still breathes, and her passion – confided to the lyre – lives').

3 *seven-tongued lute* so in Pindar's fifth Nemean ode, l. 43.

5 *Phao* Phaon was a Sicilian whom, according to legend, Sappho loved but who rejected her. *H/S* follow Whalley in reading *Phaon*, the more common form, but Jonson could easily have followed Lyly's version (in his play *Phao*, *1584*).

6 *Anacreon* see *Underwoods* II. 5, 14 and note. What fragments of his work survive suggest that he wrote mainly light, clear love songs. The *boy* of the preceding line seems to have been called Bathyllus.

8 *Maro* Virgil, in *Eclogues* IV.

9-11 *Lesbia ... Delia ... Cynthia* the mistresses in the erotic elegies of the three Latin poets named.

15 *Lycoris, Gallus' choice* Gallus is reputed to have written four books of elegies to Lycoris.

17-19 Jonson assumes that Corinna is Caesar's daughter Julia. Ovid's banishment from Rome may have had something to do with an association with Julia. The poem relevant to these lines is the *Tristia*.

21 *Laura* the mistress of Petrarch's *Canzoniere*.

23 *His new Cassandra* the *Premier Livre des Amours* by Pierre Ronsard (1524-85) is made up of sonnets called 'Amours de Cassandre'. The old Cassandra is the daughter of Priam who prophesied the fall of Troy.

25 *Stella* the mistress in Sidney's *Astrophel and Stella*.

27-8 *Constable ... Dian* Henry Constable's *Diana* (1592) was one of the sequences of the sonnet boom of the early 1590s.

30 The reference is to Hugh Holland's *Pancharis* (1603).

XXVIII

Title See *Epigrams* CIII and note. Lady Wroth published *Urania* (1621), a volume which includes a number of sonnets.

3 *exscribe* copy out (Latin 'exscribo').

14 *Venus' ceston* the famous girdle of Venus (Jonson may be referring specifically to a group of Lady Wroth's sonnets called 'A Crowne of Sonnets Dedicated to Love').

XXIX

3 *conceit* thought.

17 *Parnassus* the mountain of the muses in central Greece.

19 *Pegasus* the winged horse of the muses.

20 *wells*] well *H/S*. Since Jonson may have in mind Aganippe and not just Hippocrene the emendation to *well* seems unnecessary, despite the singular *fountain* of l. 22.

27 *Worth crowning*] Worth a crowning *H/S*. The emendation is presumably to make a four-syllable line to match l. 30. But there are several three-syllable lines in the poem as well as a number of four-syllable ones and the folio use of the apostrophe at line-endings like *banish'd*, *vanish'd* (ll. 15, 18) suggests contentment with this slight variety.

30 *Pallas* (Athene) goddess of wisdom.

48 *caesure* caesura.

56 *tumour* swelling.

xxx

Title *William, Lord Burl[eigh]* (1521–98); Baron of Burleigh (1571); knight of the Garter and Lord Treasurer (1572).
Rob[ert] . . . Treasurer Robert Cecil became Treasurer in 1608.
8 *field* the *just servants* of the preceding line could gain sustenance from him as a herbivore does from grazing in a field.
17–19 Thomas, William's eldest son, was Earl of Exeter and had thirteen children: Robert had two.

xxxi

Title See *Epigrams* LXXIV and note. Ellesmere's last term as Chancellor was Hilary term, 1617.

xxxiii

2 *a more than civil war* Lucan, *Pharsalia* I. i,: 'Bella plus quam civilia' (Jonson translates literally).
6 *Benn* the folio leaves a blank here – for no obvious reason except, perhaps, modesty on the part of the recipient of the poem – and *Benn* is Whalley's suggestion. Apart from the rhyme the conjecture seems sound for Sir Anthony Benn was a lawyer prominent enough to be satirized (see *H/S* XI, 65) and Recorder of London.
9 *Hook-handed harpies* Sidonius Apollinaris, *Letters* V. vii, 4: 'In exactionibus Harpyiae' ('exactionibus' here = 'debt-collectors', which helps define the force of Jonson's adjective).
   gownèd vultures Apuleius, *The Golden Ass* X, 33: 'vilissima capita, immo forensia pecora, immo vero togati vulturii' ('the basest of people, court-beasts, and lawyers that are only vultures in gowns').
14 'You have made me reconsider my view of lawyers.'
23 *the touch* close examination (with reference to the sense of 'touchstone' as something which reveals truth or guilt).
30 *Armed at all pieces* completely armed (French *armé de toutes pièces*).
31 *stile* playing on the Latin 'stylus', a pointed writing instrument.

xxxiv

7 *Sir Hugh Plat* the author of *Delights for Ladies to Adorn Their Persons* (1602).
10 *Madam Baud-bee* not identified: the name is of the kind found many times in *Epigrams* and may very well be a derisive name for the function rather than a reference to a real person.
11 *Turner's oil of Talc* 'Mistress Turner, the Overbury poisoner, who set the fashion of wearing yellow starch' (*H/S* XI, 66) – as a cosmetic. This fashion is frequently satirized, as for example in the pamphlets *Hic mulier* and *Haec vir* (1620; reprinted by *The Rota*, 1973).

XXXV

This is for Elizabeth, daughter of Sir George Chute. She died in 1627 and Jonson's lines were on the memorial tablet.

2 *pretty*] sweet what *tablet.*
4 *blessed*] one *tablet.*
6 *roll* record.

XXXVII

Title   The friend has not been identified. Lines 19-33 also occur in *MP* CXIV.

XXXVIII-XLI

This group of poems has been the object of a long debate over authorship. The only one of these for which there seems good reason to deny Jonson's authorship is XXXIX where the MS evidence in favour of Donne's authorship is strong. For the other poems there is no MS evidence against Jonson and the internal evidence seems quite inconclusive, particularly since Jonson's achievement is marked by his range of manners. As XXXIX is printed by A. J. Smith in a companion volume in this series (*John Donne: The Complete English Poems* – as *Elegy 15*, p. 116) I shall not print it here, particularly as I accept the ascription to Donne. Since, however, there is a traditional numbering of the poems in *Underwoods* I have not renumbered the poems which follow, despite omitting XXXIX.

XXXVIII

27 *arraigned*   called to account.
    cast   discarded, condemned.
62 *starve*   kill (Old English 'steorfan').
99 *chore*   company (Latin 'chorus').

XXXIX

See note above.

XL

1 *love's a bitter sweet*   Plautus, *Cistellaria* 69: 'Namque ecastor Amor et melle et felle est fecundissimus' ('For indeed love overflows both with honey and bitterness').
29-30 See *Discoveries 1885f.*
48 *not*] *F3*; nor *F1*.

XLII

1 *as Virgil cold* Suetonius, *Vita Virgili*: 'Cetera sane vitae et ore et animo tam probum constat ut Neapoli Parthenias vulgo appellatus sit' ('As for the rest of his life, he was considered so irreproachable both in speech and character that he was widely known in Naples as "the maiden" ').

2 *As Horace fat* Suetonius, *Deperditorum Librorum Reliquiae*, ed. Tuebner (1922), 292: 'Habitu corporis fuit brevis atque obesus' ('The appearance of his body was of shortness and stoutness').

as Anacreon old Lucian, *Octogenarians* (*Longaevi*) 10, 26 refers to Anacreon as living to an advanced age.

16 *purl* ornamental loop of fabric.

17 *matter* material, concern.

19 *But then content*] *F1*; Be then content *Gifford*; But then consent *H/S*.

42 *preoccupy* make use of before others.

43 *Put a coach-mare in tissue* dress a coach-horse in fine thread.

43–4 *horse ... leap* both used sexually.

46 *caparison* rich dress; also horse's trappings (see l. 43).

50 *brave* well-dressed.

63 *Wrung on the withers* the phrase is still current – 'put to shame or discomfort'.

71 *the Spittle sermon* a sermon preached near the site of the old hospital of St Mary Spittle of Bishopsgate Without.

75 *l'envoy* conclusion.

84 *close-stool* a closed box with a chamber-pot inside.

85 *scabbard* dress.

XLIII

In 1623 Jonson's library was destroyed by fire: this poem is his revenge on the god of fire and, in a sense, an attempt to come to terms with his loss.

1 *lame lord of fire* Catullus XXXVI, 7–8: '(vovit) scripta tardipedi deo daturam' ('offers a written votive gift to the limping god').

8 *closed in horn* Plautus, *Amphitryo* 341: 'qui Vulcanum in cornu conclusum geris' ('you who carry Vulcan encased within your horn').

9 *hurled*] cast *MS*.

9–10 see Homer, *Odyssey* VIII, 266–366.

12 *to have Minerva for thy bride* Jonson takes this idea from Hyginus, *Fabulae* CLXVI.

29 *Amadis de Gaul* by Montalvo (1510), translated by Anthony Munday (1618–19).

30 *Esplandians* the son of Amadis and Oriana.

Palmerins Palmerin d'Oliva, a French version of an earlier Spanish romance, was translated by Munday (part one in 1588; part two in 1597); *Palmerin of England* (parts one, two in 1596; part three in 1602) was translated from French versions of the earlier Portuguese originals.

30–31 *all ... Quixote* see Cervantes, *Don Quixote*, book 1, ch. vi.

34] In weaving riddles in more wretched rhyme *three MSS.*

34 *logogriphs* OED defines as 'A kind of enigma, in which a certain word, and other words that can be formed out of all or any of its letters, are to be guessed from synonyms of them introduced into a set of verses'.

palindromes words which can be used backwards.

36 *eteostichs*] acrostics *one MS.* Eteostichs (chronograms) are sentences in which certain letters (usually capitalized) when run together give a date in Roman numerals.

flammes conceits.

39 *telestichs* in these the final letters of the various words spell out a word or name.

jump exactly corresponding (see *H/S* XI, 76).

45 *monies*] masking *three MSS.*

48] Or if thou wouldst enforce the power from her *three MSS.*

50 *more thrift ... variety*] more change, and taste of tyranny *three MSS.*

53] Cloth spices, or guard sweetmeats from the flies *MSS.*

poor pigs] crisp pigs *Benson duodecimo*; crisp pig *Benson quarto.*

56] Not snatched them hence in one poor minute's rage *MS.*

58 *make* sow *Benson edns.*

61-2 *that ... ream*] *MS reads*:
... many a ream
Had filled your large nostrils with the steam.

65 *Talmud* the code of Jewish civil and canon law (mishna, gemara).

Alcoran Koran, the Mohammedan scriptures.

66 *the Legend* the *Legenda Aurea*, a thirteenth-century compilation of saints' lives by Voragine.

69-70 *Turpins ... Rolands ... Oliveers* Archbishop Turpin of Rheims, Roland and his companion Oliver are all major figures in the famous French romance *The Song of Roland.*

69 *the Peers* the twelve Peers of Christendom, of whom Turpin was one. Roland and Oliver were also among this band of Charlemagne's knights.

71 *Merlin's marvels* see, for example, Malory's *Morte d'Arthur*, especially the early books.

his cabal's loss the Rosicrucians linked their doctrines with the mystical lore of the rabbis – the cabbala.

72 *chimera* here 'wild fancy'.

Rosy-Cross according to Percy Simpson (*MLR* XLI (1946), 206-7) Jonson's knowledge of the Rosicrucians is largely drawn from Theophilus Schweighardt's *Speculum sophicum* (1618). He adds that the fraternity produced much writing in Germany and Holland from about 1616. Jonson refers to the group also in *Fortunate Isles* and *News from the New World.*

73 *seals*] charms *Benson edns.*

76 *true coal* beech coal.

77 Nicholas Breton's Pasquil pamphlets were published 1600–1602. 'Meddle with your match' seems to be the name of one of them but has not been traced.

79 *Captain Pamphlet* Apparently the Captain Gainford known to have been wounded in a skirmish in Ireland is the same man who wrote voluminously in a vigorous journalistic manner (see *H/S* II, 173 note).

81 *weekly corrants* the reference is to Nathaniel Butter's weekly 'corantos' or newsletters published from St Paul's churchyard.

82 *the prophet Ball*] Baal *Benson edns*. The reference is clearly to John Ball, a tailor-turned-preacher: exactly the kind of puritan that Jonson despised.

84 *a*] fit *MS*.

85 *excite*] invite *MS*.

89-90 *Venusine . . . Stagerite* a translation of Horace's *Ars Poetica* with material from Aristotle's *Poetics*.

91 *the Grammar*] *folio*; a Grammar *H/S, MS*. Jonson rewrote his *Grammar* and it was first published in the 1640 folio.

95-7 *not afraid . . . our own*] *five MSS read:*

  . . . not amiss

Revealed (if some can judge) of Argenis,

for our own

The *Sicilian maid* is the Argenis of the MSS: James I asked Jonson to translate Buchanan's Latin romance of that name.

97-8 *in story . . . year* a history of eight of the nine years of the reign of Henry V (1413-22).

99-100] *five MSS, with minor differences, read:*

Wherein (besides the noble aids were lent,

By Carew, Cotton, Selden, oil was spent . . .

  Carew Richard Carew (1555-1620), the antiquary.

  Cotton Sir Robert Cotton (1571-1631), antiquary and librarian.

  Selden see *Underwoods* XIV and note.

101 *humanity* observations on the human condition.

103 *the Fathers* the early Church Fathers.

  wiser guides presumably pre-Reformation commentators.

104 *faction*] fashion *MS*.

  drawn] taught *six MSS*.

110] Cause thou canst do these halting tricks in fire? *three MSS*.

111-12 *II/S* (XI, 79) quote from Apollodorus and Hyginus to explain the insult.

113-14 See *Iliad* XVIII, 395-7, where Homer refers to Vulcan having a heavy fall because of his mother's wish to be rid of his lameness.

115 See *Iliad* I, 571-600.

116-17 When Vulcan was thrown out of heaven he is said to have landed on the island of Lemnos, which became the centre of his cult.

118-19 *odd . . . squibs* the reference is to John Squire's *Triumphs of Peace* for the Lord Mayor's Show of 1620.

119 *the pageant*] the next mayor's *three MSS*.

120 *Vulcanale*] Pagan prayer *three MSS*. *Vulcanale* means a hymn to Vulcan.

123 *the Bankside* the Surrey shore of the Thames.

126 *reeds*] weeds *MS*.

132 *the Globe* the theatre was near the Bear Garden and burnt down in 1613 as a result of cannons fired at the climax of a production of Shakespeare's *Henry VIII*.

134 *marish* marsh.

139] There were, that straight did nose it out for news *three MSS*; The brethren they straightway noised out for news *three MSS*.

   Brethren publishers of reports of and ballads about the fire.

142 *the Winchestrian goose* venereal disease (the brothels of Southwark were in the liberties of the Bishop of Winchester).

144 *the*] *H/S*; in *folio*. There is also strong *MSS* support for *the*.

146 *And cried, it was*] And said twas sure *three MSS*.

147 *accursèd*] prophaner *three MSS*.

148 *the nun, Kate Arden*] Venus nun *three MSS*. Kate Arden was a famous whore: the *MSS* reading helps make the point, although the nun/whore double meaning is a famous sixteenth-century one. *Kindled the fire* (l. 149) is presumably a punning reference to venereal disease. See *Epigrams* CXXXIII, 118 where there is a similar link with the bears and the Paris Garden.

153 *Fortune* the Fortune theatre was burnt down in 1621.

156 *Whitehall* the Whitehall banqueting house was burnt in 1618.

157 *his*] high *MS*.

160 In Homer Hephaestus/Vulcan was on the Greek side, while Venus was a Trojan supporter.

168 'You have uttered (*vented*) your wish to destroy but have not really succeeded.'

169 *the Rolls* the office of the Rolls was burnt in 1621. There were six Clerks of the Rolls.

171 *chronicles*] chroniclers *H/S*. The emendation has MS support, but seems unnecessary.

178 *court of Equity* a court concerned with what is equitable, by which defects in common law can be rectified and human justice done.

180] The dyers, glasshouse and the furnaces *three MSS*; The glasshouses and their furnaces *one MS*.

   dye-fats dyers' vats.

182 *that vapour might*] the vapours should *two MSS*.

183-5 *brick kilns . . . about*] *three MSS read:*

   . . . brickhills or a forge

   Some four miles hence and have him there disgorge

   Or else in penny faggots blaze about

187 *bellman's lantern* the public-crier was also a night-watchman.

188 *Burn*] Waste *Benson eds. and two MSS*.

191 *your . . . be*] the fireworks, Vulcan, if they be *three MSS*.

192 *fatal*] chargeful *three MSS*.

193 *Paul's steeple* burnt in 1561.

194 *fireworks . . . Ephesus* the temple of Diana there was burnt down in 356 BC.

195 *Alexandria* the library there was burnt down in AD 640.

196 *unrepaired*] much despaired *three MSS.*

198 *glaives* lances or swords.

199 *Bilbo* Bilbao in Spain was famous for the quality of its swords.

200 *H/S* in a note to *The New Inn* II. 5, 65 quote Coriat on Milan's fame for making sword-hilts.

201 *the friar* Roger Bacon (*c.* 1210–92) was an early advocate of empiricism in scientific experiment, but in the Renaissance is often seen as a black magician (e.g. in Greene's *Friar Bacon and Friar Bungay*). Tradition links his name with the invention of gunpowder.

202] Who with the devil did ordinance beget *three MSS.*

205–6] *MS reads:*

  Blow up and ruin, and enjoy with praise

  Of murthering of mankind many ways

206 *petards* mines.

  granats grenades.

209 *ask*] crave *two MSS.*

212 *places*] fortunes *MS.*

213 *Vulcan . . . Pandora's pox* Zeus, to avenge Prometheus's theft of fire for man's use, made Hephaestus/Vulcan make a woman (Pandora) to ruin mankind with. She had a box which contained all mankind's afflictions – including, Jonson says, the pox.

216 *Bess Braughton*] B.Bs *folio*. The MSS make the reference direct. Bess Braughton was a costly and famous whore who died of venereal disease.

XLIV

Title ˎ *Speech* in the sense of Horace's *Sermones* ('conversational poems').

5 *Gondomar* Spanish ambassador to England: he exercised considerable influence over James I until 1622 and is the Machiavellian Black Knight of Middleton's *A Game at Chess*. Here the link with Aesop makes him a teller of diplomatic fables.

6 *the last tilting* according to Fleay the relevant King's Day tilt was in 1624.

20 *Swinnerton* a captain in the Honourable Artillery Company.

21 The reference is to the training days of the amateur soldiers of whom Jonson is writing: Pimlico was fortified as part of these training manoeuvres.

27 *These ten years' day* after a year's hiatus the Company was revived in 1611. Jonson's phrase means 'ten years before this day of writing' but 1621 seems too early a date for the poem and *H/S* suggest that Jonson is referring to 1616 when the Company's Orders were issued.

28 *posture book* a book about military drill and bearing.

30 *Flushing, or the Brill* these two towns, together with Ramequeens, were handed over to Elizabeth as guarantee of repayment of English expenses incurred in Leicester's Netherlands campaign of 1586–7.

33–4 Sir Hugh Hamersley was colonel of the Company in 1619 and its president from 1619 to 1633. Edward Panton was captain in the Company from 1612 to 1618 but Hamersley was not his successor as colonel.

35 *Aelian Tactics* the reference is to John Bingham's *Tacticks of Aelian ... Englished* (1616). Bingham is, in fact, probably the man replaced by Hamersley as colonel of the Company.

38 *Tilly* Johann Tzerelaes, Count of Tilly (1559-1632), an important general on the Catholic side in the Thirty Years War.

41 *Maurice* Maurice, Prince of Orange.

42 *Spinola* Ambrosia Spinola (1569-1630) attacked Bergen-op-Zoom in 1622 and besieged Breda (1624-5).

51-4 An obvious contrasting of 'new' names with those of old aristocratic families (the traditional heroes of the military past). Jonson's *newer men* appear in contemporary records of the Company.

57-8 Noblemen tended to deride the use of guns in warfare.

70-73 See *Discoveries* 3307-11.

81 *Guy, or Bevis* Guy of Warwick and Bevis of Hampton; both heroes of medieval romances.

99 *tailors' blocks* tailors' dummies.

100-102 'Virtue, which should be most strongly found in those of noble blood, is like a damaged statue, able only to gesture in mutilation to the *empty moulds* which such noblemen have become.'

XLV

Title *Arth[ur] Squib* a teller of the Exchequer.

6 *hearkens to a jack's pulse* 'is a time-servant': a *jack* was an automatic metal figure with a hammer for hitting the bell of a clock at the quarter-hours.

21 *threads* qualities, distinguishing characteristics.

XLVI

Title *Sir Edward Coke* (1552-1634); judge and writer on law; Solicitor-General (1592); Attorney General (1593-4); Chief Justice of the King's Bench (1613). One of the most important figures in the history of law in England.

17 *Solon's self* Solon (c. 640-c. 558 BC) was an Athenian statesman responsible for a famous constitution aiming at justice for all classes.

explat'st unravels.

XLVII

Title *Tribe of Ben* see *Revelations* vii, 8: the Biblical phrase is here applied to Jonson's followers or 'sons'.

13 See *Epigrams* CXVIII.

32 *the Valtelline* a valley in the Grisons which formed a strategically important route for Spanish troops heading for Italy and Germany. It was captured by France in 1624.

33 *States'* Dutch.

35–6 The dispensation for Charles to marry the Spanish Infanta.

44 *Brunsfield, and Mansfield* Brunsfield is unidentified, but Mansfield is Ernest, Count of Mansfeld, who commanded the army of Frederick, Elector Palatine.

48 The reference is to the reception arranged for the Infanta. Inigo Jones was involved in these fruitless arrangements, as l. 50 implies, where *motions* again = 'puppets'.

52–6 *Christmas clay . . . animated porcelain . . . earthen jars . . . mine own frail pitcher* the basic imagery here is a comparison of poetry with pottery – which fits in with Jonson's linking of writing and painting in his translation of Horace's *Ars Poetica*; with his stress on poetry as 'making' (see, for example, *Epigrams* XLV, 10 and note); and with his function, as court masque writer, of uniting poetry and the plastic arts. The first two phrases refer primarily to these mixed-media offerings but both contain an element of deprecation which suggests the disillusionment Jonson felt as Jones's influence grew and his waned. This forces the awareness of how frail his *pitcher* is (how precarious his position as artist has become) and the bitterness of *earthen jars*, which I take to use the biblical sense of 'clay' = 'man' to suggest how, if he loses court support, his position will be threatened by men of inferior stamp.

64 *well-tagged* well fastened.

78 See note to this poem's title.

XLVIII

Title Inigo Jones, in his office as King's Surveyor, supervised the building of this. See *MP* CXIX, 8–9.

4 *new* now *Gifford, H/S*.

18 *Lyaeus* an epithet for Bacchus meaning 'liberator' (of cares).

28 *Hippocrené* the muses' fountain.

44 *Saint George's union* the Garter Knights assembled on St George's Day, 23 April.

54 The reference is to Charles's hope of bringing the Spanish Infanta to England as his bride.

motto Horace, *Satires* II. i, 25: 'The heat has climbed to his head and the lights shine doubly.'

XLIX

Title *the Court Pucell* basically French 'pucelle' means 'maid'/'virgin', but by Jonson's time it also carried the idea of 'slut'/'whore', and this title plays upon the double meaning (as, especially, do the poem's closing lines). The poem is directed at Cecelia Bulstrode who died in 1609. Donne and Edward Herbert wrote elegies for her and Jonson himself writes of her in a very different vein in *MP* XXIV. See *Conversations* 673–5 for the embarrassment this present poem caused him.

7 *tribade* Lesbian.

8 *epicoene* having characteristics of both sexes.

25 *divine* a churchman, priest.

40 *fits o' th' mother* hysteria (with a pun on the idea of inviting lords and sermoneers to father a child on her).

42 *Dorrel's deed* John Dorrel, a puritan preacher and exorcist, was imprisoned in 1599 following a case involving one William Sommers of Nottingham (details in *H/S* X, 251).

44–6 Here Jonson plays on the double-meaning mentioned in the note to the title of this poem. Ironically – both with regard to Bulstrode and to the court – he suggests that any Virgin Mary and any virgin birth would be seen as evidence of sexual laxity.

L

Title Cunningham suggests that the Countess addressed is the Countess of Rutland, but there is no real evidence, except that suggested by ll. 2 and 20f.

2 *a widowed wife* Lady Rutland's husband was, it seems, impotent – but the phrase could refer to other circumstances (estrangement, absence on military or diplomatic business) so it is not really hard evidence about the addressee.

20–24 Rutland was a frequent traveller. The classical allusion is to Penelope's weaving as a way of keeping suitors at bay in the absence of her husband Ulysses.

LI

This poem is for Bacon's sixtieth birthday (1621).

1 *ancient pile* York House, granted to Bacon in 1618.

8 *thy*] my *MS*.

9 Sir Nicholas Bacon was Keeper of the Seal from 1558.

13 *Chancellor* Francis Bacon became Chancellor 7 January 1618.

LII

Title *Sir William Burlase* entered Gray's Inn (1594); Sheriff of Buckinghamshire (1601); knighted (1603); died 1629.

My Answer

6 *tun*] tub *MS*. This huge cask was made by Casimir, Count Palatine, in 1596.

11 *by*] *supplied from MS to fill out the metre.*
   monogram 'a picture drawn with one line only' (*H/S* XI, 89).

12 *you had formed*] you draw *two MSS*; y'have drawn *three MSS*; you had drawn *one MS*.

17 *sprite*] light *MS*. *Sprite* = 'spirit'.

19 *But*] *H/S*; Put *F1*.

LIII

Title *William, Earl of Newcastle* William Cavendish (1592–1676); Earl of Newcastle (1628). See also *Underwoods* LIX and Jonson's Blackfriars, Welbeck and Bolsover 'Entertainments'. Cavendish wrote verse (MSS in University of Nottingham Library), was a famous horseman and wrote a book on the subject.

4 *ancient art of Thrace* the art of raising horses.

7 *Perseus upon Pegasus* strictly, Jonson has got the wrong rider: Bellerophon rode Pegasus. But G. B. Johnston (*RES* VI n.s. (1955), 65–7) has shown that Jonson is following a well-established tradition in medieval and renaissance literature and art in linking Perseus with Pegasus.

8 *Castor ... Cyllarus* see Martial IV. xxv, 6; VIII. xxi, 5–6 and xxviii, 7–8.

10 The *Legend of Sir Bevis de Wardes* was printed in 1500 and editions are recorded as late as 1569.

13–14 *your stable seen | Before* Newcastle's stable was built in 1625.

18 The reference is to Hercules' sixth labour – cleaning the Augean stables.

19–20 *H/S* (XI, 90) refer to a story in the life of Virgil sometimes attributed to Donatus about the poet judging horses and dogs in the royal stables and being paid a bread allowance as reward.

LIV

Title See *Underwoods* XLV and note.

13 *within the socket* like a dying candle.
18 *or*] *folio*; on *H/S*.

LV

Title *John Burges* one of the clerks of the Exchequer.

LVI

Title Lady Covell has not been identified.

6 *fear*] doubt *MS*.
12] Made up still, as the pocket doth abound *MS*.
18 *either ... by*] suitor, or of servant standing by *MS*.
24 *Joan*] Cary *MS*.
25 *this, although*] this time, though *MS*.

LVII

Title See *Underwoods* LV and note.

4 *Sir Robert Pie* he held the title of Treasurer's Remembrancer from 1618 and was knighted in 1621.
6 *debentur* a writing acknowledging a debt.
24 *enable* activate, make able.

26 This means, I think, that if no help is forthcoming the poet will have to go on poor relief.

LVIII

Title *My Bookseller* both Thomas Alchorne and Robert Allot have been suggested.

8 *a cramp ring* the monarch used to bless rings on Good Friday to make them charms against cramp. As is implied here they were at times made of cheap metal.

12 The blank presumably represents some obscenity, although I cannot think of a fitting one.

LIX

Title See *Underwoods* LIII and note. Newcastle wrote *The Truth of the Sorde* on the subject of fencing.

11 *shot . . . force*] with their flames and eke their force *MS*.

LX

Title *Henry L[ord] La-ware* Henry West, thirteenth Baron; born 1603; succeeded to his title 1618; died 1628.

LXI

Gifford suggests that this is for John Williams (1582–1650), Bishop of Lincoln (1621); Lord Keeper (1621–8); Archbishop of York (1642): imprisoned 1637–40.

3 *mercat* market, state of affairs.

LXII

Title The £100 was apparently sent after *The New Inn* had failed in 1629.

4 *King's evil* scrofula. This was supposed to be cured by a monarch's touch.
10 Everyone touched for the *King's evil* received an angel (ten shillings): Jonson's £100 therefore = 200 angels. On this view of the value of a poet see also *Underwoods* LXXI, 14–15.

14 In 1629 Parliament was dissolved because of its deteriorating relationship with the king.

LXIII

Title *their First-Born* this child, Charles, died on its day of birth.

7 *grutch* complain.

LXIV

Title *Anniversary Day* 27 March.

9 *you that reign*] thou that rul'st *MS*.
17 *O times! O manners!* Cicero, *In Catalinam* I. 2: 'O tempora, o mores!'
20 *The . . . gown*] cloak, cassock, robe and gown *MS*.

LXV

Title *the Prince's Birth. 1630* Charles, born 29 May.

2 *hopes . . . earth*] hopes, with thee, of spring and May *five MSS*.
3 Henrietta Maria was the daughter of Henri IV – hence the French emblem of the lily or 'fleur de lis'. The rose is the equivalent English emblem.
7] In changing let our after nephews see *two MSS*.
11 *the great eclipse* Fuller noted this phenomenon in his *History of the Worthies*, as does Bishop Richard Corbet in his poem *To the New-Borne Prince, upon the Apparition of a Starr, and the Following Ecclypse* (*Poems*, ed. Bennett and Trevor-Roper, 1955, p. 84).
12 *Sol will reshine*] And Sol will shine *MS*.
motto Martial I. xxxi: 'He who hurries to please you, Caesar, does not deserve to displease you'.

LXVII

4-5 *H/S* (XI, 93) take this and ll. 7-9 as indicating the Queen's unpopularity.
7 *2 Mel.* Melpomene.
13 *3 Thal.* Thalia.
17 *theorbo* a two-necked lute-type instrument.
18 *dainty*] learned *Benson edns*.
19 *4 Eut.* Euterpe.
25 *5 Terp.* Terpsichore.
26 *Harry!* Henri IV of France.
27 *Lewis!* Louis XIII of France.
31 *6 Erat.* Erato.
36 *Ceston* Venus' girdle.
37 *7 Calli.* Calliope.
38 Competitors tilted at a metal ring suspended from a beam.
43 *8 Ura.* Urania.
46 *the play* Thomas Randolph's *Amyntas*.
49 *9 Poly.* Polyhymnia.
54 *a Caroline* a successor to Charles.

LXVIII

Title *the Household* the king's household.

1-2 The warrant granting Jonson a tierce of sack is dated March 1630.

8 *green-cloth ... blue* the Board of Green Cloth in the royal household was concerned with royal domestic expenses.

14 *tierce* forty-two gallons.

LXIX

Title Fleay suggests that the friend may be Sir Lucius Cary.

9–13 Plutarch, *De Adulatore et Amico* xxiv: 'The man who had painted a miserable picture of some cocks ... the painter told his servant to scare all genuine cocks as far away as possible from the painting.' (Greek text in *H/S* XI. 94.)

LXX

Title *Cary ... Morison* Sir Lucius Cary (?1610–43) was made second Viscount Falkland and was famous for his learning. Henry Morison was knighted in 1627 and died two years later.

The Turn Jonson's *Turn, Counter-Turn, Stand* structure in this poem is his most serious attempt to render in English something of the structural features of Pindar's odes.

1 See Pliny, *Natural History* VII. iii, 39: 'est inter exempla in uterum protinus reversus infans Sagunti quo anno urbs deleta ab Hannibale est' ('there is the case of a child of Saguntum who returned immediately to the womb, in the year in which Hannibal destroyed the city').

3–4 The second Punic War began with Hannibal's capture of Saguntum in 219 BC.

10 *deepest*] secret *MS.*

11 *wiser*] wisest *two MSS.*

15 *hurried*] harried *MS.*

21–2 Seneca, *Epistles* XCIII, 4: 'Actu illam metiamur, non tempore' ('Let us measure acts not by their length but by their quality').

25–30 Seneca, *Epistles* XCIII, 2, 3: 'Longa est vita, si plena est. .... Quid ilium octoginta anni iuvant per inertiam exacti? Non vixit iste, sed in vita moratus est, nec sero mortuus est, sed diu' ('A life is really long if it is full. ... What does the older man gain from his eighty years spent in idleness? A person like him has not lived; he had just loafed his life away. Nor has he died late: he has merely been dying for a long time').

43–52 Seneca, *Epistles* XCIII, 4: 'At ille obiit viridis. Sed officia boni civis, boni amici, boni filii executus est: in nulla parte cessavit. Licet aetas eius inperfecta sit, vita perfecta est' ('Your other friend, however, died in his manhood's prime. But he had accomplished all the duties of a good citizen, a good friend, a good son. In no sense has he failed. His age may have been incomplete, but his life was complete').

50 *measure*] fashion *MS.*

58–9 Seneca, *Epistles* XCIII, 4: 'Octoginta annis vixit. Immo octoginta annis fuit, nisi forte sic vixisse eum dicis, quomodo dicuntur arbores vivere' ('The other has lived eighty years. He has rather existed for eighty, unless, perhaps, by "he has lived" you mean what we mean when we talk of a tree living').

68 *bald*] *MS*; bold *folio*.

73-4 Seneca, *Epistles* XCIII, 7: 'Quemamodum in minore corporis habitu potest homo esse perfectus, sic et in minore temporis modo potest vita esse perfecta' ('Just as a person of small stature can be a perfect figure of a man, so a short life can be a perfect one').

89 *asterism* constellation.

93 *the Discouri* the twins Castor and Pollux.

97-8 Persius, *Satires* V, 45–6: 'non equidem hoc dubites, amborum foedere certo / consentire dies et ab uno sidere duci' ('I would not want you to doubt this, that there is a firm bond uniting our lives, and that both come from one star').

97 *And shine*] Shine then *MS*.

100 *indenture*] indentured *one MS*, *Benson edns*, *H/S*. An indenture is a deed or agreement in law between two or more parties.

126 *lines*] lives *two MSS*.

LXXI

Title *the Lord High Treasurer* Richard, Lord Weston (1577–1635). See *Underwoods* LXXIII, LXXVII. Became Treasurer in 1628 and Earl of Portland in 1632.

5 *wants*] want *folio*. I have adopted G. B. Johnston's suggested emendation (*NQ* (November 1954), 471): this allows for word-play on the senses (a) needs, (b) moles, and makes a good link between l. 4 and ll. 7–8, as well as clarifying and strengthening *concealed*.

7 *false braies* artificial walls in front of the main walls ('faussebraies').

8 *Reducts* redoubts.
    half-moons 'demilunes' – crescent-shaped fortifications.
    horn-works outworks consisting of two half-bastions.

LXXII

7 *glad*] great *MS*.
12] Made loftier by the winds all noises else *Benson edns*, *two MSS*.
13] Squibs, and mirth, with all their shouts *Benson edns*, *two MSS*.
15] If they had leisure, at these lawful routs *Benson edns*, *two MSS*.
17] And then noise forth the burthen of their song, *two MSS*.

LXXIII

Title See *Underwoods* LXXI and note.

9 *thyself*] thy flesh *MS*.
    kind nature.

LXXIV

Title *Hierome, L[ord] Weston* Hierome (Jerome) (1603–63) was son of the Lord Weston of the previous poem; became second Earl of Portland in 1635. He was sent to Paris as ambassador extraordinary in 1630 and was again in Paris in 1632.

26 *travail*] travel *Benson edns*. The dual reading reflects the double sense ('labour', 'travel').

LXXV

Title For Weston see *Underwoods* LXXIV and note. He was married to Lady Stuart in 1632.

1 *hast*] art *MS*.
2 *help*] mend *MS*.
11 *filled*] *F3*; filed *F1*.
 caroches coaches.
17 *bevy*] *MS*; beauty *F1*.
44 *simpless* simpleness of dress.
51 *Porting* carrying.
60 *intertex* interweave (Latin 'intertexto').
67f. This is a fairly common compliment in Renaissance love poetry – the mistress becomes almost nature's creator.
75 *journals* daily travels.
99 *'say-master* the assay master was responsible for testing coin and plate.
112 *barbican* a watch-tower projecting over the gate of a castle.
123 *the holy prelate* Laud, then bishop of Lincoln.
160 *fescennine* obscene (the singing of obscene songs was a feature of Roman weddings and was intended to give the couple protection from the evil eye).
166 *find*] feel *MS*.
170–73 These names are not chosen at random. The first Earl of Portland, Jerome's father, was *Richard*; *Thomas* Weston (1609–88) was the third son of Richard Weston by his second wife; *Francis* is with reference to the bride herself; *Kate* seems to refer to Catharine de Balsac d'Entragues, wife of Esmé, first Duke of Lennox and father of the Esmé mentioned in the title as brother to Lady Frances Stuart; *Frank* refers to Frances, second wife of Richard Weston and mother of Jerome. The only child of the marriage was in fact called Charles!
171 *Francis*] sister *MS*. This MS reading reinforces the likelihood that Jonson is referring to the bride ('Francis' is a common seventeenth-century spelling of the female name).
184 Lucan, *Pharsalia* I, 140: 'trunco, non frondibus, efficit umbram' ('making shade not with leaves but with the trunk').
 now . . . the] then, not boughs, project his *MS*.
187–8 *yet . . . pay*] *MS reads*:
 . . . and the more

He asketh, she will pay

192 See Marlowe, *Hero and Leander*, sestiad II, 69: 'Which taught him all that elder lovers know'.

LXXVI

Written in 1630. See Martial IV. xxvii for a fairly general analogue. The phrase *best . . . men* is repeated in *Underwoods* LXXIX, 7.

3 *That whereas*] Whereas late *M S*.

8] To his poet of a pension *M S*.

8–9 This pension was granted by James I in 1616. *H/S* print the relevant 'patent' in I, 231–2.

9 *large*] full *M S*; *large* has here the sense of 'generous'.

12 *accepted*] thrifty *M S*.

13 *Or*] Well *M S*.

18 *less-*] brave *M S*.

19 *aim*] think *M S*.

25 *marks* a mark was two-thirds one pound. Jonson's petition was granted and *H/S* print the relevant document in I, 245–7.

30 See Aesop's fable of the countryman and the snake (LXXXVI in the Croxall and L'Estrange translation).

LXXVII

See *Underwoods* LXXI and note, LXXIII. Also see Horace, *Odes* IV. viii for a general analogue.

3 *Nuremberg . . . Turkey* Nuremberg was famous for its silver workers. *H/S* (XI, 99) suggest that the Turkey reference is to Byzantine plate.

6 *Romano* Giulio Romano (1492–1546), painter and architect, closely associated with Raphael and with a much greater reputation in the Renaissance than he has now.

Tintaret Tintoretto.

18 *compose*] compass *M S*.

22 *sweets . . . they*] fame and honour you *Benson edns, two M S S*.

26 *glorious*] stately *M S*.

27 *tune*] voice *Benson edns, two M S S*.

LXXVIII

Title *the Lady Digby . . . Sir Kenelm Digby* Venetia Digby was the daughter of Sir Edward Stanley and married Sir Kenelm in 1625. He lived from 1603–65, was a writer, seaman and diplomat, and was responsible for the publication of the 1640 folio. See *Underwoods* LXXXIV.

8 *dwell*] *Benson edns, M S S*; dwelt *folio*. The folio reading is an obvious misprint.

13–14] *Benson edn read*:
   Witness his birthday the eleventh of June,

And his great action done at Scanderoon.

Digby won a sea-fight against French and Venetian ships at Scanderoon, near Aleppo. The discrepancy between the folio and Benson edns as to whose birthday is referred to is odd. The Harleian MS reads *my* and there is a MS in Digby's autograph which says that he was born 11 July, but *H/S* quote from an epitaph by Ferrar which speaks of Digby as born on 11 June.

15 *Barnaby the bright* the feast of St Barnabas is on 11 June. The epithet *bright* echoes Spenser's *Epithalamion* 1265: 'With Barnaby the bright'.

17–18 *Benson edns and MS read*:

That day, which I predestined am to sing,

For Britain's honour; and to Charles my king.

19–31 See Martial VII. xcvii for a fairly general analogue to these lines.

24 (*next ... book*) Digby was interested in Spenser and wrote on him.

LXXIX

Pre-title lines, title See *H/S* for details of Jonson's reworking here of old material and on the allegorical flattery of the king and queen. There is some difficulty in sorting out the allocation of parts in places and I have followed *H/S* in this respect.

2 *theorbo* a type of lute with two necks.

7 *best ... men* see *Underwoods* LXXVI, title.

9 *Janus* this Roman god developed into the god of beginnings, especially of the first hour of the day and the first month of the year (hence January). He also seems to be connected with one of the Latin words for 'door' ('janua') and Jonson appears to play on this idea (see also Ovid, *Fasti* I, 89 and 117).

18 *Mira* Henrietta Maria.

22 *Sylvanus* a Roman woodland god, often associated with Pan.

30 *Pales* an Italian shepherd–goddess.

LXXX

This poem is attributed to Sidney Godolphin in a Harleian MS and *H/S* accept the attribution. I print it partly because neither the MS evidence nor *H/S*' brief comment on style (XI, 102) is decisive; partly because it is a good poem and not well-enough known.

LXXXI

Two MSS and *Reliquiae Wottonianae* (1651) attribute this poem to Sir Henry Wotton and it may well be his. The evidence, however, is inconclusive and it is very difficult with this sort of celebratory poem to use stylistic evidence to any effect.

4 *Phrygian harp* Phrygia was an ancient country in Asia Minor which gives its name to a musical mode or scale.

21 See *Underwoods* LXV, 3 and note.

23 *ideas* in the sense of ideals or Platonic forms.

LXXXII

Title   The future James II was born 4 October 1633 and christened by Laud on 24 November.

8   *seisin*   possession.
15   *triple shade*   the three royal children.
16   *rose, and lily*   see *Underwoods* LXV, 3 and note.
motto   The source of this has not been identified ('safe in my ocean, safer in my shades').

LXXXIII

Title   *Lady Jane Pawlet*   daughter of Thomas, Viscount Savage; married the fifth Marquis of Winchester (1622); died in 1631.

2   *yew*   a common symbol of sadness.
7   *a name*] a lasting name *MS*.
10   *Great Savage of the rock*   Viscount Savage was of Rock Savage in Che-shire.
17   *the poet*] her poet *H/S, Benson edns, one MS*.
21   *Earl Rivers*   Thomas Darcy, whose daughter was the wife of Viscount Savage.
25   *dotes*   natural gifts.
25-7   Virgil, *Georgics* II, 42-4: 'Non ego cuncta meis amplecti versibus opto, / non mihi si linguae centum sint oraque centum / ferrea vox . . .' ('I do not wish to embrace the whole of life in my verse − not even if I had a hundred tongues, a hundred mouths and an iron voice').
27   *carract*   value: the worth or fineness of gold is measured in carats.
45   *institution*   position.
     fact   natural reality.
50   *assure*   make her confident to overcome.
57   *blessed her son*   Charles Paulet: sixth Marquis (1674); Duke of Bolton (1689).
58   *her fair sisters*   Elizabeth and Dorothy Savage.
66   *complement*   union.
69   *circumfusèd*   suffused.
70   *nature's*] natural *one MS*.
71   *discourses*] *Benson edns, Edinburgh MS*; discovereth *folio*; discourseth *Gifford, H/S*. The folio clearly needs emendation. Since *discourses* is a per-fectly proper form of the verb, even if less common at this time than the 'eth' ending, there is little need of Gifford's emendation which *H/S* follow.
72   *hierarchy*   rank of angels.
98-9   *bruiseth . . . head*   see *Genesis* iii 14-15.

LXXXIV

Title   See *Underwoods* LXXVIII. *Eupheme* seems to be Jonson's own coinage and means 'fair fame'.

motto Statius, *Silvarum*, preface: Jonson omits 'est' after *voluptas*: 'It is a pleasure to love her in life; an obligation in death'.

1

14 *crepundia* rattle (Latin).
17 *timbrels* tambourines.
21 *prime coats* short clothes.
26 *cauls* small caps (Old French 'cale').
31 *take tent* take care.
36 *'gree* degree, status.
38 *Jacob's ladder* see *Genesis* xxviii 12.

2

1 *uncontrolled* undisputed.
7 *penates* Roman household gods.
13 *Aldeleigh* according to Camden the Stanleys were descended from one Adam de Aldeleigh.
16 *Meschin's honour* Ranulf, called Le Meschin, was the grandson of Maud, daughter of Hugh d'Avranches, a supporter of William I and Earl of Chester. He was known as 'Lupus' (wolf).
    Cestrian pertaining to Chester.
17 *Lupus* see note to l. 16 above.

3

2 *makes*] *folio*; make *MSS*, *H/S*; mean *three MSS*. The *H/S* emendation seems unnecessary in terms of Elizabethan grammar.
4 *takes*] looks *three MSS*.
10] We fitly interpose for view *one MS*.
15 *her face*] a fire *one MS*; the sun *one MS*.
17 *let*] like *two MSS*.
    beams] light *one MS*.
20 *adore*] admire *one MS*.
21] Then next her neck draw but a spring *one MS*.
22 *youth, or it*] it and youth *one MS*; art and youth *one MS*.
23 *Four rivers* see *Genesis* ii 11–14.
    branching] breaking *one MS*.
24 *confining* bordering on.
25 *the ... globe*] a circle like the globe *one MS*.
26 *And ... be*] And set thereby *one MS*.

4

6 *may no*] must more *two MSS*.
15 *report*] express *one MS*.
18 *brave*] strange *one MS*.

27 *disdaining*] disclaiming *one MS*.
33 *notions*] motions *seven MSS*.
35] And music to the optic ear *one MS*.
36 *planted*] painted *two MSS*.
38 *stroked*] struck *five MSS*.
42 *apply*] ally *two MSS*.
44] Our gladness shows the hour and why *one MS*.
    Earth's] Our *five MSS*.
46 *stuck*] shrunk *two MSS*; sunk *one MS*.
51 *all the*] fleshly *one MS*.
    bounds] bonds *one MS*.
52 *to inhabit*] to inherit *two MSS*.
58 *gently*] greatly *one MS*.
60 *and . . . drops*] or the drops *one MS*.
61 *soft*] calm *one MS*.
64 *odorous . . . gums*] odours, spice, and gums *Benson edn, two MSS*;
odours, spices, gums *two MSS*; spices, odours, gums *nine MSS*.
72 *But*] By *one MS*.
    God] good *one MS*.
prose link *quaternion* a group of four (here, poems).

8

Title Kenelm junior died in 1648 in the battle of St Neots: John succeeded to the family estates; George died young.

1–2 Seneca, *Hercules Furens* 340–41: 'qui genus iactat suum, aliena laudat' ('he who boasts about his ancestry is just praising other people'); Ovid, *Metamorphoses* XIII, 140–41: 'Nam genus et proavos et quae non fecimus ipsi, / vix ea nostra voco' ('For as to race and ancestry and deeds done by others than ourselves, I call such things not our own in any real sense').
8–9 Juvenal, *Satires* VIII, 74–6: 'sed te censeri laude tuorum, / Pontice, noluerim sic ut nihil ipse futurae / laudis agas. miserum est aliorum incumbere famae' ('but, Ponticus, I cannot wish you to be valued because of your glorious ancestry while you do nothing to bring yourself fame in future days. Leaning on the glory of others is a poor thing').
11–12 Juvenal, *Satires* VIII, 19–20: 'tota licet veteres exornent undique cerae / atria, nobilitas sola est atque unica virtus' ('even if you decorate your hall from one end to the other with wax images, Virtue remains the one and only real nobility').

9

motto Statius, *Silvarum* V. i, 16: 'A remedy for such pain comes too late'.

6 *the old nine* the nine muses.
11 *corse* corpse.
18 *cleies* claws.

40 *greet* weep for.
    euthánasee here, easy death.
46–7 See *1 Corinthians* xv 52.
51–5 *schoolmen* a general term for medieval philosophers whose great master was Aristotle. In medieval thought there is a division between body (*corporal*) and soul (*spiritual*). The third *nature* is their union in a living being.
70 *interpell*] interpose *one MS*. *Interpell* means 'break in on' (Latin 'interpello').
90 See *Exodus* iii 14.
96 *victrice* female victor.
101 See *Psalms* xlv 7.
102 *heaven empire*] this folio reading makes sufficient, though rather clumsy, sense and the various emendations used by earlier editors are not strictly necessary.
132 See *1 Corinthians* xiii 12.
153 *creeks* crannies.
156 *formed*] framed *one MS*.
167 *awful* in the root sense of 'causing awe'.
172 *sweet commandèments* the 'e' has been retained here for metrical reasons.
177 *petite* petty, minor.
181 *essays* periods, passages.
187 See *Revelation* viii 3–4.
225 *ecstasy* in the metaphysical sense of 'a going out of her bodily self'.

LXXXV

In the folio Jonson's translation is printed facing the Latin text. Jonson read his version to Drummond (*Conversations* 65–7) which means that the translation must, in some form, be before 1618.

2 *race*] stock *MSS*.
9–10] *MSS read:*
    There, or the tall witch-hazel he doth twine
    With sprouting tendrils
12 *sets*] grafts *MSS*.
21 *Priapus* god of gardens.
    thank] greet *MSS*.
22 *Sylvan* woodland god and guardian of boundaries.
33 *subtle* subtler *MSS*.
41 *blowse* a plump woman.
42 *Apulian's* Apulia was a district in Italy.
50 *golden-eyes* another sea fish.
51 *bright* East *MSS*.
53 *godwit* a bird rather like a curlew.
57 *sorrel* a plant used in salads.

58 *mallows* a herb used medicinally.
    loosing] good for *M S S*.
59 *the feast of bounds* the reference is to the feast of the Roman god
Terminus. In Roman custom 'termini' were boundary stones between
properties.
61 *cates* dishes, dainties.
67 *thoughts*] things *one M S*.
    Alphius the spokesman of Horace's poem.
68 *mere*] *H/S*, *two M S*; more *folio*. The *H/S* emendation seems closer to
Horace's meaning. The Loeb translation has 'on the very point of beginning
the farmer's life'.
69–70 *ides ... calends* days in the Roman year for the settlement of debts.

LXXXVI

Printed in the folio with the Latin text facing the translation.

4   *Cynara* a real or fictitious mistress also mentioned in *Odes* IV. xiii, 21–2.
10 *swans* traditional companions of Venus.
    Paulus Maximus consul (11 BC); friend to Ovid and Augustus.
14 *files* smooths, polishes.
20 *sweetwood* probably a reference to the North African cedar.
24 *Phrygian hautboy* the pipe used in the worship of Cybele.
27 *Salian* the Salii were priests of Mars who danced with his sacred shields
in Rome.
31 *propound* propose.
33 *Ligurine* a probably imaginary boy, to whom *Odes* IV. x is addressed.

LXXXVII

Printed facing the Latin text in the folio.

3   *acceptable*] acceptably *F3*.
8   *Ilia* the mother of Romulus and Remus.
14 *Thurine* of Thuria in south Italy.
23 *Adria* the Adriatic sea.

LXXXVIII

Referred to in *Conversations* 68–70. The Latin is not by Petronius but was
printed as his in the 1585 edition of Linocerius.

LXXXIX

This, like LXXXVIII and the other translations, is printed facing the Latin
text in the folio.

Miscellaneous Poems

See the Preface for remarks on the arrangement of these poems. Where a poem has been taken from a play or masque the source is indicated in the text. I have usually used the Yale edition of the masques for my master-text of masque-songs.

Title *Thomas Palmer* a Roman Catholic scholar from Oxford; sometime fellow and lecturer in rhetoric at St John's College. His *The Sprite of Trees and Herbs* is a book of emblems composed 1598–9.

1 *graffs* grafts.

7–8 Referring to the difficulties Palmer faced because of his religion.

12 *simples* medicinal herbs.

14 See *Exodus* xxviii 17 and xxxix 10.

15 *the seven-fold flower of art* the trivium and quadrivium of scholastic education.

26–7 I know of no explanation of this lacuna.

30 *Palmer, thy travails* Jonson plays on the travails/travels pun together with the meaning *palmer* = pilgrim, traveller. Since Palmer was a scholar 'travails' is the primary meaning here.

motto Horace, *Odes* IV. viii 28: 'It is the muse that forbids that the hero who is worthy of fame shall perish'.

II

Title A prefatory poem for Breton's book *Melancholike Humours* (1600). Breton (1545–1626) was a prolific and versatile minor poet and prose writer.

III

Title The full title makes the provenance of this poem clear: *To Lucy, Countess of Bedford, in a Gift-Copy of* Cynthia's Revels, *1601* ... (H/S (VIII, 662) print the verses among *Inscriptions*.)

2–3 *bright* ... *Lucy* Jonson's usual play on Lucy/'lux' (Latin light, bright).

IV

Title The author is Thomas Wright and the poem was printed with Wright's *The Passions of the Mind* ... (1601). Wright was a Yorkshireman and Jesuit who studied at Rome and Milan; lectured at Louvain and Douai; returned to England as a missionary in 1577 but was imprisoned and banished in 1585. He died in 1624.

5 *scanned* examined.
6 *limiting* specifying.

V

Title Printed with Fletcher's play *The Faithful Shepherdess*: the quarto is not dated but was probably 1608. See *Conversations* 220–21.

4 *pucel* maid.
7 *sixpence* the cheapest admission price to the theatre.
14 *thy murdered poem* the play failed when first produced.

VI

Title *Coriat* Thomas Coriat (1577–1617) was born at Odcombe in Somerset and educated at Westminster and Oxford. He is remembered largely for his walking tour of France, Italy and Germany and for his account of this tour in *Coriat's Crudities* (1611) for which Jonson's acrostic lines are part of the prefatory material. See *Epigrams* CXXIX, *Underwoods* XIII, 128, *MP* VII.

1 *Try and trust Roger* H/S (XI, 133) quote the proverb 'experto crede ruperto' ('trust the experienced Rupert'). *Roger* = a plain, honest man.
10 *born . . . thigh* Bacchus was said to have been born from Jove's thigh, where he had been placed when his mother Semele died.

VII

See note above. These verses were printed with Coriat's sequel to the *Crudities* – *Coriats Crambe* (1611) – although the remarks which precede the lines make it clear that they were meant to accompany the earlier volume.

   Polytopian a coinage from Greek; literally 'many-placed' and hence 'well-travelled'.

4–5 Horace, *Epistles* I. vii, 98: 'metiri se quemque suo modulo ac pede verum est' ('it is proper that each person should assess himself by his own rule and measure').
6 *noddle* head.
19 *Helvetia* Switzerland.
20 *Rhetia* originally a Roman province south-west of the Danube.
22 *Pies* pox, plague.
34 *pediculous* lousy.
37 *Tergum O* 'Oh, my back': Coriat speaks of being egg-pelted by a Venetian whore.
43 *'pistle* epistle, letter.
45–6 *And seven . . . eleven* in his *Epistle to the Reader* Coriat names twelve famous scholars and seems to have met seven of them in his travels.

VIII

A dedicatory poem for John Stephens's *Cinthia's Revenge* (1613).

4 The play was apparently meant to be anonymous.
5 *rove* in archery, 'draws a bow', 'shoots to get the range'.

IX

Title *The Husband* This work was registered in 1614 but the author is unknown.

8 *the Wife* Sir Thomas Overbury's poem *A Wife, now a Widow*.

X

Title *Richard* Christopher Brooke's *The Ghost of Richard the Third* was registered in 1614. Brooke (1570–1628) was a close friend of Donne's and was imprisoned for giving away the bride at Donne's wedding to Anne More. He served in six parliaments and is the addressee of Donne's *The Storm* and *The Calm*.

1 This line refers to the other writers who wrote commendatory verses (Chapman, Browne, Wither, Daborne, Dynne).
3 *broad seals* guarantees.

XI

Title *Browne . . . His Pastorals* William Browne (?1590–?1645) of Tavistock was educated at Oxford and the Inner Temple. He wrote a lot of verse (largely influenced by Spenser). Jonson's lines appeared with Browne's *Britannia's Pastorals. The Second Book* (1616).

XII

Chapman's translation of Hesiod was registered in 1616.

3 Chapman's *Iliad* was published in 1613 and *Odyssey* in 1618.
10 *returns* a mercantile image which refers to the profit on an investment in a voyage.

XIII

Title The *Author* is Matheo Alman, the *Work* is his *The Rogue* (a Spanish romance) and the *Translator* is the Oxford scholar Thomas Mabbes (1572–?1642). The translation was registered in 1621 (Part one) and 1622 (Part two).

5 *Proteus* the archetypal shape-changer (see the *Odyssey* IV, 351ff.).

XIV

These lines are from the Shakespeare first folio of 1618.

1 *This figure* the Droeshout portrait on the title-page of the folio.
5–8 Martial X. xxxii, 5–6: 'Ars utinam mores animumque effingere posset! / pulchrior in terris nulla tabella foret' ('O that art could imitate his mind and personality! There would be no more beautiful painting in the whole world').

XV

This famous poem is again from the first folio.

5 *suffrage* agreement.
7 *seeliest* blindest (basically a term from falconry: the eyelids of young hawks were 'seeled' or sewn together as part of their training).
28 *commit* unite (also with the theological sense of 'inter').
29 *Lyly* John Lyly (?1554-1606) the dramatist of *Endymion, Midas* and other plays.
30 *sporting Kyd* Thomas Kyd (1558-1595), author of *The Spanish Tragedy*. *Sporting* is a pun on Kyd (kid, meaning 'little goat').
35 *Pacuvius, Accius* see Horace, *Epistles* II. i, 56, where they are mentioned in a broadly similar context. Pacuvius (*c.* 220-*c.* 130 BC) was a Roman tragic writer, fragments of whose work survive and who was influenced by the Greek tragic writers. Accius (or Attius) (170-*c.* 86 BC) was a Latin poet and a younger contemporary of Pacuvius. He was a prolific writer of tragedies which have not survived.
   him of Cordova dead Seneca the younger, born in Corduba in Spain, whose tragedies had such influence on the Elizabethan theatre.
36-7 *buskin ... socks* the *buskin* is the English equivalent to the classical 'cothurnus' (the footwear for tragedies); while *socks* is an anglicized version of 'soccus' (the light slipper of the comic actor).
45-6 *Apollo ... Mercury* the former the god of music, the latter associated with good luck and enchantment.
57 *matter* raw material (the relationship between art and nature was widely discussed at this time).
68 *true-filèd* truly polished.
69 *shake a lance* an obvious pun on Shakespeare's name.
78 *influence* as *Shine* in the previous line suggests, Jonson is here using *influence* in the astrological sense of 'benign effect'.

XVI

Title *The Touchstone of Truth* is a 'puritan' collection of scriptural references. The author, James Warre, is not otherwise known. These verses appeared in the second edition of Warre's book (1624) which was initially registered in 1620. H/S (XI, 146) express doubts about Jonson's authorship and it is certainly odd that he should have associated himself with such a compilation.

9 *Word* word of God = the scriptures.

XVII

Title Thomas May (1595-1650) translated Lucan (1627), Virgil's *Georgics* and some Martial. Jonson's verses preface the 1627 edition of the translation of Lucan's *Pharsalia*.

1 *thy mighty pair* Caesar and Pompey.

7 *peized* balanced.

11 *start* swerve.

24 *son of May* Jonson puns here on the myth that Mercury/Hermes (see l. 17) was the son of Maia (May).

XVIII

Prefixed to Drayton's *The Battle of Agincourt* ... (1627). This volume also contained other of the poems referred to in the course of Jonson's poem.

8 *Hanch* haunch.

10 *conferring symbols* comparing tallies. The reference is to the Greek custom whereby parties to a contract broke a token in half, each keeping a piece.

20 *regions seven* the title-page of Drayton's *Poems* of 1619 contained seven headings, as does that for this volume of 1627.

23 *Ideas* *Idea* (1593).

25 *Legends three* *Piers Gaveston* (1593/4), *Matilda* (1594), *Robert Duke of Normandy* (1596). Jonson forgets the fourth 'legend': *Great Cromwell*.

27 *Theocritus* the Greek pastoral poet. Jonson, at ll. 26–7, is comparing the Drayton of *The Shepheards Sirena* with him. Drayton's poem was first published in this 1627 volume.

29 *Heroic Songs* *England's Heroicall Epistles* (1597).

34 *the wise Athenian Owl* Drayton's poem *The Owl* (1604) is linked with Minerva (*the wise Athenian* = the wise owl of Athene/Minerva) because that bird was her emblem.

35 *Orpheus* in classical mythology, charmed birds by his playing.

36 *volary* a large bird-cage.

50 *periegesis* literally *circumduction* (l. 51) = travels around.

61 *Thy catalogue of ships* in *The Battle of Agincourt* 345ff.

68 *Tyrtaeus* a Spartan poet of the mid-seventh century BC. He wrote elegies and also war-songs to encourage the Spartan troops.

79–84 The poems mentioned in these lines are all in the 1627 volume.

86 *Lapland* ... *Cobalus* Lapland was famous for its witches; German 'kobold' = a mine-demon.

87 *Empusa, Lamia* Empusa is a demon in Aristophanes' *The Frogs*; Lamia is a child-eating ogre (see Horace, *Ars Poetica* 340).

89 *thy ends* the elegies at the end of the 1627 volume.

XIX

Title *Sir John Beaumont* (1583–1627), brother of Francis Beaumont. His poems (*Bosworth Field: with a Taste of the Variety of other Poems*) were published in 1629; Jonson's poem is among the elegies printed with this posthumous volume.

1 Martial, VI. xli, 10: 'victurus genium debet habere liber' ('to live a book must possess genius').

4 *ravelins* outworks in front of the curtain wall.

9 *muniments* fortifications.
22 *ethnicism* paganism.

XX

Title *Edward Filmer* son of Sir Robert Filmer; died 1669. The work to which Jonson's poem is attached is *French Court-Aires, With their Ditties Englished* ... (1629). The songs are from the French of Guedron and Boesset.

12 *The fair French daughter* Henrietta Maria.

XXI

Title *M[r] Rich[ard] Brome* Jonson's lines preface Brome's play *The Northern Lass* (1632). Brome (died ?1652) is best remembered for *The Antipodes* (1646) and *A Jovial Crew* (1652). He was at one time apparently Jonson's manservant and, despite the suggestion of some breach around the time of the failure of *The New Inn* in 1629 (see *MP* XXXIII, 27), was perhaps Jonson's most faithful follower in the English comic tradition.

12-16 Horace, *Epistles* II. i, 114-17: 'navem agere ignarus navi timet, habrotonum aegro / non audet nisi qui didicit dare; quod medicorum est / promittunt medici; tractant fabrilia fabri: / scribimus indocti doctique poemata passim' ('a man who knows nothing of a ship is afraid to handle one; nobody dares give southernwood to the sick unless he has learnt its proper use; doctors take on the work of doctors; carpenters use carpenters' tools – but, skilled and unskilled alike, everyone scrawls verses').

15 *Bilbo-smith* a sword-maker of Bilboa.
17 *nall* awl.
18 Persius, *Satires* V, 102: 'navem si poscat sibi peronatus arator' ('if a hobnailed yokel were to seek command of a ship').

XXII

Title From *Meditation of Man's Mortality* ... *By Mrs Alice Sutcliffe wife of John Sutcliffe Esquire, Groom of his Majesty's most honourable Privy Chamber* ... (1634; first edn 1633). Little more is known of the authoress than is given in the title.

12 *Celia* St Cecelia.

XXIII

Jonson's lines are from *The Shepherd's Holiday* (1635), the first play of Joseph Rutter, who also wrote *The Cid* (1637). F. L. Townsend (*MP* LIV (1946-7), 238) has an interesting article on the relationship between Jonson's poem and Rutter's play.

25 *the pix* a box for specimen coins at the Royal Mint. The 'trial of the pix' was the testing of such coins.
30 *carract* carat, which is one twenty-fourth of pure ('fine') gold.

XXIV

This epitaph on Cecilia Boulstrode is in stark contrast to the fierce attack on her in *Underwoods* XLIX. The contrast cannot be explained by any external evidence I know of, but one remembers Drummond's comment that Jonson was 'passionately kind and angry' (*Conversations* 689-91). Cecilia died in August 1609.

H/S (VIII, 372) print the letter to George Garrard with which the epitaph is enclosed. In it Jonson says 'For till your letter came, I was not so much as acquainted with the sad argument, which both struck me and keeps me a heavy man. Would God I had seen her before that some that live might have corrected some prejudices they have had injuriously of me.' This is interesting in that although it does not explain the gap between satire and epitaph it suggests that the embarrassment which the satire – *Underwoods* XLIX – caused him was something he much regretted, for whatever reasons. See *Conversations* 673.

6 There were three Graces, the daughters of Zeus.

7 *Pallas* came to be regarded as patroness of arts and crafts, and hence as the goddess of wisdom. I do not know of a specific connection of her with language but her other roles imply one.

Cynthia Cynthia/Diana, goddess of chastity.

8-9 *harmony/Of spheres* the harmony made by the spheres as they moved in perfect order and cohesion was a symbol of the working of the universe.

10 *sole*] best *MS*.

votary a person dedicated to the worship of a religion or way of life.

12 *'Sell* Cecilia.

14 *Fable of Good Women* Chaucer's *Legend of Good Women*.

XXV

Title *a Tilting ... S[ir] Robert and S[ir] Henry Rich* the tilting took place in March 1613. Robert Rich was the first son of Robert, Lord Rich (Earl of Warwick, 1618) by Penelope Devereux. He was knighted in 1603 and became second Earl in 1619. Henry Rich (1590-1649) was the second son, was knighted in 1610, made Baron Kensington in 1623 and first Earl of Holland in 1624.

12 *prospective*] perspective *Gifford*. *Prospective* is an authentic variant (so Baxter, *Saints' Rest* iv, 8: 'This is the prospective glass of the Christian, by which he can see from earth to heaven').

XXVI

Written for Somerset's wedding in December 1613.

12 *that Wife ... thy friend* Thomas Overbury's poem mentioned in *MP* IX, 8 and note; see also *Epigrams* CXIII and note and *Conversations*, 206-10.

23-4 Martial IV. xiii. 9-10: 'diligat illa senem quondam, sed et ipsa marito / tum quoque, cum fuerit, non videatur annus' ('may the wife love her husband even when he turns grey; and she, when she herself is old, not seem so to her husband)'.

XXVII

Title *Charles Cavendi.h* Cavendish is buried at Bolsover Castle and Jonson's lines are carved on the monument. The Bolsover inscription also includes a prose eulogy of Cavendish. It is printed in *H/S* VIII, 387-8.

10 *nephews* in the sense of descendants (Latin 'nepotes')·

XXVIII

Title *Lady Jane* married the eighth Earl of Shrewsbury in 1618 and died in 1625.

1 *'Here lies'* English for the Latin 'hic jacet', both being commonplace formulas for opening epitaphs (Jonson himself uses the formula – see *Epigrams* XXII).
7 *table . . . church*   *table* = memorial tablet. Jane was buried in St Edmund's Chapel, Westminster Abbey, but Jonson's lines do not appear on the monument.

XXIX

Title *Katherine, Lady Ogle* daughter of Cuthbert, Lord Ogle; made Baroness Ogle in 1628; died in 1629 and is buried at Bolsover.
motto 'Jove looks at the records in the fulness of time'.

8 *digests, pandects* the code of Roman common law.
sub-heading *Diphthera Jovis* 'the record of Jove'.

XXX

Title *Robert Dover* (?1575-1652); the founder of the Cotswold Games, held near Chipping Camden. *Instauration* means 'instituting, establishing'. Jonson's poem is from *Annalia Dubrensia* (1636) and is one of the thirty-three items which make up this anthology.

1 *drop her vies*] I follow other editors in accepting the insertion of *her* to preserve the metre. The phrase means 'to distinguish between' and is basically a card term – 'to bet on tricks'.
2 Jonson's linking of the Cotswold Games with the Olympics is suggested by the reference in the full title of *Annalia* to *Mr Robert Dover's Olympic Games*.
9 *hypocrites* probably an anti-puritan gibe.

XXXI

This, like *The Forest* X, XI and *MP* CXII, is from Chester's *Love's Martyr* (1601).

1 *Splendour! O*] Beauty *MS.*
3 *illustrate*] admired *MS. Illustrate* means 'illustrious'.

XXXII

From Hugh Holland's *Pancharis* (1603). See *Underwoods* XXVII, 30 and note. Holland may also be the author of the Welsh play *Troelus a Chresyd* (*c.* 1600–1610).

2 *black swan* something very rare. See Gosson, *The School of Abuse* ed. Arber (1906), 30: 'the abuse of (theatres) was so great, that for any chaste liver to haunt them was a black swan . . .' (cf. the pamphlet *London's Liberties, The Rota*, 1973.)
8 *Tamesis* the Thames.
17 *the hoof-cleft spring* Hippocrene, the spring of Helicon, was made by a blow from a hoof of Pegasus.
18 *Thespiads* the muses.
19 *Dircaean fount* the spring of Dirce at Thebes, Pindar's birthplace.
21 *pale Pyrene* a sacred spring at Corinth.
     the forkéd mount Persius, *Satires* prologue 2: 'nec in bicipti somniasse Parnaso memini' ('nor, so far as I can remember, did I dream on the double topped Parnassus').
24 See Ovid, *Fasti* V, 183ff.
38 *Mone* Anglesey.
39 *Cluid* Clwyd in Denbighshire – of which Holland was a native.
42 *Iërna main* the Irish sea
43 *Eugenian* anglicized name of the Eoghanachts of Munster (see *H/S* XI, 127).
45 *pale* limits (the Pale in Ireland in the sixteenth century was that part of eastern Ireland – the territories of Louth, Meath and Kildare – which was most firmly under English control).
50 (*Charles Montjoy*) Charles Brooke Blount, eighth Lord Mountjoy, born in 1563, was an experienced military figure by the time he succeeded Essex as Lord Deputy in Ireland. He had served under the famous soldier Sir John Norris and commanded a ship against the Armada. He took over Essex's campaign against the 'rebel' Tyrone and defeated him at the siege of Kinsale.
53 *kern* light Irish foot-soldier – the term is often used contemptuously, as here.
57 Pausanius connects the Baphyrus with Helicon, the river of the muses: hence Jonson means 'anyone who has tried to write poetry'.
61 *entheate* inspired.
     publish . . . tracts make known their illustrious career.
66 *Hebrid Isles* the Hebrides.
67 *Orcades* the Orkney and Shetland Isles, apparently discovered by the third-century Greek navigator Pytheas and visited by Agricola's fleet in the first century AD.

69 *utmost Thule* the 'ultima Thule' of early maps: a northern land first described by Pytheas (possibly Norway or Iceland) which came to be regarded as the northernmost part of the inhabited world.

70 *Caledon* Caledonia (Scotland).

71 *Grampius' mountain* the Grampians divide the Scottish lowlands and highlands.

72 *Lomond Lake* Loch Lomond.

Tweed's . . . fountain Twede's Well in Peeblesshire.

82–4 H/S (XI, 128) suggest that the reference is to Biron's visit of 1601 or to that of the Duc de Nevers in 1602.

98 Hugh Holland.

99 *Cycnus* was changed into a swan: in Ovid he is variously said to be the son of Sthenelus, Apollo, Neptune but the swan-change is consistent (see *Metamorphoses* II, 367ff.; VII, 371; XII, 72).

104 *Leda's white adulterer* Jupiter, who – in the shape of a swan – raped her.

109 *Eridanus* (a) a river identified with the Po; (b) the river of Elysium; (c) a constellation.

117 *Arar* the river Saone in France.

XXXIII

This poem was provoked by the failure of Jonson's play *The New Inn* in 1629.

11–12 See Ascham : 'as a man that would feed upon acorns, when he may eat as good cheap the finest wheat bread' (*The Schoolmaster*, Book II, *Works* III, ed. Giles (1864–5), 223) and Dryden, *Selected Criticism*, ed. Kinsley and Parfitt (1970), 145 and note.

13 *fury* madness.

18 *draff* lees, dregs.

21–2 *mouldy . . . Pericles* this is usually taken as a reference to Shakespeare's *Pericles*, which was acted 1607–8, but – so Jonson implies – still popular some twenty years later. Jonson's remark is derogatory but the sneer is primarily at audiences rather than at the play (although *Pericles* would hardly have appealed to Jonson's views of drama anyway).

23 *the shrieve's crust* the reference is to gaol food; *shrieve* means 'sheriff'.

27 *Broome's sweepings* for Jonson's relationship with Brome see *MP* XXI and note.

33 *orts* scraps.

42 *the Alcaic lute* Alcaeus was a lyric poet of the sixth or seventh century BC, born in Lesbos and a contemporary of Sappho. His name is associated with the Alcaic stanza, a lyric form adopted and adapted by Horace.

XXXIV

14 *country*] courtly *MS*.

22 *tunes*] times *MS*.

38 *crystal shield* an attribute of Athene/Minerva.

41 *The rebel giants* the giants who warred against Zeus.

Gorgon envy Medusa, one of the Gorgons, was killed by Perseus; her head is often depicted on Athene's shield.

XXXV–XXXVIII

Songs from *Cynthia's Revels* (1600–1601).

XXXV

Sung by Echo in I. 2. It was set to music by Henry Youll in his *Canzonets to Three Voices* (1608) and is discussed by Catherine Ing, *Elizabethan Lyrics* (1968), 119.

XXXVI

Sung by Hedon in IV. 3 and set to music by Henry Lawes. The standard book on the relation between Jonson's songs and their settings is still Willa McClung Evans's *Ben Jonson and Elizabethan Music* (1929).

XXXVII

This is recited by Amorphus in IV. 3, who introduces it by saying 'I composed this ode, and set it to my most affected instrument, the lyra'.

9 *his mother's doves* doves are traditionally Venus' birds.

XXXVIII

Hesperus sings this to Diana, goddess of moon, hunting and chastity, in V. 6.

XXXIX–XLIII

Songs from *The Poetaster* (1600–1601).

XXXIX

The first part of this is sung by Crispinus, the second by Hermogenes: a short piece of prose dialogue separates the parts. The song was set to music by Henry Lawes and comes from II. 2.

XL

Horace 'composes' this short piece in III. 1.

2 *Lyaeus* an epithet for Dionysus.

XLI

Played and sung by Crispinus in IV. 3.

9 *Cypris* Cyprus; the island was closely connected with the cult of Venus Aphrodite and is used here as a synonym for the goddess.

XLIII

The first and second parts of this are separated by a short prose speech by Ovid (IV. 4).

XLIV–XLVI

From *Volpone* (1606). See also *The Forest* V, VI.

XLIV

Sung by Nano and Castrone (I. 2).

10 *free from slaughter* without fear of reprisals.
13 *trencher* wooden plate.

XLV

Sung by Nano (as Zan Fritada) in II. 2.

1 *Hippocrates* Greek physician (born *c.* 460 BC); mentioned by Plato in *Protagoras*; gave his name to the Hippocratic oath.
   Galen (AD *c.* 129–199), born at Pergamum but lived for many years in Rome. One of the most influential of ancient doctors and a voluminous writer, six of whose works are translated by Thomas Linacre, who was one of Henry VIII's physicians.
8 *sassafras* a medicine from the bark and root of the sassafras tree.
9 *guacum* a medicine from the resin of the West Indian tree guaiacan.
10 *Lully ... elixir* Raymond Lully (1235–1315), Spanish scholar and astrologer, was traditionally regarded as an alchemist and as the discoverer of the elixir of eternal life.
11 *Danish gonswort* not certainly identified, but referring perhaps to Berthold Schwarz (Konstantin Anklitzen) of Fribourg, the inventor of guns.
12 *Paracelsus* see *Epigrams* CXXXIII, 76 and note. He carried about with him a sword with a hollow pommel to hold his drugs.

XLVI

Sung again by Nano (II. 2).

2 *coil* fuss.
5 *Tart* keen (of taste).
7 *Moist of hand* commonly an indication of a sensual disposition.
12 *for the nones* here 'to serve the purpose'.

XLVII–XLVIII

From *Epicoene* (1609).

XLVII

Sung by a boy in I. 1. Set by William Lawes for a revival of 1665 (Hunter attributes the music to Henry Lawes, without giving reasons).

5   *causes*] secrets *M S.*
6   *sweet*] well *M S.*
7   *look*] form *M S.*
9   *flowing*] hanging *M S.*
10   *taketh*] please *M S.*
11   *adulteries*   adulterations.

XLVIII

Read by John Daw in II. 3, who refers to it as his own work and 'a madrigal of modesty'. The reading is interspersed by comments and discussion involving Dauphine, Clerimont and Daw himself, so that although Daw begins his reading at l. 22 he does not make the ending until l. 117.

XLIX

Sung by Nightingale, 'A Ballad-singer', in III. 5 of *Bartholomew Fair*, to the tune of 'Peggington's Pound' (III. 5. 56). Here again the singing of the ballad is interspersed with prose comment, mainly from Cokes. The song is given a setting in D'Urfey's *Wit and Mirth* (1700) and in *Songs Compleat*, by Bow, Purcell, *et al.* (1719). The irony of the situation while the ballad is being sung adds considerably to its effect.

18   *Westminster Hall*   where courts of Common Law and Chancery sat.
23-9   It is not known to what incident this refers.
40   One John Selman was executed in 1612 for doing this.

L

Sung by Lovel in IV. 4 of *The New Inn.*

LI

From *The Sad Shepherd* I. 5. Sung by Karolin; set by Nicholas Lanier (*Select Musical Ayres and Dialogues . . .*, 1652).

LII-LIV

From *The Masque of Blackness*: 'Personated at the court at Whitehall on the Twelfth-night, 1605'.

LII

Sung by a tenor and two trebles.

4   'All rivers are said to be the sons of the Ocean, for, as the ancients thought, out of the vapors exhaled by the heat of the sun, rivers and fountains were

begotten' (part of Jonson's own note: he goes on to cite *Orphica* LXXXIII and *Iliad* XIV).

11 *feature* form.

LIII

'A song of two trebles, whose cadences were iterated by a double echo.'

LIV

1 *Dian* the moon (the goddess Diana became thought of as a moon-goddess through her association with Artemis).

LV–LIX

From *The Masque of Beauty*: 'which was presented . . . at Whitehall, on the Sunday night after the Twelfth-night, 1608'.

LV

'The musicians . . . came forth . . . singing this full song, iterated in the closes by two echoes.'

1 *Love* Hesiod says that Eros was the first thing to emerge from chaos.
9–10 'An agreeing opinion both with the divines and philosophers, that the great artificer, in love with his own *Idea*, did therefore frame the world' (Jonson's note).

LVI

Set by Alphonso Ferrabosco (see *Epigrams* CXXX, CXXXI) and printed in *Ayres* . . . (1609). 'Sung by a loud tenor.'

2 'As in the creation he is said by the ancients to have done' (Jonson's note).

LVII

Set by Ferrabosco. See note to previous song. The first verse was sung 'by a treble voice', the second 'by another treble', the third by a tenor.

1–2 As he explains in his note Jonson is drawing a distinction between love as 'blind with desire or wanton' and 'chaste Loves that attend a more divine beauty': the distinction is common enough (see, for example, Henry Reynolds, *Mythomystes* (1632), 15f).
8 *polity* policy.
9 *Albe* although.

LVIII

Again set by Ferrabosco. See previous note. Sung 'by the first tenor'.

2 The question of whether or not women had souls is discussed quite often at this time – not always wholly seriously (see *H/S* X, 464 and Erasmus, *Praise of Folly*, Penguin trans., p. 887).

6 'The platonics' opinion. See also Macrobius, *In Somnium Scipionis* I and II' (Jonson's note).

LIX

'The scene closed with this full song.'

LX–LXV

From the *Masque of Hymen* (1606), written for the marriage of the Earl of Essex and Lady Frances Howard – unfortunately the marriage ended in scandal and divorce. The songs were set by Ferrabosco.

LX

'The musicians ... with this song began.'

LXI

'This song was sung at the altar.'

3 *genial* pertaining to marriage (Latin 'genialis').
7 *coyings* caressings.
11 *Hesperus* the evening star.

LXIII

'This song importuned them to a fit remembrance of the time.'

8 *make* mate.

LXV

In his linking passage Jonson says that only one 'staff' (verse) was actually sung at the performance.

4 *stay* delay.
6 *turtles* turtle doves.
10 *prove* experience.
12 *pressèd* Jonson plays here on a double-meaning, based on the traditional analogy between love and war. So *pressed* means (a) embraced (b) forced into military service.
19 *rap* seize.
31–2 Earlier in the masque Jonson had referred to the 'Idalian star': part of his note to that reference (l. 319, Yale edn) explains the comparison here: 'Stella Veneris ... when it goes before the sun is called Phosphorus, or Lucifer; when it follows, Hesperus, or Noctifer ...'.
38–40 In his note Jonson speaks of this as another classical wedding rite, which he regards as designed to bring good luck to the bride.
46 *mead* meadow.

53–5 '"By each of which deeds the other's early death is thought to be desired". Festus, ibid' (Jonson's note).

84 *Cypris* Venus (see *MP* XLI, 9 and note).

93 *Genius* 'The god of nature, or of begetting. . . . Hence the "genial" bed, which is made at weddings in honour of the Genius' (Jonson's note). The idea is a feature of Roman religion.

99–100 The rhyming of *womb* and *tomb* is frequent in Jonson. For its use as a common topos in Renaissance poetry see Parfitt, 'Renaissance Wombs, Renaissance Tombs', *RMS* XV (1971).

102 *Cynthia* Artemis/Diana, goddess of childbirth.

LXVI

From *The Haddington Masque* 'at court, on the Shrove Tuesday at night, 1608'. The marriage was between John Ramsey, Viscount Haddington (*c.* 1580–1626) and Elizabeth Radcliffe, daughter of the Earl of Sussex. She died in 1616. Ferrabosco set ll. 45–54.

26 *kind* nature.

70 See note at head of poem.

LXVII–LXIX

From *The Masque of Queens*. 'At Whitehall, February 2, 1609'. LXVII is the third of the nine 'charms' in the masque.

LXVII

2 *cat-a-mountain* wildcat.

14 *little Martin* the *little Martin* of the witches 'is he that calls them to their conventicles, which is done in a human voice; but coming forth, they find him in the shape of a great buck-goat, upon whom they ride to their meetings' (part of Jonson's note: he goes on to quote from Del Rio and Bodin who also refer to 'Master Martinet, or Martinel').

LXIX

'This last song, whose notes, as the former, were the work and honour of my excellent friend Alphonso Ferrabosco': it is not clear whether 'former' refers only to the immediately preceding song (not printed here) or also to LXVIII, although it seems likely that it does.

LXX–LXXVII

From *Oberon the Fairy Prince. A Masque of Prince Henry's* (1611).

LXX

A 'catch' sung by satyrs. It was set to music by Edmund Nelham (*Catch that catch can . . .*, 1667).

7–8 *He . . . he*   these two 'he's refer to two 'sylvans' in the masque.

LXXI

3 *the boy*   This is Endymion, son of Calyce and Aethlios, or – in another version – a shepherd on Mount Latmos. He was the most beautiful of men and was loved by Selene (the moon in Greek mythology).

4 .Juno presided over childbirth and is also sometimes associated with the moon. Jonson goes on in this song to play upon the idea of the moon being pregnant and yet wishing to hide the fact.

LXXII

1–2   The four elements are named in ascending order of refinement.

3 *Arthur's chair*   the traditional throne of British monarchs.

LXXIII

'A full song . . . by all the voices.'

LXXIV

2 *stay*   stop, cease.

7 *plants*   feet.

LXXV

5 *these beauties*   the ladies watching the masque.

7 *call them forth*   to dance in the closing revels of the masque.

LXXVI

Sung by one of the sylvans, addressing the male gentleman masquers.

2 *measure*   moderation.

5–8   A graceful compliment to the ladies and their dancing.

LXXVIII–LXXX

From *Love freed from Ignorance and Folly* (1611).

LXXVIII

'Here is understood the power of wisdom in the muses' ministers, by which names all that have the spirit of prophecy are styled, and such they are that need to encounter ignorance and folly, and are ever ready to assist love in any action of honour and virtue, and inspire him with their own soul' (Jonson's note).

5 *Sphinx* in the masque the sphinx is seen as the mother of folly and ignorance.

LXXIX

This is the song of the Graces 'crowning Cupid'.

LXXX

3 *his crime* Time's crime is described in ll. 7–8.

LXXXI–LXXXIV

From *Love Restored* (1612).

LXXXIII

6, 8 *greater powers ... brighter planets* the watching ladies who will *mix/ Their motions* (join in the dancing) with the gentleman masquers in the closing revels.

LXXXV–LXXXVI

From *The Irish Masque at Court* (performed December 1613 and January 1614).

LXXXV

'Here the bard sings to two harps.'

7 *slough* outer skin.

LXXXVI

'After the dance the bard sings this.'

3 *source of price* springs of value, beauty.

LXXXVII–LXXXVIII

From *Mercury Vindicated* (performed twice in January 1616).

LXXXVII

'A cyclop, tending the fire, to the cornets began to sing.'

3–4 The cyclop expresses the view that nature is progressively decaying and in doing so touches on one of the great seventeenth-century controversies (see V. Harris, *All Coherence Gone*, 1949). An alternative view is expressed by Nature in the next song (see also *Discoveries* 154–9, 370f.).

LXXXVIII

9 *prove ... the numbers* try the dances (*numbers* refers, strictly, to musical units)

10 *absolve* make perfect.

13 *stealing fire* there is a cross-reference here to Prometheus (a character in this masque) who stole fire from heaven.

15 *orbs ... seven* the seven basic spheres of Ptolemaic astronomy, each one of which contained one of the seven mobile heavenly bodies.

19 *gain* permit.

LXXXIX, XC

From *Christmas His Masque* (1616).

LXXXIX

Sung by the figure of Christmas.

1 *cony* rabbit, but also dupe and whore.

3 *stake* the pole for dancing around.

6 *roll* bustle.

farthingale hooped skirt.

15 *Tom of Bosom's Inn* a London tavern where carriers stayed.

22 *kill-pot* a solid drinker.

24 *Fill-pot* an appropriate place for a hard drinker to live.

29 *trace* line.

31 Refers to the story of Hercules being made to spin with Omphale's distaff, during a year in which he acted as a female domestic to her as ordered by Apollo.

36 *card-makers* with a pun on mapmakers.

Pur Alley not a street, but a pun on 'puralé', meaning 'a survey'.

38 *MacPippin* a reference to the fact that many London costermongers were Irish.

47 *ell* one and a quarter yards in cloth-measuring.

XC

Again sung by Christmas.

1–2 Christmas speaks of himself at the beginning of the masque as 'Christmas of London, and Captain Christmas', and his sons and daughters (the subjects of LXXXIX and whose costumes are described in the prose notes before that song in the text of the masque) are London citizens. Here, then, Christmas speaks up for the ordinary London citizen (see *Underwoods* XLIV).

7 *tires* clothing.

to ... fires shoot blanks.

19 *spare ... belly* they will give up food to save money for their Christmas performance.

XCI

From *The Vision of Delight* 'presented at court in Christmas, 1617'.

6 *blood ... phlegm* two of the humours of the body: blood was held to produce a hot and lively temperament ('sanguine') where it predominated, while phlegm produced one that was moist and dull ('phlegmatic').

XCII–XCV

From *Pleasure Reconciled to Virtue* 'presented at court before King James. 1618'.

XCII

This 'Hymn' opens the masque.

5 *the hopper* the funnel in a mill into which the grain is poured.
6 *hutch* bin.
  boulter sifter.
7 *bavin* bundle of stove or oven wood.
  mawkin baker's mop.
  peel baker's shovel.
8 *dog ... wheel* dogs were used to turn spits in kitchen ranges.
10 *gimlet and vice* which make up the tap of a cask.
11 *Hippocras bag* a cloth-filter used in straining wine.
12 *cries swag* shows his drooping belly.
13–16 The gist of this is that although the belly grows fatter it will do nothing to restrict itself or to help the back to support its weight.
19 *sod* boiled.
22 Playing on the double-meanings of *pudding*, meaning 'dessert' and 'rope tied around a ship's mast'; and of *laced*, meaning 'have added to' and 'tied in'.

XCIII

Sung by Daedalus: in legend he was an Athenian craftsman of outstanding skill.

2 *curious* complex.
7–8 According to a story in Xenophon, *Memorabilia* II. i, 21–34 Hercules, when young, came to a crossroads where he met the goddesses of pleasure and virtue, each of whom urged him to follow her path (he chose that of virtue).
12 'Yet not lead to confusion.'
13 *numerous* made up of rhythmical movements.

XCIV

Again sung by Daedalus.

1 *prove* test, try out.
12 *go less* be of less value.

XCV

Sung by 'two trebles, two tenors, a bass and the whole chorus.'

XCVI, XCVII

From *News from the New World* 'as it was presented at court before King James, 1620'.

XCVII

10 *measure* (a) standard, moderate position; (b) a slow dance.

XCVIII–CI

From *The Gypsies Metamorphosed*, which was performed twice in August and once in September 1621.

XCVIII

Sung by the Jackman (an educated beggar). Nicholas Lanier composed the music for this masque: this song is also set by Robert Johnson (John Playford, *The Musical Companion*, 1673).

2 *the Devil's Arse* a cave in Castleton, Derbyshire, now politely called Peak Cavern.
4 *Egyptians* gypsies.
11 *Ribands* ribbons.
16 'Will not make the ladies faint' (which would mean that the laces of their bodices would be cut to allow the blood to flow more freely). For the performance at Windsor this line was replaced by 'And not cause you quit your places'.
23 *Burleigh* this is where the first performance took place (the second was at Belvoir and the third at Windsor).
24 *hurly* disturbance, affray.

XCIX

2 *glister* glisten, shine.
5 *fire-drake* here, probably, in the sense of 'meteor', but also possibly 'fire-breathing dragon'.
7 *the boy with the bow* Cupid.
8 *aye* always.

CI

Sung by the Jackman. At the Windsor performance three additional stanzas were given, which are not included here.

1 *Cocklorrel* name for an outstanding rogue.
6 *crudities* undigested matter.

11 *Promoter* informer.
15 *bawd* the secondary, culinary, meaning here is 'hare'.
    bacon with the slang meaning of 'flesh', 'body'.
18 *Sempsters* seamstresses.
    tirewomen dressmakers.
20 *sallet* salad.
22 *green sauce* a spiced vinegar sauce for mutton and veal.
25 *carbonadoed* scored.
34 *pudding of maintenance* the reference is to the cap of maintenance which mayors carried at official processions.
36 *hinch-boys* pages.
41 *chine* edible area around the backbone (usually of an animal).
43 *pettitoes* basically pig's trotters.
51 *sippits* croutons.
63 *flirted* flicked.

CII, CIII

From *The Masque of Augurs*, 'presented on Twelfth-night, 1622'.

CII

This ballad is introduced by the stage-direction 'Enter John Urson with his bears, singing'. *Urson* is from the Latin 'ursus', bear.

9 *St Katherine* the 'presenters' (performers) of the first anti-masque, who include Urson, are said in the introductory passage to the masque to be from this area of London around the Tower. The district was well known for its breweries.
22 *Vintry Cranes* a public house called *The Three Cranes* in a part of London called the Vintry.
23 *St Clement Danes* Clement's Inn, near St Clement Danes' church in the Strand.
24 *the Devil* a tavern near Temple Bar: one of Jonson's own favourites (see *MP* CXIII).
30 *aqua-vitae* literally 'water of life', here referring to alcohol (particularly with reference to distilled spirits).
34–5 A Catherine Wheel decorated the gate mentioned in l. 34.
36 An odd fragment of local history-cum-legend which is found in several other places apart from this reference, but which has not been pinned down to any specific incident.
47 *single coin* small change.
48 *budget* leather bag.
54 *jordan* chamber-pot.

CIII

Sung by Apollo.

5ff. 'The science of augury was called "divination from birds": from birds, or divining birds, or prophetic birds. Divining birds are the ones that give an augury by their song, prophetic birds by their flight. Young birds give augury by eating greedily. Propitious and prophetic birds are the eagle, the vulture, the osprey or sea-eagle, the buzzard or falcon, the *immusulus*, the hawk, the swan and the dove. Divining birds are the crow, the raven, the goose, the stork, the heron and the owl. The unpropitious ones are the kite, the barn-owl, the night-raven, the screech-owl, the swallow, the woodpecker, etc.' (Jonson's note.)

8 *erne* eagle.

13 *night-crow* night-heron.

CIV

From *Neptune's Triumph for the Return of Albion*, 'in a masque at the court on the Twelfth-night, 1624'. There is a setting by William Webb in *Select Ayres and Dialogues* (1659).

7 *Pallas ... Arachne* both outstanding weavers of classical myth.

17 *ambergris* a secretion of the whale, valued for its use in perfumery.

18–19 Jonson seems to be linking the sea connections of ambergris (which is often found floating on the surface of the water) with the legend that Venus Aphrodite was born from the sea-foam which gathered round the genitals of Uranus which were thrown into the sea after Cronos had castrated him.

CV

From *Love's Triumph through Callipolis*, 'performed in a masque at court, 1631 ...'.

Title *Euclia* described in the prose link as 'a fair glory'.

Ingemination Repetition.

CVI

From *Chloridia*, 'personated in a masque at court ... at Shrovetide, 1630'.

Zephyrus the west wind.

10 *emulation* competition.
   jars disagreements.

20 *humour* moisture.

24 *quickening* bringing to life.

CVII

Title Both this and CVIII come from the Newcastle MS (Harleian 4955) but nothing is known of the occasion for which they were written.

CVIII

1   *the wonders of the Peak*   St Anne's Well, Eldon Hole, Poole Hole.
3-4   'To tell you what I am thinking.'
15   *Morts*   women (a gypsy word: granted the textual problems connected with *The Gypsies Metamorphosed* it is just possible that this song may have, at some stage, been part of the masque – even if only during drafting).
      mirkins   malkins, slatterns.
27   *standard*   ensign.
39   Pem Walker is also mentioned in the *King's Entertainment at Welbeck*. On the quality of Derbyshire ale see *The Gypsies Metamorphosed* 230f.

CIX

Title   H/S print this as part of *The Forest* X as an earlier draft of *And must I sing?* .... It clearly is that and it provides almost the same lead-in to *The Forest* XI.

CX

16   *damps*   poisonous vapours.
20   *Themis*   Hesiod presents her as a Titaness and in Homer she is an officer of Zeus. Later she becomes a personification of justice, as here.
21   *that rich chain*   see Homer *Iliad* VIII, 19. In a note to *The Masque of Hymen*, Jonson draws on Macrobius to explain the concept: 'since Mind emanates from the Supreme God and Soul from Mind, and Mind indeed, forms and suffuses all below with life ... and since all follow on in continuous succession, degenerating step by step in their downward course, the close observer will find that from the Supreme God even to the bottom-most dregs of the universe there is one tie, binding at every link and never broken. This is the golden chain of Homer ...' (Yale ed., 520-21).
24   *Dice*   Justice.
      Eunomia   Order.
25   *her daughters*   this follows Hesiod, *Theogeny* 901-3, where Dice and Eunomia are said to be daughters of Themis and Zeus.
27   *Irene*   peace.
40   *red*   Hudson suggests 'glowing': more probably, perhaps, Jonson means 'ashamed at their inarticulateness'.
47   *four ... before*   James had made a progress through London on 15 March.
48   *gladding look*   look making other people glad.
53   *this town*   Westminster (as distinct from *her great sister*, London, of l. 55).
54   *tire*   clothing, attire.
72   *tempered*   combined.
129   *eyne*   eyes.
130   *Iris*   the daughter of Thaumas and Electra; wife of Zephyrus; goddess of the rainbow.

144–5 *greater bodies . . . lesser fires*   son, moon . . . stars, planets.
145 *access*   approach, or – slightly metaphorically – rising.
153–4 *the artillery | of heaven*   thunder.
motto   'Only the king and the poet are not of everyday birth' (Florus).

CXI

These little pieces are taken from Robert Allot's anthology *England's Parnassus* (1600) which gives, in all, fourteen items from Jonson.

Murder   Juvenal X, 112–13: 'ad generum Cereris sine caede et volnere pauci / descendunt reges et sicca morte tyranni' ('Very few kings go down to the son-in-law of Ceres except by sword or murder; few are the tyrants who die a bloodless death').

CXII

Title   From Robert Chester's *Love's Martyr*: see *The Forest* X, XI and *MP* XXXI.

CXIII

Title   *the Apollo*   the room in the Devil tavern where Jonson drank with his friends.

3 *pottle*   a two-quart tankard.
4 *tripos*   a three-legged vessel (one was used at Apollo's shrine at Delphi).
8 A reference to Simon Wardlow who kept the tavern (*skinker* = tapster).

CXIV

Title   See *Underwoods* XXXVII, of which this seems an altered version.

CXV

Title   See *Epigrams* CXXIX, 16–17 and note; *Underwoods* XIII, 128.

1 *Arion*   a semi-legendary poet said to have been born in Lesbos. The point of the allusion is the story that, while returning by sea from Italy to Corinth, he was thrown overboard by sailors but saved by a dolphin which had been charmed by the song he had been permitted to sing before being tossed over the ship's side.
3 *up Holborn*   on the route to Tyburn (for execution).
7 *plain . . . Dunstable*, *H/S* (XI, 132) quote the proverb 'As plain as Dunstable Road', part of Watling Street with its long stretches in a straight line. Here again the local allusion is being set against an incident reported in the *Crudities*.
14 *rabbin*   rabbi. Coriat had to be saved from a Jewish mob by Sir Henry Wotton after getting into a dispute with a rabbi.
19–20 'Coming from his courtesan, a freshman (*F*), and now having seen

their fashions. . . . He will shortly be reputed a Knowing (*K*), proper, and well travelled scholar . . .' (Jonson's gloss).

CXVI

1] 'Our king and queen the Lord God bless *one MS*; God bless the king, the queen, God bless *one MS*.

2 Princess Elizabeth married the Palsgrave of Bohemia in 1613. In the Aubrey MS this line is followed by:

And God bless every living thing,

That lives, and breathes, and loves the king.

3] God bless the council of estate *one MS*.

Pembroke see note to dedication of *Epigrams*.

4 *Buckingham* George Villiers was created Earl of Buckingham in 1617.

5] God bless them all, and keep them safe *one MS*.

5-6] *One MS reads:*

God bless me, and God bless Rafe,

And then the kingdom be shall safe.

6 *Rafe* Aubrey explains that Rafe was the tapster at the Swan near Charing Cross – and adds that James gave Jonson £100 for the joke.

CXVII

7 *gait* going, journey.

CXVIII

Title This and the two poems that follow relate to Jonson's quarrel with Inigo Jones about whose work on the masques *Love's Triumph* and *Chloridia* should have priority on the title pages of the printed texts. See also *Epigrams* XCVII, CXV, CXXIX.

2 *pipkins* goods, commodities.

4 *Euclid* the Greek geometrician (*fl.* Alexandria *c.* 300 BC).

5 *Archimede* Archimedes (*c.* 287–212 BC) was born at Syracuse; a great mathematician and astronomer; an inventor in physics and mechanics.

Architas fl. c. 400 BC; a Pythagorean philosopher and geometrician; said to have invented the screw and the pulley.

7 *Ctesibius* Alexandrian engineer of about 250 BC.

8 *Vitruvius* first century BC; author of the treatise *De Architectura* which greatly influenced Renaissance architecture.

10 *architectonic* the art of building.

13 *Visors . . . antics* masks . . . grotesque costumes.

16 *tire-man, mountebank* dresser, charlatan.

Justice Jones Jones was a Westminster J.P. from 1630.

20 *asinigo* little ass (with play on Inigo).

22 *Langley* Francis Langley, who built the Swan Theatre.

26 *velvet sheath* fashionable velvet scabbard.

27 *wooden dagger* a property of the Vice of morality plays.

32–9 *H/S* (X, 682) suggest that these remarks refer to *Chloridia*.

38 *brought*] held in *MS*.

60 *Skeuopoios* preparer of stage properties.

64–5 *dominus-do-/All* 'magister factotum'.

66 *whistle* parasite.

72 *lantern-lerry* a device for producing artificial light.
fuliginous sooty, smoky.

78 *solemn*] serious *one MS*.

79 *firk* jerk, jump.
Adam Overdo the incompetent justice in *Bartholomew Fair*.

90 *twice conceived* twice used.

91 Jonson may have in mind the image in *Daniel* iii 5, 9.

94 *cinnopar* crimson.

96 *Aimed at in*] Produced by *one MS*.

99 *the Worthies* the nine Worthies of Christendom.

101 *the Feasting Room* at Whitehall, which burnt down in 1619.

104 *remonstrance* formal rebuke.

CXIX

Title *Corollary* here, something added.

1–2 Philip IV made his architect Crescenzio Marquis della Torre.

4 *deeds*] things *two MSS*.

8 *a cave for wine* see *Underwoods* XLVIII and note.

11 *quadrivial* having four streets meeting in a point.

12 *Thumb the pigmy*] Thumb, with Geoffrey *two MSS*. Tom Thumb appears in an antimasque to *The Fortunate Isles*.

16 *Dowgate torrent* *H/S* (IX, 481) quote from Stow's *Survey*: 'Downe gate, so called . . . of the sodaine descending, or downe going of that way from S. Iohns Church upon Walbrook into the River of Thames'.

17 *brown paper fleet* perhaps another reference to *The Fortunate Isles* (see l. 421, Yale edn).

20 *Pancridge earl* Henry VIII made the Finsbury Archers a fraternity of St George in 1539. The members took mock-titles, among them that of Earl of Pancridge. Jonson's reference to the *Marquis of Newditch* seems an analogous coinage although it is not known quite what ditch he was referring to.

21 *work*] worth *one MS*.

CXX

Title See Martial XII. lxi for a fairly close analogue.

CXXI

The verses Jonson replies to are by one John Eliot.

16 *the dog days* the hottest and most unhealthy part of summer.

CXXII

The verses Jonson answers are by Alexander Gill. Gill's reference to Lowen and Taylor in l. 11 is to John Lowin and Joseph Taylor who were both actors in the King's Servants' productions of *The New Inn* and *The Magnetic Lady*. His last line echoes the first line of *MP* XXXIII – a poem provoked by the failure of *The New Inn*. The gibes about bricklaying are linked with Jonson's probable apprenticeship to his step-father early in his life.

1-6 Gill was degraded from the church, fined and sentenced to ear-lopping in 1628 for disrespect to the king. He was, however, later pardoned.
7 *Denis* this seems to refer to the tyrant Dionysius of Syracuse, reputed to have kept himself after his fall by teaching. Gill's father was high-master of St Paul's School.

CXXIII

There has been some doubt about the ascription of this poem and CXXIV to Jonson, but there seems little reason to deny his authorship of them. Both poems come from Anthony Strafford's *The Female Glory* (1635).

7 *implexèd* enfolded.
9-10 See Spenser, *The Faerie Queene* I. vii, 32.
17 *intersert* set among.

CXXIV

9f. These are conventional epithets for the Virgin Mary.
19-20 'Who made us all happy by following you in your joy on giving birth to Christ.'
28 See Donne, *La Corona* 2. As Smith says in his note (*John Donne: Complete English Poems* (1971), 620) this kind of paradox is found in the Church Fathers and is inherent in Christian doctrine.

CXXV

See *Conversations* 13-14. This poem was quite often translated at this period (for example, by Surrey and Randolph).

CXXVI

Translated from *Pharsalia* VIII, 484-95.

1 (*he saith*) the speaker is Photinus, who is speaking to Ptolemy at Alexandria.

Horace, of the Art of Poetry

The version printed here is taken from the 1640 folio. This is the text which Jonson had revised from an earlier version which is printed in the 1640 duodecimo edition, using Heinsius' 1610 text of Horace as his model. Horace's poem is addressed to the Piso family, one of some standing since the father, Gnaeus Calpurnius, was Consul in 23 BC; one son, Gnaeus, held the same office in 7 BC and another, Lucius, in 1 BC.

8–9 Jonson's syntax rather obscures the point, made clearer by the Loeb translator, Fairclough: 'Believe me, dear Pisos, quite like such a picture [Jonson's *piece*] would be a book, whose idle fancies . . .'.

20 *Diana's grove* this was in Africa in the Alban hills, where she was worshipped with the male forest god Viribius.

25 *H/S* (XI, 114) quote a Greek proverb, 'Do you want a bit of Cypress too?' and refer to a story which makes much the same point as Horace does. See also *Conversations* 504–7.

28 Horace's 'fractis . . . navibus' means 'wrecked vessel'.

33 See heading note on the Pisos.

38 *low by lee* on the calm side of the ship.

46 *The Aemelian school* Aemilius Lepidus built a school for gladiators near the Forum; part of it was apparently rented to a sculptor.

62 *mought* might; *mought* was still a fairly common variant at this time.

71 *well-trussed* refers to the Latin 'cinctuti', a loincloth worn under the toga by the early Romans.

72 *Cethegi* an old patrician family.

76 *not . . . wrested* Horace's 'parce detorta' means, more exactly, 'drawn from sparingly'.

77 *Caecilius* (*c.* 219–*c.* 166 BC); a friend of Ennius and the chief comic dramatist of his time.

79 *Varius* a friend of Virgil and Horace; author of epics on Julius Caesar and the wars of Augustus.

81 *Cato* Marcius Porcius Cato (*d.* 149 BC); an early important Latin prose writer.

Ennius Quintus Ennius (239–169 BC); wrote tragedies and the epic *Annales*; one of the great early figures of Roman literature.

91 *the sea* the Portus Julius in Campania.

93 *barren fen* the Pontine marshes.

105 *gests* deeds.

107 *verse unequal* the elegiac couplet.

110 *dapper* neat, slight.

113–17 This passage only names one poet, Archilochus (seventh century BC – known chiefly for his iambic lampoons), but ll. 113–15 are usually taken to refer to Pindar (ll. 113–14), Sappho and Alcaeus (love) and Anacreon (wine).

118 *socks . . . buskins* see *MP* XV, 36–7 and note.

122 *Thyestes' feast* Seneca's tragedy *Thyestes* deals with Atreus' revenge upon Thyestes by tricking him into eating a meal of the flesh of his own children.

125 *decent* Latin 'decenter' ('fitting attributes').

126 *turns* differences between the tragic and comic manners.

colours rhetorical ornaments.

133 *Chremes* the irascible old man in Terence's play *Heautontimorumenos*.

135 *Telephus* son of Hercules.

136 *Peleus* father of Achilles.

157 *truch-man* Latin 'interpres' (interpreter).

167 *of Colchis born* that is, a fierce barbarian.

in Assyria bred that is, effeminate.

168 Aeschylus' tragedy *The Seven against Thebes* tells how seven Argive heroes challenged seven Theban opponents at the seven gates of Thebes.

175 *Medea* killed her own children as in Euripides' tragedy of 431 BC.

176 *Ino* her husband, Athamus, killed ones of their son, so she threw herself and their other son into the sea.

Ixion murdered his father-in-law; later, in heaven, he tried to seduce Juno and was punished by being chained to a wheel which turns unceasingly in Hell.

177 *Io* Jupiter loved Io but transformed her into a cow to avoid Juno's wifely jealousy. The latter, however, sent a gadfly which drove the bovine Io from one country to another in search of relief from its stings.

Orestes was tormented by the Furies after killing his mother Clytemnestra.

184 *a rhapsody* 'the Rhapsodists, who handed down the Homeric poems, recited them' (*H/S* XI, 116).

195 *that circler* Jonson's phrase is very obscure: Horace is referring to the so-called Cyclic Poems, out of the lays of which was built up a body of legends making the basic material of Greek tragedy. Horace's word is 'cyclicus' and Jonson has translated literally.

196 *Priam* king of Troy, killed by Neoptolemus at the sack of that city.

202 *tract* treat, deal with (Latin 'tractare').

205 *Antiphates* king of the Laestrygones in *Odyssey* X.

206 *Scylla, Charybdis* see *Odyssey* XII.

Polypheme see *Odyssey* XIX.

208 *Meleager* uncle of Diomedes; at his birth the Fates decreed that he should live as long as a brand on the fire was not consumed. His mother, Althaea, seized the brand and preserved it.

210 *the two eggs* Leda hatched two eggs: one contained Helen, the cause of the Trojan War, the other the twins Castor and Pollux.

231 *the open field* the Campus Martius.

263 *Medea* see l. 174 and note.

265 *Atreus* see l. 121 and note.

266–7 *Progne ... swallow* Procne's husband Tereus raped her sister Philomela and cut out her tongue. In revenge Procne killed her own son (Itys) and served his flesh to Tereus. When he sought to kill both sisters they were transformed into a swallow and a nightingale. The two birds are, in various versions of the story, not always identified with the same sister, although Philomela is now usually associated with the latter.

267–8 *Cadmus ... snake* Cadmus, son of Agenor, King of Tyre, had a rather turbulent career and finally asked the gods to turn him into a snake as a relief.

270 *fable* plot (Latin 'fabula').

273 *To ... in* that is, as a 'deus ex machina' to unravel the plot.

275 *fourth man* in classical drama there was a maximum of three speaking characters on stage at any one time.

276 *choir* the classical stage chorus.

279 *'grees* agrees, fits in.

285 *Hide faults* Horace's 'tegat commissa' is more strictly 'keep secrets'.

287 *hautboy* Jonson substitutes the hautboy (from the oboe family) for the 'tibia' or double flute of the ancients.

304 *swooping* sweeping.

306 *a music new* Horace's 'fidibus ... severis' is more specifically a reference to 'the sober lyre' regarded as more appropriate accompaniment for tragedy than the flute.

311 *Thespis* semi-legendary poet from Attica (*fl. c.* 534 BC) usually regarded as the inventor of tragedy.

319-21 Goats were apparently prizes for competitions in tragic singing. Also, however, 'the singers were satyrs, dressed in goat-skins. Satyric drama, the subject of this passage, is closely concerned with tragedy ...' (Fairclough's note in the Loeb text of Horace's poem).

345 *Davus* type name for a slave in Roman comedy.

346-7 *Pythias ... Simo* apparently characters in a lost Roman comedy.

348 *Silenus* usually the senior of the satyrs; sometimes in Greek mythology he is the tutor of Dionysus/Bacchus.

357 *the hall* Horace's 'paene forenses' means 'nearly inhabitants of the forum', with the forum being regarded as central to the life of the city. Jonson's *hall* may be intended to suggest a London equivalent, Westminster Hall.

362 *chiches blanched* fried peas.

363 *nut-crackers* noisy members of the audience.

373 *trimeter* of three dipodies or feet.

382 *Accius* see note to *M P* XV, 35.

Ennius see l. 80 and note.

399 *Plautus* Titus Maccus Plautus (*c.* 254-184 BC); one of the two great Roman comic dramatists whose work survives in bulk.

407 *tracts* tracks, paths.

409 *guarded tragedy* a rather cloudy reference to the Latin 'praetexta', which alludes to the purple-edged togas of Roman magistrates: hence Horace is speaking of tragedies with Roman themes.

410 *gownèd comedy* the Latin 'togatae', the dress of Roman comedy.

415 *Pompilius' offspring* the Pisos claimed descent from Numa Pompilius, the legendary successor to Romulus as king of Rome.

418 *corrected ... nail* a metaphor from sculpture: the artist would use a finger nail to test the smoothness of the marble he had been working. Jonson uses a similar image in *Discoveries* 2561-4.

419 *Democritus* Greek philosopher, born at Abdera *c.* 460 BC; sometimes

called 'the laughing philosopher'. Cicero (*De Divinitate* I. xxxvii, 80) says he denied the value of poetry.

422 *sort* number.

427 *Licinus* unidentified.

428 *Anticyras* Anticyra was a town in Phocis where hellebore, which was used in the treatment of madness, grew abundantly.

429 *left-witted* the Latin 'laevus' simply means 'left', as opposed to 'right'.

436 *fet* fetch.

442 *Socratic writings* the reports of Socrates' teaching in Plato and Xenophon.

457 *specious* Latin 'speciosa locis'; Jonson is anglicizing too closely for the Latin means 'brilliant passages' or, perhaps, 'commonplaces of rhetorical ornament'.

467f. Jonson does not make it clear that in Horace this is a dramatization of a school lesson in arithmetic.

475 'Ancient rolls were preserved from decay by smearing the unwritten side of the writing with the resinous sap of the . . . juniper tree' (*H/S* XI, 121).

479 *Orpheus* in Jonson's *Masque of Augurs* Orpheus appears in attendance on Apollo.

483 *Amphion* the legendary harpist whose music drew the stones into place to create Thebes.

490 *laws . . . wood* very thin planks of wood were used as an early way to inscribe such material as the laws of a state.

493 *Tyrtaeus* a seventh-century Spartan poet whose work, which included war-songs, survives only in fragments.

510 *Lamia* Queen of Lybia. She was loved by Jupiter, and Juno killed her children through her jealousy: Lamia responded by killing and eating other people's children.

517 *Sosii* Roman booksellers.

529 *scrivener* scribe or copyist.

534 *Choerilus* a poet of Samos who wrote an epic on the Persian wars.

552 *Messalla* Marcus Valerius Messalla, a member of an old Roman aristocratic family, was an outstanding orator.

553 *Cassellius Aulus* (*fl. c.* 58 BC); another famous pleader at the bar.

559 Sardinian honey, being bitter, spoilt the taste of the delicacy made from honey and roasted poppy seeds.

576 *Metius* Maecius Tarpa was superintendent of plays for Pompeius' new theatre in 65 BC.

591 *Pythian rites* at the Pythian Games a flute performance celebrated Apollo's victory over the python.

594 *The great scurf* the 'scab', a disease like scabies.

594-5 Horace is making the point that people play at poetry as children play games. Fairclough, in the Loeb edition, refers to a Roman tag-game.

605 *happy man* *H/S* (XI, 122) attack Jonson's 'happy' but it is upheld by the Loeb translation.

623 *Quintilius* Quintilius Varus, a critic-friend of Catullus and Virgil.

639 *Aristarchus* of Samothrace; head of the famous library at Alexandria from *c.* 180 to *c.* 145 BC; editor and commentator.

660 *Empedocles* a fifth-century poet and philosopher from Sicily. There is a story that he killed himself by leaping into Mount Etna's volcanic crater and another that he did so because he wanted to convince people of his divinity.

669 *famous death* here again criticism in *H/S* of Jonson's *famous* for the Latin 'famosae' is not supported by the Loeb version, which reads 'notable' rather than *H/S* 'notorious'.

Appendix 1

TIMBER : OR DISCOVERIES

As will become evident in the course of these notes *Discoveries* is a kind of commonplace book. Some passages amount almost to self-contained essays, while others are more in the nature of jottings. The work of scholars over the years has increasingly shown how far Jonson's book draws on other writers – in this respect it is again like a commonplace book – but *Discoveries* does not become a work of plagiarism as a result of this. The basically derivative nature of the work is admitted in the prefatory note: he takes material from others which interests him or which expresses views with which he agrees, adding his own comments and illustrations whenever he wishes. The process is not unlike that found in the poems and it should be remembered that borrowing can be as selective and personally revealing an activity as invention.

Since this volume is primarily an edition of Jonson's poems I have not thought it appropriate to annotate the prose works as fully as the poems. In particular I have not reproduced texts and translations in the way done with the poems. Readers who wish or need fuller annotation are referred to *H/S* I, VIII, XI.

Prefatory note

2 *reflux* literally 'flowing-back'; the passage means 'had a relevance to his particular view of his own times'.

5-10 'The fundamental material of facts and ideas, the wood – so to speak – and called so as a result of the variety and multifarious nature of the contents. Exactly as we call a great number of trees growing at random 'a wood', so the ancients use the word "wood" or "timber-trees" for those writings of theirs which had in them material on a range and diversity of things collected at random.' (The basic image is that used for *The Forest* and *Underwoods*.)

1-13 *Ill fortune ... mixed* Seneca, *De Consolatione Helviam* V, 4; *De Providentia* III, 3; IV, 6, 7; II, 1.

13-14 *Yet ... every man* Publius Syrus is quoted to this effect by Seneca, *De Tranquillitate Animi* xi, 8.

14-15 *But ... make it* Plutarch, *De Tranquillitate Animi* XVII, quotes Menander to this effect.

16 *Casus (margin)* literally 'fall', used with the sense of the 'de casibus' idea of tragedy as the fall of great men from power.

30-31 *the man ... hated* Tacitus, *History* I. vii.

32 *not easily emergent* Juvenal, *Satires* III, 164.

39-42 *There is ... is there* Euripides, *Phoenissae* 358-60.

43 *Ingenia (margin)* Latin 'ingenium', inborn dispositions.

47-51 *We praise ... by the other* Velleius Paterculus, *Historia Romana* II. xcii. 5.

52 *Opinio (margin)* reputation.

55-7 *We labour ... us* Seneca, *Epistles* XIII, 4.

66 *gut ... groin* see *Epigrams* CXVIII.

68 *Iactura vitae (margin)* a throwing away of life.

68-73 From Pliny, *Epistles* I. ix; Quintilian, *Inst. Orat.* XII. xi, 18.

71 *venting* releasing, giving out.

74-80 'A puritan is a heretical hypocrite, whose balance of mind has been disturbed by his confidence in his own perspicuity, because of which he flatters himself that – with a few others – he has found out certain flaws in Church dogma, as a result of which he – urged on by a sacred rage – fights insanely against civil authority, believing that he is, in this way, showing his obedience to God.' (The Latin has not been traced to any source.)

81 *Mutua auxilia (margin)* mutual help.

81-215 Jonson now begins to incorporate material from Juan Luis Vives (1492-1540), one of the great humanists and a friend of Erasmus and More. He taught at Oxford for a while and was tutor to Princess (later Queen) Mary. Jonson owned a copy of his *Works*.

81-91 From Vives, *Epistola Nuncupatoria*.

83 *consociation* union, joining.

92-104 Vives, *De Consultatione*.

104-115 Vives, *De Consultatione*.

105 *Consiliarii adjunct. (margin)* The joint councillors.

111-15 See *Epigrams* XCVIII, 10-12.

114 *Vita recta (margin)* a proper, morally good, life.

116 *Obsequentia (margin)* compliance.

116-32 Vives, ibid.

121 *humanity* courtesy (Latin 'humanitas').

124-5 *(Dat nox consilium)* 'night provides council.'

127 *extemporal* That is, make up their statements on the spur of the moment.

133-143 Vives, ibid.

134 *Parrhesia (margin)* frankness, freedom of speech.

135 *empire* display of power.

136 *precept* command, order.

140 *reprehended* rebuked, checked.

142-3 *Absit ... ego* Jonson takes this direct from Vives. The source is

Plutarch, *Orationes* II. i but, as *H/S* (XI, 216) point out, Jonson follows Vives in applying the story to Alexander rather than to his father, Philip. ('Far be it from you, O king, to know these things better than I do.')

144–53 Vives, *In Libros de Disciplinis Praefatio.* (This is perhaps a good place to make the general point that Jonson does not use Vives passively, but selects, paraphrases and adds as he sees fit.)

144 *Perspicuitas* (*margin*)   clarity.

146 *discipline*   subject, learning.

150 *braky*   rough, thorny.

154–9 Vives, ibid. For the relation of this remark to contemporary controversy see V. Harris, *All Coherence Gone* (1949).

160 *Non ... antiquitati* (*margin*)   'do not put too great a reliance on the ancients'.

160–96 Vives, ibid.

165 *precipitation*   rash speed to condemn or reject.

172 *Non ... fuere*: quoted direct from Vives (with 'fuere' for Vives' 'sunt'): 'they were not our masters, but our leaders'. The source is Seneca, *Epistles* XXXIII, 11.

173 *several*   private possession.

173–5 *Patet ... relictum est*: quoted from Vives: *Patet ... occupata* is translated by Jonson. The rest means 'much remains for those of the future'.

176 *Dissentire licet* (*margin*)   'dissent is permissible'.

180 *Sed cum ratione* (*margin*)   'but with reason'.

185 *Non mihi cedendum* (*margin*)   'submission is not due to me.'

190 *evict*   establish by argument.

    fautor   partisan, advocate.

191 *addict*   attach, devote.

197–206 Vives, *De Causis Corruptarum Artium.*

205 *acquiesce*   rest easily content.

206 *Opere pascitur*   condensed from Vives; translated in the words immediately preceding.

207 *Non vulgi sunt*   'they are not for the mob'.

211 *carat*   worth.

216–19 Pliny, *Epistles* IX. xix, 3, 8.

219 *leave*   permission.

220 *Maritus improbus* (*margin*)   'a shameless husband'.

224 *Afflictio pia Magistra* (*margin*)   'affliction the mistress of prayer'.

226 *Deploratis facilis descensus Averni* (*margin*)   see *Aenied* VI.

231 *Aegidius cursu superat* (*margin*)   'Aegidius wins the race.' A condensed version of a proverb in Augustine, *Sermones* CLXIX (Migne, *Patrologia Latina*, vol. 38, p. 926).

233 *Prodigo nummi nauci* (*margin*)   sense given in text.

236 *Munda et sordida* (*margin*)   sense in text.

239 *Debitum deploratum* (*margin*)   'a hopeless debt'.

241 *Latro sesquipedalis* (*margin*)   'with a great belly' (Latin 'sesquipedalis' literally means a 'foot and a half long'.)

244 *Com. de Schortenhein* (*margin*)   although the anecdote in the text sounds quite plausible I cannot find any other reference to this *German lord*.

245–6 *to have ... up* as great noblemen did when travelling.

246 *herborough* inn.

252 *Calumniae fructus* (*margin*) 'the fruit of calumnies'.

256 *Impertinens* (*margin*) literally, 'not belonging to': here, 'silly', 'absurd'.

260–61 *touched ... earth* Petronius, *Satyricon* 44.

263–4 Erasmus, *Adagia, Opera*, MDCCIII, vol. 2, III, iv, 35.

267 *Bellum scribentium* (*margin*) 'the writers' war'.

268 *ceremonies* empty, trifling issues.

270 *fires ... altars*: see Jonson's *Catiline* V, 16 – the gist is 'fighting as if for the things most sacred to mankind'.

275–6 *Sed ... usus* 'But I have had the pleasure of a mind and disposition superior in all ways to my fortune.'

277 Martial I. cvii, 8 (Jonson omits Martial's 'ipse').

278 *Differentia ... sciolos* (*margin*) 'the difference between scholars and dilettantes'.

281 *disquisition* inquiry into.

286 *welt* edge, border.

288 *Impostorum fucus* (*margin*) sense given in text.
   specious deceitful.

293 *Icuncularum motio* (*margin*) 'puppet-play'.

294–5 *Et sordet gesticulatio* 'and the action is disgusting.'

305–6 *Finis ... promptissimo* 'We should wait for the end-product of every man's career, for man is an animal very subject to change.' (P. J. McGinnis, *NQ* (April 1957), 162–3, has pointed out that Jonson has taken the Latin direct from Vives, *Libri de Disciplinis*.)

307 *Scitum Hispanicum* (*margin*) sense given in text.

308 *artes ... dividi* 'a man's achievements are not divisible among his heirs.'

313 *frontless* shameless.

315–75 Jonson here draws on J. J. Scaliger, *Confutatio Stultissimae Burdonum Fabulae* (*Opuscula* (1612), of which Jonson owned a copy).

318–19 *quorum ... placet* 'whom, abandoning virtue, it gives pleasure to hate.' Quotation from Scaliger with 'quorum' added by Jonson, and 'placet' for 'placent'.

315 *Non ... livor* (*margin*) sense given in text.

334 *Nil ... lib.* (*margin*) sense given in text.

344 *Iam ... sordent* (*margin*) sense given in text.

349 *Pastus ... Ingenu.* (*margin*) 'the time's diet'.

370f. Compare ll. 154–9 and note.

376 *Alastor* a god of revenge.

378 *licentious* indiscriminate.

382 *spit in his mouth* that is, show contemptible sycophancy.

386. *Mali choragi fuere* (*margin*) 'they were only property-men.'

391 *meritorious* earning money by prostitution (Latin 'meritorius').

395 *630* 1630.

398 *cast* the amount of bread baked at one time (see Malory, ed. Vinaver, 234).

403 *Archy* Archibald Armstrong, court fool to James I and Charles I.

406–78 This passage is made up of pieces from Aulus Gellius (*Noctes Atticae* I. xv, 1–18) and Claude Mignault's 1573 edition of Alciati's *Emblems* (see *H/S* XI, 222 f.).

406 *Lingua . . . optanda* (*margin*) sense given in text.

410 *that philosopher* Plutarch, *De Garrulitate* 3.

412 *petulancy* rashness.

425 *Bethlem-like* insane (lunatic asylums in the seventeenth century were often called Bethlem houses).

426–7 *without . . . mixed*: without any real substance or understanding.

433 *mountebank* quack.

435 *Homer's Thersites* see *Iliad* II, 212, 246 (the Greek that follows means 'senseless talker').

437–8 *Loquax . . . facundas* Jonson follows Mignault in attributing this to Sallust, whereas it comes from Quintilian, *Inst. Orat.* IV. ii. 2: 'Noisy rather than eloquent'.

438–9 *Satis . . . parum* 'much talk but little wisdom.'

440–41 The quotation comes from Hesiod, *Works and Days* 719–20, via Gellius: 'Notice that among men the best treasure is a careful tongue, and he who moves evenly has the most grace'.

442–3 The Latin is a version of the Greek immediately above it.

445–6 Chronologically impossible since Pindar died about seventy years before Epaminondas: Jonson carelessly follows Mignault's error.

448 *Demaratus* a king of Sparta; Jonson follows Mignault in the anecdote told here. *Plutarchi* (margin) is a reference to the source in Plutarch's *Apophthegmata Laconica*.

452 *indice* mark.

453–4 Mignault's version of lines from the *Anthologia Graeca* X. 98: 'While the fool keeps quiet he may be thought wise, for he conceals by silence the ills of his mind'.

453 *Vid . . . Megabizum* (*margin*) 'Aelian, *Vera Historia* ii, has a story of Megabyzuz in Zeuxis' studio talking ignorantly of art, and the painter politely asking him to be silent, as the colour-grinders were laughing at him' (*H/S* XI, 224).

462 *Zeno* fifth century BC; founder of the Stoics (see Plutarch, *De Garrulitate* 4).

469 *Argute dictum* (*margin*) Jonson's *wittily said*.

473 *beadle of the ward* a minor public official.

473–4 "Ἔχε μυθία . . . *laudabilis* 'How worthy of praise is the silence Pythagoras recommends.'

474–5 The Greek is a Pythagorean saying preserved by the neoplatonist

Iamblichus: 'Above everything, control the tongue, following the example of the gods'.

475 *Vide Apuleium* (*margin*) see *Golden Ass* i, 8.

476–7 *Digito . . . labellum* Juvenal, *Satires* I, 160: 'Fasten your lips with your fingers'.

478–80 Cicero, *De Oratore* I. xxv, 116. The sense of the marginal note is given in the text.

485 *comic poet* Plautus (see *Poenulus* 625–6).

488 Jonson refers in the margin to Plautus' *Trinummus* 520 ff. but his text slightly misrepresents Plautus' meaning.

490–99 See *Trinummus* 533–53.

495 *murrain* cattle-disease.

498 *Hospitium . . . calamitatis* 'it was the lodging-house of disaster.'

500–509 M. Seneca, *Controversiae* IV, preface.

510 *Claritas* (*margin*) in the sense of 'fame'.

517–541 M. Seneca, *Controversiae* IV, preface.

527 *mooting* students at the Inns of Court discuss imaginary cases or 'moots'.

532 *umbratical doctors* see Petronius, *Satyricon* 2, 'umbraticus doctor': sedentary scholars, as opposed to active participants.

533 *sub dio* in the open light of day.

542–51 Seneca, *De Beneficiis* VI. xxv (Jonson also makes heavy use of this treatise in *Underwoods* XIII).

549 *courtesy*] Swinburne, *H/S*; country *folio*.

552–84 Seneca, De Beneficiis VI. v, 1; vi, 2–3; viii; ix, 2; xii.

584 *Smithfield* the main London cattle-market.

611 *stops* delays.

630–35 Pliny, *Epistles* II. xii.

630 *Comit.* (*margin*) abbreviation of 'comitia' (Jonson's *Parliament*).

636 *Stare a partibus* (*margin*) 'to support one's party.'

648 *Deus in creaturis* (*margin*) sense given in text.

649–50 *creature of glory* Tertullian, *De Anima* I. ii.

652 *For to utter . . .* Lipsius, *Politica* I. ii.

659–65 Lipsius, *Politica* I. i.

659 *Veritas . . . hominis* (*margin*) sense given in text.

661 *Ethnic* here, 'pagan'.

665 *Homer says* in *Iliad* IX, 312–13.

671–3 'From Hippolytus a Collibus, *Palatinus*, 1595, p. 31 . . .' (*H/S* XI 228).

674–706 Made up of selections from Seneca, *Epistles* CXVI, 2, 8; CXXII, 2; CXII, 3–4.

674 *Nullum . . . patrocinio* (*margin*) sense given in text.

684 *Antipodes* opposites.

707 *De vere Argutis* (*margin*) 'of those truly witty.'

714–27 Quintilian *Inst. Orat.* II. v, 11–12.

718 *Cloth . . . tissue* rich silk fabric or cloth of fine gold threads.

721   *wresting*   twisting.

732–4   See *Epigrams* III and note.

733   *vouchsafe*   permit, condescend.

742–5   Both quotations, as the marginal note indicates, are from Martial IV. x: (a) 'Let a sponge from Carthage accompany the book'; (b) 'Many erasures are not enough: one sponging would be'. The second quotation condenses ll. 7–8 of Martial's poem. The connecting words *Et paulo post* mean 'a little after'.

750   *Cestius*   L. Cestius Pius, an anti-Cicero rhetorician.

757   *Heath*   John Heath, *Two Centuries of Epigrams* (1610).

758   *the sculler*   John Taylor (1580–1650), the Water poet; *Works* (1630) (see *Conversations* 377, 629).

763–4   *Non illi . . . iudicant*   translated in the previous sentence.

774–80   *H/S* (XI, 230) suggest that Jonson is glancing at such men as Donne and Bishop Hall.

787–801   Quintilian, *Inst. Orat.* II. xii, 1–3.

802   *De . . . nostrat (margin)*   'Of our companion Shakespeare.'

816   M. Seneca, *Controversiae* IV, preface.

818   *sufflaminandus erat*   'he needed strength.' Haterius (l. 619) was a rhetorician who died in AD 26.

823–5   See *Julius Caesar* III. 1, 47–8; Jonson's remark, in relation to the received text of the play, is exhaustively discussed in *H/S* XI, 231–3.

829   *Ingeniorum discrimina (margin)*   sense clear from text.

829–44   Quintilian, *Inst. Orat.* II. viii, 1, 7–11.

845–56   Quintilian, *Inst. Orat.* I. iii, 3–5.

855   *ingeni-stitium*   'a wit-stand' (margin): that is, they reach a point beyond which they do not develop.

862–75   Seneca, *Epistles* CXIV, 15, 21.

863–4   *Quae . . . cadunt*   the second line of the Martial epigram noted in the margin. For translation see note to l. 3498.

866   *rubs*   so the proverbial 'rub of the green', a bowling term referring to unevenness in the turf.

875–9   Seneca, *Epistles* CXIV, 18.

880–81   Seneca, Epistles CXIV, 15.

885–6   Verses unidentified: Jonson may well have made them up to illustrate his point (but see *Underwoods* XL. 29–30).

900   *bring it to the stake*   wager, bet on it.

904–9   Quintilian, Inst. Orat. I. viii, 21.

911   *venditation*   Latin 'venditatio': literally 'putting up for sale'; figuratively 'boasting', 'ostentation'.

912   *naturals*   natural capacity.

922–40   Quintilian, Inst. Orat. II. xi, 1–3; xxi, 1.

941–65   Quintilian, *Inst. Orat.*, 5–7; x, 13; xii, 8.

946   *sentences*   statements (Latin 'sententia').

953   *copy*   abundance of material or invention (Latin 'copia').
      election   selection.

962 The two parts of Marlowe's *Tamburlaine* are now usually dated 1587–8. *Tamarchams* seems to refer to a lost play (*Tamar Cam*) known to have been acted by the Admiral's Men in 1596.

965–91 Quintilian, *Inst. Orat.*, II. xii, 11, 12; v, 8–10.

992 *Ignorantia animae* (*margin*) sense given in text.

1002–3 Seneca, *Epistles* xxxi, 6.

1012 *indagations* inquiries (Latin 'indagatio').

1015 *Otium Studiorum* (*margin*) sense given in text.

1019–44 Seneca, *Epistles* I, preface.

1045 *Et stili eminentia* (*margin*) 'Greatness of style.'

1046–7 There is fragmentary classical evidence that Virgil's prose was inferior to his verse, while Cicero's verse was inferior to his prose.

1048 *Sallust's orations* the speeches he composed for Caesar and Cato in his *Bellum Catilinae*.

1049–50 *Plato's speech . . . for Socrates* the *Apology*.

1051 *patron* advocate (Latin 'patronus').

1063 *panniers* baskets slung over horses for load-carrying.

1064–90 Seneca, *Epistles* III, preface.

1064 *De . . . Oratoribus* (*margin*) 'Of famous orators.'

1090 *chosen* carefully selected.

1091–4 Seneca, *Epistles* III, preface.

1091 *Dominus Verulanus* (*margin*) Lord Verulam, Francis Bacon, the *one noble speaker* of l. 1025.

1094–1108 Seneca, *Epistles* III, preface. Seneca is speaking of Cassius Severus, for whom Jonson substitutes Bacon.

1098 *censorious* severe.

1099 *presly* concisely.

1101 *member* section (as in the organization of Burton's *Anatomy of Melancholy*).

1105 *devotion* power of arguing.

1109 *Scriptorum Catalogus* (*margin*) 'List of writers.'

1109–10 Seneca, *Epistles* I, preface (where Jonson's Latin tag, translated in his text, is taken from).

1113 *seculum* Latin for 'age', 'generation'.

  Sir Thomas More (1478–1535); his main English work is the *History of Richard III* (*c.* 1513).

  the elder Wyatt Thomas Wyatt (1503–42) the poet.

1114 *Henry . . . Surrey* Henry Howard (?1517–47) the poet.

  Chaloner Sir Thomas Chaloner (1513–77), translator of Erasmus' *The Praise of Folly* (1549) and of *An Homilie of Saint John Chrysostome* (1544).

  Smith Sir Thomas Smith (1513–77), author of *De Republica Anglorum* (1583).

1115 *Elyot* Sir Thomas Elyot (?1490–1546), author of *The Boke Named the Governour* (1531).

1115   *B. Gardiner*   Bishop Stephen Gardiner (?1483–1558), author of several Catholic tracts.

1117   *Sir Nicho[las] Bacon*   (1509–79); Keeper of the Seal (see *Underwoods* LI); mentioned here for oral eloquence rather than written.

1119   *Sir Philip Sidney*   the author of *Astrophel and Stella* and the *Arcadia*.

1120   *Mr Hooker*   Richard Hooker (1533–1600), author of *The Lawes of Ecclesiasticall Politie* (?1594–7; full version 1617). See *Conversations* 128.

1123   *Earl of Essex*   Robert Devereux (1566–1601), second Earl of Essex; Spenser's patron, Elizabeth's favourite, minor writer. See *Conversations* 372.

1124   *Sir Walter Raleigh*   (1552–1622); sailor, courtier, poet, author of *The History of the World* (1614). See *Underwoods* XXIV, *Conversations* 189f.

1126   *Sir Henry Savile*   (1549–1622); translator of Tacitus (1581). See *Epigrams* XCV.

1126–7   *Sir Edwin Sandys*   (1561–1629); author of *A Relation of the State of Religion* (unauthorized edn, 1605; authorized version, retitled *Europae Speculum*, 1629).

1127–8   *Lo[rd] Egerton*   Thomas, Lord Egerton (?1540–1617). See *Epigrams* LXXIV and note; *Underwoods* XXXI, XXXII.

1131   *successor*   Francis Bacon (*L.C.* in the margin against Egerton and Bacon = Lord Chancellor).

1132–8   Seneca, *Epistles* i, preface. For the epithets for Greece and Rome see MP XV, 39.

1140   ἀκμή   highest point.

1141   *De Augmentis Scientiarum (margin)*   the title of the first chapter of Bacon's *Instauratio*: Of the Advancement of Learning.

1150   *his books of Analogy*   Caesar's lost treatise *De Analogia* was partly written during his crossing of the Alps to rejoin his army in Gaul.

1151   *Lord St Albans*   Francis Bacon

1152   *Novum Organum*   published 1620.

1154   *nominals*   the names of things, as opposed to the realities.

1158   Horace, *Art of Poetry* 346: 'et longum note scriptori prorogat aevum' ('with honour make the far-known author live' – Jonson).

1159–71   From a letter from Father Fulgenzio Micanza to the first Earl of Devonshire (for details see *H/S* XI, 244).

1172   *De ... morum (margin)*   'Of the corruption of manners.'

1172–84   Seneca, *Epistles* CXIV, 3, 11.

1174   *vitiated*   corrupted, faulty.

1185–94   Seneca, *Epistles* CX, 3.

1185   *De rebus mundanis (margin)*   'Of worldly things.'

1197   *venery*   sexual intercourse.

1201   *Vulgi mores (margin)*   'The manners of the vulgar.'

1204–5   *Hercules ... bull*   the capture of the Bull of Crete was the seventh (in some versions eighth) labour of Hercules.

1211   *Morbus Comitialis (margin)*   'The sickness of Parliament.'

1225–33   'Cf. Henry Garnese *Diphthera Iovis* ... 1607, pp. 107–8' (*H/S* XI, 245).

1229 *with Orpheus* see *Argonautica* 128–9; *Iliad* IX, 524 f.

1234 *De . . . Iacobo (margin)* 'Of James the best of kings.'

1238–47 Jonson is here drawing upon traditional views of the importance of wisdom for monarchy. *H/S* (XI, 245) quote from Erasmus, who provides the substance of Jonson's remarks, and from Franciscus Patricius, who mentions Lycurgus (a legendary Spartan law-giver), Sylla (138–78 BC – dissolute himself, but nevertheless aiming through law to reform public morals) and Lysander (a Spartan naval commander in the Peloponnesian War; died 395 BC).

1247–58 *H/S* again quote from Farnese (XI, 246). Cyrus founded the Persian empire and died in 529 BC. For the story of his being nursed by a bitch see Lucian, *De Sacrificiis* V.

1259 *De . . . studentium (margin)* 'Of the malignity of the learned.'

1260–61 *habent . . . deliciis* 'they have poison as a way of living: indeed as luxuries.'

1265 *hint* chance, opportunity.

1277 *feign* imaginatively create.

1281–9 Quintilian, *Inst. Orat.* I, proemium 9–14.

1285 *embattling* setting in opposition.

1290 *controverters* disputants (the sense of the marginal note is in the text).

1294 *More . . . pugnant (margin)* 'The way of the andabatae, who fought with their eyes covered.'

1294–5 *The one . . . sieve* see Lucian, *Demonax* 28.

1296 *fluxive* unstable

1305–10 Erasmus, *Hyperaspistae Diatribes.*

1306–8 a medieval belief.

1309 *dissimuled* concealed.

1311–19 Pliny, *Epistles* I. viii, 15.

1311 *Iactantia intempestiva (margin)* inopportune boasting.

1320 *Adulatio (margin)* cringing.

1322–5 Seneca, *Quaestiones Naturales* IV, praefatio 7.

1331 *springes* traps.

1342–3 Seneca, *Epistles* LIX, 11.

1344 *suits* requests.

1346 *livery-friends* sycophants.

1358 *De . . . probis (margin)* 'Of the upright and the good.'

1361–3 See Paul's *Epistle to the Hebrews* XI, 4–8.

1370 *Mores Aulici (margin)* 'Of the ways of courtiers.'

1377–84 Suetonius, *The Twelve Caesars*, 'Caligula' 31.

1377 *Impiorum querela (margin)* 'Complaint of the unrighteous.'

1381 *Varus* the Roman general who, in AD 9, was lured into the Teutoburgian forest by the German chief Arminius and had three legions decimated.

1383 *Fidenae* see Suetonius, *The Twelve Caesars*, 'Tiberius' 40.

1386–7 Dio, *Roman History* lix. 30. 1ᶜ.

1389–91 Quintus Curtius, *Historiarum Alexandri* IV. xiv, 18.

1392 *Nobilium Ingenia (margin)* 'Of the main qualities of noblemen.'

1392–1406 Machiavelli, *Il Principe* IX, 4.

1407-13 *Principum . . . Principis (margin)* See *Il Principe* II, 1: 'I say, then, that with hereditary states, accustomed to that prince's family, there are far fewer problems in maintaining one's rule than in new principalities'.

1407-29 Machiavelli, *Il Principe* IX, 2-7.

1430-34 Machiavelli, *Il Principe* VII, 4.

1430 *Clementia* mercy.

1438-46 Seneca, *De Clementia* I. xxiv, 1, 3; viii, 6-7; x, 4.

1454 *factors* agents.

1455 *St Nicolas (margin)* facetiously, Niccolo Machiavelli.

1455-9 Machiavelli, *Il Principe* VIII, 8.

1462 *obnoxious* dependent on (Latin 'obnoxious').

1465-78 Seneca, *Epistles* I. xiii, 2-5.

1479 Farnese, *op. cit.*, 105.

1480 *The Palladium* Greeks and Romans thought that this image of Pallas guaranteed a city's safety. As Troy could not be taken while the image was in the city Diomedes and Odysseus stole it.

1486-90 Seneca, *Epistles* I. i, 9.

1491 *capital* liable to execution (Latin 'capitalis').

1499 *Euripides saith* *H/S* (XI, 250) quote from Menander.

1503 *Terminus* the Roman god of boundaries; symbolized by a sacred stone which stood in the temple of the Capitoline Jupiter.

1504 *in the fable)* of Reynard the Fox (see, for example, Spenser, *Mother Hubberd's Tale*).

1520-22 Pliny, *Panegyricus* LXIV.

1525-32 Iustus Lipsius, *Politica*, praefatio (*Opera* (1628), vii, 6).

1536-7 Plutarch, *Quomodo adulator ab amico internoscatur* 16.

1545 *Character principis (margin)* 'The nature of a prince.'

1550-72 Lipsius, *Politica* ii. 75, who collects these names from Tiberius, Erasmus, *Proverbs*, Cicero, Pliny, Tacitus (see *H/S* XI, 251 for details).

1551 *flea* flay.

1552 *fells* skins.

1568 *affect* seek for (Latin 'affectare').

1578 *price* bribery.

1578 *disquisition* careful investigation (Latin 'disquisitio').

1595-6 *H/S* (XI, 252) have a long note on this but the basic point is that the sword was 'Proverbial in Greece for an instrument which served two purposes'.

1598 *De Gratiosis (margin)* 'Of the favoured.'

1598-1604 See *Underwoods* LXXV, 115-20.

1605 *Divites (margin)* the rich.

1609 *Haeredes ex asse (margin)* 'Heirs to the whole property.'

1615 *lightly* usually.

1621 Juvenal, *Satires* II, 63: 'He pardons ravens, but treats the doves with the greatest severity'.

1622 Terence (not Plautus as margin), *Phormio* 331: 'Nor is a fowling net set for the hawk or kite'.

1625 *They* the *wise masters.*

1625 *huff* bluster.

1627 *place the counter* the counter is a unit of varying value, ranging from gold to nothing. The point is that the *wise masters* can control the *great thieves of state.*

1629 The *clerk* has not been identified.

1630 *device* a picture, usually accompanied by a motto, expressing a person's aspirations or principles.

1636 *De . . . malis* (*margin*) 'Of the good man and the evil.'

1636–69 Apuleius, *Apologia sive de magia* 377–90 (*Opera Omnia*, ed. Oudendorp and Bosscha, vol. 2, 1911).

1648 *precipices* dangerous situations (Latin 'praeceps').

1649–51 Jonson had his fair share of brushes with authority: imprisonment for his part in *The Isle of Dogs* (1597) and in *Eastward Ho* (1605) – *Conversations* 252 – and being called before the Privy Council for *Sejanus* (1603) – *Conversations* 324.

1656 *starting-holes* loop-holes, ways of escape.

1659 *engineers* planners.

1664–5 *granted to* to be expected from.

1681–98 Apuleius, *Opera Omnia*, vol. 2, 432–4.

1686 *impertinences* things contrary to decent behaviour.

1699 *Amor nummi* (*margin*) 'Love of money.'

1699–1750 Seneca, *Epistles* CXIX, 9–11; CX, 9, 10, 12; CXIX, 13, 14; CXIX, 6; CX, 14–19.

1718 *contemn* despise.

1724 *brought . . . praemunire* originally 'praemunire' was a writ issued for the offence of introducing a foreign power into the kingdom; more generally – the sense here – incurring a praemunire meant the penalty of having one's goods etc. forfeited to the sovereign.

　　　proscribed banished.

1729 *stews* ponds where fish were kept until ready for eating.

1730 *tissues* see l. 718 and note.

1737–41 The reference is to the visit in July 1606 of King Christian IV of Denmark to James I.

1751–1815 Seneca, *Epistles* CXV, 2, 6–18; CXIII, 32.

1751 *De . . . effoeminatis* (*margin*) 'Of the effeminate and unmanly.'

1752 *kempt* combed, tidy.

1754 *curious* fastidious, over-particular.

1756 *morphew* a scurfy eruption.

1757 *gumming* stiffening.

1758 *bridling* trimming.

1760 *pickedness* affectation.

1768 *commission* mandate.

1779 *De stultitia* (*margin*) 'Of folly.'

1781 *fairing* a trifle bought at a fair.

1800 *De sibi molestis* (*margin*) 'Of those who are a nuisance to themselves.'

1805 *others' envy* their own envy of other people.

1816–29 Seneca, *Epistles* CXIV, 23, 25.

1816 *Periculoa melancholia* (*margin*) 'a dangerous disease'.

1825 *drabbing* whoring.

1830 *Falsae . . . fugiendae* (*margin*) 'Even a semblance of evil should be avoided.'

1830–52 Plutarch, *Quomodo quis suos in virtute sentiat profectus* 11.

1834 *Black Lucy* a contemporary whore of some repute (see *H/S* XI, 257).

1837 *keep* stay in.

1841 *Decipimur specie* (*margin*) 'The appearance of truth deceives us.'

1848 *original* origin.

1853 *endenisen* naturalize.

1857 *Dejectio Aulic.* (*margin*) 'The despondency of courtiers.'

1868 *of* by.

1868–9 Plutarch, *De gloria Atheniensium* III, 346 f.

1878 *err* wander (Latin 'erro').

1882 Philostratus, *Imagines* I. i.

1885–90 J. K. Houck (*NQ* (October 1968), 367–8) has pointed out that this is from Quintilian, *op. cit.*, XI. iii, 67.

1890–1900 Quintilian, *op. cit.*, XII. x, 6–9.

1901–1904 Quintilian, *op. cit.*, XII. x, 4.

1901 *Zeuxis* (*fl.* fifth century BC); from Heraclea in Southern Italy; particularly famous for his painting of women and for his ability to create llusions of reality.

      Parrhasius (*fl. c.* 400 BC); from Ephesus; often linked with Zeuxis as the paradigm of the great classical painter.

1905–11 Pliny, *Epistles* III. xiii, 4; IV. vii, 7 (the reference to M.A. Regulus – informer and orator, hated by the younger Pliny but praised by Martial – comes a few lines earlier in the latter letter).

1911 *obscene* here primarily 'unfortunate', 'inappropriate', but also in its modern sense so far as '*occupy*' (l. 1812) = 'use sexually' is concerned.

1916–38 *H/S* (XI, 257) quote from Possevino's *Bibliotheca Selecta*, 1593.

1916 *De . . . picturae* (*margin*) 'Of the progress of painting.'

1917 *compass* range.

1923 *Eupompus* of Sicyon; Greek painter and contemporary of Zeuxis and Parrhasius.

1925 *optics* perspective.

1929 *recessor* background (Latin 'recussus').

1935 *Plin.* (*margin*) Possevino makes use, in the section Jonson is drawing on, of Pliny, *Natural History* XXXV. x, 67; xi, 126–7.

1935–8 *all . . . breaking* following Pliny, *Natural History* XXXV. xi, 127: 'all solid objects on an uneven ground'.

1938 *he* Vitruvius. Jonson's marginal reference is to *De Archtectura* 3 (not 8) and 7: the Vitruvian section on *chimeras* is vii, 173.

1943 *Horace . . . at* see *Ars Poetica* 9–14.

1948 See Xenophon, *Memorabilia* III. x.

      Clito Cleiton in Xenophon – nothing is known of him.

1950 *Polygnotus* Greek painter (*fl.* 475-447 BC) regarded by many later Greeks as the first great Greek painter.

1951 *Aglaophon* Greek painter of *c.* 420 BC

1952 *lawgiver* see Quintilian, *Inst. Orat.* XII. x, 5.

1953-5 Jonson misreads here (see *H/S* XI, 259-60).

1956-61 Jonson again follows Possevino closely – to the extent of naming seven painters despite the reference to six. *Sebastian of Venice* is Sebastian del Piombo (*c.* 1458-1547); Romano (1492/9-1547) was an assistant to Raphael for some time.

1963 *oraculous* having the power of an oracle.

1974 *compound* settle matters.

1975 *delate* inform against (Latin 'delator').

1997 *simulties* arguments (Latin 'simultas').

2001 *pies* magpies.

2005 *Imo serviles (margin)* 'Slaves indeed!'

2017 *undertaken* dealt with.

2025 *De . . . educandis (margin)* 'Of the education of children.'
   your lordship H/S (XI, 260) are confident that this relates to the Earl of Newcastle: this is a possibility, but scarcely the only one.

2030-31 *just . . . propounded* adequate treatment of what had been asked for.

2033 *venter* utter.

2035-45 Quintilian, *Inst. Orat.* I. i, 21; iii, 1.

2042 *apting* making apt, fitting.

2055-9 Quintilian, *Inst. Orat.* I. 1, 20.

2059-2100 Quintilian, *Inst. Orat.* I. ii, 1, 4, 6, 18, 20, 21-2, 31; iii, 7, 8, 10, 11, 13-14.

2063 *willing* wishing.

2075 *commonwealth* nation.

2078 *age* old age.

2083 *singulars* individuals.

2093 *reprehension* rebuke.

2099-2100 Jonson is saying that the use of the cane is perverted/perverting and cowardly/conducive to servility.

2101-48 Quintilian, *Inst. Orat.* X. iii, 4-10.

2101 *De . . . genere (margin)*: 'Of style and the best way of learning to write.'

2106 *excogitate* consider.

2112 *laboured* carefully considered.

2113 *conceits* ideas.

2115 *order . . . approve* arrange carefully what we have decided is adequate.

2118 *juncture* the connection between what we have already written and are proceeding to write.

2123 *fetch . . . largest* take the longest run-up.

2125 *loose* release, discharge.

2125-7 'I do not forbid a free release of our imaginative resources, so long as we do not make an error about our inspiration.'

2153-72 Quintilian, *Inst. Orat.* II. vii, 2-5; viii, 12, 13, 15.

2172 *consent* harmony, accord (Latin 'concentus').

2173 *Praecipiendi modi (margin)* 'Methods of teaching.'

2180–92 Quintilian, *Inst. Orat.* I proemium 26.

2194–2254 Quintilian, *Inst. Orat.* II. iv, 3, 4, 6, 14, 10–11; I. i, 5; I. ii, 27–8; II. v, 19, 21, 23; I. viii, 5–7, 9.

2197 *winding* indirect, full of circumlocutions.

2237 *squalor* roughness.

2248 *manners* moral disposition.

2251 *the later* That is, Greek 'new' comedy, imitated by the Romans.

2253 *sentences* 'sententiae' or moral maxims.

2255 *Fals . . . fugiend. (margin)* 'False quarrels should be avoided.'

2255–99 Quintilian, *Inst. Orat.* I. xii, 16; i, 1–2; xii, 11, 15, 2–5, 7. Cicero, *De Finibus* V, 87.

2269 *Platonis . . . Italiam (margin)* Plato's journey to Italy (this took place much later than the Egyptian venture mentioned in l. 2173).

2300 *Praecept. Element. (margin)* in 'Elementary precepts.'

2306 *elementarii senes*: 'old men stuck in the rudiments (of learning).' See Seneca, *Epistles* XXXVI, 4.

2315–16 *Pure . . . customary* Quintilian, *Inst. Orat.* VIII proemium, 23, 25.

2320 Quintilian, *Inst. Orat.* II. xxi, 14.

2326–7 Quintilian, *Inst. Orat.* I proemium 25.

2328–70 Vives, *De Ratione Dicendi* i.

2328 *De . . . dignitate (margin)* 'Of the dignity of speech.'

2332 *deorum . . . interpres* 'interpreter for gods and man' (see *Aeneid* IV, 356).

2339 *Ἐγκυκλοπαιδείαν* general education.

2341–2 *verborum . . . eloquentiae* 'the choice of words is the start of eloquence.' See Cicero, *Brutus* 253 (referring to Caesar's lost *De Analogia*). Jonson's Latin is adaptation rather than quotation.

2342–5 *Of words . . . 1.8 (margin)* *Ars Poetica passim*; Quintilian, *Inst. Orat.* VIII. vi, 5, 6, 15–17.

2349 *translation* figure of speech (Latin 'translatio').

2350–51 *(nam . . . prudenti)* '(a wise man uses no metaphor at random).'

2352 *commodity* convenience, profit.

2358 *property* propriety.

2359 *farfet* obscure, far-fetched.

2363 *ordinary* see *Epigrams* XII, 11 and note.

2370 *boulin* bowline.

2371–4 Jonson here makes direct use of Quintilian (VIII. vi, 5, 6, 15–17) who was also Vives' source.

2377–80 Quintilian, *Inst. Orat.* I. v, 71–2.

2382–4 Quintilian, *Inst. Orat.* I. vi, 2.

2385–2407 Quintilian, *Inst. Orat.* I. vi, 3, 39–41, 43–5.

2390 *perspicuity* clarity.

2391 *vicious* incorrect, deformed.

   Venustas (margin) beauty, charm.

2396 *intermission* the period when they were not in use.

2407–9 Quintilian, *Inst. Orat.* I. vii, 18. 'Aquai' and 'pictai' were archaic genitives in Virgil's time.

2409 *scabrous* rugged.

2411 *Chaucerisms* English archaisms.

2420 *paranomasies* either what Peacham calls 'A figure which of the word going before deriveth the word following' (giving as example 'The wisdom of the wise') or what Scaliger defines as 'Words which are similar in sound but which through slight alteration differ in meaning' (fasting/feasting). See Lee Sonnino, *A Handbook to Sixteenth Century Rhetoric* (1968), 24, 26–7.

2421–2 Martial XI. xc, 2 (for translation see ll. 3488–90 note).

2424 *grateful* pleasing.

2424–2514 Vives, *De Ratione Dicendi* i.

2425 *accurate* careful.

2433–4 *veer out of sail* change course.

2440 Jonson substitutes Tacitus for Vives' Lysias as the example of the *strict and succinct style.*

2446 *breaches* elisions, compactings.

2448 *Fabianus (margin)* a Greek rhetorician (*fl.* AD 14–41); criticized by M. Seneca for obscurity: Vives quotes this criticism, so the marginal note should read 'Secena de Fabianus'.

2459 *marking* paying due attention.

2465–6 Quoted straight from Vives: 'Directness throws light, while ambiguity and circumlocution darken'.

2471 *Obscuritas . . . tenebras (margin)* 'obscurity encourages darkness.'

2473 *pearl . . . fable* in Aesop's fable of the cock and the jewel (XLIV in the Croxall/L'Estrange translation).

2475 *found* there is quite a good case for emending to 'wound'.

2477 *Superlation* hyperbole (Latin 'superlatio').

2477–88 Jonson here inserts two phrases from M. Seneca, *Sausoriae* I, 11, 12: 'The ocean raves as if indignant at your leaving dry land' and 'One might think that the Cyclades were torn up and swimming on the sea'.

2480 *Cestius* Pius Lucius Cestius; Greek, popular teacher and wit, who disliked Cicero.

2484–5 *Aeneid* VIII, 691–2; the second piece translated above.

2490–91 Vives, who is misquoting the boast attributed to Caesar in *De Bello Hispaniensi* XLII. (In Vives and Jonson *P.R.* = 'populi romani'.) 'Are they the armies of the Roman people which can burst the barriers of heaven?'

2494 Quintilian, *op. cit.*, VIII. vi. 50. The warning is against mixed metaphors.

2507 *circumstance* circumlocution.

2515–87 Vives, *De Ratione Dicendi* ii.

2515 *Oratio . . . anim. (margin)* 'Speech is the image of the soul.'

2515–16 *speak . . . thee* Erasmus, *Apophthegmata* III, 70 (*edn cit.*, vol. IV, col. 162).

2525 *pumila (margin)* dwarfs.

2526–7 *absolution . . . poured out* the delivery flows readily

2533 *pleasing* Vives' 'placida' is more 'gentle', 'easy'.

2542 *tumorous* pompous, bombastic

2547 *trunk-hose* the part of the hose which covers the trunk, usually loose and baggy. Here it is obviously part of a style of dress inappropriate for a *councillor of state.*

2548 *hobby-horse cloak* a long cloak.

2557 *answerable* appropriate, decorous.

      Cutix sive Cortex (margin) skin, shell.

2560 *coagmentation* combination (Latin 'coagmentio').

2561–4 See Horace *Of the Art of Poetry* 418 and note.

2567 *Carnosa (margin)* fleshy.

2568 *Adipata (margin)* fatty.

2568–9 *arvina orationis* (from Vives); speech well filled-out.

2572 *picked* carefully arranged.

      Oratio . . . pasta (from Vives); speech smooth and plump.

2574–5 *Redundat . . . est* 'It is abundant in blood, because of which more than is necessary is said.'

2577 *signifying* meaningful.

2578 *Jejuna (margin)* meagre, dry.

2579 *macilenta (margin)* thin, lean (so also *strigosa*).

2586–7 *ossa . . . nervos* 'They have bones and sinews.'

2588–2631 Jonson here follows Bacon's *Advancement of Learning* I. iv (especially 2, 3, 5, 8, 12), often using Bacon's own language.

2590 *distemper* illness.

2614 *fierce undertakers* echoing Bacon's reference to the Schoolmen as 'great undertakers indeed, and fierce with dark keeping' (*Advancement of Learning* I. iv, 7).

2618 *digladations* disputes, arguments (Latin 'digladatio').

2620 *concatenation* linking.

2622 *animadversion* censure, rebuke.

2629 *monte potiri* Ovid, *Metamorphoses* V, 254 ('monte potita').

2632 *De . . . scriptore (margin)* 'Of the best writer.'

2635–2836 Jonson here uses John Hoskyns's *Directions for Speech and Style* (ed. H. H. Hudson (1935), 2f.). Hoskyns was a friend of Jonson.

2643–5 *Cicero said Brutus* VI, 23, but Jonson follows Hoskyns in reading *recte* for Cicero's 'bene': 'No one can be a good speaker who is not a sound thinker.'

2656 *preposterous* having first what should be last (Latin 'praeposterus').

2700 *some earnest* something of real substance.

2710 *brief* summary, epitome.

2732 *cense* rank (Latin 'census').

2743 *reaches* ranges, extents.

2746 *discharges* duties, commitments.

2749 *breviates* précis, summaries.

2759 *baits* periods of rest and refreshment.

2760   Quintilian, *Inst. Orat.* IV.ii, 41.

2770   *appeached* impeached, accused.

2778   *Bill of Chancery* until 1873 Chancery was, next to Parliament, the highest court in England.

2781   *this* perspicuity.

2783–4   *distinctly . . . yourself* working out clearly what you want to say.

2790–92   *like . . . shop* like a rich man who, because he does not attend to the details of his business, cannot quickly produce any particular item from his shop.

2799   *curious* over fastidious.

2817   *not to cast a ring* not to make a special effort to draw in the fashionable contemporary words.

2825–6   *the Courtier* Castiglione's *Il Cortegiano* (1528).

2833   *as . . . saith* Lipsius in *Epistolica Instituto* (*Opera*, 1623) – Lipsius is a prime source for Hoskyns.

2739   *primogeniture* birth, beginning.

    peccant erring, imperfect.

2843   *charact* worth.

2848   *the professors' estimation* the estimation in which those who profess poetry are held.

2852   (*Placentia College*) a *placentia* or 'pleasance' was a secluded pleasure garden. Jonson seems to use the phrase as a sarcastic comment on the surface sophistication of the court.

2854–91   Erasmus, *Epistola Apologetica ad Martinum . . .* (*edn cit.*, vol. IX, col. 4–6 – selectively used).

2858–9   Erasmus quotes from memory Jerome, *Epistulae* CXXV (Migne, *op. cit.*, I, 934–5): 'Where there is a broad-based discussion of faults no individual is wronged'.

2864   Persius, *Satires* I, 107–8: 'Sed quid opus teneras mordaci radere vero/auriculas?' ('But why rasp people's tender ears with biting truths?') (Jonson reads *rodere* – gnaw – for 'radere').

2865   *Remedii . . . spes* 'When it is a question of remedy, hopes are always more prominent than expectation.' The margin claims this for Livy, but where in his work remains a mystery.

2896   *several* particular possession.

2905   *concomitancy* connection.

2907   *κατ'εξοχὴν, ὁ Ποιηγὴς* the maker par excellence.

2911   *Aristotle Poetics* I, 2–4.

2922   *verse* line.

2927   *Aeneid* III, 288 'Aeneas hangs on these doors the arms won from Danaan conquerors.'

2929–30   Martial VIII. xcviii: 'You buy everything, Castor; so the result will be that you sell everything.'

2932   Martial VIII. xix: 'Cinna wishes to be poor and is poor.'

2934   *designs* names, designates.

602 NOTES FOR PP. 445-8

2936 *De Rerum Natura* VI, 937: 'which is clearly shown in the beginning of my poem too.'

2938 *sentence* idea, statement.

2943-50 From Johannes Buchler, *Reformata Poeseos Institutio . . .* (1633) see *H/S* XI, 282.

2956-7 *if . . . Aristotle* possibly referring to *Poetics* 1451ᵛ5 and/or *Politics* 7. 1336ᶜ30.

2960f Cicero, *Pro Archia* 16.

2965 *earnest* work, serious occupation.

2966 *recesses* retreats.

2985 *Ingenium (margin)* Jonson's *natural wit*.

2988 *For whereas all other. . .* Cicero, *Pro Archia* 18.

2991-3016 Seneca, *De Tranquillitate Animi* XVII. 10, 11.

2992-3 The quotation is from Seneca, but *secundum Anacreontem* is an insertion (see *Anacreon*, ed. Bullen, xiii): 'At times Anacreon finds it pleasant to be mad.'

2995 *Phaedrus* 245 A: 'He who is sane wastes his time seeking poetical inspiration.'

2996-7 *Problems* XXX. 1.: 'There was never any one of great ability who had no element of madness.'

2997-8 *Nec . . . mens* from Seneca, *op. cit.*, 10: 'Nor is it possible for the mind to speak highly and, so to speak, above itself, unless it is stirred up'.

3007-8 A fusion of *Fasti* VI, 5 ('There is a god within us; it is when he stirs that we burn') with *Ars Amatoria* III, 549-50: 'Est deus in nobis; et sunt commercia caeli/Sedibus aetheriis spiritus ille venit' ('There is a god within us: and there are dealings with heaven. That inspiration comes from heavenly sources').

3009-11 Lipsius, *Electa* II. xvii (*Opera* (1623)/, 427): 'I know there has never been a great poet who was without a more than ordinary share of divine inspiration.'

3013 *imos* inferiors.

3015-16 *solus . . . nascitur* 'Only a king or a poet is not born every year.'

3029 *the first quarter* within the first three months of trying.

3034 *It is said . . .* by Donatus, *Vitae Virgilianae* 78-82.

3036 *Scaliger, the father* J. C. Scaliger.

3040 *Valerius Maximus Factorum et Dictorum memorabilia* III. vii. 11 ext. i

3058-71 From Buchler, *op. cit.* (see *H/S* XI, 284).

3064 *concoct* digest (Latin 'concoque').

3066 *as Horace saith Ars Poetica* 131-5.

3072 *Statius* AD *c.* 40–*c.* 96; from Naples; author of *Silvae* and *Thebaid*.

3073 *Archilochus* Greek poet, probably of the fifth century BC. Only fragments of his work survive.

       Alcaeus Greek lyric poet of the seventh and sixth centuries BC; from Lesbos; fragments survive.

3082-5 *And not . . . Helicon* Persius, *Satires* prologue 1-4.

603 NOTES FOR PP. 449–51

3092 *Cicero (margin)* *Pro Archia* 15.

3094 *conformation* adaptation (folio reads 'confirmation', but Jonson is surely following Cicero's 'conformatioque').

3096 *Simylus* Athenian writer of comedies; *fl. c.* 354 BC.

    Stobaeus: compiler of an anthology *c.* 500 BC (see *H/S* XI, 285–6 for details of the Greek quotation).

3110–29 Jonson here starts to use Daniel Heinsius, *De Tragoediae constitutione* (1611), ch. 1.

3123 *prudence* sagacity, wisdom.

3127 *declaimers' gallery* Jonson's point here, that the writer must have broad experience rather than merely specialized training, is similar to that made at l. 396 ff.

3129–31 Cicero, *De Oratore* I. xvi, 70.

3131 *numbers* metrical writing.

3138 *Lysippus* a sculptor, of Sicyon, contemporary of Alexander the Great.

    graver engraving tool.

3139 *Apelles* fourth-century BC painter from Ionia and a favourite of Alexander the Great.

    pencil brush.

3149 *comic poet* Gneaus Naevius (*c.* 270–*c.* 199 BC); author of comedies, tragedies and an epic. The epitaph Jonson quotes, said to have been composed by Neavius himself, is preserved in Gellius, *Noctes Atticae* I. xxiv, 2: 'If immortals might weep for mortals then divine Camoenae would weep for Naevius. For after he was consigned as treasure to Orcus, the Romans at once forgot how to speak Latin'.

3155f. Stilo was an early Roman grammarian who instructed Varro and Cicero. The quotation is from Quintilian X. i, 99, somewhat mangled: 'If the muses wished to speak Latin, they would speak in Plautus' words'.

3158 *M. Varro* (116–27 BC); poet, satirist, grammarian, scientist. Little has survived of his 600 volumes.

3159–60 See Gellius, *op. cit.*, VI. xviii, 4.

3161–82 Heinsius, *op. cit.*, i.

3161 *conclude* restrict (Latin 'concludo').

3169 *Demosthenes* (?382–322 BC); great Greek orator.

3170–71 See Aristophanes, *Acharnians* 530–1.

3172 *Alcibiades* an Athenian (*c.* 450–404 BC); friend of Socrates. Demosthenes considered him the most gifted speaker of his period. See *Acharnians* 407–79, *Thesmophoriazusae*.

3184–5 J. J. Scaliger, *Confutatio Fabulae Burdonum* (Opuscula, 1612).

3189–90 *in Lil. Gre. (margin)* as the reference is to the critic Giraldi of Ferrara (1479–1552) this should read 'in Lil. Gir.'

3190–92 *Nemo ... scripsit* 'No one has judged poets so infelicitously as he who writes about poets.'

3198–204 Heinsius, *Ad Horatii de Plauto et Terentio ...* (prefixed to his Terence edition of 1618).

3211 *Cato* Valerius Cato, quoted to this effect by Suetonius, *De Grammaticis* 11, ed. Roth, 262 (265 in the margin should be 266).

3212 *Lucilius* (*c.* 180–102 BC); Founder of Roman satire.

3213-14 'Cato, the Latin siren, alone taught grammar and made poets.'

3215 The *heresy* was defending Lucilius (Quintilian, *op. cit.*, X. i, 93–4); the rejection is by Heinsius.

3216 *Chaerilus*: see *Ars Poetica*, 534 of Jonson's translation and note.

3218 *Laberius* a Roman knight whom Caesar forced, in 45 BC, to act in his own mimes in a dramatic contest with Pubilius Syrus, another writer of mimes.

3233-46 Heinsius, *Ad Horatii de Plauto et Terentio . . . .*

3233 *so gracious* so much in favour (Latin 'gratiosus').

3233-6 see Suetonius, *Deperditorum Librorum Reliquiae*, ed. Roth, 296 f. (Teubner edn).

3240 See *Epistles* II. i (but Jonson confuses the reference, for Horace does not associate Terence with Menander).

3247-313 Heinsius, *Ad Horatii de Plauto et Terentio . . .*

3255 Jonson follows Heinsius in misinterpreting Aristotle, *Poetics* V. i, 7.

3259 *deformed vizard* a reference to the grotesque masks of Greek comic actors.

3264 Plato, *Republic* III, 388 (and see *Iliad* I, 599).

3267 *Poetics* IV. v, 2.

3277 *sinister* malicious, base.

3293f. In Aristophanes, *Clouds* 218f.

3298-300 *Measure . . . scale Clouds* 144f.

3300 *engine* the crane-like machine used on the Greek stage.

3307-11 See *Underwoods* XLIV, 70–73.

3312 The *tumbril* connects with the Thespian cart of *Ars Poetica* 311–13, but Jonson may also have in mind the carts of early English drama.

3323 *proportionable . . . members* the parts of the whole structure should be in proportion to their place in the whole.

3348-490 Heinsius, *De Tragoediae constitutione* iv.

3353 *convenient* appropriate.

3358 *rhinocerote* rhinoceros.

3359 *absolute* complete, perfect.

3367 *Tityus* a giant of Greek mythology, killed by Apollo and Artemis because he showed violence to Leto, their mother. As he lay in Hades his body covered nine acres of land (see *Odyssey* XI, 576; *Aeneid* VI, 595).

3371 *entire* complete, single.

3377 *pismire* ant, emmet.

3397 *one day* see *Poetics* V. 5: Jonson follows many other Renaissance writers in making a rule of Aristotle's recommendation.

3404 *considerable* to be considered.

3431 *pretermitted* omitted.

3432-3 *fought with Achilles* see *Iliad* XX, 156–352.

3434 *by Venus* see *Iliad* XX, 297–318.

3435 *prosecutes* follows.

3436 *error* wandering.

3447 *Codrus* Juvenal, *Satires* I, 2 (Jonson is muddling Cordus mentioned in I. 2 with the Codrus of III, 203).

3481 *of which hereafter* as *H/S* suggest (*XI*, 294) this seems to imply that Jonson planned to translate the twelfth chapter of Heinsius' treatise.

3482 *the single combat . . .* see *Iliad* VII, 181–312.

3488–90 Martial XI. xc, 2, 6, 5: 'You approve of no verses that run smoothly, but only of those that seem to leap over hills and crags; you read with pleasure words like "terrai frugiferai" as well as all the splutterings of Accius and Pacuvius.' (For Accius and Pacuvius see *MP* XV, 35 and note.)

Appendix 2

BEN JONSON'S CONVERSATIONS WITH WILLIAM DRUMMOND OF HAWTHORNDEN

There is no way of knowing how accurately Drummond's notes reflect what Jonson said to him during his stay. There is an aggressive directness in these *Conversations* that sounds like genuine Jonson but Drummond may well report mainly the more memorable and belligerent things Jonson had to say and may also have tended to précis statements which, in a fuller form, might seem less pungent. It is important too, I think, to remember that Jonson was the great man up from London visiting someone who was out of touch with the London literary scene and anxious to get the latest news. Jonson, especially when he had been drinking, was not the man to underplay his role and much of what he said to Drummond must have been deliberately provocative and pointed. This is simply a reminder that *Conversations* should not be read as if everything reported in it reflected Jonson's most mature views.

5 *against . . . Daniel* Campion's *Observations on the Art of English Poesie* was published in 1602 and Daniel's *A Defence of Rhyme* at about the same time. Jonson's *discourse* is not extant but see *Underwoods* XXIX.

7 *broken* with a caesura.

8 *cross-rhymes* rhymes that run over the rhyme/line-ending.

12 *Plinius secundus* Pliny the younger, the letter-writer, as distinct from his uncle, author of the *Natural History*.

13 *Epigrams* X. xlvii (translated as *MP* CXXV).

15–17 See ll. 54, 633.

19–20 See ll. 168–70.

23 *Poly-Olbion* published in 1613.

23–4 *if he had performed . . .* see Quintilian, *Inst. Orat.* X. i, 89.

26–8 See *Epigrams* CXXXII and note.

28 *confer* to compare translation with original.

    Fairfax Edward Fairfax's translation *Godfrey of Bulloigne* (1600).

29–30 Presumably referring to Arthur Hall's *Ten Books of Homer's Iliades* (1581) and Chapman's *Seaven Bookes of the Iliades* (1598), both written in fourteeners. Also to the *Aeneid* of Thomas Phaer (Books I–IX, 1562) and Thomas Twyne (remaining books, 1584), again in fourteeners.

31 *John Harington* his translation of Ariosto's *Orlando Furioso* was published in 1591.

33 Harington's *Epigrams* (1613, 1615, 1618) are pleasant poems but Jonson's distinction between *narrations* (l. 34) and real epigrams is fair comment.

36–7 William Warner's *Albion's England* is a verse history of England. The third edition (1592) went up to Elizabeth's accession and that of 1612 – presumably the one Jonson objects to – covered events in the early part of James I's reign.

38 *Anniversary* the *Anatomy of the World* (1611).

41 *idea* ideal, platonic form.

43 *Fletcher* H/S (I, 155) suggest that Beaumont's *Masque of the Inner Temple* ... (1613) may be meant (compare the Beaumont/Fletcher fusion at ll. 220–21).

Chapman the only surviving Chapman masque is *The Memorable Masque of the Two Honourable Houses* ... (1613).

46 *Sharpham* author of the comedy *The Fleire* (1616).

Day John Day, author of *The Isle of Gulls* (1606), *Law Tricks* (1604) and *Humour out of Breath* (1607–8).

Dekker Thomas Dekker, prolific playwright and pamphleteer – probably mentioned here because of his part in *Satiromastix* (1601), an element in the 'War of the Theatres'.

47 *Minshew*: John Minshew, lexicographer, author of *The Guide into Tongues* (1617) and of a Spanish dictionary and grammar.

48 *Francis* Abraham Fraunce, who wrote *The Lamentations of Amintas* (1587, a translation) and *The Countess of Pembroke's Yvy-church* (1591–5), both in hexameters.

50 For Bartas see l. 25 and note. See Quintilian X. i, 89, where Cornelius Severus is said to be 'versificator quam poeta melior' ('a better versifier than poet').

52–3 Like the bed of Procrustes, the legendary brigand of Eleusis. He had travellers laid on the bed, trimming or stretching them so that they fitted its length exactly.

54 *Pastor Fido* (1585): see ll. 15–17, 633.

56 *Lucan* see l. 636 and *MP* CXXVI and note.

58 *Bonefonius* Jean Bonnefons, lived at Clermont towards the end of the sixteenth century: the poem, like almost all record of the writer, is lost. See ll. 390–91.

59 *de Perron* on the connection between Jonson and Duperron see H/S I, 71 f.

62 *his Odes* *Les Quatre premiers livres des Odes* (1550); *Ensemble le Cinquième des Odes* (1552).

65 Horace, *Epodes* II, translated as *Underwoods* LXXXV.

68   Properly 'Foedo est in coitu et brevis voluptas': translated as *Underwoods* LXXXVIII.
71   *the preface* lost; apparently written as a dialogue.
74   *an ... Herbert's* Sir Edward Herbert (1583–1648); Lord Herbert of Cherbury, 1629; historian, philosopher, poet; elder brother of George Herbert. The poem referred to, 'To his Friend Ben. Jonson of his Horace made English', was printed in Herbert's *Occasional Verses* (1665).
75   *Lord Aubigny* see ll. 250–51 and *Epigrams* CXXVII and note.
76   *ten years since* ten years before the production of *Bartholomew Fair* in 1614.
77–8   *dialogue pastoral* *Underwoods* III.
79   *Ferrabosco* see *Epigrams* CXXX and note, CXXXI. Any of several pieces by Ferrabosco could be meant.
      with his letter with Jonson's words to his music. I have accepted Paterson's emendation of 'Parabostes Pariane', but see *H/S* (I, 156) for a defence of this reading.
79–80   *epigram of gut* *Epigrams* CXVIII.
80   *my ... buck* *Epigrams* LXXXIV.
80–81   '*Drink ... eyes*' *The Forest* IX.
81   '*Swell me a bowl*' *MP* XL.
82–7   A bad misquotation of *Underwoods* II, 7.
88   Not extant.
88–9   *verses ... Bulstrode* *Underwoods* XLIX Donne's epitaph *An Elegy upon the Death of Mistress Boulstred* is on p. 251 of A J. Smith's edition (1971).
90–92   *a satire ... the world* not extant.
92–3   See ll. 13–14 and note.
95   *my ... prince* 'Tears on the Death of Moeliades' (1613).
96   *Schools* see *Underwoods* LXXIV, 9, 51–5 note.
98   *verses ... running* see ll. 7–8 and note.
99   '*Forth Feasting*' 'Forth Feasting, A Panegyricke to the Kings most Excellent Majestie ...' (1617).
102   *verses ... chain* Elegy XI (p. 107 f. of A. J. Smith's edition of Donne's poems (1971)).
103   *The Calm* p. 199 of A. J. Smith's edition (1971). Drummond refers to ll. 18–19.
106   *Sir Henry Wotton* (1568–1639); diplomat and poet. The poem referred to begins 'How happy is he born and taught', most easily accessible in *The Tribe of Ben* (1966), ed. A. C. Partridge.
107–8   Compare ll. 29–30 and note.
109–10   *epitaph ... faith* 'Elegy upon the untimely Death of the Incomparable Prince Henry' (A. J. Smith edn (1971), 253). The remark about matching Herbert for obscurity may refer specifically to the latter's 'Elegy for the Prince' (1612).
112   *Calendar* *Shepherd's Calendar*, 'October, Aegloga Decima'.
113   For *Colin* read 'Cuddy'.

114–22 that is, *The Progress of the Soul, Infinitati Sacrum. Metempsychosis* (A. J. Smith edn (1971), 253).

121 Donne became D.D. in 1615.

125 *Perse* Persius.

126–7 *Hippocrates* the Greek physician (*fl.c.* 460 BC). Some of his writings survive and – with Galen – he was a standard reference point in medicine even as late as the early seventeenth century.

128 Books I–IV of the *Ecclesiastical History* were published *c.* 1594; Book V in 1597. Hooker died in 1600 and the later books of his *History* were published posthumously (1617). See *Discoveries* 1120 and note.

130 *Titles of Honour* published in 1614; *De Diis Syris* (of which Jonson had a copy) in 1617. See *Underwoods* XIV and note.

141 See ll. 21–2.

142 But compare *MP* XVIII.

143–4 See Quintilian, *Inst. Orat.* X. i, 88, where Ovid is said to be 'unduly enamoured of his own gifts', and compare *Epigrams* LV.

145 *Sir John Roe* see *Epigrams* XXVII (and note), XXXII, XXXIII.

146–9 See *Epigrams* LXVII and note. Roe's poem, 'The State and men's affairs are the best plays/Next yours ...' (sometimes wrongly attributed to Donne and printed in Grierson's edn, pp. 414–15) is dated 6 January 1603, so the masque in question presumably Daniel's *Vision of the Twelve Goddesses*.

150 See ll. 282–4. Jonson's relationship with Marston was unstable; it formed a part of the 'War of the Theatres' but Marston was a t times distinctly conciliatory to Jonson.

151 *Sir W. Alexander* William Alexander (?1567–1640): poet and statesman; knighted in 1609 and made Earl of Stirling in 1633. He was a friend of Drummond and wrote introductory verses to 'Tears ... Moeliades' (see l. 95 and note).

153 *Sir R. Ayton* Sir Robert Ayton was private secretary to James's wife Anne and died in 1638.

154 *Ned Field* Nathaniel Field (1587–1637); actor–dramatist; as a child he acted in *Cynthia's Revels* (1601).

156 *Markham* Gervase Markham (?1568–1637); author of *The English Arcadia, alluding his beginning from Sir Philip Sydnes ending* (1607) and *The Second and Last Part of the First Book of the English Arcadia* (1613).

158 *Day* see l. 45 and note.

Middleton Thomas Middleton (1570–1627); one of the major playwrights of the period.

160–61 See Epigrams CXIII and note: since the epigram is friendly the quarrel presumably came later. See also ll. 206–10 below.

162 *apothegms* pithy sayings.

163–7 One of the periodic O'Neill uprisings led to the burning of Kilcolman Castle in 1598 and Spenser, with his family, fled to Cork. The poet died at an inn in King Street in 1599. The details of the burnt child (which syntactically need not have been Spenser's) and of Spenser's *lack of bread* do not have corroboration.

168-70 See ll. 19-20 and 'The Letter of the Author's' prefixed to the *Faerie Queene*. The *blating beast* = the 'blatant beast' of the *Faerie Queene* VI. i, 7. For *Duessa* see *Faerie Queene* V. ix, 38-50.

171 *Southwell* Robert Southwell (?1561-95) Jesuit missionary and poet, was hanged, drawn and quartered for high treason.

174 Beaumont actually lived to be thirty-two (1584-1616).

175 *Roe* see l. 145 and note.

180 *Mortimuriades* (1596), rewritten as *The Barons' Wars* (1603). He was *challenged* (taken to task for) apparently for calling a one-book poem by so resounding a name. See Drayton's note to the 1603 volume.

181-4 The poems are Sir John Davies's *Epigram* 25 and Drayton's *Idea* 18 (*Poems* (1619), 259). Dametas is a clown in Sidney's *Arcadia*, but the remark attributed to him is not there. Drayton's point is that his mistress is such as to displace any of the nine worthies. See *Epigrams* XVIII and note for Davies.

185 *Heywood* (?1497-1580); father of Donne's mother Elizabeth.

191f. See *Underwoods* XXIV and *Discoveries* 1124 and note. Raleigh was helped by many scholars; his life of Elizabeth is not extant.

196-7 Mary Sidney (1561-1621), Philip's sister, married Henry Herbert, second Earl of Pembroke, and helped Sidney translate the *Psalms*.

198-9 Wood says that Marston's father-in-law was William Wilkes, a chaplain to James I.

203 *Civil Wars* published 1595-1609: Jonson's remark is unfair.

205 *Countess of Rutland* see *Epigrams* LXXIX and note, *Forest* XII.

207 *'Wife'* 'A Wife now the Widow', a poem printed in 1614.

212-14 See *H/S* I, 163.

215 *Owen* John Owen (1560-1622), master of King Henry VIII school at Warwick. He had a European reputation as an epigrammatist in Latin and does not really deserve this comment.

218 'The Divine Poem of Musaeus . . .' (1616). Musaeus was a Greek poet of the fourth or fifth century AD who wrote a poem on Hero and Leander.

220-21 *The Faithful Shepherdess* (1608). Probably by Fletcher alone.

222 *Dyer* Sir Edward Dyer (?1545-1607); a poet best known in his lifetime for his elegies.

225 *my lord Lisle* Robert Sidney (1563-1626); Philip's younger brother; knighted in 1586, created Viscount Lisle in 1605 and Earl of Leicester in 1618. His eldest son was also called Robert.

234 (*his master Camden*) see l. 259 f. and *Epigrams* XIV and note.

235 *wright* artificer, craftsman.

236f. See *Epigrams* CVIII.

240 *opima spolia* great spoil.

241 *his adversary* Gabriel Spencer, the actor. He was imprisoned with Jonson over the *Isle of Dogs* incident (see *Discoveries* and note) and was a sufficiently distinguished actor for Henslow to note his death with anger in a letter of September 1598.

247-8 That is, he did not study for these degrees but they were awarded *honoris causa.*

250–51 See l. 75 and note.

256 *Epigrams* LIX.

257 *the pest* the plague of 1603, the year of James's accession to the English throne.

258–9 *Cotton* knighted in 1603 and had been at Westminster School with Jonson.

259 *Camden* see l. 234 and note.

264 *apprehension* delusion.

265 *disjected* dejected.

270 *delated* informed against.

271 *Eastward Ho* (1605); contains various remarks which might well upset James and London-based Scots. Murray (l. 270) was knighted in 1603 and in 1610 was a Gentleman of the Privy Chamber to Prince Henry.

283 *Poetaster* (1601); Marston = Crispinus.

294–304 The young Walter Raleigh (b. 1593) was killed at San Tomás in 1618, while with his father on his final expedition.

299 *car* cart.

pioneers here 'people going before'.

301 *lively* lifelike.

312 See the dedication of *Epigrams* and note.

316–20 See *Epigrams* XLIII and note, LXIII, LXIV, where Jonson is complimentary.

324 *Northampton* Henry Howard was made Earl of Northampton in 1604.

326 *Sejanus* acted 1603, published 1605.

339f. The evidence that Jonson is not just gossiping is given in *H/S* I, 166.

346 *Monsieur* the Duc d'Alençon, brother of Henri III: he came to England in 1579 to try to persuade Elizabeth to marry him.

350–52 Lady Sidney caught small-pox in 1592. Jonson's anecdote is supported by Fulke Greville's *Life of Sir Philip Sidney* (1652).

353 *Earl of Leicester* Robert Dudley (1532–88), made Earl in 1564, died, officially, of a fever. Jonson is the only known source of this particular view of his death but there were other contemporary rumours of mysterious circumstances.

357 See ll. 316–20 and note.

359 *Lady Wroth* see *Epigrams* CIII and note; *Underwoods* XXVIII; also *Forest* III.

361 *my lady Rutland* see l. 205 and note.

365 *Lord Chancellor* Francis Bacon became Chancellor in 1617. See *Underwoods* LI and *Discoveries* 1131, 1151, etc.

368–71 The poem is *Forest* VII (and see note).

372–5 In 1604 Sir Henry Savile's translation of four books of Tacitus' *History* and Greneway's of *The Annals ... The Description of Germany* were printed together. The 'epistle to the reader' prefacing Savile's part is signed A.B. For Savile see *Epigrams* XCV and *Discoveries* 1130; for Essex see *Discoveries* 1123. Patterson's explanation of the remark about the Jews (*Ben Jonson's Conversations* 32) is not very convincing but I cannot offer a better one.

377   *the sculler*   Taylor the Water Poet: see *Discoveries* 757–8 and *Conversations* 629.

384–5   See *Discoveries* 2920 f.

388   *Sir John Davies*   see ll. 181–4 and note.

389   *running verses*   see l. 8 and note.

plus . . . complacet   'more than pleases me.'

390   *He imitated . . .*   this imitation is not extant.

392   *transponed*   transposed without affecting the sense.

393–4   The opening couplet of Davies's poem *Orchestra* (1596).

399   *The May Lord*   not extant, but it must have been written by 1612, as Lady Rutland died in August of that year.

400   *Countess of Bedford*   see *Epigrams* LXXVI and note.

401   *Overbury*   see ll. 160–61 and note.

Countess of Suffolk   Catherine, daughter of Sir Henry Knevet, widow of Richard Rich, married Thomas Howard (*c.* 1586) who became Earl of Suffolk in 1603.

402   *Pembroke*   see ll. 368–71 and note.

403   *Countess of Rutland*   see l. 205 and note.

Lady Wroth   see l. 361 and note.

409   *That epithalamion*   *MP* LXV.

411–12   If he did it does not survive.

413   The allusion is presumably to *Underwoods* XLIII, 93–5.

415–21   Nothing more is known of this incident. Fitz Dottrell in the play aims to be Duke of Drounland. The Greek word ('by-play', 'secondary concern') suggests that any local satire in the play was incidental.

416   *comedia vetus*   old comedy.

422–3   See l. 71 f.

424–5   *The Art of English Poesy* (1598); perhaps by George Puttenham or his elder brother Richard. Jonson owned a copy.

432f.   Henri IV abandoned Protestantism in 1593. Pasquil and Marforius were two famous Roman statues; poems, usually attacking Pope and church, were often attached to Pasquil. In stories of this type Marforius usually does the questioning and Pasquil the answering.

438–9   This is rather obscure, but Ferdinand of Aragon was given the title of Rex Catholicus for expelling the Moors from Spain, while – since 1469 – kings of France have held the title Christianissimus.

440–41   Pliny, *Epistles* ii, 6.

442   *that panegyrist*   not identifiable, but pattern-poems were made popular by Puttenham. Jonson also attacks them in *Underwoods* XLIII, 32f.

443–4   *homo miserrimae patientiae*: 'a man of the most wretched endurance.'

446–7   Martial II. lxxxvi, 9–10: 'Turpe est difficilis habere nugas/et stultus labor est ineptiarum' ('It is humiliating to undertake difficult trifles; and the effort spent on idiotic tasks is foolish').

452   *chase*   H/S (I, 170) quote the OED: 'Applied to the second impact on the floor (or in a gallery) of a ball which the opponent has failed or declined to return; the value of which is determined by the nearness of the spot of impact to the end wall. If the opponent, on sides being changed . . . can "better" this stroke (i.e. cause this ball to rebound nearer the wall) he wins and scores it; if not, it is scored by the first player; until it is so decided, the "chase" is a stroke in abeyance.'

460 *An Englishman* probably Nicholas Hill in his *Philosophica Epicurea* (1601).

Democritus see *Epigrams* CXXXIII, 108 and note.

468 *Butler* probably the celebrated and eccentric doctor, William Butler (1535-1618).

470 *mustered* needed.

472-4 Patterson, *Ben Jonson's Conversations* 40, suggests that this picture was Dieric Bouts's *Last Supper*.

479f. See *Epigrams* XCVII, CXXIX; *MP* VI, VII.

489 *Easter* Esther.

490 *Assuerus* Ahasuerus.

492-4 'Will he even force the queen before me in the house?' (*Esther* VII, 8).

495 *goodman* head of the house.

510-15 See l. 102. According to Walton's *Life* (*World's Classics* edn, 110-11) Wotton was sent by Ferdinand, Duke of Florence, to Scotland disguised as an Italian, carrying antidotes against poison for James (then James VI of Scotland) who Ferdinand thought was in danger of being murdered.

532 *Mr Dod* John Dod was a fellow of Jesus College, Cambridge, who was suspended for nonconformity in 1604. There is quite a lot of information about him in Haller, *The Rise of Puritanism* (1957).

536 Scaliger *Epistles* IV, 362 (to Ubertus, not to Casaubon).

540-41 See ll. 393-4 and note.

543 *demonstrate* that is, answered the question asked in Davies's lines.

546 *cockered* pampered.

552-4 '*Dominum cognoscite vestrum*' Ovid *Metamorphoses* III, 230: 'Actaeon ego sum:dominum cognoscite vestrum' ('I am Actaeon, recognize your own master'). Actaeon was an Elizabethan prototype for a cuckold.

557 *ta'en* taken, caught.

560 *Cardan* Girolamo Cardano, a famous Milanese doctor who visited London in 1552. The remark has not been identified.

566 *facere periculum* to make trial of: 'periculum' usually means 'danger' which makes the point of l. 564.

567 The reference seems to be to *The booke of the life of . . . Mark Aurelye Anthony*, early sixteenth century.

569 '*harlot*' the derivation of the word from Harlotha, mistress of William I, goes back at least asfar as Lambarde (*c.* 1570).

570-71 Presumably a joke.

572 *Percy* Sir Josceline Percy (d. 1631), a son of the eighth Earl of Northumberland.

577 Sir Jerome Bowes (d. 1616) had been an ambassador to Russia in 1583.

581 *Buchanan* George Buchanan (1506–1582), scholar and historian of considerable reputation, was tutor to James from 1570–78.

584–5 Walsingham went to Scotland in 1583 to persuade James not to negotiate with Spain on behalf of his mother. The Latin may be related to that of *Luke* xix 14: 'Nolumus hunc regnare super nos' ('We will not that this man reign over us').

590 *Guyse*] Gryse H/S. H/S identify this with one Robert Gryse, knighted in 1628.

590–91 *consumed* presumably with venereal disease.

591 *occupied* possessed sexually.

    dildo artificial penis.

592 *sleppery* sleepy.

593 *Heywood the epigrammatist* John Heywood (?1497–?1580); dramatist and epigrammatist; a favourite of Mary when she was princess and queen.

598 *impresa* see *Epigrams* LXXIII, 15 and note.

599 *Deest . . . orbem* see Ovid, *Metamorphoses* VIII, 249: 'altera pars staret, pars altera duceret orbem' ('one part might stand still, while the other traced a circle').

600 *Mr Devereux* Walter Devereux was born 1569 and died in a skirmish before Rouen in 1591.

601 *void* blank.

601–2 *Par . . . dolori* 'No emblem of grief equals this.'

603 *ashes* dust.

604 *Dum formas minuis* 'Until the image is made smaller.'

605 *the prince* probably Prince Henry.

    Fax . . . honestae Silius Italicus vi, 332: 'An honest mind is the torch of glory.'

608 *His arms . . . rhombi* Symonds has shown that this is to be identified with the arms of the Johnstones of Annandale (see l. 228f.): this does not prove a family connection.

609 *Percunctator . . . Perscrutator* both words mean 'inquirer'.

619 *John Stow* (1525–1605); historian and antiquary; brought up as a tailor; best known now for his *Survey of London* (1598). He was very poor in his old age – hence the rather bitter joke.

623 *a whole oration* as Cordus' speech in III, 407–60, translated from Tacitus, *Annals* IV, 34–5 – hence the harsh remark of ll. 624–5 is directed at Greneway's translation of 1598 (see ll. 372–5 and note).

626 *Selden* see l. 130 and note. *Titles of Honour* is dedicated to Edward Heyward, 'my most beloved friend and chamberfellow'. See *Underwoods* XIV and note.

629 *Taylor . . . him* Taylor had mocked Coriat's journey (see *MP* VI) in his *Three Weeks . . .* (1617) and undertook to walk to Edinburgh moniless and without begging. He made the journey between July and October, 1618, and published *The Penniless Pilgrimage* about this journey (see also ll. 667–8).

630 Camden's *Remains . . . Concerning Britaine* was published anonymously in 1605.

631 *Hall* Bishop Joseph Hall was rector of Hawsted in Suffolk from 1606–8. This was where Sir Robert Drury lived, for whose dead daughter Donne wrote his *Anniversaries*. The 'Harbinger to the Progress' (i.e. 'Of the progress of the Soul . . . The second Anniversary') is on p. 286 of A. J. Smith's 1971 edition. A 'harbinger' was 'an official who went on ahead of an army or royal progress to make preliminary arrangements' (Smith (1971), p. 606).

632 *The . . . Verpum* Martial XI. xciv. Jonson is claiming to have elucidated (*exponed*) the famous crux of Martial's last line.

633 *Lucan* now joins Sidney (l. 17) and Guarini (l. 54) in this reiterated criticism. For *Dametas*, see l. 183.

636 See l. 56 and note.

646–7 *quintessenceth their brains* his brain contains the quintessence, or most precious qualities, of theirs.

648 *that . . . Plinius* Pliny, *Epistles* II, 6.

648–51 This is rather a muddle. Pliny tells an anecdote (*Epistles* IV. 22) of the depraved Messalinus and Veiento. Patterson thinks that Drummond's *Marcellinus* should read *Messalinus* and that Jonson has in mind Juvenal, *Satires* IV, where Veiento and Messalinus are again coupled (l. 113) and a *gross turbot* is mentioned (l. 39).

652–4 For an explanation of this anecdote see *H/S* I, 176–7.

655 Davies's epigram 'In Katum'.
    C. cunt.

656 *coul* a cowl is properly a monk's hood or cloak: here it is used with reference to the 'buff jerkin' of Davies's poem.

666 *Darnton* Darlington.

667–8 See l. 629 and *Epigrams* CXXIX; *Underwoods* XIII; *MP* VI, VII, CXV.

668 *excoriate* an obvious pun. *Excoriate* here means 'to lose the skin (of one's feet)'.

671–2 *borough-laws* bye-laws.

673–5 See *Underwoods* XLIX and note.

686 *dissembler* concealer.

701 '*plaudite*' 'let it be applauded.'

Index of First Lines

Index of Titles